THEOLOGICAL ETHICS AND HOLY SCRIPTURE

THEOLOGICAL ETHICS AND HOLY SCRIPTURE: THE USE OF SCRIPTURE IN THE WORKS OF JAMES M. GUSTAFSON, R. PAUL RAMSEY, AND ALLEN D. VERHEY

(with a summary in Dutch)

LAURENS WOUTER BILKES

Canadian Cataloguing in Publication Data

Bilkes, Laurens Wouter, 1943 -
Theological ethics and Holy Scripture

Includes summary in Dutch.
Includes bibliographical references and index.
ISBN 90-5030-868-6 (Uitgeverij J.J. Groen en Zoon) – ISBN 0-921100-98-1 (Inheritance Publications)

1. Gustafson, James M. 2. Ramsey, Paul. 3. Verhey, Allen. 4. Christian ethics. I. Title.
BJ1251.B54 1997 241'.092'2 C97-910927-2

Cover design: Steven van der Gaauw

Photographs rights:
Emory University-USA (James M. Gustafson)
Princeton University Libraries (R. Paul Ramsey)

ISBN 0-921100-98-1

Promotor: Prof. dr. W. H. Velema

Co-promotor: Prof. dr. J. W. Maris

THEOLOGICAL ETHICS AND HOLY SCRIPTURE: THE USE OF SCRIPTURE IN THE WORKS OF JAMES M. GUSTAFSON, R. PAUL RAMSEY, AND ALLEN D. VERHEY

Preface

The subject matter of this dissertation is the role of Scripture in theological ethics. The specific inquiry is after the level at which and the manner in which Scripture informs ethics. The issue is broached by way of the work of James M. Gustafson, R. Paul Ramsey, and Allen Verhey, three representative ethicists on the recent American Protestant scene. The perimeters of inquiry are thus delimited according to the American context and Protestant affiliation of the authors. The discussion of Gustafson, Ramsey, and Verhey reveals the important components of the question as to the role of Scripture in ethics, namely, the role of reason, the character of the community, and the place of practice. These components become guiding concepts for the whole inquiry into the role of Scripture in ethics.

The selection of James M. Gustafson, R. Paul Ramsey, and Allen D. Verhey as representatives of modern American Christian ethics produces a tender equilibrium of commonality and diversity. All three have been active in the second half of the 20th century in the chronological order of Ramsey, Gustafson, and Verhey. All three identify themselves as constructing a *Christian* ethics. All three move within Protestantism, respectively, Methodism, Lutheranism, and Calvinism, though some connections with Roman Catholic natural law are evident (particularly Ramsey). Beyond this, all three confirm indebtedness to some type of Reformed theology.

Educationally, they share Ph.D. degrees from Yale University, Ramsey having graduated in 1943, Gustafson in 1955, Verhey in 1975. The first two benefited from the strong presence of H. Richard Niebuhr at Yale, while Verhey received training from Gustafson, who returned to teach at his *alma mater*. The dissertations of all three ethicists interact with spokespersons of modernism, in the case of Ramsey, Josiah Royce, an American idealist philosopher and Bernard Bosanquet, a British Hegelian, in the case of Gustafson, Josiah Royce, George Herbert Mead, Henri Bergson, and Wilhelm Dilthey, and in the case of Verhey, Walter Rauschenbusch.

The diversity occasioned by the selection of Gustafson, Ramsey, and Verhey is evident in the subsequent chapter headings. Gustafson has emphasized the *theocentric* perspective in ethics, Ramsey specifically the *Christian* character of ethics, and Verhey's work has focused on the role of *Scripture* and the authorization thereof in ethics. This is not to say that they have a monopoly on these perspectives or subject matter. For to a lesser or greater extent they would all align themselves with the designations, theocentric,

Christian, and Scriptural. Nevertheless, the differences in emphasis lend a diversity of voices to this project.

The organization of this dissertation intends to achieve three things: 1) an opportunity for three recent or contemporary ethicists on the American Protestant scene to speak individually, specifically on the function of Scripture in ethics; 2) an examination of their work against their American background and within their American context; and 3) a response to these ethicists on the matter of the role of Scripture in ethics.

The first point receives shape in individual chapters (2, 3, and 4). These chapters combine a descriptive and analytic treatment of the author and conclude with some focused questions. The second point is begun in the introductory chapter on American background and context and forms a recurrent motif in the subsequent chapters. As far as the third point is concerned, it has proven most advantageous to present the response in the fifth chapter, in which some suggestions are made toward a foundation of ethics on the Scriptures of the Old and New Testament.

The advocacy for a theological ethics entails that the shift to theological categories and exegetical lines is not viewed as problematic, but precisely the solution of a Christian ethics. It parallels the relationship between theology and science, soteriology and epistemology, and faith and reason. At the same time, its function as a solution must be carefully delineated. Finally, at the heart of the proposal for theological ethics stands the proper configuration of law and gospel. The omission or misconfiguration of this linchpin of theological ethics, jeopardizes the basis and character of Theocentric and Christian ethics.

Acknowledgments

Looking back over the process of the writing of this dissertation, I wish to acknowledge with heartfelt gratitude those who have in varied ways contributed toward making possible the completion of this dissertation.

The research for and the writing of this dissertation was pursued over a period of 12 years and on both sides of the Atlantic.

I count the opportunity I have had to study at the Theological University in Apeldoorn a singular privilege, not only in Christian ethics under Prof. Dr. W. H. Velema, but also during the pre-doctoral study in Systematic theology under Prof. Dr. J. van Genderen and in New Testament studies under the late Prof. Dr. J. P. Versteeg. I wish to thank Prof. Dr. J. W. Maris for joining Prof. Dr. W. H. Velema during the past four years in directing me in the writing of the dissertation. His competent involvement has been helpful and profitable. I express also gratitude to the other members of the Faculty of the Theological University for their demanding discipline and stimulating vision. The study under Prof. Dr. W. H. Velema has been an invaluable experience and highly rewarding. I am grateful to him for suggesting the topic of this dissertation and for directing me in the writing of this dissertation. I am indebted to his scholarly and pastoral direction. From his lectures and writings as well as from personal association with him I have reaped a rich harvest of blessings. I appreciate deeply his boundless interest, his friendly criticisms and suggestions, his many tokens of ready and expert helpfulness, which contributed much to making this work enjoyable and enriching.

I am very grateful to my friend Dr. Allen C. Guelzo for his interest in my study and for some helpful points he gave me in an early discussion as I was attempting to put American Protestant ethics in historical perspective. I wish to express appreciation to Dr. Stanley J. Grenz for carefully reading through an earlier edition of my proposed dissertation and making various critical and constructive comments.

I wish to thank Prof. Gustafson for his words of encouragement by way of letter and telephone, as well as for the photograph he sent me to be used in this dissertation. I am deeply grateful to Prof. Allen Verhey for the kind contact I had with him by way of telephone and the to me unforgettable time we spent together one day discussing his perspective on the use of Scripture in ethics. I also thank him for sending me his photograph as it appears in this dissertation. Although there are considerable differences in how they and I do theology and ethics, they have challenged me to think through the use of Scripture in ethics. I have come to appreciate very much the nuanced way in which they handle this very topic. I wish to thank "Princeton University Library" for the right of using Paul Ramsey's photograph from "University Archives, Department of Rare Books and Special Collections, Princeton University Library."

It is privilege to acknowledge the kindness of various colleagues in the Netherlands and North America, in whose fellowship my wife and I have learned to appreciate the richness of the Church and the variety of graces with which it is crowned.

This dissertation was written while serving the congregations in Ermelo and in Abbotsford. I thank the congregations not merely for allowing me some time to study but also for always reminding me to make sure that my studying be in the light of God's Word.

I can never fully repay the debt of gratitude which I owe my wife and our sons. They not only endured my studies with fortitude and patience, but also showed loving interest in my studies and sacrificed liberally and cheerfully while still loving me to the full. Apart from my loving and loyal wife, Jane, I could not have accomplished this work. Every comment she made to me in relation to this study was a challenge afresh, which I have valued and respected. Brian Mark patiently helped me make the transition from type-writer to computer, Lawrence James assisted in proof-reading and discussing various aspects of the fifth chapter, and Gerald Michael gave perceptive comments and constructive criticisms and encouraged me to complete this work.

I wish to thank my nephew Dave van Grootheest for his careful and accurate reading. He suggested many corrections, which have saved me from errors and obscurity, and provided me with a good start on writing the Dutch summary.

The responsibility for all remaining errors and opinions remains mine.

I wish to thank various friends, among whom are Dick & Mary Anne Westeringh, Edi and Aty de Vin, and Jaap and Krijnie van der Steege for their friendship and assistance during the various years of working on the dissertation. I am in special debt to Zion Building Society for financial assistance related to the completion of this project. I am in special debt to Renger and Gerda Guliker for their friendship and love since 1980, as well as for enabling publication of this dissertation.

I dedicate this project to my mother and in memory of my father, who together brought me up with the Word of God as a lamp unto my feet and a light upon my pathway unto heaven.

In all the blessings of which I have been an unworthy recipient I recognize the beneficence of my Heavenly Father, Who wisely uses the common experiences of His children to demonstrate His love and to introduce them to the fullness of salvation which He has provided His people in Jesus Christ. Of Him and through Him and unto Him are all things. To the Triune God alone be glory (Romans 11:36).

Table of Contents

La vérité est une reine qui habite en elle-même sa félicité. Toutefois, pour la bien des hommes, elle a voulu régner, et Jésus-Christ est venu au monde pour établir cet empire par la foi qu'il nous a prêchée. ...
[L]a vérité chrétienne n'a point cherché son appui dans les raisonnements humains; mais qu'assurée d'elle-même, de son autorité suprême et de son origine céleste, elle a dit, et a voulu être crue; elle a prononcé ses oracles, et a exigé la sujétion. Elle a prêché une Trinité, mystère inaccessible par sa hauteur; elle a annoncé un Dieu-Homme, un Dieu anéanti jusques à la croix, abîme impénétrable par sa bassesse. Comment a-t-elle prouvé? Elle a dit pour toute raison qu'il faut que la raison lui cède, et qu'elle est née sa sujette.

> Jacques Benigne Bossuet, "Sur la Devinité de Jésus-Christ" [Sermon preached on Matthew 11:5,6, December 6, 1665], *Oeuvres Oratoires de Bossuet*, Vol. 4 (ed. J. Lebarq; Paris: Brouwer, 1921), 656 [652-675].

Chapter 1: Introduction: Historical Background and Contemporary Context

1.1. The American Character

In the study of the history of ethical thought, consideration of geographical constellations has proven to be useful. Discussions of the history of ethical reasoning usually delineate both chronologically and geographically. Thus there are, for example, separate chapters or volumes on American ethical thought. As most scholarly delineations involve a degree of artificiality, so also geographical boundaries. American ethical thought has never been as disjunctive as its geographical landmass, nor has it been internally so unified that one could speak of a singular American ethics. On the one hand, American ethical thought has had its sources mainly in European thought and the contact with Europe has been sustained ever since the constitution of America. On the other hand, America has been composed of heterogeneous religious and philosophical movements with innumerable practical manifestations.

For all the exterior influences and forces on American thinking, it has been recognized that there is an independent internal development within American thought in general, and ethical thought in particular. Gustafson begins an essay on Christian ethics by stating: "Scholarship in Christian ethics in the United States has developed in a particularly American way."[1] According to Gustafson, this "American way" has manifested itself in a focus on practical ethical issues rather than theoretical problems. In addition, Americans have had a peculiar mix of social and individual concern in their moral discussions. Thus the "Social Gospel" could to some extent be considered a typically American phenomenon. The impetus to collectively and individually conform to a social standard such as "the Social Gospel" could be seen as characteristically American. Gustafson's comments illustrate the usefulness of geographical delineation in the case of ethics.

The solution to this ambiguity in the scholarly task has been to retain the delineations, but to refine the distinctions by acknowledging variegated external influences. Yet within this solution there is a whole continuum of possibilities. One could study American authors in conversation with authors from another geographical entity, such as Europe. The emphasis in such an international dialogue would be on the conjunctiveness or disjunctiveness of American and European ethical thought. The other option would be to study American authors in intra-national dialogue, which would highlight the internal connections and

---

[1] James M. Gustafson, "Christian Ethics," in *Religion*, ed. Paul Ramsey (Englewood Cliffs, N.J.: Prentice-Hall, Inc., 1965), 287 [285-354].

differences within American ethical thought. These are not mutually exclusive options but rather tendencies. As indicated above, the present study focuses on strands within American ethics and the weight of the discussion will therefore fall on the intra-national dialogue. This study will largely limit itself to those influences and sources which are explicitly acknowledged by the authors. Fortunately, the authors themselves point in similar directions for their sources and influences. Gustafson's observations about the practical (pragmatic) and collective character of American ethics will serve as key points.

1.2 American Protestant Ethics in Historical Perspective

1.2.1. The Emergence of Collective Character: Puritanism

As in Western Europe, the legacies of the Reformation and the Enlightenment have exerted their influence on America, in a particular form. For instance, the Puritans in America were early descendants of the European Reformation. The European Enlightenment also made its impact on America's beginnings via rationalists and deists such as Thomas Jefferson and Benjamin Franklin. These two heritages intermingled on the American continent (as they did in Western Europe) and became so intertwined that today the debate on the origins of the republic of America still continues.

In the sixteenth and seventeenth centuries, the Puritans in New England wrote comparatively little on ethics in the sense of an ethical system, but many systems of casuistry from Old England, such as William Perkins' *A Golden Chaine* (1590), William Ames' *On Conscience* (1639; Latin 1630) and Richard Baxter's *A Christian Directory* (1673) were widely read on the new continent. What emerges from these writings is a sense of absolute sovereignty of God, a pattern of order, godliness, and sobriety, and finally, a life directed by vocation and stewardship. It is important to realize that Puritan ethics was not solely a matter of regulating conduct. Although the Puritans of New England are notorious in American history for what their communities forbade their members to do, speak, or wear, the restrictiveness of Puritan community does not differ from what prevailed in most northern European communities of the time. What makes them seem peculiar against the American background is their determination to persist in these structures for regulating public conduct, when in other places in North America, the diversity of ethnic and settlement patterns helped to derail notions of a common and enforceable public ethics.[2]

A more important consideration for these purposes was the large place occupied by the idea of the "national covenant." Rooted in the covenant

[2] Allen C. Guelzo, *Edwards on the Will: A Century of American Theological Debate* (Middletown: Wesleyean, 1989), 19. Guelzo's book is a masterful and fascinating account of 18th century American theology. The title encapsulates the methodology of the book: taking its point of departure in Edwards, specifically his treatise on the freedom of the will, it pursues the debate between Calvinism and Arminianism throughout the shifting contexts.

theology of their English Puritan forebears, the settlers in New England conveniently applied the idea of a covenant to the public realm. The notion of the "national covenant," which was in place from the 1630's until the mid-18th century, entailed that the New England settlements were a particularly religious effort, created as an expression of the Puritans' longing to establish a godly community, and that God recognized and sanctified this effort by establishing a personal, national relation between himself and New England for as long as New Englanders were true to their loyalty to God.[3] So, in addition to cohesive community, New Englanders had ever before them the need to demonstrate their faithfulness to this covenant, and therefore the need to erect a variety of public and private ethical safeguards to prevent an apostasy which would then result in God forsaking them and bringing disaster. This idea of covenanting was not just a theological idea but a whole way of Puritan life.[4]

In the eyes of the Puritans, ethical concerns were intimately bound up with public ethics; introspective as the Puritans often were in their preoccupation with purity and obedience, much of that introspection was a satellite to the central anxiety that New England might manifest a public ethic consistent with its national covenant. Private ethics, in this case, were almost subordinate to public ethics. With Puritanism, then, one can clearly speak of the emergence of a collective or public ethic.

1.2.2. The Emergence of Practical Character: The Awakenings

It is difficult to conceive of the significance of the spiritual revivals which swept the colonies in the years 1740-1742. The emphasis which emerged in what was later called an awakening was the experience of spiritual quickening or conversion or rebirth, sparked under the preaching of both itinerants like George Whitefield, and parish pastors like Jonathan Edwards. Naturally, this had been part of Puritanism from its origins in England, but the concentration and amount of attention which it has received left a stamp upon the American church and nation. The revivals effected some polarization among the clergy as to how to evaluate the phenomena of the revivals. Those negatively impressed received the name "Old Lights" and were represented by the Boston clergyman Charles Chauncy. In their estimation the revivals were substituting true Christianity with diabolical enthusiasm and antinomianism. This charge was made by the association of the revivalists with the early dissenter, Anne Hutchinson, who held that union with the Holy Spirit made the moral law

[3] Allen C. Guelzo, *Edwards on the Will*, 148.

[4] When many children of the early settlers did not have a personal conversion experience as their parents had and therefore did not seek full membership in the church, the Puritans resorted to practice of the "half-way covenant." By this "half-way covenant" baptized adults who professed faith and lived uprightly, but who had had no conversion experience, were accepted as church members. They were, however, not allowed to take communion or vote in church, but their children were baptized.

superfluous and was therefore exiled from the Boston colony in 1638. The "New Lights" defended the revivals as inspired by the Spirit of God. Jonathan Edwards (1703-1758) arose as the defender of the revivals in all but their extreme forms. In his *Treatise on the Religious Affections*, Edwards appealed to the fact that true religion was a matter of the heart rather than simply the intellect.[5] The heart was the seat of the will or the affections, from which arises action. Divine love or goodness will only be known subjectively when this love is revealed to the heart. Edwards did urge the testing of the emotions in order to manifest whether they were of God or not. The emotions could be considered from God when they directed themselves toward the love of God and neighbor.

This defense of the revivals had thus an immediate connection with ethics.[6] The revivals drew attention to the will and this was to largely determine the discussion as well as the character of American ethics. Edwards elaborated on his ethics with the heritage of Puritanism, as is evident from his ethical writing, *The Nature of True Virtue*.[7] Though Edwards engaged philosophical concepts here and sought to establish natural morality, he also transformed his conclusions theologically.

True virtue for Edwards consists in "love to Being in general." Edwards specifies that this particularly holds for God, who is the "Being of Beings." God is called the Fountain of all Being and the sum of existence and excellence. This love of Being is a matter of the heart, which orients itself to the well-being of this Being. We see again that the experience of the heart, the will, source of which is the heart, is important in ethics. Benevolence or the ethics of love is not prior to God's benevolence, but rather the reverse: God's goodness produces existence and also the virtue of benevolence. Edwards promotes an ethics based on the primacy of God's love.

The focus of our love ought to be chiefly God. Edwards reproaches the moral philosophers who marginalize benevolence towards the Deity in favor of benevolence to the "created system." Instead, our love should be supremely focused on God, since without that focus, the ground of virtue is lost. Thus private affections left alone tend to exert hostility to love to Being in general. But love for particular beings which flows from love for God is virtuous.

---

[5] Jonathan Edwards, *Treatise on the Religious Affections* (ed. John E. Smith; New Haven: Yale University Press, 1959 [1746]), first preached as a series of sermons in his own parish in 1741-1742.

[6] The standard work on Edwards' ethics is Norman Fiering's, *Jonathan Edwards' Moral Thought and Its British Context* (Chapel Hill: University of North Carolina Press, 1981). Cf. also chapter 2 of Stephen D. Crocco's dissertation, "American Theocentric Ethics: A Study in the Legacy of Jonathan Edwards," Ph.D. diss., Princeton University, 1986. Cf. Gerald McDermott, *One Holy and Happy Society: The Public Theology of Jonathan Edwards* (University Park: Penn State University Press, 1992).

[7] Jonathan Edwards, *The Nature of True Virtue* (Ann Arbor: University of Michigan Press, 1960 [1765]). *The Nature of True Virtue* was written in 1755, during the Stockbridge years and published posthumously in 1765 as one of Two Dissertations, the other being *Concerning the End for Which God Created the World*. Ann Arbor: University of Michigan Press, 1960.

The ultimate focus is thus the glory of God. Here the union with God is as important, for in it the glory of God is most supremely realized in a person. Correspondingly, the love for created things should thus also seek God's glory in particular beings. God must be both first and last, the ground and the end, and his glory is thus the *telos* of our life and ethics.

The natural order somewhat reflects these matters, according to Edwards. He is willing to engage in moral discussion on this level. He speaks of the workings of the conscience and the sense of just deserts, the law of proportion, etc. Nevertheless, Edwards is quick to admit the corruption of this natural law. Only if the conscience were properly illumined by God, a concurrence with the law of God would develop. Ultimately, therefore, it is the revealed law of God which becomes the criterion and revelation of the true virtue.

Edwards' argument will be clear: the moral life consists in love, rooted in God, directed to God, though also involving other particular beings. In everything the glory of God is both end and goal. Conscience and natural law point to this and, if properly illumined by revelation, establish love to God as the nature of virtue and the moral life. The will is vital in this regard, for from it issues forth love, when it has been awakened by the Spirit of God.

The preoccupation with the will continued on a somewhat more philosophical level in Edwards' treatise entitled *The Freedom of the Will* and its subsequent legacy.[8] In this treatise Edwards makes a case for protecting a theistic form of determinism (Calvinism) as the basis for fending off not only atheism (as in the atheistic determinism of Hobbes), but also defective forms of theism, such as "Arminianism."[9] The intricacies of Edwards' argument cannot occupy us here. Its legacy was to inspire Edwards' successors Samuel Hopkins and Joseph Bellamy to promote "New Divinity," a theology focused on the will. In their preaching the New Divinity clergy denounced the older Puritan system of "preparationism" or "gradualism" which had sought to lead sinners from sin to grace along various stages. Their disdain for the "use of means"--often advocated in Puritan preaching--is related and obvious. Furthermore, the New Divinity clergy were reluctant to tolerate those in the church who were merely Christians by profession and without faith in Christ. Finally, the New Divinity departed from the standard Calvinist view of the atonement by not understanding it as the substitution of Christ imputed to the elect. Their view of the atonement has been termed "governmental," since it conceives of God as the supreme Governor, who sovereignly and graciously forgave sins, but not because of Christ. Christ's sacrifice was to show that God was indeed serious about sin and could punish it as he did in Christ. Christ's sacrifice served to ensure that God's glory would be maintained before the eyes of humanity.[10] It is not difficult to recognize the irony that, as Hendrikus Berkhof notes, "the Arminianism which had been banished from the front door finally conquered the

[8] Allen C. Guelzo, *Edwards on the Will*.
[9] Guelzo, *Edwards on the Will*, 24-25, 40-53.
[10] Guelzo, *Edwards on the Will*, 124-135.

temple of theology through this back door."[11] This was not an immediate development and Edwards can not be faulted with this charge, but the later explicit Arminianism of the nineteenth century evangelist Charles Finney was prepared by the New Divinity movement in New England.[12] Besides such transformation of Calvinist circles, there was of course the already Arminian doctrine and preaching of Methodists and many Baptists, which had as important a role, especially outside of New England, in setting the tone of the spiritual life of the young nation.

In fact, the whole character of the Second Great Awakening (especially 1840-1857) was remarkably different from the First, and partly as a result of the developments described above with the New Divinity. One could say that during this second Great Awakening American Protestantism discovered voluntarism to an extent not even realized before even within groups such as Methodists and Baptists. Beginning with Timothy Dwight (1752-1817), president of Yale, his students Lyman Beecher (1775-1863) and Nathaniel W. Taylor (1786-1858), and reaching to Charles Finney (1792-1875), intentional measures were employed to occasion the revival of the spirits of the laity. Camp meetings, rhetorical technique, the so-called "anxious benches," were all seen as "new measures" to promote and encourage the motion of the affections of persons to the embrace of God's grace.

The voluntarism of this revivalism also manifested itself in the fervor for social reform.[13] Countless voluntary societies sprang up, distinguishing themselves in immediate ends, whether missions, revivals, education, charity, prohibition, or the abolition of slavery, but unified in the objective of the betterment of society as a whole. The motivation for these activities lay in the revivals and particularly the sanctification which they stressed to persons who became converted. This emphasis on sanctification was cast in different terminology and had different theological backgrounds, from Wesleyian perfectionism to "disinterested benevolence" (Edwards). Conversion was seen to be only the beginning of a life of service. One can recognize how, despite the distinct individualism of the revivals, the collective nature, evident earlier in the Puritan idea of "national covenant," had again arisen to the fore and combined itself with the voluntaristic spirit of the revivals. This union of collectivism and voluntarism was to be continued in the Social Gospel movement later in the nineteenth century and into the early twentieth century. Before we turn to this union, however, we must take a look at the emergence of a third element in the spirit of the American nation, namely, the emergence of rational character through the Enlightenment.

---

[11] Berkhof, "North America: From Social Gospel to Neo-Orthodoxy," *Two Hundred Years of Theology: Report of a Personal Journey*, trans. John Vriend (Grand Rapids: Eerdmans, 1989), 258.

[12] Guelzo, *Edwards on the Will*, 234-235.

[13] Cf. Timothy L. Smith, *Revivalism and Social Reform: American Protestantism on the Eve of the Civil War* (Gloucester: Peter Smith, 1976).

1.2.3. The Emergence of Rational Character: The Enlightenment

The influence of the Enlightenment on America occurred at different times to different degrees at different levels. In the second half of the 18th century, the Enlightenment began to influence American political life under the leadership of Deists such as Thomas Jefferson, Benjamin Franklin, and Thomas Paine.

In ethics, the Enlightenment declared reason to be the source of moral discussion. The focus was turned to human nature and its capabilities, and literally, "man became the measure of all things." So the Anglican bishop Joseph Butler (1692-1752) could write:

> The nature of man, considered in his single capacity, and with respect only to the present world, is adapted and leads him to attain the greatest happiness he can for himself in the present world. The nature of man ... leads him to a right behavior in society to that course of life we call virtue.[14]

For Enlightenment ethics, revelation was only useful to the extent to which it corresponded to insights derived from reason. At first, Christianity was seen as compatible and the teachings of Jesus were even recommended as moral guidelines. Later, however, the relationship between Enlightenment ethics and Christianity was seen as more competitive. The subsequent history of Enlightenment ethics has developed separately from the Christian church in the various movements of transcendentalism, idealism, pragmatism, naturalism, etc.[15] For our purposes it would have little benefit to go into detail on these different schools of thought. Allow us simply to mention the American philosopher-ethicist Josiah Royce (1855-1916), who became somewhat important to both James Gustafson and Paul Ramsey. Royce was largely influenced by Kant, Hegel, and German Idealism and his ethics reveals this commitment. He proposed his ethics chiefly in response to pragmatism and William James as its teacher. Royce's discussion of ethics centers on "loyalty."

Royce defined loyalty as "*the willing and practical and thoroughgoing devotion of a person to a cause.*"[16] Royce sees human nature as naturally autonomous. However, in the social context of our life, we must assert our autonomy by being loyal to a cause. Royce combats individualism, for he sees it as indulgent or apathetic in its ethics. Royce formulates this loyalty as a loyalty to loyalty. Whoever seeks to further the cause of loyalty is doing a service to humanity as a whole. The relationship of this to Kant's categorical imperative--the duty of each for all--will be evident.

This philosophy of loyalty comes from nature, particularly the conscience. The ideal plan or loyalty to a cause is presented by conscience.

---

[14] Butler, *Sermons* (New York: Robert Carter & Bros., 1858).

[15] Cf. Guy W. Stroh, *American Ethical Thought* (Chicago: Nelson-Hall, 1979).

[16] Josiah Royce, *The Philosophy of Loyalty* (New York: MacMillan, 1908), 16-17.

Royce says: "The conscience is the ideal of the self, coming to consciousness as a present command. It says, *Be loyal.* If one asks, *Loyal to what?*, the conscience, awakened by our whole personal response to the need of mankind replies, *Be loyal to loyalty.*"[17] Are there further criteria in the particular criteria to exercise this? Royce advocates following the decision which the conscience--"the ideal expression of ... personal nature"--finds best.[18]

Royce sought to be social in his orientation in contrast to the individualism of the pragmatists. Moreover, Royce's idealism is clear in his argument. The realm of the mind, the conscience, decides moral action. We see how the ground of Enlightenment thinking has provided the ground for Royce: human nature is the source of morality. It is interesting that Royce raises the conscience, the awareness of loyalty to loyalty to the position which traditionally has been reserved for God: "Through our actual human loyalty, we come, like Moses, face to face with the true will of the world, as a man speaks with his friend." Royce calls this "the creed of the Absolute Religion."[19] This religion is the religion of human nature.

James M. Gustafson relates that H. Richard Niebuhr led him to a serious study of Josiah Royce.[20] In his dissertation Gustafson wrote on ecclesiology from a sociological and social philosophical perspective. Here he made substantial use of Royce's emphasis on community.[21] Paul Ramsey, also a student of Niebuhr at Yale, wrote his dissertation partly on the anthropology of Josiah Royce.[22] Also in his book *Basic Christian Ethics*, Ramsey uses Royce's concept of human sin as a source.[23] Royce symbolizes for both Gustafson and Ramsey one of the figures of Enlightenment ethics with whom both Gustafson and Ramsey had to come to terms.

The ethics of Royce, as well as other above-mentioned non-Christian schools, does not exhaust the extent of the influence of Enlightenment on the moral life of America. For within Christianity, the ideas of the Enlightenment had their impact upon Protestant theology particularly from the middle of the nineteenth century on. The movement of liberalism or modernism gained ground particularly in the latter part of the nineteenth century, partly in reaction to the

---

[17] Royce, *The Philosophy of Loyalty*, 195.

[18] Royce, *The Philosophy of Loyalty*, 195-196.

[19] Royce, *The Philosophy of Loyalty*, 390-391.

[20] *Treasure in Earthen Vessels: The Church as Human Community* (Chicago: University of Chicago Press, 1961), xi.

[21] James M. Gustafson, "Community and Time in the Christian Church: A Study of the Church from a Sociological and Social Philosophical Perspective," PhD. diss., Yale University, 1955.

[22] Cf. Paul Ramsey, *The Essential Paul Ramsey: A Collection*, eds. William Werpehowski and Stephen D. Crocco (New Haven: Yale University Press, 1994), viii. The title of his dissertation was "The Concept of Man in the Philosophy of Josiah Royce and Bernard Bosanquet." Werpehowski and Crocco relate that he "never thought much of his dissertation ... but it does illustrate his early interests in philosophical idealism." Bernard Bosanquet (1848-1923) was an English philosopher, the last major representative of Neo-Hegelianism in England.

[23] Paul Ramsey, *Basic Christian Ethics* (New York: Charles Scribner's Sons, 1950), 321-325.

revivalism dominant up till that point. Largely through contact with European sources, such as the philosophy of Kant and the theology of Schleiermacher and Ritschl, the tradition of liberalism made inroads in Protestant seminaries and churches. Horace Bushnell (1802-1872) is usually considered one of the early nineteenth century liberals.[24] One of his first theological publications entitled *God in Christ* (1847) asserted that religious language is always figurative and that behind the various symbols lay concealed the "essential meaning" to be considered normative. A treatise on religion and science, *Nature and the Supernatural* (1858), sought to accommodate the new scientific discoveries of the day. His book *The Vicarious Sacrifice* (1866) propounded a form of the "moral influence" theory of the atonement. Though he allowed that the sacrifice of Christ had some effect on God, the main tenor of the atonement is that the love demonstrated therein should move us return such love to God. Like Schleiermacher in Europe Bushnell sought to reformulate traditional dogma to suit the experience of contemporary people. With Hendrikus Berkhof, one could say that Bushnell began a process of "anthropolization" in Protestant theology which has been dominant ever since.[25]

Partly then out of reaction to the pervasive revivalism, and partly owing to the impact of the publication of Darwin's *Origin of Species* and the consequent popularity of evolutionary theories, theology, particularly in the Protestant North, adjusted drastically. In general, the liberalism of the late nineteenth century was one characterized by an emphasis on the immanence of God in the processes of nature, the goodness and freedom of humanity, experience as the source of Christian belief, and the inevitable progress of the human race. Biblical criticism was used in the interpretation of Scripture in order to rid the church of believing in its archaic aspects. Ethics lay at the center of the church's proclamation and its message focused on bringing in the kingdom of God through education and social reform. It can easily be seen how one of the most famous of liberalism's children was the Social Gospel. To this peculiarly American phenomenon we turn our attention.

1.2.4. The Convergence of the Collective, Practical, and Rational I: The Social Gospel

In his dissertation on *The Background of the Social Gospel in America*, W. A. Visser 't Hooft wrote: "The social gospel, therefore, in the sense in which we are going to speak about it, is more than an application of Christian principles to society; it is also an application of social principles to Christianity; or to put it shortly: it is a form of interpenetration of religious and social

[24] Cf. D. A. Smith, *Symbolism and Growth: The Religious Thought of Horace Bushnell* (Chico, CA: Scholars, 1981); Claude Welch, *Protestant Theology in the Nineteenth Century* (New Haven: Yale University Press, 1972).

[25] Hendrikus Berkhof, "North America: From Social Gospel to Neo-Orthodoxy," 259-260.

thought."[26] The collective, practical, and rational elements which emerged in the American character did not find a wholly developed fusion till the idea of the Social Gospel began to be articulated and adhered to within the Protestant tradition. One needs to note that the social problems which attended the rise of industrial America after the Civil War (1861-1865) demanded an extraordinary and practical response from the churches.

The Congregationalist clergyman Washington Gladden (1836-1918) is usually heralded as one of the first to be identified with this movement.[27] As a personal friend of Horace Bushnell and a practitioner of biblical criticism, Gladden discovered that the situations in which he found many of his parishioners required a prophetic response from the church, not unlike that of Amos. In his voluminous writings he sought to relate the gospel to the social problems of labor, race, taxation, etc.

The most important theological representative of the Social Gospel is undoubtedly Walter Rauschenbusch (1861-1918). The line from the Enlightenment to Rauschenbusch runs partly through Albrecht Ritschl. Ritschl focused on the human effects of God's work on earth under influence of Kant's stating the impossibility of knowing anything about the absolute world. Kant had emphasized the practical postulates for moral behavior. Along those lines Ritschl focused on what we could see of God's work in the world. The emphasis was laid on the person of Jesus as the founder of the Kingdom of God on earth.[28]

Furthermore, one should keep in mind the Darwinian philosophy of evolving history, which was current at the turn of the century. When combined with the above view of the kingdom of God, it was believed that God was operative in the processes of history, which were always ameliorating.[29] Both Ritschl's and Darwin's influence on Rauschenbusch symbolize the Enlightenment's focus on the mere historical.

For Rauschenbusch the Bible did play a part, particularly as it spoke about social justice of the Kingdom of God. Rauschenbusch advocated a social interpretation of the Bible. The message of Scripture comes to us only as we have been taught to listen to it. In Rauschenbusch's view the social message of the Bible had been numbed by dogmatic interpretation. However, the historical interpretation had rendered things more "life-like" and thus called attention to the social aspects.[30] The doctrine of the Kingdom of God was important for Rauschenbusch, because it linked religion and ethics: "When our moral actions

---

26 Quoted in Berkhof, "North America: From Social Gospel to Neo-Orthodoxy," 260-261.

27 Cf. J. H. Dorn, *Washington Gladden: Prophet of the Social Gospel* (Columbus: Ohio State University Press, 1966).

28 Cf. Waldo Beach and H. Richard Niebuhr, *Christian Ethics: Sources of Living Tradition* (New York: Ronald Press, 1955), 444-445.

29 Beach and Niebuhr, *Christian Ethics: Sources of Living Tradition*, 447-448.

30 Walter Rauschenbusch, *Christianity and the Social Crisis* (New York: MacMillan, 1908), 45, 196, 209.

are consciously related to the Kingdom of God they gain religious quality." Rauschenbusch understands sin primarily socially. When we sin against humanity, we are sinning against God. Rauschenbusch even advocates a "democratizing of the concept of God." Conversely, redemption involves co-operating and laboring for the good of others. Rauschenbusch even calls this labor "one of the conditions of salvation."[31] The Kingdom will be realized more and more when we promote a good social order, exercise love as the law of Christ, surrender opportunities to exploit others, and labor towards the unity of humans. This is the ethics which flows from Rauschenbusch's Social Gospel.

The connections with the Enlightenment should not be lost from view. The focus primarily on history, the positivism, and the practicality flowing from the surrender to ignorance regarding the absolute marks the Social Gospel's inheritance from the Enlightenment. In his dissertation on Rauschenbusch, Allen Verhey admits that the slogan, *sola scriptura*, is "methodologically deceptive." He states that the argument for the very authorizations licensing the use of Scripture can be traced back to other sources of data.[32] Accordingly, Verhey proposes that interpreters of Scripture must exhibit openness to other authorities, such as the community, the tradition, new experience, and reason.[33]

In the practice of thc Social Gospel an interesting shift took place. We noted above that the revivalism of the second Great Awakening had prompted much social action through its beliefs in holiness, perfection, and "disinterested benevolence." This social action had not been partisan or reserved to one segment of the Protestant church. In the later nineteenth century with the more distinct problems of modernization this non-partisanship stopped. The Social Gospel was largely practiced by liberal Protestantism and the baton of social action was, so to speak, left in their hands. This was the era of the growing divergence between conservative and liberal elements in the Protestant church and the emergence of the fundamentalist movement.[34] The fundamentalists adopted millenarian positions and promoted a very individualistic concept of salvation. The liberal, pragmatic, and evolutionist commitments of the Social Gospel also effected the distance between fundamentalism and social action. Yet, the mainline churches were characterized by much action in political and economic spheres. The practical character which had emerged during the revivals became under Enlightenment philosophy what one could call "pragmatic."

---

[31] Walter Rauschenbusch, *A Theology for the Social Gospel* (New York: MacMillan, 1918).

[32] Allen D. Verhey, "The Use of Scripture in Moral Argument: A Case Study of Walter Rauschenbusch," Ph.D. diss., Yale University (Ann Arbor: University Microfilms, 1975), 221, 222.

[33] Verhey, "The Use of Scripture in Moral Argument," 222.

[34] Cf. George M. Marsden, *Fundamentalism and American Culture: The Shaping of Twentieth-Century Evangelicalism 1870-1925* (Oxford: Oxford University Press, 1980), esp. 85-93.

Though the practical impulses of American religion are distinctly operative in the Social Gospel movement, one can as well recognize the old emphasis on a collective ethic. America was intended to have an extraordinary place in the world and its own social and collective life had to be exemplary. The utopian ideals of the colonists and the republican aspirations of the early nation could only survive the crisis of industrialization, interpreted by means of the Social Gospel. Josiah Strong (1847-1916), for example, combined the Social Gospel with a type of Christian "imperialism." In his book *Our Country: Its Possible Future and Its Present Crisis* (1885), Strong outlined the various social perils facing America and advocated reform led by the Anglo-Saxons, representatives of civil liberty and "pure, spiritual Christianity." These last two ideals were for Strong "the forces which, in the past, have contributed most to the elevation of the human race, and they must continue to be, in the future, the most efficient ministers to its progress."[35] Though the character of Strong's imperialism is defined to a great extent by a liberal and social thought foreign to the Puritan idea of national covenant, some degree of continuity with this Puritan idea ought not to be excluded. With Strong, then, the prominent collective element of the Social Gospel movement is thus evident.

After a few decades of the twentieth century, the Social Gospel began to lose its strength as a distinct movement. It seems that the social reform emphases were to some extent sublimated into the political fabric of society, though they were to re-emerge as the situation requires, even to this very day. In that regard, the Social Gospel movement has not disappeared, but instead been assimilated into other movements and processes. Yet, spokespersons for such a movement of the caliber of Walter Rauschenbusch have not arisen. Instead, the theological momentum turned to Existentialism and Neo-Orthodoxy, as it had arisen in Europe, and received its own definition in the United States.

1.2.5. The Convergence of the Collective, Practical, and Rational II: Neo-Orthodoxy and the Niebuhrs

Though in many ways a child of Social Gospel theology, Reinhold Niebuhr (1892-1971) recognized that despite the efforts of the Social Gospel, the developments in society failed to confirm the hopes of the Social Gospel. Instead, his pastoral experience in the automobile manufacturing capital of America, Detroit, caused him to recognize the disparity between "moral man and immoral society." His book by that title (1932) sketched the hollowness of the optimistic idealism of liberal theology and called for a Christian realism which ascertained that in contrast to individuals, for collective groups and human societies "there is less reason to guide and to check impulse, less capacity for self-transcendence, less ability to comprehend the needs of others

[35] Quoted in Winthrop S. Hudson, *Religion in America: A Historical Account of the Development of American Religious Life*, 4th edition (New York: MacMillan, 1987), 297-299.

and therefore more unrestrained egoism."[36] As an extension of the Social Gospel, Niebuhr began to advocate justice through force as a means to render societies as moral as individuals.

Niebuhr's pessimism concerning human possibilities increased, however. His ambiguous statement "man sins inevitably, but not necessarily" is well-known. The Christian response to sin Niebuhr encapsulated in the term "Christian realism." Christian realism maneuvered between the dialectic of the absolute standard of love and the rational standard of justice. On the one hand, Niebuhr realized that an ideal social order could not be realized by persuading people to love each other. On the other hand, he regarded the law of love as the full requirement of God. It stands above history and occurs infrequently in history in the self-sacrificing *agape* love, but does not sustain itself. The standard of justice is the most Christians can hope for, and it is the imperfect product of a given community, in which various perspectives on various problems merge.[37]

Reinhold's brother, H. Richard Niebuhr (1894-1962), stood less in continuity with the Social Gospel movement and more directly with theological liberalism as it existed in Europe. Yet, Richard Niebuhr also represents a voice in American theology and ethics which some have labelled neo-orthodox. Like his brother, he was dissatisfied with the optimistic liberalism of the turn of the century and sought for more theological depth structure to respond to the non-abating problems of modern society. Richard Niebuhr's thought has had quite a bit of influence, in part through his writings, in part through his students.[38] In the Netherlands there was recognition of his work particularly in the 1960's.[39]

Niebuhr pointed to Karl Barth and Ernst Troeltsch as his primary teachers.[40] Though this combination might seem surprising, the manner in which Niebuhr sought to combine relativism and theocentrism indeed confirms this

---

36 Reinhold Niebuhr, *Moral Man and Immoral Society: A Study in Ethics and Politics* (New York: Charles Scribner's Sons, 1932), xi-xii.

37 Reinhold Niebuhr, *The Nature and Destiny of Man*, Vol. 2 (New York: Charles Scribner' Sons, 1943), 253-258. Cf. Paul Ramsey's discussion of the relationship between love and justice in Reinhold Niebuhr: "Reinhold Niebuhr: Christian Love and Natural Law," in *Nine Modern Moralists* (Englewood Cliffs, N.J.: Prentice-Hall, 1962), 141-185.

38 Cf. the various essays in *Faith and Ethics: The Theology of H. Richard Niebuhr*, ed. Paul Ramsey, (New York: Harper & Row, 1957); and those in *The Legacy of H. Richard Niebuhr*, ed. Ronald F. Thiemann, (Harvard Theological Studies 36; Minneapolis: Fortress, 1991).

39 Cf. e.g., J. van den Berg, "Tussen Troeltsch en Barth: Enkele inleidende opmerkingen over het leven en het werk van de Amerikaanse theoloog H. Richard Niebuhr," in *Gereformeerd Theologisch Tijdschrift* 63 (1963), 161-175; J. Brinkerink, "Richard Niebuhr, een te weinig bekend theoloog," in *Wending* 16 (1961), 470-482; E. J. Beker, "The Sovereignty of God in the Thought of H. Richard Niebuhr," in *Nederlands Theologisch Tijdschrift* 15 (1960-1961), 108-130.

40 H. Richard Niebuhr, *The Meaning of Revelation* (New York: MacMillan, 1941), x. Cf. van den Berg, "Tussen Troeltsch en Barth."

statement. Niebuhr subscribed to the historicism of Troeltsch.[41] Spacial and temporal relativity, the discovery of science and philosophy, encloses all our knowing.[42] Niebuhr remarkably calls this awareness "an act of faith," inevitable and justified by its results.[43] From this acceptance of relativism we must move to revelation. In revelation our relativity is addressed and its disclosure invites us to devotion.[44]

This revelation is of a particular nature. On the one hand, since we are historical and social beings, revelation comes to us through those means. Thus we have Scripture as a historical book. But as such mere Scripture can not be revelation. Revelation can not simply be Scripture, but only Scripture read from the point of view of church history. As a community we listen for the word of God in the reading of Scripture.[45] Revelation as God coming to us cannot be history. Niebuhr is sensing the tension: revelation is necessarily historical, but it cannot be history.

In order to deal with this tension, Niebuhr distinguishes between internal history and external history. External history refers to those aspects of experience intelligible to all sharing the same cultural values. Internal history is that history which impacts the destiny of the self. Internal history can thus only be confessed by those in community. Internal history can also impact the present.[46] Here Niebuhr is using Kant's distinction between pure and practical reason.[47]

Niebuhr refers to the common error of locating revelation in external history. Instead, revelation takes place in internal history and the proper response is faith. To move into the apprehension characteristic of internal history occurs through "a leap of faith, a *metanoia* or revolution of the mind." Internal history is also nurtured in a community of symbols, traditions, and rituals. Thus this history receives life and practicality. The Christian community should not neglect external history, though, for external history is "a medium in which internal history exists and comes to life."[48]

---

[41] A standard study on the development of Troeltsch's thought is J. Klapwijk's *Tussen Historisme en Relativisme: Een studie over de dynamiek van het historisme en de wijsgerige ontwikkelingsgang van Ernst Troeltsch* (Assen: Van Gorcum, 1970). On Niebuhr's theological background, cf. Hans W. Frei, "Niebuhr's Theological Background," in *Faith and Ethics: The Theology of H. Richard Niebuhr*, ed. Paul Ramsey (New York: Harper & Brothers, 1957), 3-64.

[42] H. Richard Niebuhr, *The Meaning of Revelation*, 7ff.

[43] Niebuhr, *The Meaning of Revelation*, 20.

[44] Niebuhr, *The Meaning of Revelation*, 22. Paul Ramsey discusses this thought as "transformation" in his chapter, "H. Richard Niebuhr: Christ Transforming Relativism," in *Nine Modern Moralists*, 187-223.

[45] Niebuhr, *The Meaning of Revelation*, 51.

[46] Niebuhr, *The Meaning of Revelation*, 67-74.

[47] Niebuhr, *The Meaning of Revelation*, 65.

[48] Niebuhr, *The Meaning of Revelation*, 83, 89-90.

Niebuhr's focus on revelation is revolutionary compared to the Enlightenment. Barth signified this same revolution. Nevertheless, this turn to revelation should not be understood as a return to the pre-Enlightenment understanding of revelation. It is an understanding of revelation closely related to Troeltsch's historicism. Niebuhr explicitly adopts Troeltsch's view of understanding. Moreover, Troeltsch reached to transcendence through a religious *a priori* located in human nature. With this religious *a priori* Troeltsch can still bring in the absolute and transcendent spirit into the lives of persons. Niebuhr takes a slightly different route by delimiting an area and function of so-called "internal history" in which revelation comes to the community engaged in ritual and tradition.

After laying these grounds of revelation Niebuhr proposed an ethic of responsibility and radical monotheism.[49] In light of the emerging religious pluralism of America, attention to the principle of monotheism can clear the way for at least a "monotheistic ethic." Monotheism also challenges the adherence to other gods, whether they be American nationalism, capitalism, and all other principalities and powers which would assert themselves in place of God. Niebuhr writes: "Radical monotheism dethrones all absolutes short of the principle of being itself. At the same time it reverences every relative existent. Its two great mottoes are: 'I am the Lord thy God; thou shalt have no other gods before me' and 'Whatever is, is good.'"[50]

In his posthumously published book, *The Responsible Self* (1963), Niebuhr gives most concrete expression to his dispositional ethic. Niebuhr advocates close attention to the "symbolism of responsibility": it connotes "the image of man-the-answerer, man engaged in dialogue, man acting in response to action upon him."[51] Niebuhr's theory of responsibility contains the following elements: 1) we *respond* to actions upon us; 2) we respond in terms of our *interpretations* of those actions; 3) we are *accountable* (answerable) for our actions; 4) we construct our answers in the *context* of the community.[52] The horizons of relationships within which this responsibility is exercised are vertical and horizontal. Within these contexts, the Christian operates and acts as an ethical agent.

These ethical views are the product of Niebuhr's effort to combine the transcendence of God and the relativity of the human situation. The community has been put forward as the determining context for ethical decisions. When the lines are drawn, the ground for ethical action lies in the experience of the community and their discernment of the proper response. This ethic has received

---

[49] H. Richard Niebuhr, *The Responsible Self: An Essay in Christian Moral Philosophy* (New York: Harper and Row, 1963); *Radical Monotheism and Western Culture* (Louisville: Westminster/John Knox, 1993; orig. published 1943).

[50] Niebuhr, *Radical Monotheism and Western Culture*, 37.

[51] Niebuhr, *The Responsible Self*, 56.

[52] Niebuhr, *The Responsible Self*, 47-68.

an indelible imprint from rational Enlightenment thinking. And it articulates itself within the practice of ethics, as the practice requires.

Community, reason, and practice: these three elements have arisen within the history of American ethics and have blended themselves in a peculiarly American fashion. H. Richard Niebuhr characterizes well the contemporary scene of options in the mainstream of American ethics. As this project now turns its focus to some of Niebuhr's students, the subsequent and present developments will be traced in detail and the horizons for the future of American ethics will receive attention.

1.2.6. Heirs to the Convergence: Gustafson, Ramsey, and Verhey

Contemporary American ethics is almost endlessly diverse. The older ethical schools of pragmatism, idealism, naturalism, transcendentalism, socialism, and existentialism are being supplemented by situationism, egalitarianism, feminism, passivism, and liberationism. Within any distinctly Christian ethics there can be any mix of the above movements, plus an attachment to key principles such as narrrative, character, virtue, *agape*, justice, covenant, etc. The confusion of schools has become somewhat irrelevant, due to the fact that the agenda in ethics is largely being set by the practical issues at hand. Yet the heritage of the practical, the collective, and the rational, as sketched above, is still fundamental to much of these ethics. The following chapters will signal the prominence of these elements in the works under examination

When one traces the sources for Gustafson, Ramsey, and Verhey, one begins to notice patterns. For instance, all three men completed their Ph.D. study at Yale University, Ramsey and Gustafson partly under H. Richard Niebuhr, Verhey partly under Gustafson. This establishes the connection with Richard Niebuhr, one of the most important Christian ethicists of this century. This superficial connection with Niebuhr is substantiated by a closer reading of their works.[53] With Niebuhr we enter into the realm of neo-orthodoxy, also linked to the names of Barth and Bultmann. There is then, first of all, a common connection with neo-orthodoxy.

Secondly, we see all three of them struggle with some aspect of modern philosophy or ethics in their dissertations. Ramsey wrote on the anthropology of Josiah Royce, an American idealist philosopher, and Bernard Bosanquet, a British Hegelian. Gustafson wrote an ecclesiology from a sociological and social philosophical perspective, using authors such as Josiah Royce, George Herbert Mead, Henri Bergson, and Wilhelm Dilthey. Verhey wrote on the

---

[53] According to David H. Smith, referring to H. Richard Niebuhr's growing influence in theological ethics, the "clearest line is from Niebuhr to the work of James M. Gustafson," "Religion and the Roots of the Bioethics Revival," in ***Religion and Medical Ethics: looking back, looking forward***, ed. Allen Verhey, (Grand Rapids: William B. Eerdmans Publishing Company, 1996), 11.

Social Gospel reformer Walter Rauschenbusch and his use of Scripture, with the help of logical and philosophical categories from Stephen Toulmin and Henry D. Aiken. Their respective dissertations show an effort to come to terms with some aspect of modern, post-Kantian philosophy or ethics. This strand of modernity would return in later writings, particularly in Gustafson, but to a milder extent also in Ramsey and Verhey.

In spite of common themes in their backgrounds, these three men display diversity in emphasis, which provides rationale for selecting them as representatives. The titles to the individual chapters illustrate the difference in emphases. Gustafson seeks to construct a theocentric ethics: an ethics in which God is the critical reference point. Ramsey's ethics often receives the label "Christian ethics," because he seeks to make ethics christocentric. With Verhey it is more difficult to attach a single term to his ethics. In Verhey's work the problem of the place of Scripture in moral discussion has received most explicit attention. By dealing with Gustafson, Ramsey, and Verhey together, theocentricity, christocentricity, and the place of Scripture are all brought to bear upon moral discussion.

1.3. Scripture and Ethics in the Contemporary American Discussion

To simply discuss the individual ethical models of three ethicists would lack coherence, unless a specific issue would bind the discussion together. In this study the methodological issue of the use of Scripture will serve that function. What role is attributed to Scripture in the construction of an ethical model? At what level does Scripture function in the discussion of the practice of Christian ethics? What uses of Scripture are rejected and for what reasons? What relationship does Scripture have to other possible sources of ethical authority? These questions will set the agenda for the discussion of the authors. This issue will also constitute the subject of the response in the final chapter.

Though Scripture has been a significant force in the history of American Protestant ethics, the methodological discussion on Scripture has been a relatively recent concern. Biblical studies and ethics in America have suffered from the compartmentalization standard in all academic fields today. Rare were the ethicists who were competent to follow biblical discussion at the level at which they retained credibility for the biblical scholar. On the other hand, seldom did biblical scholars venture into the field of ethics, but stop short of making ethical claims. In their book entitled *Bible and Ethics in the Christian Life*, Bruce Birch and Larry Rasmussen ascertain what they term a "gap" or a "divergence" between the two disciplines.[54]

---

[54] Bruce C. Birch and Larry L. Rasmussen, *Bible and Ethics in the Christian Life* (Minneapolis: Augsburg, 1976), 15-44. Their book is one of the more recent attempts to effect the rapprochement of the two disciplines. Cf. Gustafson, "Christian Ethics," 337-338.

This discontinuity between the disciplines was experienced by others as well. Scholars had begun to wonder whether the disjunction was not just a matter of the academic disciplines, but whether there was simply an irreconcilability between the Bible and the moral life. Edward LeRoy Long's 1965 article "The Use of the Bible in Christian Ethics" is usually heralded as one of the first of a new generation of attempts to deal with the problem.[55] Long's article delineates three ways in which theologians have employed Scripture in moral discussion: prescriptively, principledly, exemplarily. The first attends to the direct commands or directions of Scripture (Calvin, John Murray, C. H. Dodd). The second derives and deduces principles from scriptural material (von Harnack, Reinhold Niebuhr, Andrew R. Osborn). The third group finds scriptural morality a pattern or model for ethical reasoning (Paul Lehmann, Joseph Sittler). In his article Long does not opt between the alternatives, but simply classifies and describes the usage of the Bible in ethics.[56]

Others have opted for distinct alternatives, among whom Gustafson, Verhey, and Ramsey. Since the following chapters of this study focus on their work, I will leave them outside of consideration at this point. Their work is only part of a whole forum of views. Since this introduction intends merely to survey the territory to be discussed below, I will suffice with sketching some lines representative of the recent discussion.

The book by Bruce Birch and Larry Rasmussen, referred to above, advocates a position which is rather typical of a certain consensus on the relationship between Scripture and ethics. Their emphasis is, first of all, on the function of the Bible in the formation of character. The variety of materials and emphases in the Bible will mould a full character, which could very well be different in different instances.[57] The authors outline, secondly, how the Bible ought to influence specific actions and decisions. They speak here of the Bible as a source of moral rules and principles, which prescribe a Christian's identity, the boundaries for proper conduct, and locate where the weight of normative action falls and where exceptions might be permitted.[58] Crucial here is the locus of the church as the community context: it shapes moral character, carries the moral tradition, and provides the context for moral deliberation.[59] Birch and Rasmussen are therefore reluctant to invest single authority in the Scripture. In their view, it negates the ongoing activity of God and the other sources through which God discloses himself.[60] Yet, the Bible should be considered the primary

---

[55] Edward LeRoy Long, Jr., "The Use of the Bible in Christian Ethics: A Look at Basic Options," *Interpretation* 65 (1965), 149-162.

[56] Similar in intent is William C. Spohn, S.J., *What Are They Saying About Scripture and Ethics?* (New York: Paulist Press, 1984). His discussion is not limited to American ethicists, but does include a discussion of H. Richard Niebuhr, Gustafson, Hauerwas, Yoder and others.

[57] Birch and Rasmussen, *Bible and Ethics*, 104-112.

[58] Birch and Rasmussen, *Bible and Ethics*, 113-123.

[59] Birch and Rasmussen, *Bible and Ethics*, 127-141.

[60] Birch and Rasmussen, *Bible and Ethics*, 147, 150.

source "to insure that Christian decision-making is dialogic--biblical faith interacting with the best wisdom of our modern world."[61] The main tenor of this study is that the Bible constitutes the primary source for ethical reflection which takes place dialogically within the community of the church. The word "dialogically" has two senses: Scripture in dialogue with experience, and persons with persons.[62]

Thomas Ogletree is one who has practiced this dialogue fashion and offers one reading of the significance of Scripture for the ethics of the community.[63] Ogletree's practice of interpretation is informed by Hans-Georg Gadamer's hermeneutical theory developed within the existentialist tradition of Heidegger. Ogletree begins with a treatment of what he sees as the various preunderstandings (Gadamerian term: the pre-existing framework and assumptions of persons and communities) of the moral life: the utilitarian ethic, the deontological ethic, and the perfectionist ethic. These ethical theories take shape in the finite realm of historical contingency (contextualism). Scripture then enters into the discussion as a dialogue partner and its eschatology confronts the pre-understandings with its importance. It demands a transformation in which the Christian community receives an eschatological identity and is impelled to live out an eschatological existence in this world. The eschatological identity and ethic of the church transforms the utilitarian, deontological, and perfectionist ethic and makes the church 1) a community alien to the world, and 2) an instrument of change within social existence.[64] Ogletree suggests, for example, that inwardly the church become a community in solidarity with the marginalized of society and thus live out its eschatological existence of grace. In its mission to the outside world, the church ought to challenge the fixed hierarchies of power and modes of economic, social, and cultural oppression.[65] To effect these objectives Ogletree has felt free to embrace critical theory as a tool of critique offered by modern society itself. He finds that "[c]ritical theory is itself motivated by experiences of alienation in the everyday life world."[66] Within our historical context, it coincides to some extent

---

[61] Birch and Rasmussen, *Bible and Ethics*, 158. Cf. Robin Scroggs, "The New Testament and Ethics: How Do we Get From There to Here?", in *Perspectives on the New Testament: Essays in Honor of Frank Stagg*, ed. Charles H. Talbert, 77-85 (Macon, GA: Mercer University Press, 1985). Her discussion concludes with the encouragement to take the biblical message seriously, but also "in Christian freedom" risk contrary to it, if our deliberations lead us to that point (93). Also here the dialogue between Scripture and our own judgment is the framework within which the Christian moral life takes place.

[62] Michael G. Cartwright has also ascertained this as the scholarly consensus at the present ("The Uses of Scripture in Christian Ethics--After Bakhtin," *The Annual of the Society of Christian Ethics* 12 [1992], 263-265).

[63] Thomas W. Ogletree, *The Use of the Bible in Christian Ethics* (Philadelphia: Fortress, 1983).

[64] Ogletree, *The Use of the Bible in Christian Ethics*, 182-206.

[65] Ogletree, *The Use of the Bible in Christian Ethics*, 185, 191-192.

[66] Ogletree, *The Use of the Bible in Christian Ethics*, 184-185.

with the alienation of Christian eschatological existence, though the latter goes beyond it. For eschatological existence is witnessed by the horizon of the Scripture and an encounter with this horizon effects this dialogical transformation necessary for the identity and ethic of the Christian community.

Ogletree has exemplified a dialogical method in which again the Christian community is constitutive for the effect of Scripture. This dialogical method has a Gadamerian form for Ogletree and highlights the eschatological quality of Christian identity and ethic.

Similar in their emphasis on the context of the Christian community are the conclusions of the well-known ethicist Stanley Hauerwas.[67] In reference to the term "the authority of Scripture," Hauerwas argues that authority needs a community. In the case of Scripture there is the Christian community, upon which Scripture exercises authority in a formative manner, in the process of Christians remembering the narrative of God's actions.[68] Scriptural authority is therefore, according to Hauerwas, in practice mediated through the community. It is interesting that Hauerwas, following Yoder, ascribes this insight to the Free (Anabaptist) Church, which discerned the significance of the spiritual community appropriating Scripture, in contrast to the "extreme" (Lutheran and Calvinists) Protestants insisting on the objective authority resting in Scripture.[69] For Hauerwas, who follows David Kelsey at this point, authority is contained in the "hermeneutical circle" of "church, Scripture, and theology."[70]

In his book surveying the recent uses of Scripture in theology, David Kelsey argued that to speak of the authority of Scripture means to speak of its function for the church.[71] The authority of Scripture is not a property of Scripture, nor based on the properties of Scripture, according to Kelsey.[72] The authority of Scripture exists in its being *for* the church. Kelsey proposes that the locus of Scripture in systematic theology should therefore be treated as part of "the shaping of Christian existence, both communal and individual, i.e., a part of doctrines of 'sanctification' and 'ecclesiology.'"[73] Hauerwas has drawn the proper conclusion of this view for ethics: Scripture can offer guidance for the

---

[67] Cf. his *A Community of Character: Toward a Constructive Christian Social Ethic* (Notre Dame: University of Notre Dame Press, 1981) and *Vision and Virtue* (Notre Dame: University of Notre Dame Press, 1974). A representative piece of his on this subject is "The Moral Authority of Scripture: The Politics and Ethics of Remembering," *Interpretation* 34 (1980), 356-370. Reprinted in, *Moral Theology No. 4: The Use of Scripture in Moral Theology*, eds. Charles E. Curran and Richard A. McCormick (New York: Paulist Press, 1984), 242-275.

[68] Hauerwas, "The Moral Authority of Scripture," 361-365.

[69] Hauerwas, "The Moral Authority of Scripture," 357-358.

[70] Hauerwas, "The Moral Authority of Scripture," 363.

[71] David H. Kelsey, *The Uses of Scripture in Recent Theology* (Philadelphia: Fortress, 1975), 89, 93-94 *et passim*.

[72] Kelsey, *The Uses of Scripture in Recent Theology*, 29-30, 108-109.

[73] Kelsey, *The Uses of Scripture in Recent Theology*, 208-209.

moral life only in the context of the community and its reflections and deliberation.[74]

John Howard Yoder's book *The Politics of Jesus* was influential as a discussion of the use of the Bible for moral problems. Yoder points out how Jesus' ethic is unacceptable to the modern world. Instead, the mainstream ethical consensus seeks to bridge the gap to the present. But Yoder finds that only a "certain very moderate amount of freight can be carried across this bridge: perhaps a concept of absolute love or humility or faith or freedom. But the substance of ethics must be reconstructed on our side of the bridge."[75] Yoder finds this, however, identical with a "theology of the natural," and pleads instead for an ethics "rooted in revelation, not alone in speculation, nor in a self-interpreting 'situation.'"[76] In a subsequent book *The Priestly Kingdom* Yoder moves from what this ethic is about to how this ethic takes shape in the world. This argument unfolds mainly in his chapter entitled: "The Hermeneutics of Peoplehood." Yoder draws upon the experience of the Free Church (the Anabaptists) during the Reformation and finds there a "procedure for doing practical moral reasoning."[77] Yoder builds on Matt. 18:15,18 ("Whatever you bind on earth ... " etc.) and states: "A transcendent moral ratification is claimed for the decisions made in the conversation of two or three or more, in a context of forgiveness and in the juridical form of listening to several witnesses."[78] The Anabaptist community could fulfill this more closely than the other communities of the Reformation, since it did not align itself with the civil powers of the state. Yoder elaborates on the components of this practical moral reasoning, but the focus is on the action of the community. As with Hauerwas and Kelsey above, ethics is constructed from Scripture (or the ethics of Jesus, in the case of Yoder) only in the context of the community.

There have been a few scholars which have offered challenges to the consensus as described above. Michael Cartwright, for instance, points out the danger of "dissolving the particularity of Christian traditions and implicitly supporting one or another individualist ideology."[79] If the moral decisions are left to the community's deliberations, who will guarantee that the character of Christianity is not be replaced with random and private impulses? Cartwright himself proceeds to propose a view which, building on the work of the literary

---

[74] This line of thinking culminated in Hauerwas' recent book, *Unleashing the Scripture: Freeing the Bible from Captivity to America* (Nashville: Abingdon, 1993). Provocatively, Hauerwas advocates that we "take the Bible out of the hands of individual Christians in North America" (15). He further states: "[I]f we are to understand Scripture it is necessary that we place ourselves under authority, a placement that at least begins by our willingness to accept the discipline of the Church's preaching" (38).

[75] John Howard Yoder, *The Politics of Jesus* (Grand Rapids: Eerdmans, 1972), 19.

[76] Yoder, *The Politics of Jesus*, 20, 239.

[77] John Howard Yoder, *The Priestly Kingdom: Social Ethics as Gospel* (Notre Dame: University of Notre Dame Press, 1984), 27.

[78] Yoder, *The Priestly Kingdom: Social Ethics as Gospel*, 27.

[79] Cartwright, "Uses of Scripture--After Bakhtin," 267.

theorist Mikhail Bakhtin, advocates a reading of Scripture in community with attention to "the chains of signification" in order to challenge ideological oppressive prescriptions.[80] One could classify this view within the emerging school of post-modernism.

An essay by William Schweiker likewise struggles with oppressive interpretations of Scripture.[81] Schweiker advocates a pragmatist reading, which reads the text in such a way that "the creative, liberating, judging, and transformative ways of God are enacted in the world for all." Schweiker's liberationist perspective takes the form of an explicit pragmatist hermeneutic to safe-guard against oppressive moral interpretations of Scripture.

As a final example of a voice of challenge to the consensus we will mention James Childress. His critique comes less from a post-modern perspective than the ones above. In an article entitled "Scripture and Christian Ethics," Childress highlights the importance of justification in the moral life.[82] The notion of responsibility in Christian ethics, derived in the main from H. Richard Niebuhr, includes the element of being answerable for decisions. However, this item has often been ignored, partly out of fear for legalism. Childress emphasizes the importance of reason-giving and justification and recommends a certain use of Scripture to that end. He states: "I propose that we think about some of Scripture's moral statements in terms of principles and rules, especially in terms of principles that establish presumptions and burdens of proof for the moral life."[83] His use of the term "presumptions" in this context means that a certain rule or command establishes "a *prima facie* case for a course of action."[84] There might be exceptions, but the burden of proof points in a certain direction. These presumptions, if conclusive, might even be called absolutes. Childress uses the commandments "Thou shalt not kill" and "Thou shalt not lie" as examples. Childress finally notes that the Bible is not only a "resource" for moral dilemmas, but should also be seen as a "source of dilemmas."[85] Were it not for Scripture, we would not be clear of certain dilemmas which confront us.

The tone and emphasis of Childress' article points in a different direction than the perspective of consensus outlined above. Scripture for Childress can have the function analogous to rules in a court of law. Though there remains the act of deliberation as essential to the moral life, there is also the necessity of justifying behavior by something exterior to the self, and Scripture has a primary place in this regard.

---

80 Cartwright, "Uses of Scripture--After Bakhtin," 274-276.

81 "Iconoclasts, Builders, and Dramatists: The Use of Scripture in Theological Ethics," in *The Annual* 1986, 129-162.

82 James F. Childress, "Scripture and Christian Ethics: Some Reflections on the Role of Scripture in Moral Deliberation and Justification," in *Interpretation* 34 (1980), 371-380.

83 Childress, "Scripture and Christian Ethics," 378.

84 Childress, "Scripture and Christian Ethics," 379.

85 Childress, "Scripture and Christian Ethics," 380.

Many more names could be mentioned from the plethora of those who have offered a contribution to the discussion of Scripture and ethics. Yet, the present author presumes it clear that the recent discussion has produced some lines of consensus. The prominence of the datum of experience draws upon the rational strand in American ethical thought. The role of the Christian community is stressed as the framework within which Scripture has (and receives) authority. The aspect identified as "collective" in the discussion above has been raised to the prominent level of the determinative context in which and through which Scripture receives authority. The rational and the collective aspects make the term "dialogue" popular. The basis for ethics has been fixed upon the processes of a conversation within communities facing issues from out of their experiences in encounter with Scripture. Voices have begun to ask whether there are safeguards against the loss of the particularity of the Christian tradition. To what extent is this approach an apparition of the pragmatism characteristic of American society in general? The consensus shows few signs of disintegrating, however. If this era in theological study is indeed a transitional one, as is being suggested by the increasing popularity of references to the "post-modern age," the issue of the authority of Scripture is indeed of great importance.[86] It is then at this juncture that the present study seeks to offer a contribution. Central to the discussion will be the theory and practice of the use of Scripture in the writings of three respectable Christian ethicists, James M. Gustafson, Paul Ramsey, and Allen D. Verhey.

---

[86] Stanley J. Grenz and Roger E. Olson even suggest that the whole 20th century is in some regards "a transitional age" in theology in the title of their book: *20th Century Theology: God and the World in a Transitional Age* (Downers Grove: Intervarsity Press, 1992).

Chapter 2: James M. Gustafson: The Use of Scripture in Theocentric Ethics

2.1. Introduction

James Moody Gustafson is considered by many as one of America's foremost Christian ethicists.[1] He was born on December 2, 1925 in Norway, Michigan as the youngest child of his parents. His father was a minister in a Swedish immigrant denomination in the Lutheran pietist tradition. He spent his boyhood in Michigan's Upper Peninsula.[2] In 1939 his family moved to a rural farming community in Kansas.[3] In his teenage years James M. Gustafson distanced himself from his church, which he felt lacked intellectual and social awareness and missionary outreach. After W.W. II he joined the Congregationalist Church, which has its roots in the Puritan tradition. In 1947 he married Louise Roos. They have a family of 4 children, two sons and two daughters, grown and scattered throughout the USA.

Gustafson began his academic work at North Park College, Chicago, Illinois. In 1944, during the second World War, he interrupted that work for military service, overseas in Burma and India. In 1946 he returned and received his Bachelor of Science degree from North Western University, Evanston, Illinois. He went on to Chicago Theological Seminary for his Bachelor of Divinity degree and earned his Ph.D. in 1955 from Yale University, New Haven, Connecticut. His dissertation is entitled "Community and Time in the Christian Church: A Study of the Church from a Sociological and Social Philosophical Perspective." During the years of his studies in theology H. Richard Niebuhr, along with James Luther Adams, Claude Welch, Julian Hartt,

---

[1] I have gleaned much of this biographical information from M. A. Flanagan, "The Theological Ethics of James M. Gustafson: His Methodology and Fundamental Concerns," Ph.D. diss. Katholieke Universiteit at Leuven, 1974, x-xii.

[2] Many of his "experiences there helped form...[his] devotion to and respect for the natural environment," Gustafson, *A Sense of the Divine: The Natural Environment from a Theocentric Perspective* (Cleveland: The Pilgrim Press, 1994), 3. "The Upper Peninsula provided social as well as natural resources" for his theology, Lisa Sowle Cahill, "James M. Gustafson," in *A New Handbook of Christian Theologians*, eds. Donald W. Musser and Joseph L. Price (Nashville: Abingdon Press, 1996), 179.

[3] In this Midwestern community Gustafson witnessed tornadoes and "the outcomes of the sustained drought of the thirties," Gustafson, *A Sense of the Divine*, 4. In a recent article on Gustafson, Lisa Sowle Cahill makes clear that the "relation between aspects of Gustafson's theology and his personal history are important, complex, and recognized by the theologian himself as foundational for the texture and shape of his cumulative project, "James M. Gustafson," 179.

and Kenneth Underwoods, guided him.[4] In Gustafson's own words, Niebuhr taught him how to place his interests in social science and social philosophy in a theological context.[5] Gustafson found the thought of Ernst Troeltsch and G. H. Mead helpful for that purpose.

Gustafson was ordained to the ministry in the United Church of Christ. While working on his Ph.D., he was a minister in the Congregational Church, Northford, Connecticut. In 1955 he returned to Yale University and spent 17 years in the department of Religious Studies. From 1972 to 1988 Dr. Gustafson was at the University of Chicago as the University Professor of Theological Ethics in the Divinity School and in the Committee on Social Thought. In 1988 he moved to Emory University, Atlanta, Georgia, to be the Henry R. Luce Professor of Humanities and Comparative Studies. Here he conducts seminars for faculty persons from various disciplines and fields.[6] He has received many academic awards. In 1953 he was a Kent Fellow, Society of Religion and Higher Education. He was a Guggenheim Fellow on several occasions--at one time (1959-1960) at Lund University, Sweden, at another time (1967-1968) at Princeton University. He has been awarded honorary doctorates from 6 different institutions.

In addition to a host of articles and chapters, Gustafson has published 14 books on moral theology, including *Treasure in Earthen Vessels* (1961), *Christ and the Moral Life* (1968), *Christian Ethics and the Community* (1971), *Can Ethics Be Christian*? (1975), *Protestant and Roman Catholic Ethics* (1978), his two-volume masterpiece, *Ethics from a Theocentric Perspective: Theology and Ethics* (1981) and *Ethics and Theology* (1984), and recently *A Sense of the Divine* (1994) and *Intersections: Science, Theology, and Ethics* (1996).

Gustafson has engaged in ethics primarily because in his judgment it provides the best means in our day to do theology proper. Gustafson has provided careful and informative analyses of past and present thinkers and provided philosophically incisive discussions of perennial methodological and substantial issues, in an effort to create and sustain the disciplined discourse necessary for theological ethics. His overriding intention throughout his works has been to show how theological convictions make a difference for ethical reflection and practice. For instance, in his *Can Ethics be Christian?* (1975), he explicitly claims that "religion *qualifies* morality."[7] This claim sets

---

[4] Cf. James M. Gustafson, "Community and Time in the Christian Church: A Study of the Church from a Sociological and Social Philosophical Perspective." Ph.D. diss. Yale University, 1955, ii-iii.

[5] Gustafson, *Treasure in Earthen Vessels: The Church as a Human Community* (Chicago: The University of Chicago Press, 1961), xi.

[6] In a letter addressed to the present author, dated September 26, 1989, Gustafson writes: "The program is an effort to sustain and develop interdisciplinary discourse in a university that is also proceeding apace to foster specialized research and graduate education." His latest book, *Intersections: Science, Theology, and Ethics* (Cleveland: The Pilgrim Press, 1996) refers to him as "Robert W. Woodruff Professor of Comparative Studies and Religion at Emory University."

[7] Gustafson, *Can Ethics Be Christian?*, 173.

Gustafson apart from those who claim that ethics cannot (and should not) be Christian, as well as from those who hold to the view that Christian ethics is entirely disjunctive from "secular" reflection on human experience.[8] This delineation of the place which Gustafson occupies on the spectrum of ethical thinking is characteristic of Gustafson's method, also as it concerns the place of Scripture within moral reflection.

The previous chapter sketched in brief outline the historical background to the present discussion of the use of Scripture in moral discourse. The terms "practical," "collective," and "rational" were employed to characterize the development of ethical thought on the American scene. Turning now specifically to Gustafson, this chapter uses as it were a longer lens to focus on the minute movements of the argument. The continuities with the previous discussion should, however, not be lost from view. Gustafson's view of the function of Scripture is determined by an ethical framework similar to that described above for Niebuhr and others. In terms of intellectual movements, Gustafson can be best placed at the cusp of the neo-orthodoxy and modernism. With both heritages, certain commitments of authority are in place, in tension, and in development. The following discussion will trace these commitments and attempt to discern outlines for the future of this discussion in American ethics. First of all, Gustafson theologically qualifies the immediate authority of Scripture. Secondly, he asserts "theocentrism" defined in opposition to pragmatism and utilitarianism as the proper perspective from which to formulate ethics.

2.2. Theological Qualifications to the Authority of Scripture

To begin a discussion of Gustafson's ethics with attention to the issue of the authority of Scripture is admittedly somewhat artificial. In his own discussions, the subject of Scripture and its authority is not a point of departure. Instead the topic is raised in typically three settings: 1) in polemical discussion with fundamentalists on authority; 2) in sympathetic discussion as an example of the development of religious tradition; 3) in qualified discussion on the source of Christian theology. For instance, in his *Ethics from a Theocentric Perspective* (vol. 1), Gustafson raises the issue of Scripture in the context of the development of tradition, which in turn becomes a source for Christian theology, and in disagreement with those who cling too closely to revelation as their source for morality.[9] In each instance, Gustafson's discussion of Scripture is highly *qualifying* in nature.

---

[8] Cf. Allen Verhey, "On James M. Gustafson, Can Medical Ethics Be Christian?" in *Second Opinion* 7 (March 1988), 106.

[9] Gustafson, *Ethics from a Theocentric Perspective*, Vol. I: *Theology and Ethics* (Chicago: The University of Chicago Press, 1981), esp. 144-150 and 339. Cf. also Gustafson, "The Changing Use of the Bible in Christian Ethics," in *Readings in Moral Theology No. 4: The Use of*

The following discussion will examine the qualifications which Gustafson employs for the authority of Scripture. These qualifications are made by disjoining various aspects of revelation and Scripture. One could group these qualifications together under four distinct, though related, tenets:

1) Scripture is the record of experiences and represents a multitude of views. This could be conveniently termed the Experience-Revelation disjunction.

2) Scripture reveals reality, not morality. Ethics is a response to that reality. This could be conveniently termed the Reality-Morality disjunction.

3) Faith is in Christ and not in the Bible. This could conveniently be called the Christ-Bible disjunction.

4) Biblical teachings are not easily applicable as norms, but seem to inform Christian character. This could conveniently be called the Character-Norm disjunction.

2.2.1. The Experience-Revelation Disjunction

Under this heading, Gustafson makes three distinct submoves, each of which brings Scripture to the level of experience. First of all, Gustafson explicitly regards the Bible as "the record of experience." In the Scriptures we have "the record of a people of piety who, under their historical and natural conditions, did discern what was morally required of them. The changes that occurred in their perceptions and discernments are in the biblical record." Although there are commandments in the Bible "that one cannot foresee being broken without moral guilt (such as condemning murder and adultery and attitudes such as covetousness)," the morality recorded in the Bible is "not timeless and changeless."[10]

Does Gustafson simply assert this as a presupposition, or does he ground this observation in anything? For Gustafson the ground to legitimate this assertion lies within the Bible itself. After all, there is evidence in the Old Testament "that a process of development of a moral tradition has taken place." The morality recorded in the Bible "is distilled by a community of piety and faithfulness from their own perceptions and understandings of the divine governance through the course of their history."[11] The Bible records "how a community of Israel came to understand moral responsibility under God--in terms of their actions and historical events, in terms of distillations into moral laws, in terms of abstractions such as justice and righteousness." It delineates "the actions and sayings of Jesus Christ, a life that was so faithful and obedient to God that it reveals God's will toward man." It narrates "the beginnings of a Christian tradition in which the community expresses in word and deed what manner of life was worthy of the gospel of Christ." He immediately adds that

---

Scripture in Moral Theology, eds. Charles E. Curran and Rickard A. McCormick, S.J. (New York/Ramsey: Paulist Press, 1984), 133-177.

[10] Gustafson, *Theocentric Perspective* I, 339.

[11] Gustafson, *Theocentric Perspective* I, 339.

the Bible is not "a book of rules for moral conduct which merely need to be applied through the processes of moral discourse." Rather the "Christian moral tradition itself developed as this biblical norm was lived and thought out in relation to both the moral ideas and the historical events engaged by Christians under diverse circumstances."[12]

In this line of argument, Gustafson grounds his assertion that the Bible is a record of experience in his observation that there is an apparent discontinuity within the tradition of the Bible. There are points of disjunction which emerge from the line of tradition. The assumption here is that, if the tradition had been continuous and without disjunction, the assertion that the Bible is a record of experience would simply be an assertion. The question can be asked, whether this is a legitimate ground to hold the assertion that the Bible is a record of experience. Does the fact that Scripture shows progression and development necessitate its classification with "mere" experience? Moreover, should experience be so easily contrasted to revelation? Gustafson's argument implies that something which is a "mere" record of experience, cannot be seen as authoritative as "revelation" in the traditional theological sense of the word.

The second aspect to the claim that the Bible is a record of experience is that human experience is also the means of knowing this record. To those who claim "God can be known only through revelation," Gustafson responds that they "cannot deny that human experience is an indispensable aspect both of how it is known and what is known through it."[13] For rightly understanding the Bible, "... the medium of human reflection, symbols, and language has to be taken into account."[14] If "there is knowledge of God it is human knowledge of God; it is knowledge of God mediated through human experiences ...."[15]

Experience is not only the nature of the construction and existence of the Scriptures, but also the framework or medium through which we receive, understand, and interpret this record. As with the first aspect under this heading, this description of our relationship to the Scriptures sets it entirely on a subjective level. The implication is that human knowledge completely determines the nature of the comprehension of Scripture and leaves it indelibly subjective and subjected to the whim of human experience.

The third aspect under this heading intends to be somewhat of a recovery of the Bible. Gustafson says that what "gives the scriptures some authority for us is ... that the perceptions of the meaning of God's presence recorded there are to some extent confirmed in our current experience in the Christian and wider community."[16] Scripture "is the principle [*sic*] source of the Church's

---

12 Gustafson, *The Church as Moral Decision-Maker* (Philadelphia: United Church Press, A Pilgrim Press Book, 1970), 87.

13 Gustafson, *Theocentric Perspective* I, 147.

14 Gustafson, *Theocentric Perspective* I, 148.

15 Gustafson, *Theocentric Perspective* I, 186.

16 Gustafson, *Can Ethics Be Christian?*, 161.

language,"[17] whereby "a common ethos in the community" is made possible.[18] The Bible does delineate God as "its object of loyalty" and tells the story of Jesus Christ as "the center of the Church's life,"[19] but the Bible "is the record of the lived experience" of Israel and of "early Christians, and the meaning of the person and event of Jesus Christ ... who brought the community into being, and gave it its identity."[20] Within this community there are professional theologians who stand between the Bible and some other points. The role of the Biblical scholars is to "clarify the meaning of the Bible in relation to historical evidence, literary styles, linguistic problems, and what they take to be the most significant themes in the book." The role of the ethicists is to "interpret the moral problems and condition of man in the light of the Church's knowledge of God in order to give some direction to Christian behavior."[21] The role of the clergyman as preacher is "to bring a particular people into a more significant relation to the meanings of the Church." The clergyman's role as pastor is to bring the various difficulties and aspirations of the persons to whom he pastors "under the light of the Church's distinctive ethos as it is expressed in the Bible and in the life of the community."[22] Gustafson underlines that when he makes use of Scripture, he is making use of "human statements about God as these statements are forged from Scripture and from the theological tradition."[23]

There is thus a possibility for the Bible to have authority. It does not derive that authority from itself or from God, but from the coincidence of present and past experience. The means or method for establishing authority lies in the activity of the community, that is, professional theologians, clergy, laity, etc. One should note two things at this point. Firstly, the authority of Scripture is spoken of as a possibility; it is *in potential*. Secondly, the Christian community is determinative for the realization of this authority.

In comparison to what was described above under the history of American ethics, one could see the strong emphasis on the collective nature of ethical character. The role of this collective nature is as catalyst for the realization of the authority of the Bible. The collective emphasis at the same time entails subjectivizing the authority of Scripture to the experience of the community. At the same time, the influence of the tenet of the "rational" character is as well visible. The rational basis of the Enlightenment has modified the character of the Scriptures and relativized them to experience.

---

[17] Gustafson, *Treasure in Earthen Vessels*, 46. Allen D. Verhey refers to this book as "a work too much neglected," "Scripture and Ethics: Practices, Performances, and Prescriptions," in *Christian Ethics: Problems and Prospects* [Essays in honor of James Gustafson], eds. Lisa Sowle Cahill and James F. Childress (Cleveland: The Pilgrim Press, 1996), 27.

[18] Gustafson, *Treasure in Earthen Vessels*, 49.

[19] Gustafson, *Treasure in Earthen Vessels*, 71.

[20] Gustafson, *Treasure in Earthen Vessels*, 75.

[21] Gustafson, *Treasure in Earthen Vessels*, 58-59.

[22] Gustafson, *Treasure in Earthen Vessels*, 63-64.

[23] Gustafson, "Moral Discernment in the Christian Life," in *Norm and Context in Christian Ethics*, eds. Gene H. Outka and Paul Ramsey (New York: Charles Scribner's Sons. 1968), 32.

Below we will trace more precisely Gustafson's indebtedness to the Enlightenment.

2.2.2. The Reality-Morality Disjunction

Although Gustafson calls the Bible "the charter document" for Christian ethics, he immediately adds that "what it charters depends upon a number of other things that the ethical thinker brings to it."[24] He expresses appreciation for insights of Ernst Troeltsch and Max Weber[25] as well as for "the impact of the crisis theologians, and particularly Karl Barth." He concurs with the thinking that the Bible does not reveal morality but rather "the living God," or better yet that the Bible reveals not morality but rather reality.[26]

At this point Gustafson is indebted to men such as Karl Barth and H. Richard Niebuhr. The Bible is the revelation of the reality of the living God, a person, not a proposition. The Bible itself points beyond itself to the living Lord and is therefore of "penultimate significance."[27] In grammatical terms, one could say that the Bible provides the indicative, for which ethics must then follow with the imperative. With these terms the whole issue of law and gospel is introduced, even though Gustafson does not elaborate at this point. Yet, if one would wish to apply these terms to the discussion, it is evident that for Gustafson the Scriptures at some level reveal the gospel, or rather, point to the person of Christ, who is the content of the gospel. As for the law, the imperative of Christian ethics, it flows in some way from the reality of the gospel, but falls outside the boundaries of the Scriptures.

The question can be asked, in which specific ways the Bible reveals the reality of the gospel. Gustafson isolates four distinct avenues. First of all, there is the reality of Scripture's "pervasive significance," particularly in the Western world. The tradition of the West and especially of the Christian community have been indirectly informed by Scripture. This tradition "is always in a process of development or change in the light of new historical events and unfolding awareness of the meaning of biblically informed morality for new issues." This process does not only unfold the biblical tradition but also often revises and judges the biblical tradition as being "wrong in the light of historical developments."[28]

In second instance, Gustafson sees Scripture as providing "data and concepts for understanding the human situation," on the one hand "in terms of its limits," which are a result of "moral evil in the world," man's "finitude" which prohibits him from "achieving that position of the 'ideal observer' who can judge events as God himself would judge them." These "limits" also are a

---

[24] Gustafson, "The Changing Use of the Bible in Christian Ethics," 133.
[25] Gustafson, "The Changing Use of the Bible in Christian Ethics," 134.
[26] Gustafson, "The Changing Use of the Bible in Christian Ethics," 140-141.
[27] Gustafson, "The Changing Use of the Bible in Christian Ethics," 142.
[28] Gustafson, "The Place of Scripture in Christian Ethics: A Methodological Study," 168-169.

consequence of "his sin: his bondage ... pride ... failure to consider the purposes of God," which "all keep him from hitting the moral mark." In this way the Bible teaches the Christian community to be profoundly dissatisfied with those events that destroy "human life and value." On the other hand, Scripture "provides a vision of human possibilities." It gives man "clues to what God is enabling as well as requiring" him "to be and to do." It teaches the Christian community both to believe "that the unknown future is in care of a Being who is ultimately benevolently disposed toward his creation," and to long for and work toward "a future which is more fulfilling for all God's creation."[29]

In third instance, Scripture specifically shows which "sorts of human actions and events" in the past were considered "to be in accord and out of accord with the purposes of God for man." In this way we can formulate "[c]ertain generalizations about God's prevailing aspirations and purposes for human life," whereby we can judge present "human actions and events ... to be more or less in or out of accord with those purposes."[30]

Finally, various other types of discourse in Scripture, such as narratives which express "the judgment of God," parables, and wisdom sayings, can function as "informing sources of judgment and as corroborations of judgments ... made in the light of the more general theological ethical principles."

The above four points are avenues in which the reality of the gospel has found and continues to find inroads into the community of men and women who seek to respond to the reality of the gospel. There is the tradition which the Bible has inspired, its understanding of the human situation, its depiction of human possibilities, and its different types of discourse. This is the form in which the reality of the gospel touches upon the modern situation. Gustafson himself concludes that he is not proposing *sola Scriptura*; instead, a "biblically informed theology," or a "dialectic between more intuitive moral judgments and both scriptural and nonscriptural principles."[31] Again the Christian community is the locus where this biblical influence takes place.

2.2.3. The Christ-Bible Disjunction

Gustafson's qualifies the immediate authority of Scripture also by insisting that one must place the "prime point of reference for all thinking in ethics and all moral activity on the part of Christians" not on "moral teachings, particularized or generalized" but rather on "God in his living, free activity."[32] What "distinguishes the morality of the Christian community is the root and ground of its moral faith, its allegiance to Christ." It "is an expression of trust in the goodness and power of God, the creator and orderer and redeemer of life; a goodness made known in the advent, the birth, the words and deeds, the death

[29] Gustafson, "The Place of Scripture in Christian Ethics: A Methodological Study," 169-170.
[30] Gustafson, "The Place of Scripture in Christian Ethics: A Methodological Study," 170.
[31] Gustafson, "The Place of Scripture in Christian Ethics: A Methodological Study," 170-172.
[32] Gustafson, "The Place of Scripture in Christian Ethics: A Methodological Study," 141.

and the new life of Jesus Christ."[33] Gustafson does not regard Scripture as God's rule for faith and life. He does not believe "that truth in Christianity was given once and for all time in a given person and set of historical events, and in the record of these events and the early articulations of their meaning (that is, in the Bible)." He rejects the view that "God ... chose to reveal the eternal and immutable truth about himself through the events in the history of a particular historic people, and in the events and life of one man who came to a particular place in a particular time with its particular religious and political conditions, and its particular mode of execution of criminals."[34] To him, it is important to "acknowledge changes in religious ideas in the Bible itself."[35] What happened in the process of writing the books of the Bible, is this: "Received traditions are reinterpreted in the light of the religious and theological needs of other historic periods in the life of the Jewish people, and even within the short historic span of the New Testament community."[36] He therefore concludes that the "divine governance is not revealed to us in its moral details in the Scriptures." Christian ethics thinks not about "morality reduced to propositions, but about God and how life ought to be rightly related to his power and his presence."[37] It "is not an objective moral truth from the ... Bible that can become a guide for social policy or for personal moral life to all who require of it." The parable of the good Samaritan, for example, takes the place of a discourse on general principles.[38] It is faith in Christ, the Redeemer and Creator, that results particularly in a certain "basic attitude or disposition."[39]

Nevertheless there is more to the Christian moral life than certain dispositions and intentions in which Christ is to function "normatively, particularly in the formation of intentions." There is also the "matter of specific judgments, choices, and actions." For this Gustafson suggests Christ "as an objective norm among others ...."[40] Gustafson explores three aspects of this "'normativeness' of Christ."

(a) "Christ is the norm for the Christian's theological interpretation of what God wills that life should be among men." He becomes "the content-filled symbol for man's efforts to discern what God is enabling and requiring in the world." One might call this the symbolic aspect of Christ.

---

33 Gustafson, "Faith, Unbelief, and Moral Life," in *Theology and Christian Ethics* (Philadelphia: United Church Press, A Pilgrim Press Book, 1974), 55.

34 Gustafson, *Theocentric Perspective* I, 138.

35 Gustafson, *Theocentric Perspective* I, 138.

36 Gustafson, *Theocentric Perspective* I, 152.

37 Gustafson, "The Changing Use of the Bible in Christian Ethics," 140-141.

38 Gustafson, *Theology and Christian Ethics*, 67.

39 Gustafson, *Christ and the Moral Life* (Chicago: The University of Chicago Press, 1968), 54-55. Cf. his "The Relation of the Gospels to the Moral Life," *Theology and Christian Ethics*, 148f.

40 Gustafson, *Christ and the Moral Life*, 264.

(b) Christ is "the norm for illumination of what the Christian ought to be and do in his actions," as he seeks to express his "faith in words and deeds." This is the paradigmatic aspect of Christ.

(c) Christ is among other norms "the central obligatory norm for those who would order their lives in discipleship to him."[41] One might call this the centralizing, or unifying aspect of Christ.

Gustafson himself uses the term "paradigm" with reference to point (b).[42] One wonders whether the two other points are not restatements of the paradigmatic aspect of Christ. Point (a) might mention the symbolism of Christ and point (c) the central character of Christ among other norms, but the Christ normative function in all three cases is a paradigmatic one. Christ as norm functions to shed light on alternatives and direct the choice of the Christian. For example, the problem of euthanasia is not solved by a reference to Christ, but Christ can illumine the problem and condition an answer. Sometimes this takes place because a parable activates the imagination, or a specific command is closely considered. Christ functions as a norm in the confrontation of the Christian with the gospel.

In "The Relation of the Gospel to the Moral Life," Gustafson refers extensively to John 13. Although, according to him, the purpose of John 13 is not primarily moral, nevertheless this account "flows into and informs the bearing toward one another that arises out of life in Christ Jesus and the manner of life that is worthy of the gospel of Christ."[43] The narrative is "a paradigm of action," which "makes its point more concretely than does the ... command to love the neighbor." With a specific reference to John 13:1 and 15, Gustafson insists that the actions and dialogue in this passage, which point to the "dispositions of love and humility," are "paradigms both of God's own readiness to loving and humble service and of the manner of life ... that is to characterize the community and its members." Similarly, as is also clear from Philippians 2:5-8, the accounts of the crucifixion of Jesus function as "paradigms of intentions and dispositions that ought to characterize the manner of life ... of the community and its members." Just as Jesus acted "in perfect obedience to the Father, in perfect fidelity, and in love," so the community and its members are to be ready "to be faithful to God and to others, to be loving and merciful to others, to sacrifice their own interests and even lives."[44]

Gustafson's maintains that within the New Testament texts there are several Christologies. He takes the liberty to build his Christology selectively. He prefers a Christology based mainly on the narratives in the synoptic gospels.

---

[41] Gustafson, *Christ and the Moral Life*, 265.

[42] Gustafson, *Christ and the Moral Life*, 264.

[43] Gustafson, "The Relation of the Gospels to the Moral Life," *Theology and Christian Ethics*, 156.

[44] Gustafson, *Theology and Christian Ethics*, 157-159.

To explain this preference he simply cites his appreciation for narrative and his suspicion of a pre-existent Christ, as described in Colossians and Ephesians.[45]

2.2.4. The Character-Norm Disjunction

Gustafson insists that the teachings of Jesus "are not so important for their moral details, for the specific rules and precepts, but for the direction and the way they show Christians to go," namely, to perfectly and completely "trust in God." They, "as part of the whole revelation," make clear to men in faith that they "are to be obedient, to be loving," to have a basic attitude and "disposition in accord with the gift of God in Jesus Christ." So the teachings of Jesus "are not easily applicable as a norm, but must be brought to bear together with other considerations and principles derived from them in one's decisions." In His teachings Jesus evokes, commends, and commands loyalty as "an inner commitment ... toward God and neighbor." This loyalty "often does, can, and ought to give" a Christian "a particular perspective on" life and "a particular posture" or orientation toward God, "the Creator and Sustainer of the world," and toward "the self, others, and the world."[46] This orientation gives "shape and movement to a certain disposition,"[47] or as Paul put it in Phil. 1:27, a "manner of life ... worthy of the gospel of Christ," or as he put it in Phil. 2:5, "your bearing towards one another ... out of your life in Jesus Christ."[48] Also 1 John 4 indicates "how religious faith and belief are claimed to affect moral dispositions," how a "moral imperative to love is inferred from a religious belief." Believing in "the proposition 'God is love'" implies "a disposition to be loving, a commandment to love, and even rules of conduct."[49] This disposition or set of dispositions is "part of what is given to them 'in Christ Jesus,'" a "'gift of the Spirit,'" but it is also "a requirement of Christians." The only two aspects of this disposition that Gustafson delineates are "hope and freedom." Hope as a disposition in the life of a Christian "comes into being through faith" and is a "confidence" that "God enables out of his goodness new possibilities for humane life, that men are the agents of hope actualizing the good as they share in the development of history and in the building of the human community."[50] Freedom as a disposition in the life of a Christian comes into being "in response to God's love and goodness" and is an inner freedom of spirit "to give oneself in love for the neighbor, to seek the other's good rather than one's own, to identify with the oppressed and the anxious, to participate in causes to seek justice and peace in spite of their ambiguities ...." It enables him "to risk the unusual word

---

[45] Gustafson, *Theocentric Perspective* I, 275. Cf. also his footnote 65.

[46] Gustafson, *Christ and the Moral Life*, 242, 245, 248.

[47] Gustafson, *Christ and the Moral Life*, 194-195, 203.

[48] As the New English Bible renders it. Cf. Gustafson's *Theology and Christian Ethics*, 149-150.

[49] Gustafson, "Education for Moral Responsibility," *Theology and Christian Ethics*, 70-71.

[50] Gustafson, *Christ and the Moral Life*, 249, 252.

and deed when it seems to be required, to do more than or even other than the 'law' requires when such deeds would restrain destructive forces or bring new good into being."[51]

The Christian moral life is, however, not only the expression of a certain disposition but also of a specified moral intention, by which Gustafson means "a basic direction of activity" evoked by, and consonant with his faith in Jesus Christ and "his bearing toward the world." Gustafson suggests that Paul's words, "Do all to the glory of God" (1 Cor 10:31b) "can function as a touchstone for various moral intentions of Christians," although he recognizes that there are in this Corinthians passage other statements of what Christians are to do and not to do. They are to seek their neighbor's good, not their own. "They are to do what is helpful, what builds up. They are to imitate Christ ... [and] preserve the liberty of their consciences." Jesus' teachings "commend certain intentions and actions" to them and "shed light in a particular direction" along which their behavior is and ought to go. "From these biblical statements and from the reflection of members of the Christian community," they can "form more particular intentions ... consonant with these." So the idea is not that they form specific moral intentions merely "on the basis of a central or general intention." The moral intention to seek the neighbor's good "needs specification in the light of other considerations." Their central intention "becomes one of the norms" involved in their "specific moral judgment in a complex and specific situation."[52]

Recent theological developments have made it more difficult to view the teachings of Jesus as normative for Christians.[53] Gustafson cites three reasons:

1. The "serious questions" that "biblical scholars" have "raised about the ethicists' assumption that the teachings of Jesus were of timeless applicability," have "created an uncertainty from which ethicists have never been relieved."
2. The radical question that "form-critical scholars" have raised "of whether or not verifiable historical authenticity could be a ground for the authority of much that was attributed to Jesus by the nonscientific writers of the Gospel narratives," have made or kept the ethicists uncertain. After all, if "the so-called teachings of Jesus" are "not the words or teachings of Jesus himself ... what reliance and authority" can they carry?
3. Ethicists in recent decades have become keenly aware of the view of those Protestants who "affirmed ... in the theological revival of 1920-60 ... that the revelation given in the Bible was one basically of the deeds of God, and not of morality," and that the "teachings of Jesus must be seen in relation to the theological significance of Jesus."[54]

---

[51] Gustafson, *Christ and the Moral Life*, 253, 255.

[52] Gustafson, *Christ and the Moral Life*, 255-256, 261-263.

[53] Gustafson, *Christ and the Moral Life*, 149.

[54] Gustafson, *Christ and the Moral Life*, 192-193.

The developments in biblical research and theology warrant for Gustafson that the teachings of Jesus are not without hesitancy accepted as normative. Thus Gustafson again qualifies the normativity of Scripture.

2.2.5. Conclusion

It is evident, then, that for Gustafson the qualifications to the authority of Scripture for Christian ethics are *theological* in nature. On the one hand, Gustafson loosens the connection between the Scripture and the revelation from God (1, 2, 4) and from the other side, Gustafson detaches the revelation of God from Scripture (3). By loosening this connection the authority of Scripture in ethics becomes less direct and is instead mediated. That Gustafson takes his starting-point in experience and views Scripture as a record of experience, shows his indebtedness to rationalism. The Christian community functions to mediate the Scripture to the present in this sense that the community combines an understanding of the contemporary situation with an understanding of the Scriptures and tradition. Here one can recognize the *collective* element indicated in the history of American Protestant ethics (chapter 1), which also here has assumed the place as the locus of ethical decision making. These theological qualifications to the authority of Scripture beg the question how the Christian community and the individual can and should move from the Gospel to the practice of Christian ethics. It is here that for Gustafson, the term "theocentrism" becomes important.

2.3. The Theocentric Perspective for Ethics

2.3.1. Theological Foundations

Gustafson's project of bringing theocentrism and ethics together began in a diagnostic study on Protestant and Roman Catholic ethics: *Protestant and Roman Catholic Ethics: Prospects for Rapprochement* (1978). He typifies the modern Protestant as one who tends to look at life more as a *movement* than as a *structure*. The modern Protestant looks at life as a network of physical and spiritual dynamics moving human history into ever new and changing patterns. His moral response to life tends to be innovative, creative, and ready for change, tied to neither the ways of the past nor any universal law supposed to reflect a stable order or design for life. Protestant ethics tends to be relativistic, forward-looking, ready to judge human behavior by its results rather than by its conformity to a natural law or sacred order. This Protestant tendency for relativity and freedom is rooted in both philosophical and theological premises.

Philosophically, modern Protestant ethics have been influenced by Kantian philosophical presuppositions. The question has become whether there can be any rational knowledge of a universal moral order and universal principles.[55] Two post-Kantian movements have subsequently exercised much influence: historicism and existentialism.

The tenets of historicism are captured well in the work of Ernst Troeltsch. Gustafson explains: When Protestants became convinced that there was no harmony between the active human mind and an established rational order in nature, they considered all knowledge "to be historically situated."[56] Consequently, they said, we cannot expect our thinking to reflect abiding moral values that "are applicable to all persons."[57]

Existentialism was the second post-Kantian philosophical movement to influence Protestant theological ethics deeply. In light of the shattering of illusions of universal moral principles, this movement emphasized "radical human freedom," the "need for a subjective confirmation of moral choices" and "occasionalism." The latter is the view which recognizes the value in each occasion of decision making.[58]

Modern Protestant theology has blended well with this philosophical background. God is no longer considered the Creator of the world, to Whose moral law He wills His free human creatures to adapt their lives. Rather He is considered and experienced as a God Who freely decides and freely acts in ways that may be surprising and offensive to the human mind, but to which we respond and in which we may participate for our salvation. Words that fit well into the theology of the free God are *grace*, *good news*, *new creation*, *freedom in Christ*.

An ethic that fits the theology of freedom is likely to stress a morality of freedom. Its key phrases will be selected from a list like *freedom*, *responsibility*, *obedience to the Lord's command*, *acting in love*, *care for persons*, *following the Lord's guidance*, and *making one's own decisions*. According to Gustafson, Protestant ethics has tended to be ethics of freedom as opposed to ethics of law.

Roman Catholic ethics, by contrast, is rooted in philosophical and theological perspectives that see the world in terms of order and law. The natural order and the natural tendency of things are the embodiment of God's rational design for human life. Moral law is a mirror of that design which summons us to bend our lives to the shape of God's design. God's design, built into the energies of life, is not only the plan we ought to follow; it is the goal

---

[55] Gustafson, *Protestant and Roman Catholic Ethics: Prospects for Rapprochement* (Chicago: University of Chicago, 1978), 61.

[56] Gustafson, *Protestant and Roman Catholic*, 65.

[57] Gustafson, *Protestant and Roman Catholic Ethics*, 66. Cf. Gustafson, *Protestant and Roman Catholic Ethics*, 68: "Theological ethics ... involves a process of interpreting how God acts in current events. The norm is not grounded in ... universalizable moral principles, but in a historical source used to interpret subsequent historical events." Cf. Gustafson, *Protestant and Roman Catholic Ethics*, 69: "It is a fairly short step from the theology of God's actions in history to an affirmation of 'historicism' in another sense, that is, historical relativism or 'relationalism.'"

[58] Gustafson, *Protestant and Roman Catholic Ethics*, 71.

toward which we are naturally inclined to move. By nature we tend to follow the channels that lead us to our ultimate happiness. Further, we recognize God's design and call it "natural law." The Bible also tells us what to do, although for the most part it reaffirms what we already know (in part and sometimes confusedly) from nature. Tradition does the same. When the Pope speaks authoritatively on morals, he almost always appeals to natural law. On the whole Jesus, too, confirms natural law.

Gustafson in this book[59] argues for a theology of God which embraces both order and freedom. In this book he is seeking normative principles which require from us imagination and freedom as much as fidelity to principle. Ethics should not be limited to the job of solving every new moral problem that emerges. What is needful is a fundamental ethic whose theological roots are clearly exposed, whose main trunk stems organically from those roots, and whose branches are all of a piece with the trunk.[60]

If such an ethic is to provide Christian consensus, Gustafson maintains, more agreement will be needed than the agreement managed up till now on "*the basic outlook, principle, or metaphor that is appropriate to Christian theological ethics*."[61] What is necessary is consensus on the doctrine of God, an area often avoided by moral theologians. Gustafson proposes "a view of God as a gracious ordering dynamic presence and power in nature and in history whose being and purpose are not fully known or disclosed."[62]

This is a very striking ending to this book. We need an ethics that is drawn from the doctrine of God. What does Gustafson mean by that?

In 1981 and 1984, Gustafson published his *opus magnum*, *Ethics from a Theocentric Perspective* I and II. He characterized it as "a coherent interpretation of theology and ethics," a realization of his proposal in his *Protestant and Roman Catholic Ethics*.[63] His *opus magnum* is not only "the product of at least thirty years of" studying but also "the product of fifty-five

---

[59] Gustafson, *Protestant and Roman Catholic Ethics*.

[60] It is remarkable that eleven years after publishing this book Gustafson returns to this particular theme in the March 1989 issue of *Theological Studies*, entitled, "Roman Catholic and Protestant Interaction in Ethics: An Interpretation." In this article he calls attention particularly to the following points: (i) "An issue that has always been present between Protestant ethics built on the principle of Scripture alone and the Roman Catholic tradition continues to be debated with great vigor" (59). (ii) "The role of the Bible in Christian ethics has been more consciously addressed by Protestants in the last decades .... Some of the work attempts to relate both biblical theology and biblical ethics to more systematic ethical positions. For example, after the publication of a very useful article, 'The Use of Scripture in Ethics,' Allen Verhey wrote *The Great Reversal*, which is a study of New Testament ethics and a 'modest proposal' for using them. Verhey's work is a rare combination of competence in biblical scholarship and moral philosophy" (65-66).

[61] Gustafson, *Protestant and Roman Catholic Ethics*, 153.

[62] Gustafson, *Protestant and Roman Catholic Ethics*, 158.

[63] Gustafson, *Ethics from a Theocentric Perspective*, Vol. 2: *Ethics and Theology* (Chicago: University of Chicago Press, 1984), 143.

years of living." He calls it in part the result "of reflection on events in which I have participated or which I have observed, on the lives of persons and communities that have been part of my own life, and on experiences of the worlds of nature and culture."[64]

His *Ethics from a Theocentric Perspective* is almost a systematic theology. In it he argues that ethics should begin and end with a theological, rather than an anthropocentric perspective. By "theological perspective" he means a perspective whose critical reference point is God[65] "as the power that bears down upon us, sustains us, sets an ordering of relationships, provides conditions of possibilities for human activity and even a sense of direction."[66] He returns many times to Jonathan Edwards' notion of "consent of being" as the basis of true religion. That is the meaning of theocentricity. Although man is inescapably the measurer of all things, mankind is not the measure of all things.[67]

Gustafson considers much of traditional Christian thought and contends that the theological framework has eroded and that "religion is propagated for its utility value to individuals and communities."[68] For instance, on Tillich's method of correlation between human question and divine answer, Gustafson says that he "cannot avoid the strong impression" that in Tillich, as in "much of traditional Christian thought" the almost exclusive purpose of God is the enrichment and fulfillment of human life.[69] Gustafson is offended by various liberation theologies that presume to know what God is doing in the world and end up declaring that God is doing whatever their "liberationist" causes are aimed at. Proponents of this approach invoke the biblical story to justify their readings of political change, but they "move from theology to politics without passing through ethics."[70] A similarly self-serving ploy is evident in pastoral theology and counseling, except there the goals are therapeutic rather than political.[71] Gustafson also has a hard time taking seriously the "theology of hope" as represented by Moltmann, although he finds this theology "much more biblical in significant respects" than the theology of Tillich.[72] The notion that "all reality is surpassable" flies "in the face of centuries of development in the natural sciences." Such statements are either "homiletical hyperbole, or ... unintelligible."[73] The only dogma of this theological school seems to be contingency, and "it is difficult to get much particular guidance from

---

[64] Gustafson, *Theocentric Perspective* I, x.
[65] Gustafson, *Theocentric Perspective* I, 88f.
[66] Gustafson, *Theocentric Perspective* I, 264.
[67] Gustafson, *Theocentric Perspective* I, 99.
[68] Gustafson, *Theocentric Perspective* I, 18.
[69] Gustafson, *Theocentric Perspective* I, 40.
[70] Gustafson, *Theocentric Perspective* I, 73.
[71] Gustafson, *Theocentric Perspective* I, 20, 28.
[72] Gustafson, *Theocentric Perspective* I, 42.
[73] Gustafson, *Theocentric Perspective* I, 44.

contingency."[74] Gustafson concludes that he believes that all that "Moltmann can tell us" is that "God, the future, makes possible hope and courage."[75] The process theologians come off considerably better, in Gustafson's evaluation, mainly because theirs is a cosmic vision that does not necessarily put mankind at the center.[76]

2.3.2. Gustafson's Point of Departure

2.3.2.1. Contextualism

It is remarkable that whereas Gustafson argues for "*theo*logical ethics,"[77] that is, an ethics that is drawn from the doctrine of God, he at the same time takes his point of departure in the human historical experience. That is immediately evident in the very first sentence of his *opus magnum*: "Every effort to develop a coherent theology is shaped to some extent by the author's perceptions of the circumstances in his or her culture and in the churches."[78]

This point of departure, the orientation of "contextualism," is very pervasive in the latter part of the twentieth century. Contextualism is the view that humans draw their values and knowledge of all things moral from the experience of the contexts in which they live. It is a view deeply influenced by modern historicist, sociological, and psychological epistemology, and by the theories of relativity found in physics and numerous philosophies of science. This orientation of contextualism is basic to Gustafson. Thus he first of all develops a perspective on contextualist presuppositions.

Beginning with an account of how we can know anything reliable in the face of the fact that we are deeply conditioned by who and what we are in quite confined arenas of human historical existence, Gustafson attempts to take into account the experientially derived evidence from the modern natural sciences. This demands that we recognize our selves, our communities, and our species as existing in an enormously vast and dynamic context, one inevitably shaped and stamped by cosmological and biophysical relationships which we have but begun to understand. This is the context from which our sense of morality must be drawn if it is to be wide and deep. This contextual awareness gives us a perspective on the whole.[79]

---

[74] Gustafson, *Theocentric Perspective* I, 45.

[75] Gustafson, *Theocentric Perspective* I, 48.

[76] Gustafson, *Theocentric Perspective* I, 56-62.

[77] Gustafson, *Can Ethics be Christian?*, 156.

[78] Gustafson, *Theocentric Perspective* I, 1.

[79] Victor Anderson traces this concern from Gustafson's earliest book, *Treasure in Earthen Vessels: The Church as a Human Community*, to his two-volumed *Theocentric Perspective*. Anderson concludes that Gustafson has been "deeply influenced by ... the social philosophical insight of American tradition of the sociology of knowledge," Victor Anderson, "The Legacy of Pragmatism in the Theologies of D. C. MacIntosh, H. Richard Niebuhr, and James M. Gustafson" (Ph.D. diss. Princeton University; Ann Arbor, Mich.: University Microfilms International, 1992), 171. To be sure, he too acknowledges that there is on the part of

2.3.2.2. The Priority of Human Experience

Gustafson argues for "the priority of human experience," the "primacy or centrality of human experience" for inferring moral principles from religious beliefs.[80] He argues that religion and morality "are aspects of human experience; theology and ethics are ... ideas about aspects of experience."[81] Because religion and morality are thus prior, Gustafson gives them also priority in treatment. In words reminiscent of the history of religions school Gustafson traces religion to the common experiences of communities involving incidents like natural disasters, wars, suffering, etc. "Theology construes these experiences: it provides principles of explanation of their meaning and suggests ways in which life needs to be conducted in the light of that meaning."[82] Theology takes place on a level of abstraction necessary for the clear construal of the experiences, but the experiences are prior. All this is implied in the tenet, "[h]uman experience is prior to reflection."[83]

Experience for Gustafson is "always social and historical." He insists that "the meaning and significance of human experience is continually being assessed in communities which share common objects of interest and common concepts, symbolism and theories."[84] Meaningful experiences, such as love, hate, potential, fear, are practically unintelligible without a social community. Language is the chief evidence of the fact that meaning is attributed to experiences communally.[85] Here Gustafson conjoins the rational category of experience immediately with the category of the "collective." It is necessarily within a social context that experience is generated.

How do empiricism and rationalism relate to one another in Gustafson? Robert O. Johann has addressed the matter in an essay on Gustafson's ethics.[86] He points out that reason for Gustafson organizes experience: "We have said that experience, whose elements reason is to organize appropriately, is a process of interaction and interrelationship in which everything is involved and on

---

Gustafson's a "methodological solidarity with such thinkers such as Schleiermacher and Troeltsch, Weber and Bergson, as is evident in his writings--especially in terms of his historical realism," 172. That which used to be explained solely in dogmatic language, can also be understood as human and social processes. The Church is to be understood "as a human community--and not strictly or exceptionally as a faith community." He insists on understanding "the life and unity of the Church within ... two worlds: the one of natural and scientific explanation and the other of belief in 'the God' revealed 'in Christ ... from the perspective of social inquiry and theological belief.'"

80 Gustafson, *Theocentric Perspective* I, 115, 191. Cf. Gustafson, *Can Ethics be Christian?*, 148.

81 Gustafson, *Theocentric Perspective* I, 129.

82 Gustafson, *Theocentric Perspective* I, 135.

83 Gustafson, *Theocentric Perspective* I, 115.

84 Gustafson, *Theocentric Perspective* I, 115.

85 Gustafson, *Theocentric Perspective* I, 121.

86 Robert O. Johann, "An Ethics of Emergent Order," in *James M. Gustafson's Theocentric Ethics: Interpretations and Assessments*, eds. Harlan R. Beckley and Charles M. Swezey (Macon: Mercer University Press, 1988, 95-118), 101.

whose patterns and structures (which Gustafson insists are patterns of interdependence) all things depend for their existence and their possibilities. In other words, experience is never something without form or structure; it is always more or less organized."[87] Reason and experience are in a relationship of interdependence whereby the rational envelopes, catalogues and processes experience. Perhaps it could be said that American empiricism is combined with a European rationalism and bracketed within it.

Besides theology being rooted in experience, it is methodologically important to view experience as unified. Though reflection on experience makes differentiations between religious, aesthetic, and moral experiences, experience itself comes uncategorized and unified. Likewise, the distinctions between affection, cognition, and volition might be used to the end of constructing an ethic, but "all three aspects are present in the ordinary course of moral experience."[88]

Gustafson makes explicit what this unity and priority of experience entails for ethics: "[p]rescriptive moral theories all rest upon descriptive accounts of human life."[89] Gustafson points to the inherent "circularity to moral theory." This is the refrain of the section on the priority of human experience: a certain amount of anthropocentrism is unavoidable and its circularity must be acknowledged and embraced.

If one were to cite the undisputed progress in natural scientific work or the quest for universality as evidence for the existence of objectivity or an independence from culture and history, Gustafson notes that history should make us hesitant to accept such claims. For even science can only measure progress within communally agreed upon standards.[90] Gustafson does not advocate relinquishing goals of progress and universality, but cautions against unrealistic expectations.

For Gustafson the most important dimension of experience is an encounter with the crisis of meaning in the vast fabric of the universe. Gustafson confronts this crisis by a response of piety, marked by a "consent to being." He is "persuaded that the primary moment in a religious view of the world, and therefore an assumption in theology, is the affection of piety: a sense of dependence on, and respect and gratitude for, what is given."[91] By piety he means "an attitude of reverence, awe, and respect which implies a sense of devotion and of duties and responsibilities as well."[92] Piety, in a sense, is "the

---

[87] Robert O. Johann, "An Ethics of Emergent Order," 103.

[88] Gustafson, *Theocentric Perspective* I, 119. Cf. *Theocentric Perspective* I, 116-119.

[89] Gustafson, *Theocentric Perspective* I, 118.

[90] Gustafson, *Theocentric Perspective* I, 125.

[91] Gustafson, *Ethics from a Theocentric Perspective* I, 61. Echoes from Schleiermacher are easily heard here.

[92] Gustafson, *Theocentric Perspective* I, 163.

hinge which joins the frame of the moral natural ordering of life to the door of human duties and obligations." Piety intertwines both religion and morality.[93]

Gustafson makes two fundamental claims about the theological enterprise, in which he draws together his thinking about his point of departure. 1) Piety "is a necessary condition for ideas of God to be subjectively meaningful and intellectually persuasive." 2) The "'substantial content' of ideas of God cannot be incongruous (rather than must be 'in harmony') with well-established data and explanatory principles established by relevant sciences, and must 'be in some way indicated by these.'" Gustafson follows Ernst Troeltsch at this point and insists that if the "substantial content of theology ... is not in perfect harmony with scientific knowledge, [it] cannot be in sharp incongruity with it."[94] Moreover, "what we say about God must be congruent in some way with what we know about human experience and its objects through the sciences."[95]

It is for that reason that Gustafson spells out that he is not advocating a secular ethics or an anthropocentric ethics but rather a theocentric ethics. Such a "theological construing of the world has to view in some guarded and critical way the Deity as 'objective' to ourselves and to the world."[96] However, he argues that the "Deity toward which we are oriented must be a deity related to the natural world, the world described and explained by natural sciences as much as one related to historical experience, and to the realms of human action and their consequences."[97]

In theological terms one can easily recognize the similarity to Schleiermacher's approach. Schleiermacher begins his dogmatic endeavour with the "feeling of absolute dependence." This feeling of the community of pious persons constitutes the basis for the whole further discussion. Theology thus comes to rest on experience.[98] As Schleiermacher says: "The doctrines in all their forms have their ultimate ground so exclusively in the emotions of the religious self-consciousness, that where these do not exist the doctrines cannot arise."[99] Gustafson also begins with "piety" and "experience" and thus moves along the same lines as Schleiermacher.

What impact does a starting-point in experience have for one's understanding of revelation? In the section of his *Theocentric Perspective* I on experience, Gustafson states the implication as follows: "Whatever claims are made for revelation, one cannot deny that human experience is an indispensable

---

[93] Gustafson, *Theocentric Perspective* I, 167. Cf. Gustafson, *Theocentric Perspective* I, 195: "(1) piety, which is evoked by (2) the powers of God, (3) in relation to whom we are to relate ourselves and all things."

[94] Gustafson, *Theocentric Perspective* I, 257.

[95] Gustafson, *Theocentric Perspective* I, 251-252.

[96] Gustafson, *Theocentric Perspective* I, 61.

[97] Gustafson, *Theocentric Perspective* I, 62.

[98] Friedrich Schleiermacher, *The Christian Faith*, trans. by H. R. Mackintosh and J. S. Stewart (Edinburgh: T. and T. Clark, 1928 [orig. 1821-1822]), 17-18.

[99] Friedrich Schleiermacher, *The Christian Faith*, 76-78; quote from 78.

aspect both of how it is known and what is known through it."[100] Experience leaves its mark in the production of revelation and in the reception of revelation. In this context, Gustafson does not elaborate, but it is clear that the circularity of both the theological and moral exercises prove true for the approach to Scripture as well. In fact, as theology is a reflection on human experience, so too, "what is given in the Bible is itself reflection on the meanings of common human experience in light of an experience of the presence of God."[101] The symbols within the Bible have within the historical process provided further references for reflection. Thus it has become part of tradition and the marks to distinguish it from mere tradition are not clear, other than the fact that within history it has been thus elevated.

2.3.3. Gustafson's Preference for the Reformed Tradition

According to Gustafson, theology is primarily a way of "construing the world,"[102] that is, "relating all things (including human beings) in a manner appropriate to their relations to God."[103] Moreover, according to him, theology develops in a tradition. Of all the strands of Christian theology, Gustafson acknowledges that he has a distinct preference for the Reformed tradition, although he immediately admits that other traditions also inform his work.[104]

Gustafson stresses and affirms these three elements in this Reformed Tradition:

1. "a sense of a powerful Other, written about in the post-Calvin developments as the sovereignty of God."
2. "The centrality of piety or the religious affections in religious and moral life." Gustafson is not referring to the Protestant movement of Pietism, but rather to "an attitude of reverence, awe, and respect which implies a sense of devotion and of duties and responsibilities."
3. "An understanding of human life in relation to the powerful Other which requires that all of human activity be ordered properly in relation to what can be discerned about the purposes of God."[105]

Gustafson regards these three elements in the Reformed Tradition as "reciprocally interrelated." For "it is the powerful God who evokes piety; it is

---

[100] Gustafson, *Theocentric Perspective* I, 147.

[101] Gustafson, *Theocentric Perspective* I, 146.

[102] Gustafson, *Theocentric Perspective* I, 158, quoting Julian N. Hartt, William Kenan Professor Emeritus of Religious Studies at the University of Virginia.

[103] Gustafson, *Theocentric Perspective* I, 158.

[104] "That I am a Christian rather than a Jew is an accident of birth; that I am a Protestant rather than a Roman Catholic is both an accident of birth and a matter of conscious assent; that I choose to develop my work out of the Reformed tradition is a matter of religious and theological conviction," Gustafson, *Theocentric Perspective* I, 163.

[105] Gustafson, *Theocentric Perspective* I, 163-164.

the powerful God who is the ultimate condition of possibility for human action and the ordering of life: individual, interpersonal, social, historical, and in relation to nature."[106] In order to establish that these three general themes are in the Reformed tradition, Gustafson gives a discussion of these themes in Calvin, Augustine, Jonathan Edwards, and Schleiermacher.

Placement within a tradition is for Gustafson not simply an admittance which is of little further consequence. For Gustafson it is rather an intentional, conscientious matter and functions as more than an admittance. It functions almost as a warrant for the line which will be further pursued. If later in the argument someone would want to question certain aspects of the various conceptions, one would not argue beyond the choice for the Reformed tradition. Yet, Gustafson's construal of the Reformed tradition is rather selective and artificial in that it does not align itself with a body of confessions, but instead with a revisionist treatment of certain theologians. In fact, Gustafson opposes the limitation of any theologian to historic creeds, such as a formula of subscription, and prefers on this point the "Free Church" tradition.[107]

The importance for Gustafson of aligning himself with a tradition could be seen as part of his method and his point of departure for ethics. As discussed above, Gustafson sees theological and ethical discourse growing dynamically out of a tradition, always in dialogue with the present experience within the Christian community. In light of this one could conclude that Gustafson's preference for the Reformed tradition provides him with 1) the "soil" on which he is able to "cultivate" his discussion, and 2) the warrants for certain theological and ethical choices.

2.3.4. Gustafson's Theocentric Accent

Particularly in his *opus magnum* Gustafson takes as his task nothing less than challenging the anthropocentrism that he alleges characterizes mainstream Western Christian theology, and advocating his theocentric alternative.

2.3.4.1. Anthropocentrism Defined

Anthropocentrism is used in the sense of pragmatism, that school of thought or general proclivity, which uses religion to promote one's own personal ends. It is choosing one's belief primarily on the basis of the practical benefits they convey. It is putting religion into the service "not of gratitude, reverence, and service to God but of human interests, morally both trivial and serious."[108] In anthropocentrism God's chief concern is to promote human well-being. In anthropocentrism "God is denied as God; God becomes an instrument in the service of human beings rather than human beings instruments

[106] Gustafson, *Theocentric Perspective* I, 164.
[107] Gustafson, *Theocentric Perspective* I, 163.
[108] Gustafson, *Theocentric Perspective* I, 25.

in the service of God."[109] "Culturally, religiously, theologically, and ethically, man, the human species, has become the measure of all things; all things have been put in the service of man."[110]

Gustafson rejects all these central features of anthropocentrism. According to him, theology has succumbed to anthropocentrism when it suggests that all God's purposes and all cosmic events are "interpreted as rewards or chastisements of persons ...."[111] For example, he refers to the birth of a Down's Syndrome child as often being viewed either a divine punishment of the parents or as a God-sent opportunity for them to develop certain virtues and to increase their faith. What lies behind this view, according to Gustafson, is "the long and deeply held conviction that man is the crown of the creation, and that all that occurs is to be explained finally in the light of its meaning and significance for human beings." Gustafson does not deny that such a happening can be the occasion for beneficial human responses. What he does deny is that God has such purposes in ordaining the event.[112]

Gustafson contends that the acid of anthropocentrism has eaten very deeply into the fabric of Christian theology, so that also Reformed theology, inasmuch as it sometimes evaluates events according to their value for human beings, has been affected by it. He is convinced that most of what passes for theological ethics aims at glorifying humanity rather than God. For instance, he refers to Edwards' sermon on "The Justice of God in the Damnation of Sinners," in which Edwards clearly implies that the freedom of God is "arbitrary, that is, to not have to render an account of his choices, deeds, and will to anyone." Nevertheless, Gustafson continues by pointing out that in all instances that he is aware of, theologians who assert this radical sovereignty with such rigour, still typically conclude by asserting that God's holy will is undoubtedly beneficial to humankind. By this final admission, Christian theologians have at least introduced anthropocentric categories through the back door.

Gustafson sees another instance of anthropocentric influences in Reformed theology in the doctrine of eternal life. Though, on the one hand, the Reformed tradition has asserted that heavenly bliss is preserved for those who believe and are elected to this saving faith, nevertheless, the same theology will maintain that there are heavenly rewards and benefits for the pious.[113]

In Gustafson's own mind, theology should see the possibility of life after death as unnecessary.[114] The key to this lies within the Reformed tradition itself,

---

[109] Gustafson, *Theocentric Perspective* I, 25. Here it seems clear that Gustafson shares affinity with K. Barth.

[110] Gustafson, *Theocentric Perspective* I, 82.

[111] Gustafson, *Theocentric Perspective* I, 180.

[112] Gustafson, *Theocentric Perspective* I, 180-181.

[113] Gustafson, *Theocentric Perspective* I, 184.

[114] It is clear that Gustafson's ethic is a reactionary ethic, finding an ideological grounding point.

namely in the confession that "the chief end of man is to glorify God." The safe-guard against anthropocentrism is "to relate all things in a manner appropriate to their relations to God, in recognition of the dependence of all things upon him, and in gratitude for all things."[115]

Gustafson sees a further instance of anthropocentric influences in Reformed theology in the centrality that human guilt has had in its theology.[116] As such Gustafson has no difficulty with that. He states: "I shall retrieve and sustain" their "perception of the depth and persistence of the human fault."[117] The problem he has with it is the following: "[W]hen a particular theological tenet assumes a place of particular importance, it affects the ordering of other tenets in a coherent theological account."[118] Gustafson wonders "whether one can take the human fault with deep seriousness, establish some sense of the possibilities of human alteration, and claim some benefits of the divine benevolence, without becoming trapped in utilitarian Christianity's preoccupation with human guilt."[119] Although he does not go on to contend that Augustine, Calvin, and Edwards became "trapped in utilitarian Christianity's preoccupation with human guilt," he does say so implicitly when he states that their "confidence in the sufficiency of Scripture for various reasons is difficult to sustain in our time."[120]

From this discussion on anthropocentrism it will be evident that Gustafson's embrace of theocentrism is the embrace of an idea, formulated in reaction to anthropocentric extremes both in theology and ethics. Hereby, Gustafson can only be guided by his formulation of the idea and in reaction to excess. By his own admission, the source for true theocentrism for Calvin and others, the Scriptures, cannot be confided in, for it too displays anthropocentric tendencies. One wonders whether Gustafson's idea of theocentrism can be sustained without resorting to the relinquishment of human language, for it seems that human language, even theological language, will not avoid the anthropocentrism which Gustafson seeks to purge. The traditional treatment of revelation as "divine condescension" seemed better equipped to make head-way through this theological problem.

2.3.4.2. Theocentrism Defined

Over against the egocentric, anthropocentric orientation of Christian piety and Christian theology, Gustafson proposes a theocentric orientation. He argues that it is not God's chief concern to promote human well-being. He puts it like this: "The preoccupation with self has to be altered; the proper

---

[115] Gustafson, *Theocentric Perspective* I, 184.

[116] Here he explicitly refers to Augustine, Calvin, and Edwards; not to Schleiermacher.

[117] Gustafson, *Theocentric Perspective* I, 185.

[118] Gustafson, *Theocentric Perspective* I, 184.

[119] Gustafson, *Theocentric Perspective* I, 185.

[120] Gustafson, *Theocentric Perspective* I, 186-187.

orientation is not toward self but toward God--to the honoring of God, and to the ordering of life in relation to what can be discerned of the divine ordering."[121]

Gustafson is well aware that an ethic from such a theocentric perspective may be in radical discontinuity with the ethics of Western culture and Christianity. For no longer is the good determined by what is good for humankind, but rather the question is what is the good of the "whole of creation." Although mankind is inescapably the measurer of all things, mankind is not the measure of all things. "Man, the measurer, can no longer be the measure of the value of all things. What is right for man has to be determined in relation to man's place in the universe and, indeed, in relation to the will of God for all things as that might dimly be discerned."[122]

Belief in such a God, according to Gustafson, is more appropriate not only to what we know of the human condition but also to substantiating evidence from various sciences. Underlying Gustafson's attack on anthropocentrism is a profound sense of our dependency on and continuity with nature. He is impressed by our increasing ecological awareness that the more we seek to control nature, society, and history, the more we become controlled by them. But this is no easy attempt to provide a theology to underwrite everything undertaken in the name of ecological responsibility. Indeed, Gustafson is particularly critical of the romanticism involved in the current enthusiasm for "ecological ethics." Nor does he deny that there may be some legitimate sense to claims of human distinctiveness. Moreover, he assumes we must and should intervene in nature as well as seek more nearly just social orders.[123] Our task is not only to consent to divine governance but to cooperate with it toward those aims that we can discern.

According to Gustafson, the principal task of theology as an activity of practical reason is so "to construe the world" that all things are related "in a manner appropriate to their relations to God, in recognition of the dependence of all things upon him, and in gratitude for all things."[124] Gustafson has little use for any account of religion or theology which underwrites the assumption that Christian convictions are "useful" or functional for the flourishing of individuals or even the species. He is particularly critical of Tillich in this respect, and scorns the general preoccupation with method in modern history. We cannot determine method prior to content, for if we do so then we fail to situate human life within its appropriate limits by presuming to restrict God to our categories of meaning and rationality.

Nevertheless Gustafson knows that in dealing with questions of how we acquire and justify our knowledge of the power we call God "there is no way in which a certain kind of anthropocentrism can be avoided." For all knowledge of

---

[121] Gustafson, *Theocentric Perspective* I, 110.
[122] Gustafson, *Theocentric Perspective* I, 99.
[123] Gustafson, *Theocentric Perspective* I, 241.
[124] Gustafson, *Theocentric Perspective* I, 84.

God is human knowledge of God and it is mediated through human experience.[125] "Experience is prior to reflection," Gustafson insists, so that any "doctrine" such as "'creation out of nothing' cannot be explained without understanding that it stems from human experience of the mystery of life and efforts to provide a way of thinking about, relating, and accounting for that mystery."[126]

By arguing that experience is prior to reflection, Gustafson does not mean to deny that there are reflective elements in the ordering of even the most primary experiences. Rather there is an inherent circularity between experience and the reflective modes through which one comes to understand experience. We are inextricably creatures of history; our reliance on historical tradition is inevitable. Thus our experiences confirm that which we are predisposed to have them confirm.[127]

It is not clear whether Gustafson is committed to working within a tradition because doing so is unavoidable or because he believes certain traditions to be more nearly truthful. There seems to be an ambiguity in his thinking. On the one hand, he no doubt has gladly consented to finding himself situated within the Christian tradition, but on the other hand there remains the longing of the philosopher in him to find a place and a means to help us overcome the narrowness of the communal and cultural boundaries, the spatio-temporal constructs, in which we are confined. Thus he tells us that there "is no way in which we can be totally relieved of the boundaries of the particular communities to which we belong,"[128] but one senses that he feels powerless that such is the case and wishes for some alternative. At the same time he assumes that he needs a privileged standpoint outside any tradition that provides a more sure knowledge of what kind of God, the "power that bears down upon us," is. Such a standpoint is required by the kind of God Gustafson has depicted.

2.3.5. Theocentrism in Theology Proper

Gustafson sees theology and ethics next to each other on the second order, experience being of the first order, and is serious about engagement in actual theology. His chapters on "God in Relation to Man and the World" (chapter 5) and "Man in Relation to God and the World" (chapter 6) in his *Ethics from a Theocentric Perspective* (vol. 1) have the character of a brief

---

[125] Gustafson, *Theocentric Perspective* I, 115. James Balfour Tubbs Jr. also calls attention to this, that "despite his cogent and impassioned critique of anthropocentrism," Gustafson himself acknowledges that "'a certain kind of anthropocentrism' is unavoidable in theological reflection," James Balfour Tubbs, Jr. "Recent Theological Approaches in Medical Ethics: McCormick, Ramsey, Hauerwas, and Gustafson," Ph.D. diss. University of Virginia, 1990 (Ann Arbor, Michigan: University Microfilms International, 1990), 299.

[126] Gustafson, *Theocentric Perspective* I, 116.

[127] Gustafson, *Theocentric Perspective* I, 234.

[128] Gustafson, *Theocentric Perspective* I, 125.

systematic theology. His model for its lay-out derives from Calvin's emphasis on the dual knowledge of God and man.[129] Though the focus in this discussion does not allow us to go into detail on all Gustafson's reconstructions in systematic theology, the nature of the theocentrism as it becomes pertinent for ethics must come into view. Moreover, Gustafson brings Scripture into the discussion at a number of points. The theocentrism which he develops is gleaned partly from Scripture to the extent that it is part of the tradition which informs theology. A discussion of the function of Scripture in the ethics of Gustafson must look at the measure to which the concepts which inform ethics interact with and are built upon Scripture.

On the basis of theological sources within the Reformed tradition and the findings in various natural sciences, Gustafson portrays God as "the power that bears down upon us, sustains us, sets an ordering of relationships, provides conditions of possibilities for human activity and even a sense of direction."[130] God's transcendence makes him to be "beyond us." God is "majesty and mystery." Human efforts to speak before this Transcendent One fail. "In a very real sense, God as the Transcendent One is experienced as 'peculiarly devoid of content,'"[131] although He is "not the *totally* unknown God either," for He "has revealed Himself to a belief-full human community."[132]

Gustafson adopts and adapts the following traditional designations used for God: Creator, Sustainer, Judge, and Redeemer. Because we sense our finiteness, therefore we are justified in thinking of God as Creator. Genesis 1-11 is likewise the product of the sense of finitude, cast in the form of traditional myths and symbols. The creation narratives are affective construals of experiences which emphasize the theocentricity of reality.[133]

God is also our Sustainer as we find that we must and can trust the natural, social, cultural, and historical processes that are not of our own creation but matters to which we give our tacit consent. Rather than referring to certain "orders of creation," Gustafson raises the idea of God's continued creative ordering in the world. The moral question which belongs to this theological observation is: What does divine ordering require and how are humans accountable to divine ordering?[134]

The symbol of God as Judge also retains meaning "when we perceive that a deficiency of our activity is responsible for adverse consequences."[135] This symbol is closely connected to the social character of creation. Human life

---

[129] Calvin, *Institutes*, I,1,1. Cf. Gustafson, *Theocentric Perspective* I, 281.

[130] Gustafson, *Theocentric Perspective* I, 264. Flanagan points out that Gustafson already in 1967 referred to God as "a power bearing down" upon man [taking the phrase from Julian N. Hartt], "The Theological Ethics of James M. Gustafson," 111.

[131] Flanagan, "The Theological Ethics of James M. Gustafson," 109.

[132] Flanagan, "The Theological Ethics of James M. Gustafson," 110.

[133] Gustafson, *Theocentric Perspective* I, 236-238.

[134] Gustafson, *Theocentric Perspective* I, 238-242.

[135] Gustafson, *Theocentric Perspective* I, 246.

is ordered socially and disorder occurs actively through the transgression of limits and passively through the neglect of social duties. In Scripture, the disorder of murder, theft, and adultery are pointed to and the symbol of the judgment of God is invoked in prophetic indictments (Amos, Hosea, Micah), or presumed in various law codes.[136]

Finally, God is our Redeemer as we find ourselves constantly confronted with fresh possibilities as a sense of direction freeing us from our fatedness and sin. Here too, Gustafson invokes Scripture, since it places next to the indictments of moral infractions both the experience of forgiveness, and reconciliation with God and others. Briefly stated: "The biblical religions are salvation religions in a strong sense."[137]

Gustafson believes each of these traditional ways of speaking of God to be "in harmony" with and "indicated by" human experience and the "well-established data and explanatory principles established by the relevant sciences."[138] Scripture is brought to bear upon the subject as part of tradition and tradition as part of construed experience. But for Gustafson, tradition, to which Scripture belongs, must be in constant conversation with the sciences. It is remarkable that for Gustafson theocentrism is achieved particularly through attention to science. The reverse is true as well: the anthropocentrism of Christianity is particularly vulnerable in the light of what we are learning from physicists, astronomers, paleontologists, and biologists. Science guards the theocentrism which Gustafson pursues. One has the sense that Gustafson has a superior trust in gaining objectivity and theocentrism from science rather than theology, tradition, or revelation.

It is striking that at many points he refers to God in a depersonalized way as "the Deity." God is one which continues to "bear down upon us" and "sustain us."[139] This God, according to Gustafson, calls us to respond, to be responsible, by presenting us with the circumstances in which we find ourselves--although the circumstances do not always enable us to respond in ways that make sense to our human frames of meaning. This God may be depersonalized, but is nevertheless providential and vocationally demanding. This God provides, sustains, oversees, and anticipates purposes that are greater than all human concerns, and that sometimes contravene such concerns.

In terms of Gustafson's method, his depiction of God arises from a processing of experience and tradition. He finds that an openness to the sciences points to the propriety of a theocentric perspective of God, a God who

---

136 Gustafson, *Theocentric Perspective* I, 242-247.

137 Gustafson, *Theocentric Perspective* I, 250. Cf. Gustafson, *Theocentric Perspective* I, 247-251.

138 Gustafson, *Theocentric Perspective* I, 257.

139 Here in his doctrine of God Gustafson again moves in close proximity to Schleiermacher. God is seen as that to which our feeling of absolute dependence points back. God is called "absolute Causality" by Schleiermacher and is portrayed equally depersonalized (*The Christian Faith*, 200ff.).

is greater than our human concepts and concerns. One should note that theocentrism is not, then, the source of Gustafson's depiction of God, but its conclusion, for, as indicated above, the point of departure is necessarily that of piety and affection, or in other words experience. This is then also indicated by the qualifying clause in the heading title: "God in Relation to Man and the World."[140] Gustafson has portrayed God as God is experientially and piously evident to man and the world.

2.3.6. Theocentrism in Christology

With such a portrayal of God, constructed on the basis of human experience and piety, what does Gustafson do with the dogmatic *locus* of Christology, which has been traditionally so bound to the Scriptures? What is a Christology viewed from a theocentric perspective? What does Gustafson mean by Christology, which he calls "the most critical doctrinal issue for any Christian theology"?[141]

Already in 1968, in *Christ and the Moral Life*, he took up Christological implications for ethics.[142] According to him, the central question for every Christian as well as for Christian ethics must always be: "What is it to live, when, (in Paul's words) to live is Christ?" He takes up the positions of those who view Jesus Christ as "the Lord who is Creator and Redeemer,"[143] those who view Jesus Christ as "the Sanctifier,"[144] and those who view "Jesus Christ as the Justifier."[145] According to Gustafson, an appeal to Christology, whether

---

140 Gustafson, *Theocentric Perspective* I, 194.

141 Gustafson, *Theocentric Perspective* I, 275. Richard A. McCormick, S. J., in "Gustafson's God: Who? What? Where? (Etc.)," *The Journal of Religious Ethics*, 13:1 (Spring 1985), comments that Gustafson's Christology "is contained in five pages (1981:275-279) and appears almost as an afterthought" (58). Similarly, James Balfour Tubbs, Jr. writes that "while Gustafson may insist that Christology is a 'critical doctrinal issue' for his proposal, it does not appear that his method, or even most of his substantive conclusions stands or falls on any of his Christological claims" (James Balfour Tubbs, Jr., "Recent Theological Approaches in Medical Ethics: McCormick, Ramsey, Hauerwas, and Gustafson," 313). On Gustafson's Christology, cf. also Paul Jon-Yuan Jaw, "The Roles of Jesus Christ in the Ethics of James M. Gustafson," Ph.D. diss. Drew University (Ann Arbor, Michigan: University Microfilms International, 1990).

142 James M. Gustafson, *Christ and the Moral Life* (Chicago: University of Chicago Press, 1968).

143 He indicates particularly how Barth, Bonhoeffer, and Maurice in distinct ways focus on this metaphor and constitute variations on the inner logic of this theme, chapter II, 11-60. Paul Jin-Yuan Jaw correctly points out that although in *Christ and the Moral Life* Gustafson refers to Jesus' first role as "Creator and Redeemer," he in fact "never refers to Jesus Christ as the Redeemer or the Creator. He does mention the work of redemption in Jesus Christ. But the Redeemer is always God, not Jesus Christ," "The Roles of Jesus Christ in the Ethics of James M. Gustafson,"349.

144 In distinct ways Wesley, Schleiermacher, and St. Thomas, chapter 3, 61-115.

145 The variations of inner logic within this type are exemplified in Luther, for whom justification means the freedom to love freely; in Bultmann, for whom it means being free for the

dominated by Lord, Sanctifier, or Justifier metaphors, does not immediately solve the hotly debated questions of post-World War II ethics. For Christian ethics is directed not towards propositions, but instead towards the person of God as he is revealed in Jesus and in Scripture. Ethics is "a response not to a moral consensus drawn out of scripture or tradition, but to the promptings of the Holy Spirit as men deliberate together to discern the mind of Christ in their moral responsibilities."[146]

That Gustafson withdraws himself from the statements concerning Christ and the propositions contained in the Gospels, does not entail that he leaves Christ as norm aside. Christ as a person who reveals God deserves close attention for Christian ethics. Gustafson maintains that the Christian's loyalty to Christ demands a "responsible self." The person of Christ must be matched by the personhood of the ethical self. But the self "is not to be responsive to the movements of history, to the course of events as if in so doing one were doing what Christians ought to do, but to respond and participate in obedience to him, being directed by the discriminations and discernment that he enables."[147] The person of Christ and the person of the ethical self are brought into relation.

What are the dynamics of this relation according to Gustafson? This requires explicit, normative clarification under Christ of the fundamental concepts of the good, of the marks of faith, and of the free disposition which crosscuts both deeds and rules. In this way Gustafson attempts to break open from the inside the categories in which debates have been conducted and to move theological ethics beyond both the imperialism of certain neo-orthodox motifs and the rather tired practice of choosing sides between principalists and contextualists.[148]

Jesus Christ to Gustafson is "the One through whom ultimate powers and realities of life are known and understood, the One who represents as an historical figure the origin of a continuing historical community of trust and loyalty."[149] This sentence combines both "high" and "low" Christologies: Christ is the revelation of the Transcendent One and Christ is the incarnation of

---

future; and in Reinhold Niebuhr, for whom it means being free to engage pragmatically as participant in the struggles of life, Gustafson, *Christ and the Moral Life*, chapter IV, 116-149.

146 James M. Gustafson, *Christian Ethics and the Community* (Philadelphia: United Church Press, A Pilgrim Press Book, 1971), 99.

147 Gustafson, *Christ and the Moral Life*, 270.

148 Flanagan is right when she writes that Gustafson's *Christ and the Moral Life*, even though its "aim was to set forth in systematic fashion some theologians" claims about Jesus and his relationship to the believer's moral life," and "although indications of his own view can be noted within the summaries of exposition chapters and in his own constructive statement in Chapter VII," in fact is "more a composite text book of varying Christological positions than it is a personal Christological statement of the author." She adds that "Gustafson's interest in reflecting about God tends to be more broadly theological than Christological," "The Theological Ethics of James M. Gustafson," 116.

149 Gustafson, *Christ and the Moral Life*, 241.

theocentric piety. Christ manifests God before humankind but also represents the faithful community before God. Gustafson explains Christ's theocentric piety as follows: "Through the gospel accounts of his life and ministry we can see and know something of the powers that bear down upon us and sustain us, and of the piety and the manner of life that are appropriate to them."[150] He adds that this "in no way denies continuity between Jesus and the Jewish history and tradition of which he was a part; indeed what was known through him is so dependent upon that history and tradition that its distinctiveness could not have occurred in other cultures."[151]

But what is then the relationship between Christ and the testimonies to him found in the gospel? They portray with power the unique life of Jesus in relationship to God and the world.[152] Gustafson reserves his statements to the human nature of Christ. In fact, in a footnote[153] he expresses his "suspicion of the meaningfulness ... of claims about the nature and activities of the 'pre-existent Christ,' of Colossians and Ephesians ...." He writes that Jesus Christ "is the revelation of God; in him believers know God's mercy and wrath, God's grace and judgment." However, he does not write that Jesus Christ is God. He writes that "some plainly say 'Jesus Christ is God,'"[154] but he clearly does not belong to these "some."

Perhaps one could phrase it as follows: Gustafson's aversion to metaphysical and ontological speculation entails that his Christology is probably best understood in comparison with e.g. Schleiermacher. Christ for Schleiermacher is the one in whom complete God-consciousness developed. Thus in Christ the creation of human nature was completed, since perfect God-consciousness was intended for humanity, but disturbed through sin.[155] Believers are assumed into communion with Christ, who thus imparts his God-consciousness. This is his redemptive activity.[156] The pre-existence of Christ is marginalized to point to Christ as the human with the most complete God-consciousness. It can be asked of Gustafson why Jesus is singled out as particularly unique for the incarnating of theocentric piety--surely there are others, such as Gandhi, who are also compelling. Gandhi, for one, seemed to

---

150 Gustafson, *Theocentric Perspective* I, 276.

151 Gustafson, *Theocentric Perspective* I, 276. Nevertheless Yoder rightly remarks that Gustafson "has little space for history" ("Theological Revision and the Burden of Particular Identity," in *James M. Gustafson's Theocentric Ethics: Interpretations and Assessments*, eds. Harlan R. Beckley and Charles M. Swezey. Macon, Georgia: Mercer University Press, 1988, 76). Earlier in his presentation he argued that "with regard to Christology, Gustafson would seem to stand closer to Calvin's victim, Servetus, than to the Reformer" ("Theological Revision and the Burden of Particular Identity," 69).

152 Gustafson, *Theocentric Perspective* I, 276.

153 Gustafson, *Theocentric Perspective* I, 275, Note 65.

154 Gustafson, *Treasure in Earthen Vessels: The Church as a Human Community* (Chicago: University of Chicago Press, 1961), 104.

155 Friedrich Schleiermacher, *The Christian Faith*, 385, 389, 397.

156 Schleiermacher, *The Christian Faith*, 425-433.

have quite an understanding of the relationship between humans and other forms of life. Gustafson, no doubt, would reply that his identification with Jesus is but an attempt to remain true to the tradition in which he finds himself. But in what way is Jesus to Gustafson such a compelling example of theocentric piety? And how can he show that the "power that bears down on us" in fact is the God of Abraham, Isaac, and Jacob, the God and Father of our Lord Jesus Christ? What to Gustafson is the continuity between Yahweh and Gustafson's God who creates, sustains, judges, and redeems?

To be sure, Gustafson gives in some way an intriguing account of how God can be understood as an ever present reality "sensed" through the "aspects of piety." He does not try to "prove" God, but rather to show how our sense of dependence, gratitude, and so on, makes belief in a monotheistic theism intelligible. Gustafson manifests a pervasive sense of God's presence. Yet the question remains: Has he given us sufficient grounds for believing his God has a reality transcendental to our experience? He clearly does not regard Jesus Christ as God-become-man in Whom God has come to seek and to save lost man, to reconcile him to God and to bring him into the Kingdom of God.

2.3.7. Theocentrism in Anthropology and Soteriology

Since ethics ultimately concerns *human* action, it is interesting to examine how Gustafson moves from God to man. At some level, Gustafson has already made this move in his discussion on Christ. But Gustafson himself chooses to continue the dogmatic *loci* of anthropology, harmotology, and soteriology as he lays his theological foundations. Gustafson acknowledges Calvin's distinction of knowledge of God and knowledge of self and proceeds to speak of "Man in Relation to God and the World."[157] This heading articulates the concern to view anthropology from a theocentric perspective.

What does his theocentric perspective produce in terms of anthropology? Gustafson finds human life to be characterized by dependence, interdependence, valuing, and agency.[158] For society as a whole Gustafson advocates an interactional view, one which sees actions, individual and collective, within a context of processes. Human action is then determined, not in the sense of theologically pre-determined, but sociologically and culturally.[159]

Gustafson's anthropology is constructed with exclusive reference to experience though in comparison with theological and philosophical tradition. This is the case as well with Gustafson's harmotology, or in his term "the human fault." Human experience prompts the consciousness of "fault," "obligation," and "remorse." Human sin has been experienced as "misplaced trust or confidence," "misplaced valuations of objects of desire," "erroneous perceptions of the relations of things to each other and of our understanding of

---

[157] Gustafson, *Theocentric Perspective* I, 280-281.

[158] Gustafson, *Theocentric Perspective* I, 282-293.

[159] Gustafson, *Theocentric Perspective* I, 293.

things," and as "unfulfilled obligations and duties."[160] The human fault exerts itself in human life and destroys proper loyalty, reason, and love. The implication for ethics is that right action cannot be assumed.

Likewise, soteriology, or in Gustafson's term "the correction," is likewise constructed on the basis of experience in conversation with theological tradition. "The correction" to "the human fault" can be explained in three parts: 1) an "alteration and enlargement of vision, which is in part a correction of the flaw of our rational activities"; 2) an "alteration and enlargement of the 'order of the heart,' which is in part a correction of the flaws of idolatry and of disordered loves and desires"; and 3) different "standards for determining proper human being and action as a result of the other corrections, which is in part a correction of the flaw of 'disobedience.'"[161]

Gustafson maintains that a "theocentric vision and piety can also enable a correction of the moral fault of disobedience." Quoting Edwards' metaphysical terms, Gustafson states: "The moral life becomes one ... of 'benevolence to being in general.' It becomes one of living one's life, ordering one's activities and 'all things,' in such a way that they agree more with the ends and purposes of the divine ordering of life." He calls attention to the fact that "the enlargement of vision is clearly necessary as a condition for this view of moral life." Through this correction human "responsibilities and obligations are enlarged, and particular obligations are set in a wider context of life."[162]

In his discussion of anthropology and soteriology for ethics, Gustafson has arrived at an articulation of the need for theocentricity. Yet in his methodology he has been guided by experience and tradition. The sources for knowledge concerning mankind, sin, and redemption have been in perception and interpretation. It is not clear how the qualifying aspect of the heading "Man in relation to God and the World" finds its way in Gustafson's dogmatic methodology. Instead, the qualifier "in relation to God" gives a clue to Gustafson's "dogmatic" conclusions. The necessary re-ordering of the human heart occurs under divine rule, which is identical to Gustafson's plea for theocentricity.

Besides being a "dogmatic" conclusion, the qualifier "in relation to God" is also an ethical presupposition. As Gustafson moves from theological reflection to ethical reflection, the issue of theocentricity becomes a presupposition and a theocentric perspective is deemed necessary for the moral life.

2.3.8. Rules and Discernment in Theocentric Ethics

For Gustafson, the correction and reordering of the heart leads to an expansion of loyalty and a life under divine rule. It is interesting that Gustafson

---

160 Gustafson, *Theocentric Perspective* I, 294-306.

161 Gustafson, *Theocentric Perspective* I, 308.

162 Gustafson, *Theocentric Perspective* I, 315.

brings up "the law of God" in this context. As such he is pleased with the term, since it suggests both "the theocentric focus and the religious dimensions of morality." It connotes that ethics must involve an ordering of everything after God.[163] But instead of elaborating on the expression of the law of God in the Scriptures, Gustafson sees the law more exemplarily. Responsibilities and requirements come into play, though not in a legalistic sense. Rather, Gustafson insists on them being "general rules," applied differently in different conditions. First of all, we do not have infallible knowledge of what divine rule demands. Rather, discernment develops historically, as does theology and science. Secondly, divine rule has an "ordering" rather than an immutable character. Consequently, rules will develop in parallel to societal and cultural conditions.[164]

However, Gustafson seeks to distance himself from anthropocentristic utilitarianism, which asks exclusively for the benefit of humanity. According to theocentric ethics, the moral question is: "What serves the divine purposes?"[165] In this theocentric construal the central moral question that needs to be put in every situation, therefore, is not what does the categorical imperative require here?, or what is required by the principle of utility or the pursuit of *eudaimonia*? Rather it is: "What is God enabling and requiring us to be and to do?"[166]

Gustafson's most general answer to this question is "that we are to relate ourselves and all things in a manner appropriate to their relations to God."[167] He works it out somewhat further as follows: "It is a process of discernment that we come to some certitude (but not always certainty) about what God is enabling and requiring, and about the appropriate relations of ourselves and all things to God." Gustafson offers a paraphrase of Romans 12:1-2 in which he emphasizes the discernment of ordering things properly in relation to God.[168] Gustafson gives "discernment" the sense of "keenness of perception," the ability to analyze persons and communities on the one hand, and the dynamics of divine governance on the other.

This method of discernment is separate from 1) a simple fact analysis with some moral principles or 2) moral intuition without moral principles.

---

[163] Gustafson, *Theocentric Perspective* I, 322-323.

[164] Gustafson, *Theocentric Perspective* I, 316.

[165] Gustafson, *Theocentric Perspective* I, 317.

[166] Gustafson, *Theocentric Perspective* I, 327.

[167] Gustafson, *Theocentric Perspective* I, 327.

[168] Gustafson, *Theocentric Perspective* I, 327-328. The paraphrase is as follows: "Individually and collectively offer yourselves, your minds and hearts, your capacities and powers in piety, in devoted and faithful service to God. Do not be conformed to the immediate and apparent possibilities or requirements of either your desires or the circumstances in which you live and act. But be enlarged in your vision and affections, so that you might better discern what the divine governance enables and requires you to be and to do, what are your appropriate relations to God, indeed, what are your appropriate relations of all things to God. Then you might discern the will of God."

Instead, it is a dialogical analysis of both situation and consequences of divine governance. First, an evaluative interpretation of the situation needs to be made. This is a rational and reflective activity. Secondly, there is the reflection on divine government. As said, this can only be known generally, not specifically. Gustafson rejects the view that the Scriptures give us divine rule in its moral details. There are changes within the biblical record, in fact a clear development. Morality needs to be discerned by a pious community through its perception of reality and understanding of divine governance.[169]

2.3.9. The Practice of Theocentric Ethics

Volume 2 of *Ethics from a Theocentric Perspective* is dedicated to ethical concerns. In this volume it is possible to see how the multidimensional aspects of his argumentation come to fruition. As to the question of the role of Scripture in the practice of ethics, one must not expect much direct discussion of Scripture. As the argument above has shown, the function of Scripture is qualified as the idea of theocentrism. This idea, as Gustafson elaborates on it, becomes significant as a pole within the moral discussion which takes place in the community. It is, nevertheless, useful to trace the paths along which Gustafson arranges the impact of this idea upon the practice of ethics, utilizing the arguments in three of the four areas which Gustafson takes up: 1) marriage and family; 2) suicide; and 3) population and nutrition.

2.3.9.1. Marriage and Family

Gustafson does not discuss scriptural data concerning the institutions of marriage and family. In fact, the discussion concentrates on what appears from nature and tradition. First, Gustafson connects the evidence of nature to the plan of God. Ethics is the way to give collective order to what is required by our natures. Ethics does so by ordering our relations as they most appropriately suit together and in the end pattern after God. Marriage and family are ways in which persons live socially. Gustafson's theocentrism directs his attention to the communal nature of life and duties. It directs man away from his egocentric and utilitarian interests and focuses him on the social frameworks within which he finds himself.

Gustafson's theocentrism calls to mind human finitude. Human limitations are opportunities for enrichment, since it procures diversity within social arrangments.[170] Marriage and the family are also contexts in which "the human fault" is expressed.[171] Forgiveness is possible by participating "in the

---

[169] Gustafson, *Theocentric Perspective* I, 328-338.

[170] Gustafson, *Ethics from a Theocentric Perspective*, Vol. 2: *Ethics and Theology* (Chicago: University of Chicago Press, 1984), 167.

[171] Gustafson, *Theocentric Perspective* II, 168.

sustaining and renewing powers of God that come to us through our natures and capacities as human persons."[172]

Secondly, tradition stands next to nature in providing direction for the theocentric nature of ethics. Here Gustafson turns to an examination of the "Form of Solemnization of Matrimony" from *The Book of Common Prayer* in the Anglican/Episcopal tradition. In this document Gustafson finds an ethics of marriage which directs the participants in the social patterns of the institutions of marriage. It supplies what one needs to deem a matter "ordered after God." Scripture is brought to bear only in the form in which tradition has best deemed its use.

One must add that at a deeper level it is Gustafson's own experience of tradition that judges the theocentricity of tradition. For Gustafson distances himself from some of the explicitly patriarchal elements of the form for the solemnization of marriage with a reference to the contemporary change in custom.[173] In many regards, Gustafson's discussion of the form for marriage is a processing of the data of tradition through his experience within contemporary society.

2.3.9.2. Suicide

Gustafson begins his treatment of suicide by an empathetic description of the situation in which persons have resorted to suicide. It is characterized by fundamental lack of alternatives, a sense of loss of freedom to do anything about the conditions, coupled with a fundamental loss of hope.[174]

A theocentric perspective gives attention to the relations of interdependence, and points to the responsibility of rearranging conditions to alleviate the sense of despair for persons. It also points to human limitations in the cases when suicide does take place. Gustafson speaks of a condition of tragedy in which "the powers that bear down upon them are greater than the powers that sustain them."[175] Gustafson uses the word "consent" to characterize the theocentric response to suicide that has taken place.[176]

2.3.9.3. Population and Nutrition

On a worldwide scale, threats of malnutrition and famine, like those of despair and suicide at a more personal level, suggest that neither nature nor nature's God is particularly and especially concerned about human well-being. Sometimes these realities seem to strike with the force and unintended destruction of a tornado or an earthquake. Humans, to be sure, should treasure

---

[172] Gustafson, *Theocentric Perspective* II, 167-168.

[173] Cf. e.g. Gustafson, *Theocentric Perspective* II, 183.

[174] Gustafson, *Theocentric Perspective* II, 207.

[175] Gustafson, *Theocentric Perspective* II, 209.

[176] Gustafson, *Theocentric Perspective* II, 215.

and attempt to sustain life wherever possible. And Gustafson is alert to what technology, new economic organization, and political rearrangements can do to mitigate want, suffering, and ecological destruction. He has little patience with romantic, anti-scientific, and anti-technological rhetoric that dreams of returning to primeval harmony with nature. "There is no return to a mythical Eden, and there is no assurance of a risk-proof and tragedy-free future."[177] He reminds us that from his theocentric perspective "it cannot be argued that all things were created for the sake of man." Rather than focusing solely on the need for nutrition for the human species, mankind must work towards the sustenance of nature both for the sake of the continuation of the human species and for nature's own sake.[178]

He argues against moral prohibitions of birth control and calls for voluntary restraint in procreation as long as that remains feasible.[179] Humans are to steward both production and reproduction with all the technological wisdom we can manage. And this requires awareness of the possible courses of action through the patterns and processes of interdependence around the world and in the face of ecological limits. This demands the acceptance "of responsibility for larger wholes than the immediate interests of a couple, their family, their community, or the nation." Nevertheless we must also acknowledge that we seldom have "signals of the divine ordering" which are sufficiently loud and clear that we know immediately what ought to be done.[180] Humankind must do its best to work toward the continuation of the human race and the maintenance of nature itself.

Here, as with suicide, Gustafson presses us to recognize human and natural limitations and possibilities. "Human life," he states, "remains dependent upon natural forces and powers that are not fully in human control." Moreover, "any human policies and activities to improve conditions have to take into account natural limitations and possibilities."[181] We are to actively do all that can be done, because our choices and actions are neither bound by inexorably determined laws nor necessarily in accord with some clear purpose which we can know now.[182] Yet we are accountable before other people, before history, before nature, and before God and find ourselves called (by circumstances) to respond as best we can. We must face the fact that we also are finite, that what we do is inevitably caught up in processes and patterns beyond our control, and that we are not responsible for everything we view as evil all the time in the same degree. Hence we must view ourselves as temporal participants in interdependent realities, neither underestimating nor

---

[177] Gustafson, *Theocentric Perspective* II, 243.
[178] Gustafson, *Theocentric Perspective* II, 243.
[179] Gustafson, *Theocentric Perspective* II, 247.
[180] Gustafson, *Theocentric Perspective* II, 249.
[181] Gustafson, *Theocentric Perspective* II, 236.
[182] Gustafson, *Theocentric Perspective* II, 236.

overestimating what can be done in the vast cosmos in which we find ourselves, nor bearing undue guilt when we have done what we can.

Again, Gustafson's discussion at this point is clearly guided by his idea of theocentrism. He advocates a realization that we are temporal participants in patterns beyond our control. In this language we recognize the allusion to God who is the power who bears down upon us. Gustafson proposes responsible activity which pursues possibilities and acknowledges limitations. His theocentric center forces him to acknowledge dependence upon a Being higher than human power.

2.4. Summary and Evaluation

The preceding discussion has been far from exhaustive as far as Gustafson's thought as a whole concerns. This chapter has sought to lift up main objectives, compare his practice of moral thinking, and specifically call attention to his use of Scripture. One could summarize Gustafson's project as seeking to ground moral discussion theologically, i.e. in the very doctrine of God. Thus Gustafson aims at theocentricity in opposition to anthropocentrism. For Gustafson, anthropocentrism in ethics constitutes an orientation towards the mere well-being of humans, a certain pragmatism in moral discussion. Sometimes Gustafson can detect this anthropocentrism in theologies which hinge on simply human salvation. Often these theologies emphasize sin and judgment and eternal life. For Gustafson this is part of anthropocentrism.

Theocentrism, specifically in ethics, aims at ordering all things in relation to God. Theocentrism involves a sense of dependence on God, God bearing down on us. Moral discussion therefore seeks to order life in accordance to divine governance. For Gustafson, that is a dialogical process comprising a reflection on social, cultural, and individual situations and a discernment of divine government.

For Gustafson, Scripture should not be engaged here in a casuistic manner. Rather, there might be Scriptural principles which, in the experience of piety of the Christian community, are employed with reference to the situation. Gustafson is careful not to elevate Scripture beyond such a point. Scripture is a record of experiences, in which pious people discerned the will of God in various circumstances. In the practice of moral discussion Gustafson is on his guard for anthropocentrism. In its place, he heralds a divine governance perspective.

Gustafson's moral methodology is clear in its outline. To sum up one could note a number of things. 1) Gustafson emphasizes a theocentric perspective, which in the area of moral rules takes on a concern for an ordering everything in relation to God. 2) Gustafson at the same time seeks to locate a point of departure in experience, which for the Christian is the experience of religious affectivity, or piety. 3) Gustafson aligns himself with the Reformed tradition because of its emphasis on the otherness of God, on the place of religious piety, and on the responsibility of ordering all things in relation to God. 4) In his discussion of the various dogmatic *loci*, theocentrism is not the presupposition, but rather the conclusion. Human experience in conversation with tradition is the ground of theological construal, which concludes the necessity of theocentric perspective for ethics. 5) Gustafson outlines a method for ethics which is dialogical in character, bringing situation and divine rule into unity. Theocentrism has become the key-word for Gustafson's perspective on ethics. It is that posture which Gustafson finds to mediate between God and the moral life.

Gustafson's ethics from a theocentric perspective does not produce a single principle or hierarchy of values, nor does it deliver a relativism. It brings to the situation a view of God, which calls for a response to match the divine order with a human order. It could be said that for Gustafson it is more important to enable others to view situations in light of the same theocentrism. One could almost say that for Gustafson the first volume of *Theocentric Perspective* was more significant, for it set forth a view of God, upon which communities of moral discourse can elaborate. Yet, the method of volume 2 of *Theocentric Perspective* has also shown that theological awareness is a large part of moral decision making. On the matter of marriage it entails the realization of the divine ordinance and the patterning after divine order. Concerning suicide it entails the realization that the source of life is outside our control, so that we should restrain suicide where possible, but neither deify life itself. Regarding issues of population and nutrition, a theocentric perspective directs attention to the dynamics of total communities and the realization of limitations. The role of Scripture in the application of Gustafson's ethics has been consistently qualified and mediated through his theocentric perspective, as he has constructed this from experience and tradition and as he practices it on the various issues at hand. Through the posture of theocentricity Gustafson has allowed Scripture to speak insofar as he has heretofore qualified and elaborated its place.

Gustafson's approach is to be appreciated for its polemic with the rampant anthropocentrism in the forms of pragmatism, utilitarianism, and emotivism rampant in both the theory and practice of Western Christian ethics. Not only would a reversal in such individualistic and pragmatic ethics save our societies from much egocentrism, utilitarianism, materialism and other societal ills, but it is an orientation demanded by the Christian tradition. As such this emphasis can be welcomed and valued.

Furthermore, Gustafson's emphasis on piety and its intimate relationship to morality is appreciated. Too often Christian ethicists neglect piety and its significance for moral action. The heart converted, regenerated, and kindled by the grace of God in Christ through the Spirit is also the source of new obedience (Jer 31:33-34; Ezek 36:26-27).

That Gustafson's theocentrism is contained in an ordering of the heart according to the governance of God is a significant and valuable insight. The relations with other humans and also with nature comes into proper perspective when the relationship to God is correctly perceived. Discernment is a biblical concept (Rom 12:2), as is the idea that all things are from God and to God and through God, also our moral action.

Our appreciation for Gustafson does not entail that we have no questions about his method and conclusions. The first question pertains to the area of dogmatics. This point is relevant to the question of the role of Scripture in ethics, firstly because Gustafson chooses for a theological approach to ethics, and secondly, because Scripture exerts its influence precisely through theological construal. The question is whether Gustafson's adoption of Reformed sources, such as Calvin, Augustine, and Edwards, not proved to be a serious *adaptation* of them? To some extent Gustafson is aware of this problem. He acknowledges that there is a great deal in the theology of Calvin and Augustine that is left out by the process with which he has selected these three elements. With regard to Calvin's theology he acknowledges that he has "left out the redemptive work of Christ, so central to Calvin's theology."[183] Concerning Edwards, Gustafson notes that there is much that he discards in his theology.[184] Indeed, Gustafson makes clear where he disagrees with the Reformed tradition: (1) its tendency to attribute all events to divine providence, (2) its interpretation of God's sovereignty as being good and just for man, and (3) its need for a conception of eternal life as a means to resolve the doubts that arise from our experience about the justice and benevolence of God.[185] But has Gustafson in that way not significantly distanced himself from the Reformed tradition?

Stephen D. Crocco rightly calls attention to the fact that Gustafson's "reformulation gives no place to some of the most notable features of the Reformed tradition, such as predestination, law and gospel, covenant, the Trinity, the two natures of Christ, salvation history, the atonement and eschatology."[186] Crocco also notes that, although Gustafson admires Edwards' conviction that God's glory was the last end of creation, Gustafson's criticism of Edwards seriously misinterprets Edwards. Gustafson bifurcates "divine glory and human well-being," which for Edwards are one. God's glory *is* God's righteousness and human well-being. According to Crocco, "Edwards never

[183] Gustafson, *Theocentric Perspective* I, 167.
[184] Gustafson, *Theocentric Perspective* I, 172, 176.
[185] Gustafson, *Theocentric Perspective* I, 178-184.
[186] Crocco, "American Theocentric Ethics: A Study in the Legacy of Jonathan Edwards," Ph.D. diss. Princeton University, 1986 (Ann Arbor, Mich.: University Microfilms International, 1985), 154.

spoke of the good of the creature in a way that separated it from the glory of God."[187]

One could add that Gustafson's adaptation of the classic Reformed is owing significantly to his embrace of major tenets of Schleiermacher's theology. In his time Schleiermacher substantially left the Reformed tradition in many of its articulations and thus redefined those elements he did retain. Gustafson admits to being impressed with many of Schleiermacher's points and explicitly indicates that his affinities with his theology go beyond the three elements.[188] The similarity to Schleiermacher has been noted at points above. They share a concept of God as a "power bearing down on us" (Gustafson) or "the co-determinate of our experience of absolute dependence" (Schleiermacher). Furthermore, their common point of departure in experience, piety, or the religious feeling of dependence marks their methodology. Finally, they share a strong Christology from below, wherein Christ is conceived of as the incarnation of the perfect and complete "feeling of absolute dependence" or "loyalty to divine governance." These are the main and significant points of contact between Schleiermacher and Gustafson.

A second question concerns Gustafson's qualification to the authority of Scripture. Is it not evident that the theological qualifications which Gustafson makes regarding the use of the Bible as authority do not displace the authority for the moral life from God and his Word to the human community and their experience? By means of each of his qualifications to the authority of the Word of God, Gustafson relays the center of gravity for moral decision within the Christian community and their experience. If this is so, then Gustafson is certainly in line with the collective emphasis of modern American Protestant ethics, described in chapter 1. Gustafson might respond that even those who claim to have invested full authority in the Word of God for the moral life still act upon their own impulses and motivations. The question is, however, whether Gustafson's prior commitment to a Troeltschian view of knowledge and

187 "American Theocentric Ethics," 172-173. Crocco argues that Gustafson's claim for Jonathan Edwards "as a precursor of his own position" is a mistaken claim. He compares Gustafson to a surgeon in this regard, who in his "work of retrieval and development" uses "a double-edged scalpel cutting away at the tradition." Like a surgeon, Gustafson believes that this surgery will "contribute to the health of the tradition." What does he as a surgeon cut away? "With one pass, the scalpel's Troeltschian edge cuts away those things that are no longer believable in the light of modern knowledge. With another, Gustafson's understanding of the 'glory of God' severs those beliefs which he judges dishonoring to God," "American Theocentric Ethics," 171. By way of illustration, Crocco mentions the "traditional doctrine of eschatology," which Gustafson cuts away by means of this "double-edged scalpel," because (i) he no longer considers it "believable in the light of what we know about the universe," and (ii) he considers it "largely a product of human wish-fulfillment reflecting an unwillingness by human beings to worship God unless they somehow profit from it," Crocco, "American Theocentric Ethics," 172.

188 Gustafson, *Theocentric Perspective*, I, 176-178.

religion prompts him to make this claim. The grandeur of this issue impels us to take it up more deeply in the final chapter.

A third question about the moral program of Gustafson concerns his concept of God. Other than his departure from the distinctly Reformed view of God noted immediately above, any explanation of and justification for a monotheistic piety is absent. Such piety derives from the search of the human "self" for the appropriate object of its confidence, hope, love, and desire. Gustafson does not attempt to establish or prove that the "power that bears down on us" exists, but instead to show that, given the character of our existence, loyalty to such a God is appropriate. Just as our sin or "fault" lies in our unwillingness to relate all things in a manner appropriate to their relation with God, so our redemption comes as we find in God the means of enlarging and ordering our vision and our hearts. Such an "enlargement" can be achieved from a non-theological perspective, but Gustafson wants to maintain that the theocentric enlarging of vision and ordering of the heart remains indispensable for the appropriate situating of the self in nature and history. Why at all does Gustafson call "those powers that bear down on us" *divine*? An explanation fails at this point.[189]

A fourth question, which touches the heart of Gustafson's project, is whether Gustafson achieves the theocentrism he seeks. Others have raised this precise question, such as Jaw. Jaw even asks for the motivation for the shift to theocentricity. Is it perhaps pragmatic? Has Gustafson not also indicated that "the energy crisis which we have experienced in recent history raised our consciousness toward the scarcity of natural resources, the possible demise of the world, and the sin of human abuse?"[190] Has he not made clear that "our awareness of the interdependence of the world" led us "to see more clearly that our survival depends on the survival of the rest of the world and our well-being depends on the well-being of nature?"[191] Jaw rightly comments that if this is the case, then Gustafson remains in the anthropocentric tradition and "may still have a certain degree of teleological anthropocentrism.[192]

Also regarding Gustafson's desired theocentrism, there is the question whether his starting-point in experience, human subjectivity, and piety does not condemn his theocentric aspirations to fail. Can a theocentrism which attempts to order all things in relation to God succeed when it is grounded in the thoughts and experience of the *anthropos*? Furthermore, when moral decisions need to be made in a dialogue between experience and "a discernment of divine governance," the nature of theocentrism is severely affected, in my estimation.

---

[189] Cf. Crocco, "American Theocentric Ethics," 187.

[190] Jaw refers to Gustafson's "Interdependence, Finitude, and Sin: Reflections on Scarcity," in *Journal of Religion* 57 (April 1977): 156-68.

[191] Jaw refers to Gustafson, *Theocentric Perspective* 1, 282-84.

[192] Jaw, "The Roles of Jesus Christ," 413-416.

Gustafson does little to safeguard against spiraling from an anthropocentric hermeneutic into anthropocentrism in ethics.[193]

It remains a question to what extent the idea of theocentrism and the disposition or posture which it affirms is able to stem the weight of the pragmatism which Gustafson seeks to avoid. For even the language which Gustafson uses is replete with references to the human good. It must be granted that Gustafson modifies an exclusive concentration on individual good and gain with a vision for all of society. Yet, it is impossible for Gustafson to press his claim that humans do not exist for their own good to its consistent end. For even with his wide focus, Gustafson points out for the various issues that the human duty is to aim for those things which will sustain human life and existence (albeit within a sustained nature) for the longest period of time. The question is therefore, whether Gustafson is not simply more oriented towards the totality and extensiveness of the human world but yet on a pragmatic line. It seems that issues necessarily demand attention for themselves and will inevitably require pragmatic action of some degree. The idea of theocentrism will only relay the peripheries of such demands, while maintaining the essential requirements of the issue. If this is the case, then the feature of American pragmatism (cf. chapter 1) has not been banished but perhaps sublimated. This line of thinking will need to wait till a further discussion in chapter 5.

A fifth question concerns Gustafson's understanding of piety. As Allen D. Verhey points out, "God must be knowable to some measure for piety to exist."[194] According to Gustafson, the transcendent God's character and purposes are not altogether unknowable, but they are not fully and exhaustively knowable either. How, then, can he give theocentric content to his piety? To know Christ is to know God (John 14:7, 9-11). Richard A. McCormick, S.J., in "Gustafson's God: Who? What? Where? (Etc.)" cogently states: "Knowing Jesus' qualities, ideals, and injunctions is a direct insight into God's gracious governance of the world. More importantly, knowing *who He is* is knowing both the Godhead and ourselves in relationship with the Godhead, and therefore knowing some rather basic things about God's plan for us."[195] The question remains: Can piety exist without this christological basis? This is not even to ask about a pneumatological thrust to piety. Would a theocentric piety not need to be fully Trinitarian?

---

[193] Even the Dutch ethicist H. Kuitert has pointed out this incongruity in Gustafson, "Theologie en ethiek," in *Gereformeerd theologisch tijdschrift* 85 (1985), 9: "Als je zegt dat we alleen met een niet-antropocentrische theologie en ethiek de moderne problemen de baas kunnen, is dan de keuze voor een niet-antropoccentrisch uitgangspunt niet toch weer nuttigheids-bepaald en dus weer antropocentrisch?" [If you say that we can only overcome modern problems with a non-anthropocentric theology and ethics, then is the choice for a non-anthropocentric starting-point not still utilitarian and consequently anthropocentric?]

[194] Allen Verhey, "On James M. Gustafson: Can Medical Ethics Be Christian?" in *Second Opinion*, Vol. 7 (March 1988), 111.

[195] McCormick, Richard A., S. J. "Gustafson's God: Who? What? Where? (Etc.)," in *The Journal of Religious Ethics* 13:1 (Spring 1985), 59.

The terms "practical," "collective," and "rational," utilized to describe the character of American Protestant ethics (chapter 1), suit Gustafson's discussion to a certain extent. From Troeltsch and others, Gustafson has learned to view everything within the confines of sociological and historical knowledge and to see everything from the basis of experience. Scripture is also subject to these categories and can be seen as a record of such experience. The locus of ethical decision-making then becomes the Christian community, as it discerns through the coincidence of present experience and the past experience of Scripture and tradition what is the proper theocentric response. The idea of theocentrism has difficulty curtailing the pragmatic demands of the issues which arise and runs the danger of sublimating them rather than avoiding them.

With these questions and observations our chapter specifically on Gustafson and his *theocentric* comes to a close. The discussion now turns to Paul Ramsey and his specific emphasis on a *Christian* ethics.

Chapter 3: Paul Ramsey: The Use of Scripture in Christian Ethics

3.1. Introduction

> In North America Paul Ramsey has been a towering and forceful figure for almost four decades; his writing has forced persons with alternative views to come to grips with his thought, and had a deep impact on a younger generation of authors. He has been a persistent critic of moral fads, a steadfast proponent of the Christian ethics of love, and a vigorous participant in debates about public policy and medical ethics.[1]

These words from the pen of James M. Gustafson illustrate the position and influence of the now late Paul Ramsey. On February 29, 1988, he died of a heart attack, in Princeton, N.J., R. Paul Ramsey was born on December 10, 1913, in Mendenhall, Mississippi. His parents were Rev. John William Ramsey and Mamie McCay Ramsey. On June 23, 1937, he married to Effie Register. They had three children: Marcia, Jenifer, and Janet. Denominationally he was a Methodist, as were his parents.

He began his academic work at Millsaps College in Jackson, where in 1935 he received his Bachelor of Science degree. He went on to earn his B.D. degree in 1940 and his Ph.D. degree in 1943 at Yale University, where, among others, H. Richard Niebuhr was his mentor and teacher. Already during his studies for his B.D. degree, from 1937-1939, he was an instructor in history and social sciences at the College where he had obtained his B.S. degree. While working on his Ph.D. he taught for two years as assistant professor of Christian ethics at Garrett Biblical Institute (now Garrett Theological Seminary), Evanston, Ill. In 1944 he joined the faculty of Princeton University, Princeton, N.J. (from 1944-1947 as assistant professor, from 1947-1954 as associate professor and from 1954-1982 as professor of Christian ethics). In 1957 he was named Harrington Spear Paine Professor. Upon his retirement from the faculty in 1982 he joined the Harrington Spear Paine Center for Theological Inquiry.[2]

He has authored more than a score of books, among which the widely seminary text *Basic Christian Ethics*,[3] *War and the Christian Conscience*, *Life or Death: Ethics and Options*, *Fabricated Man*, *The Patient as Person*, and

---

[1] Gustafson, *Ethics from a Theocentric Perspective* II, 84

[2] Allen Verhey, "Paul Ramsey (1913-1988)," in *The Reformed Journal* 38 (April 1988), 2.

[3] Verhey refers to it as "a classic introduction to Christian ethics; it alone would leave us in his debt," "Paul Ramsey (1913-1988)," 2. James M. Gustafson calls this book Ramsey's "most comprehensive statement of theological ethics," *Ethics from a Theocentric Perspective* II, 84.

Ethics at the Edges of Life. During the above-mentioned many years Ramsey dealt with some of the most pressing concerns of the times, from such traditional issues as premarital sexual relationships and the ethics of war to such avant-garde topics as *in vitro* fertilization and fetal research. In his ethics he always made the claim that love is the controlling moral principle. He edited a collection of essays on H. R. Niebuhr (*Faith and Ethics*, 1957), as well as two works of the eighteenth-century American Calvinist preacher Jonathan Edwards (*Freedom of the Will*, and *Charity and Its Fruits*).

Ramsey spent the first part of his career as Christian ethicist on basic Christian ethics, that is, on the basic norm and the distinctive character of the Christian life. He gave the middle part of his career to considering the relation between force and political responsibility. About the 1970's he shifted his focus to medical ethics in which he strongly defended the life claims of the fetus and the dying.[4]

As the preceding chapter pointed out, Gustafson's ethics speaks of theocentrism, though he does acknowledge the place of Jesus Christ. The heading of this chapter applies the characteristic "Christian" to Ramsey's ethics. What is the rationale for this? First of all, the ground for Ramsey's ethics is specifically Christian. Ramsey does not make an effort to arrive at a universal ethic for those both within and outside the Christian faith. Secondly, the prominence of the place of Christ in ethics is evident. Thirdly, the important force of love (*agape*) in ethics receives formulation and definition in Christ. He even calls his *Basic Christian Ethics* "an essay in the Christocentric ethics of the Reformation."[5]

As in the chapter on Gustafson we are assuming our discussion in chapter 1 on the history of American Protestant ethics under the key phrases "practical," "collective," and "rational." This chapter will closely examine the steps in Ramsey's use of Scripture, both theoretically and practically. As noted above, Ramsey was taught in part by H. Richard Niebuhr and the legacy of American Protestant ethics has moved through him, though Ramsey has reached back to older American figures such as Josiah Royce and Jonathan Edwards.

As to Ramsey's theological orientation, Oliver O'Donavan writes that he "belonged to the neo-orthodoxy of the mid-century, somewhere on an axis between Barth and Reinhold Niebuhr." Among the currents of modernism he particularly withstood "its recurrent attempt to absorb the mystery of providence," whereby modernity manipulated "it into the positivism of human planning and etherialising it into the optimism of a religious hope without the

---

[4] Cf. Charles E. Curran, *Politics, Medicine, and Christian Ethics: A Dialogue with Paul Ramsey* (Philadelphia: Fortress, 1973). With respect to his shift medical ethics, Allen Verhey refers to him "as one of the midwives at the birth or rebirth of mecial ethics," "Introduction," in *Religion and Medical Ethics: looking back, looking forward*, ed. Allen Verhey, (Grand Rapids: William B. Eerdmans Publishing Company, 1996), 4.

[5] Paul Ramsey, *Basic Christian Ethics*, xiv. The references are to the 1950 edition, except for the "Forword" by Stanley Hauerwas and D. Stephen Long in the 1993 edition, in footnote 143.

paradox of grace."[6] Yet Ramsey's relation with modernism was not only antithetical in nature. In what follows we will particularly discuss the movements of Ramsey's argument on the role of Scripture in ethical discourse. In Paul Ramsey's ethical thought there is less a direct urge to create a distance between Scripture and moral action, as with Gustafson. Yet, a certain distance is evident in the desire to construct a single unifying principle with which to meet the issues of Christian practice. The distance which Ramsey creates between Scripture and Christian ethics is a *principled* distance. The similarities in situations call for principles of action. He says this on the one hand against pure situationalism, which advocates distinct responses to distinct situations. He says this on the other hand against those who propose only rules with no attention to the situation.

This principle is what Ramsey early on called the *agape* principle, which is christocentrically grounded. Later on Ramsey preferred to speak of the covenant principle, which denotes much the same. The *agape* principle as it is taught in the Bible and manifested in Christ is the highest embodiment of the Christian moral practice. The lacuna created by the absence of immediate biblical authority is thus for Ramsey filled by a christocentric understanding of love.

3.2. Ramsey and the Interpretation of Scripture

3.2.1. The Authority of Scripture Assumed

Ramsey's treatment on the role of Scripture in ethics differs from Gustafson's polemical writing on the subject. Ramsey turns to Scripture without much explanation. He calls the Bible the traditional source of ethics in the Hebrew-Christian tradition. In his *Basic Christian Ethics* the self-evident use of Scripture is expressed as follows:

> I submit that it would never occur to an unprejudiced mind--a mind not already greatly harmed by some wrong-headed apologetic interest--to look for the meaning of Christian ethics anywhere else than in the biblical record and in the writings of men of the past whose thinking about morality has been profoundly disturbed and influenced by what they found there.[7]

Ramsey calls his *Basic Christian Ethics* "a self-contained introduction to biblical ethics."[8] He writes that this book "endeavors to stand within the way the

---

[6] Oliver O'Donavan, "Obituary: Paul Ramsey (1913-88)," in *Studies in Christian Ethics* 1 (1988), 83.

[7] Ramsey, *Basic Christian Ethics*, xiii.

[8] Ramsey, *Basic Christian Ethics*, xiii.

Bible views morality."[9] These words were penned in 1950. In 1970 it was still Ramsey's commitment to move within the field of a distinctly "biblical ethics."[10] In 1979 Ramsey was still explicit that the Bible as it found its way in liturgy was to guide the moral life. He wrote the following on the subject of abortion: "[T]here are multitudes of sincere contemporary Christian people who seem to believe that the Bible says nothing definitive to the abortion question. I can only conclude that they have not heard Biblical sermons ... "Pro-choice" opinion[s] ... are secular points of view not bent to God's *convex*."[11]

The essential character of the Bible for ethics is grounded in the connection between God and Christian ethics. Gustafson and Ramsey share the concern that ethics be theologically rooted in God. Ramsey is insistent that the very sense of obligation is related to the existence and character of God. Therefore Ramsey turns to the Bible. Though he does not explicate the nature of the connection between God and the Bible, it is evident that Ramsey considers the Bible to be the source for revelation concerning both God and the moral life. Whereas Gustafson was careful to qualify the distinction between the person of God and the Bible, for Ramsey it is the connection between the two which is self-evident.

In this connection, one must remember that Ramsey's *Basic Christian Ethics* was published in 1950, which was the period of time in which the Biblical Theology Movement was very popular within American Protestant circles. Influenced by the neo-orthodox theology of Barth, this movement emphasized the actions of God in history as revealed in the Bible.[12] Ramsey, for instance, uses the phrase "the strange new religious world of the Bible" without even documenting Barth who coined this phrase.[13] This illustrates that Ramsey's context in 1950 would have understood an unexplained move from God to the Bible. For someone as Gustafson in the 1980's this would no longer be a matter of course.

Ramsey grants that a Christian ethics would not be complete without a comparison with non-Christian moral philosophies. This comparison is not of the same nature as a comparison with the Scriptures, for Ramsey. For besides having connections with moral philosophy, a biblical ethics will often stand in

---

[9] Ramsey, *Basic Christian Ethics*, xi.

[10] Cf. his "The Biblical Norm of Righteousness," in *Interpretation* 24:4 (October 1970), 419-429.

[11] Ramsey, "Liturgy and Ethics," in *The Journal of Religious Ethics* 7:2 (1979), 161.

[12] Cf. e.g. the extremely popular book by G. E. Wright, *God Who Acts: Biblical Theology as Recital* (London 1952). Though this book is more than a decade later than Ramsey's *Basic Christian Ethics*, it characterizes the atmosphere which existed in the middle of this century in many American Protestant seminaries. On the biblical theology movement, cf. B. S. Childs, *Biblical Theology in Crisis* (Philadelphia, 1970). As will be pointed out below, Ramsey's concentration on God's action in Christ also fits the Biblical Theology Movement, which also on this point has been influenced by Barth.

[13] Karl Barth, "The Strange New World Within the Bible," *The Word of God and the Word of Man*, trans. by Douglas Horton (New York: Harper and Row, 1928) 28-50.

contrast to secular philosophies.[14] Ramsey's commitment to the Bible as a source for ethics is explicit and fundamental.

3.2.2. Scripture Interpreted "Principledly"

As obvious as it is for Ramsey to turn to the Bible as the source of Christian ethics, so self-evident is it for him to speak of biblical principles. Other terms which Ramsey utilizes as synonyms are "concept," "notion," "primitive idea," and "category." Ramsey explains this concentration on principles partly as an effort to *systematically* set forth a theory of ethics.[15] However, most of the time, Ramsey's principled use of Scripture goes without explanation and is simply practiced. In order to examine this particular use of Scripture, it will be helpful to look at the principles which Ramsey sets forth. How does Ramsey draw or distill principles from the Scriptures? Later on the concern will be how Ramsey applies these principles to ethical issues. But for now, a discussion of Ramsey's exposition of the main biblical principles.

3.2.2.1. The Principle of God's Righteousness

The first few chapters of *Basic Christian Ethics* form a convenient entrance into the question how Ramsey develops this project. Ramsey states upfront that the concept of "covenant" constitutes an appropriate summary of the ground of action. Ramsey discusses "covenant" as evident in "God's righteousness" and the "Kingdom of God."[16]

Ramsey begins by elaborating on the righteousness of God in Scripture. "Righteousness" in Scripture approximates the concept of love and should not be understood in opposition to it. God is a saving God in his righteousness and not despite it (cf. Ps. 71:2). The corollary of divine righteousness is the expectation of an ethic of righteousness as operative among humans.[17] Human ethics is rooted in divine action as a response of thankfulness. Thus in contrast to the Greek view, righteousness is not retributive but redemptive. The community is upheld by a benevolence which mirrors and flows from divine redemption. Ramsey cites the many Old Testament laws for the protection of the weak, widow, and orphan.[18]

Moving on to the New Testament Ramsey sees Jesus as confirming this same righteousness in his teaching. For the first Christians, Jesus even became "the righteousness of God." Here Ramsey speaks of the Incarnation and the *kenosis* of Christ as manifesting this saving love of God.[19] The manner of

---

[14] Ramsey, *Basic Christian Ethics*, xii.
[15] Ramsey, *Basic Christian Ethics*, xiv.
[16] Ramsey, *Basic Christian Ethics*, 2.
[17] Ramsey, *Basic Christian Ethics*, 5.
[18] Ramsey, *Basic Christian Ethics*, 14.
[19] Ramsey, *Basic Christian Ethics*, 19-20.

Christian action is rooted also in this righteousness, particularly through imitation.[20]

The eschatological concept of the "Kingdom of God" focuses the idea of righteousness. The apocalyptic framework of Jesus' life and message gives the kingdom ethic its intensity, evidenced, for instance, in the Sermon on the Mount. However, this apocalyptic is no different in its description of "God's righteousness" as God's saving love. Ramsey cautions against making too much out of differences in New Testament Theology. Instead, he emphasizes that fundamentally there is a unanimity among the biblical authors in that they ascribe a supernatural character to obedient love.[21] This emphasis on the consensus of Scripture stands in contrast to Gustafson's argument that the diversity in Scripture is evidence that Scripture is a record of experience.[22] Ramsey is pressing for the coherence of the matter.

The coherence comes in the person of Christ. In Ramsey's words: "Jesus did not bring the kingdom; his sense of the kingdom brought Jesus."[23] The meaning of this statement is that the matrix of Jewish apocalypticism produced the person of Jesus who with radicality and perfection forged the transcendent validity of the concept of love. In Christ "human thought gains an Archimedean point."[24] In him all moral conduct receives a standard which dialectically challenges all mundane habits and requires the obedience of absolute love which transcends limitation.

Ramsey anticipates the objection that the idea of the kingdom and the gift of Jesus Christ are two things by stating that both are held together by the concept of divine righteousness. In language borrowed from Albert Schweitzer, Ramsey writes: "The biblical idea of the righteousness of God was the crater from which, when stirred into renewed action by apocalypticism, burst forth the flame of the eternal religion of love."[25]

Ramsey's discussion of early Christian theology as apocalyptic is influenced by Schweitzer's findings concerning the character of Jesus.[26] Ramsey, however, is interested in more than simply the person of Jesus. Instead, he is concerned with the centrality of Jesus for ethics. In Jesus one finds the point where the righteousness of God is formulated so unqualifiedly and transcendently, that it is able to be the perpetual source of Christian action.

This ground of Christian ethics is not only the historical Jesus, but also the pre-existent Christ, and particularly the condescension of God in Christ.

---

[20] Ramsey, *Basic Christian Ethics*, 22-23.

[21] Ramsey, *Basic Christian Ethics*, 21.

[22] Cf. e.g. Gustafson, *Theocentric Perspective* I, 147. Cf. the discussion in the previous chapter.

[23] Ramsey, *Basic Christian Ethics*, 41.

[24] Ramsey, *Basic Christian Ethics*, 44.

[25] Ramsey, *Basic Christian Ethics*, 45.

[26] Cf. e.g. Albert Schweitzer, *The Quest of the Historical Jesus: A Critical Study of Its Progress from Reimarus to Wrede* (New York: MacMillan, 1964).

Specifically the moment of Incarnation is important for Ramsey. He not only follows the apostle John who emphasized that Jesus Christ was God in the flesh (John 1), but particularly Paul in his kenotic Christology, who emphasized the "cosmic-historical importance for human salvation," namely, "the fact that the pre-existent Christ became a man at all."[27] So Christocentric ethics grounds itself not simply in Christ's manhood but also His divinity, and the unity of these two natures.[28] To emphasize one nature at the expense of the other would be to dispose of all ground of knowledge, including that of moral character.[29] Ramsey's ethics, then, is based upon the revelation of the divine will in Christ as the decisive measure of human action, and it makes the love of Christ the controlling--the primary or basic--principle of moral conduct.

Ramsey does not leave behind the remainder of the Bible once he has arrived at the person of Christ. The totality of the Bible helps him get the full significance of Christ in view. In fact, though Christ is of utmost significance for ethics, Ramsey frames the biblical principle always in terms of "divine righteousness" or "love." These are the biblical ideas which ultimately supply the coherent principle which Ramsey will operate with as his ethics begins to take shape.

From this discussion of righteousness it is clear that one sense of the word "principle" is that idea or thought to which a whole can be reduced which grants coherence and simplicity to that which might seem on the surface disparate and divided. This sense of "principle" carries within it the notion that one is able to handle the idea and do justice to a whole. The term "principle" connotes that there are matters which stand in a derivative relationship to this "principle." These matters would be "secondary," "tertiary," etc., and not "principal" or "primary." At this level it is similar to the term "theme."

There is, however, a dynamic which distinguishes from that which is purely "theme." In fact, the term "principle" connotes the potential of applicability. The practical benefit of a "principle" is that it has a character which makes it suitable and able to provide direction to that which it is brought into relationship with. Undoubtedly for Ramsey, the field and issues of ethical practice will be that which the principle will be brought into relationship with. For now, however, that function can only be noted, while examination of the process will need to wait.

3.2.2.2. The Principle of Christian Liberty

The second sense of "principle" can also be made clear by what it is opposed to. Ramsey makes clear that this "principle" stands in opposition to a code morality. Ramsey cites examples of the latter in ancient Judaism or contemporary pietistic sects. In Christ this code morality, or "law" as Ramsey

[27] Ramsey, *Basic Christian Ethics*, 18-20.
[28] Ramsey, *Basic Christian Ethics*, 21-22.
[29] Ramsey, *Basic Christian Ethics*, 198-199.

also calls it, is overcome. "Righteousness" or "love" stands as a new "principle" in that it eradicates all morality guided by a code ("principles, rules, customs, and laws") and becomes the "sovereign test" of all morality.[30]

According to Ramsey, Christ raised the code to the level at which it disintegrated. His words: "You, therefore, must be perfect, as your heavenly Father is perfect" (Matt. 5:48) show how Christ fulfills the law by attacking its very nature as law. In its place Christ places that which is infinitely different: self-sacrificing love of one's neighbor.[31] Ramsey does not agree with the interpretation which sees the double love commandment (Matt. 22:37-40) as a summary or an extension of the Old Testament commandments. He suggests that this interpretation indicates more about the "rebirth of legalism" in the early church.[32]

Ramsey cites Christ's teachings of non-resistance (Matt. 5:38-42), his saving life on the sabbath day, and his polemics against the scribes and the Pharisees as evidence of the inauguration of a transcendently different principle. Ramsey also examines St. Paul's notion of "Christian liberty" as evidence of the absence of a code and independence from the law. Ramsey reads Paul in this way that the law has no "positive moralizing power," and that with the coming of Christ the law, our former custodian, has been abolished (Gal 3:28). In the end Ramsey concurs with Paul Tillich that the principle of *agape*-love is that which provides the solution to the problem of either absolutism or relativism. Love as principle challenges both, for it confronts a person with the needs of the other.[33]

It must be noted that the sense of "principle" in Ramsey is best understood as it relates negatively to code morality. That morality which bases itself on principle upon principle, law upon law, line upon line is abolished by the one principle, so infinitely and qualitatively different. There is a dialectical relationship between law and the principle of love. "Love" is that other principle which stands diametrically opposed to that principle which establishes principles.

There are thus two senses to the term "principle." The first sense is that of coherent simplicity in the form of an idea which gathers disparateness and complexity and carries the potential of being brought into relation with other matters with a certain method of appropriation. The second sense is that of a singular notion which stands in an antithetical relationship of infinite quality to that which has the potential of being pluralized and set in opposition to the singular notion. The first is centrifugal, the second centripetal. The first is prioritizing, the second dialectic. The two senses are dependent upon one another. As Ramsey "distills" the principle of "love" from the Scriptures, he finds it in an antithetical relationship to natural and human codifications. That

---

30 Ramsey, *Basic Christian Ethics*, 57.

31 Ramsey, *Basic Christian Ethics*, 73.

32 Ramsey, *Basic Christian Ethics*, 64.

33 Ramsey, *Basic Christian Ethics*, 74-91.

which he finds antithetical to the "principle" serves to confirm the antithetical character of the principle and contributes to the singularity and simplicity of the principle. With these senses to the term "principle" Ramsey engages in a principled reading of Scripture.

Both because of this second sense of the term "principle" and because of the primary sense of the term "principle," the process of "distilling" or "gathering" a principle has a hierarchalizing character to it. It not only puts things into relationship with it, but places them into relationships which are hierarchical. For singularity in this case demands superiority. An example of this is Ramsey's treatment of Matthew 22:40: "On these two commandments *depend* all the law and the prophets." Ramsey quotes in agreement the NT scholar T. W. Manson who comments that this verse is "another indication that where the Law is in question Matthew is simply not to be trusted."[34] As part of his principled use of Scripture, Ramsey betrays a preference for certain texts above other texts.

3.2.2.3. The Principles of Creation and Fall

Another example of the hierarchalizing tendency of Ramsey's principled treatment of Scripture is his discussion of creation. In his *Basic Christian Ethics* this discussion is focused on the matter of the *imago Dei*. He objects to those conceptions of the *imago Dei* which, influenced by Stoicism, use this notion to remove the line of demarcation between God and human nature. But building upon Augustine, Kierkegaard, and Barth, Ramsey advocates an understanding of the *imago Dei* as the posture of man oriented toward responding toward God. Ramsey then concludes that this notion can be considered a Christian category which "can be defined only *derivatively* by decisive reference to the basic 'primitive idea' in Christian ethics, i.e., the idea of Christian love which itself in turn can be adequately defined only by indicating Jesus Christ."[35]

The theological background for this allowance is explicated in Ramsey's referral to Barth's statement: "Creation is the external basis of the covenant, and the covenant is the internal basis of creation" (*Church Dogmatics* III, 1, sec. 41, 2, 3).[36] Prudence and love are held together as creation and covenant are, covenant and love being the controlling bases in their respective cases.

Ramsey's argument concerning the motif of the Fall follows a similar pattern. Sin is to be defined in opposition to Christian love. Human sin is any "falling short of disinterested love for the neighbor for his own sake, love cut to the measure of Christ's love, any falling short of the strenuous teachings of Jesus, any falling short of the full definition of obligation contained in 1 Corinthians 13."[37]

---

[34] Ramsey, *Basic Christian Ethics*, 64.

[35] Ramsey, *Basic Christian Ethics*, 249-259. Quote taken from p. 259. Emphasis is Ramsey's.

[36] Ramsey, *Basic Christian Ethics*, 244.

[37] Ramsey, *Basic Christian Ethics*, 290.

There is in fact an epistemological connection between sin and Christian love. We do not know about this sin simply "from analyzing the capacities and propensities within human nature as such." Rather, we are forced to this conclusion "from viewing man in the light of God as Christians know him, *i.e.*, in Jesus Christ. Ramsey emphasizes particularly a personal knowledge of sin, rather than a "general human sinfulness." The Christian doctrine of human sin teaches the need for a "personal appropriation" of this truth, which requires "a confession of one's own sinfulness," for at "the deepest level the doctrine of sin has least to do with mankind in general and most to do with one's self in the mirror of God's Word."[38]

For this Ramsey refers to St. Paul. He, indeed, taught that "all mankind was in bondage to sin." In Romans 1:21b-23, for instance, Paul taught that "men 'became futile in their thinking and their senseless minds were darkened.'" Nevertheless it is striking that Paul "paid ... tribute to man's natural powers" in two respects. (i) In Romans 2:14, 15, Paul writes that man has "a native capacity for natural morality." (ii) In Romans 1:19-21a Paul writes that "man is naturally religious." However, Paul did emphatically teach that man is plainly unable "to attain to the Christian religion and the Christian ethic, unless God gives what he commands."[39] Moreover, Ramsey insists that when Paul wrote in Romans 3:23 that "all have sinned and come short of the glory of God," he meant that all have fallen "short of Jesus Christ as standard."

How does Ramsey arrive at this interpretation? According to him, the expression "the glory of God" means "throughout the Bible God's disclosure of himself to man." In view of the fact that Paul in II Corinthians 4:6 writes that God gives "the light of the knowledge of the glory of God in the face of Jesus Christ," Ramsey concludes that for Paul this "meant, of course, God's disclosure of himself in Jesus Christ."[40] In a footnote, Ramsey refers to Karl Barth who says that "'there is no knowledge of sin except in the light of Christ's cross. For he alone understands what sin is, who knows that his sin is forgiven him.'"[41]

In this way, according to Ramsey, "the Genesis story" is placed "in proper perspective," for Christians read their Bibles *backward*, first the New Testament, then the Old." They "do not believe man sinful because of the account of Adam's first sin in Genesis." Rather, they "first have been persuaded of man's sinfulness" in the synoptic gospels. Even though the synoptic gospels themselves do not say much about sin, "the consciousness of sin arises especially from thinking about oneself in relation to this part of the New Testament Word." Christians must therefore acknowledge the "depth of sin," before they read Genesis. Then in the Genesis account they find "something of an explanation as to *why* man is what he is." The "Christian doctrine of human

---

[38] Ramsey, *Basic Christian Ethics*, 288.
[39] Ramsey, *Basic Christian Ethics*, 289-290.
[40] Ramsey, *Basic Christian Ethics*, 290.
[41] Ramsey, *Basic Christian Ethics*, 292.

sinfulness ... was never grounded primarily in Genesis but in man's understanding himself on encountering Jesus Christ."[42]

Although he regards the opening chapters of Genesis to be "ancient legends which were the repository of the earliest Hebrew thought about man in relation to God," he does insist that they "do contain profound truth concerning the nature and meaning of human sin. Genesis gives a theocentric, or a contra-theocentric definition of sin." For that matter, the whole Old Testament defines sin as "some particular act of disobedience or breach of moral law." The "quality of human sinfulness can ... best be seen in contrast to what God must do in order to correct sin and hold it within bounds: He is a zealous and a 'jealous' God who will have no other gods before *or beside* him."[43] Then the New Testament account of God's dealings with man "brings to sharper focus the sinfulness of man" simply "by bringing to sharper focus 'the righteousness of God.'"[44]

Ramsey's discussion evidently assumes some of the results of historical criticism of the Bible and its rationalistic heritage. He does not make an effort to argue the presence of myth or even explain his criteria for what qualifies as myth. But the presence of myth gives occasion to philosophical elaboration on various biblical themes.

3.2.3. Scripture Interpreted Philosophically

In his *Basic Christian Ethics*, Ramsey, particularly as it concerns public policy, argues that "contemporary Christian ethics must make common cause with the ethics of philosophical Idealism."[45] Ramsey's dissertation had arranged for a significant encounter with the anthropology of Idealism.[46] Ramsey's discussion of "original sin" is an example of a philosophical discussion of a biblical topic, which he regards as couched in myth. He defines "original sin" as sin originating "in man himself by his own will." In a sense he regards "the doctrine of 'original' sin" as "the most significant thing" that can be said about man, "because it makes him responsible for the origination of sin."[47] He distances himself from the "traditional doctrine of 'original sin.'" He argues that it "was completed by adding to the account of man's first sin a 'history' of the inheritance of sin or the transmission of sin to the entire race by biological propagation." He argues that this "idea could not have occurred to a man of the Bible," for the Bible views "the physical body and procreation ... as good" and

---

42 Ramsey, *Basic Christian Ethics*, 292.

43 Ramsey, *Basic Christian Ethics*, 294.

44 Ramsey, *Basic Christian Ethics*, 295.

45 Ramsey, *Basic Christian Ethics*, xiii.

46 Ramsey, "The Nature of Man in the Philosophy of Josiah Royce and Bernard Bosanquet"(1943). Cf. D. Stephen Long, *Tragedy, Tradition, Transformism: The Ethics of Paul Ramsey* (Boulder: Westview, 1993), 24-37.

47 Ramsey, *Basic Christian Ethics*, 287, 288.

"by no means" disparages sexual intercourse. According to him, the "idea of the biological inheritance of sin ... was a product of Greek and biblical ways of thinking in the minds of men such as St. Augustine." They were "first convinced of man's sinfulness and had in Genesis the beginnings of an explanation for it." Then they "completed their theory by making sexual propagation the vehicle for the transmission of sin, the connecting link between men's 'original' sin and our own."[48]

3.2.3.1. Existentialism

How does Ramsey then account for the origin of sin in every man? He turns to Christian existentialism and argues that "every man is his own Adam, sin originates with him, he does not sin on account of anything."[49] He acknowledges that he arrived at this thesis by, first of all, listening to "the analysis of spiritual freedom and anxiety by Christian existentialism"[50] for saying something "about the *occasion* for sinning."[51] He refers to Kierkegaard's writings on "the relationship between spiritual freedom and dread, and between dread and the act of sin."[52] He refers to Fyodor Dostoyevsky's view of freedom as the source of sin.[53] Finally, Ramsey points to Reinhold Niebuhr's discussion of "the relationship between '*justitia originalis*' or 'perfection before the Fall' and the origin of original sin." Whereas "Genesis assigns" the "real locus of original righteousness ... to the garden of Paradise," Niebuhr assigns it to "every man 'before the act.'" According to Niebuhr, "'Perfection before the Fall' means 'perfection before the act'; sin or the Fall takes place in the act." Falling into sin or sinning in the act "accomplishes every man's passage from the garden of original righteousness."[54]

---

48 Ramsey, *Basic Christian Ethics*, 293.

49 Ramsey, *Basic Christian Ethics*, 306.

50 Ramsey, *Basic Christian Ethics*, 313.

51 Ramsey, *Basic Christian Ethics*, 307.

52 Ramsey, *Basic Christian Ethics*, 307-308. Kierkegaard defined the concept of "dread" or "anxiety" as "'the reflex of freedom within itself at the thought if its possibility.'" This "dread" or "anxiety" arises in man "over the alarming 'not-yet-ness' of his future." As he looks into the future, "(...he encounters nothing at all, because the future is by definition not yet)." So man through "'his consciousness'" discovers the future, but when "'this future through the consciousness is withdrawn in the moment' ... sin is born; and this situation provides the *occasion* by which, through a free act of sin, sin comes into the world."

53 Ramsey, *Basic Christian Ethics*, 308-310. Dostoyevsky considers freedom to be the source of sin. "Out of freedom, by sin sin comes into the world, and it is always coming into the world."

54 Ramsey, *Basic Christian Ethics*, 310-312. Niebuhr "draws extensively from Kierkegaard's concept of dread," when he describes "anxiety as 'the internal condition for sin' and temptation its external precondition." Nevertheless Niebuhr insists that when "a man sins it is he who does it and not anxiety which compels him."

3.2.3.2. Idealism

Ramsey is aware of the radical individualism of Christian existentialism and advocates that it be supplemented by the idealism of philosophers such as Jean Jacques Rousseau and Josiah Royce.[55] Though they had an eye for the responsible nature of man's act, they gave a sharp analysis of the social occasion for sin. To Rousseau "'man is naturally good.'" To him man's "original condition" is that of "a being in whom the impulses of egoism and compassion are unself-consciously expressed and nicely balanced." In addition to these, man "possessed also free agency and 'perfectibility' (which simply means 'the faculty of self-improvement')." Nevertheless "'men are actually wicked.'" Rousseau "gives a mythical account of the sin and fall of man" to explain "how man, essentially good as he may be supposed once to have been, could ... produce corrupting and tyrannical political institutions, whose influence ... creates in social man such an overwhelming propensity toward evil."[56] Rousseau first presents "an external history" and "introduces the 'first revolution': 'The first man who, having enclosed a piece of ground, bethought himself of saying *This is mine*, and found people simple enough to believe him, was the real founder of civil society.'" To this "external history," Rousseau adds "an internal moment or factor in the fall of man." He writes: "From his very first social contact man began to perceive certain relations of comparative superiority between himself and ... other individuals of his own kind: 'Thus, *the first time* he looked into himself, he felt the first emotion of pride....'"[57]

Ramsey compares Rousseau's mythological account with the Genesis story, which he also regards to be "an external explanation of sin as resulting from temptation." The serpent tempted Eve, and she sinned. She tempted Adam, and he sinned. This, however, "only leads us back to an original angelic rebellion in heaven where there was no temptation." So neither "Rousseau nor Genesis really explains sin by external history; they both bring sin with them into external history." Rousseau makes use of the external history to explain "the successive revolutions which produce vested social inequality." The Genesis account tells the external history in order to explain "why woman must bear her children in pain and why man is subject to the drudgery of agriculture." They "simply refer to sin as an internal factor in order to explain certain external realities." However, neither account explains sin itself. To be sure, there is a difference between Genesis and Rousseau's account. Whereas "Genesis understands sin as sin before God ... as an ultimate infraction of man's God-relationship," Rousseau "understands sin as sin over man ... a less ultimate and appalling infraction."[58]

---

[55] Ramsey, *Basic Christian Ethics*, 307.

[56] Ramsey, *Basic Christian Ethics*, 313-315.

[57] Ramsey, *Basic Christian Ethics*, 315-316.

[58] Ramsey, *Basic Christian Ethics*, 317-318.

Next, Ramsey refers to Josiah Royce, who insists that "'Man's fallen state is due to his nature as a social animal.'"[59] Royce "distinguishes between the conduct of men and their consciousness about their conduct" and states that the "individual's conduct" may be good. "Men may keep the peace, even though in spirit they are enemies of one another." He does not assert "'that the conduct of all natural men is universally depraved,'" but he does assert that "they all do inwardly revolt and this is their sin. Their self-consciousness about their conduct inevitably has the 'form of *spiritual* self-assertion,' which is both sin and loneliness."[60] Royce speaks about social man gaining selfhood and coming to be what he is "out of mutual relationship with many factors in his environment." He also speaks about social man gaining "selfhood in relationship to the fundamental structures of any possible human life in community with other persons." Royce goes on to say that nevertheless "the self's reactions to the efforts society makes to stamp its image upon him are truly the self's own actions, his own response."[61]

Nevertheless there is also "common responsibility here." Ramsey refers to the relationship of child to parents and of church member to the congregation. Although faith is a personal thing, and no man "can have faith for another," and each member in the church says "I believe," man does not sin "quite by himself." That is the reason that when in "the congregation Christians repeat the "general confession" in unison, each individual making use of the plural form of the personal pronoun." It is "because of common responsibility for sin socially at the root of manhood," that we do this.[62]

In summary, one could say that Ramsey derives from Christian existentialism "the possibility and the proneness to sin which freedom gives"[63] and from idealism the fact that sin lies connected to "sociality" and becomes evident in "social contracts." As such, it is therefore the opposite of love, which seeks the neighbor. Therefore, Christian love in its expression often seeks social policies, such as in human rights, etc., to oppose the natural outworkings of sin. Ramsey is quick to stress that love always remains independent of such social policies, and ultimately is free. Love is free, for it does not identify with either abstract truths or the situation.

Ramsey admits that the Genesis account gives a far more theocentric definition to sin than do the philosophical accounts. Not only is there the moral command which is transgressed by the first parents (Gen 2:16-17), but there is the desire expressed to be like gods (Gen 3:5).[64] Ramsey even brings the New Testament account to bear on the matter, as pointed out above. In Christ the depth of sin is uncovered as self-interested idolatry and the "falling short of the

---

59 Ramsey, *Basic Christian Ethics*, 321.

60 Ramsey, *Basic Christian Ethics*, 322.

61 Ramsey, *Basic Christian Ethics*, 324.

62 Ramsey, *Basic Christian Ethics*, 324-325.

63 Ramsey, *Basic Christian Ethics*, 307.

64 Ramsey, *Basic Christian Ethics*, 294-295.

glory of God" (Rom 3:23). The philosophical accounts do not attain to this theocentricity or christocentricity, but are left with anthropocentric orientations, whether individualistic or collectivistic.

Ramsey does not, however, point up how the philosophical accounts lack the aspect of the *revelation of sin* by the divine Word or in the divine law. He himself does not concentrate on this either, except by noting that with Christ the depth of sin is uncovered. Yet, in the Genesis account this is indicated already in the divine command and warning in Genesis 2:16-17 and the response of God to the fall (Gen 3:9ff.). The philosophical accounts focus more on self-discovery, but are unable to speak of a remedy from the sinful condition, in contrast to the Genesis account (Gen 3:15). All these things show that a departure from close attention to the biblical record cannot benefit the clear theocentric and thus also christocentric focus for ethics.

3.2.4. Conclusion

Ramsey calls the Bible the traditional source of ethics in the Hebrew-Christian tradition. Scripture is brought to bear on ethics in the form of a single unifying principle with which to meet the issues of Christian practice. The similarities in situations call for principles of action. This principle is what early on Ramsey called the *agape* principle, which is christocentrically grounded. The totality of the Bible helps him get the full significance of Christ in view. In fact, though Christ is of utmost significance for ethics, Ramsey frames the biblical principle always in terms of "divine righteousness" or "love." A "principle" is an idea which can be prioritized, put in dialectical relationship to another idea, and be appropriated in practice. As Ramsey "distills" the principle of "love" from the Scriptures, he finds it in an antithetical relationship to natural and human codifications.

Ramsey's discussion assumes some of the results of historical criticism of the Bible and its rationalistic heritage, such as the supposed presence of myth in Scripture. This gives occasion to philosophical elaboration on various biblical themes. With the help of existentialism and idealism, Ramsey sees sin both as responsibility and socially constructed. As Ramsey sees the need to complement the existentialist understanding of sin as responsibility with the idealist view of the social context of sin, so Ramsey also strengthens the relationship between love and the biblical concept of covenant. This covenant is social in nature and love is its content.[65] In fact, on the last pages of *Basic Christian Ethics* the term "covenant" has almost replaced the term "love": "Christian love may also be reduced to a simple corollary of the idea of covenant."[66] By covenant Ramsey means the relationship with God, or philosophically speaking, the form to which the laws were the content. As

[65] Ramsey, *Basic Christian Ethics*, 367-379.

[66] Ramsey, *Basic Christian Ethics*, 388.

pointed out above, Ramsey hesitates to speak positively about laws. He does turn to the idea of covenant, which he sees a step removed from laws. It articulates a relationship, for peculiar to this covenant was the dynamic that God was transcendent over it. The sum of the covenant stipulations is again the notion of righteousness, or its equivalent "obedient love," the principle with which Ramsey began.

One can notice that again Ramsey is somewhat ambivalent about the relationship of love to the (social) reality of ethics. He adopts an idealist understanding of the root of sin to highlight the nature of love being social in nature and connecting with various social policies. Yet, Ramsey emphasizes that love remains free from and independent of these. One could ask whether such love has not become ethereal and unable to interact or affect reality. The reader will detect the same struggle on the part of Ramsey in his discussion of deeds and rules in ethics, to which this chapter now turns.

3.3. The *Agape*-Principle in the Theory of Christian Ethics

3.3.1. The *Agape* Principle in Ethics

It has been seen how in Ramsey's Christian ethics the concept of Christian love figures as "the groundfloor" of Christian morality as it lies in Jesus Christ.[67] According to Ramsey, the basic principle of New Testament ethics is *agape*-love. All other principles, such as the worth of the individual or the common good, or the quest for values, though all important, are secondary and derivative. The determinative element in the Christian ethic is *agape*-love. It determines Christian thought and action. It is the crux of the Christian ethic. It is a unique ethical category. Instead of being defined in other terms, *agape*-love defines and limits all other terms. It is not like Plato's love, a form of desire springing from want. Rather it is a form of giving, springing from abundance. The double love-command is the persistent point of orientation.[68]

The discussion above has also traced the sense of the term principle as Ramsey used it in Scriptural interpretation. At that time, the point was made that what distinguishes the term "principle" from "theme" is that "principle" has the potential of applicability. Since Ramsey's concern is ethics and the practice of ethics, it is obvious that that area of practice is the area in which the potential of applicability becomes significant. As Ramsey's discussion moves on the more theoretical plane, however, the term "principle" acquires some new dynamics and manifests certain tensions inherent in such a method. Near the end of the previous section, it was noted that Ramsey feels the tension of the application of a transcendent and potentially ethereal principle to the mundaneity of practice.

[67] Ramsey, *Basic Christian Ethics*, 115.
[68] Ramsey, *Basic Christian Ethics*, 44.

The issue is that of application or appropriation. This issue on a theoretical level will now be the focus of the discussion.

Ramsey, who interprets Christian ethics primarily in deontological terms, defines *agape* in terms of a moral principle. *Agape* defines what is "'right,' or obligatory."[69] Christian love is "obedient love."[70] This is "the positive religio-ethical category in Christian ethics."[71] Also in the areas of medical and sexual ethics Ramsey seeks to apply his deontological claims based on this *agape*-love.

Ramsey distinguishes between "principles" and "rules" in moral reasoning. He defines "principles" as "*directions* of action"[72] and "rules" as "particular *directives* of an action, prescribing or proscribing a *definite* action."[73] Principles are more general, rules more action-specific. Ramsey considers both "principles" and "rules" necessary for providing direction and guidance to the moral agent in moving from the ultimate norm of obedient love to concrete decisions. His own model of the various stages in moral reasoning moves from this "ultimate norm (*agape*, utility, self-realization, etc.)" to "general principles," from "general principles" to "*defined*-action principles, or *generic* terms of approval and *generic* offense-terms"; from there to "*definite*-action rules, or moral-*species*-terms; then to the *subsumption* of cases."[74]

Ramsey regards *agape*-love essentially as a directional principle or norm of conduct, which points the moral agent toward the neighbor. It is "a relation by which one man exists for another." It is always a "present decision" rather than a "habit" of moral behavior. Such obedient love "is not a virtue, it has virtues."[75] It is a directional response of the whole self toward the neighbor--a response which includes such qualities as those attributed to it by Paul in 1 Corinthians 13.[76]

According to Ramsey, in Christian ethics, this notion of *agape* must be continually nourished by liturgy and the entire biblical narrative; otherwise it loses its meaning and collapses into a pale philosophical concept.[77] Particularly the Eastern Orthodox tradition brings out this relation of liturgy and morality. It is the liturgy that contains, subsumes and conveys "theology and ethics (almost

---

69 Ramsey, *Basic Christian Ethics*, 115. Cf. Ramsey, *Deeds and Rules in Christian Ethics* (Edinburgh/London: Oliver and Boyd, 1965), 108.

70 Ramsey, *Basic Christian Ethics*, xi, 388. Although Ramsey is strongly opposed to any teleology, it is not so that consequences are unimportant to him in so far as the moral quality of decisions is concerned. Consequences are a necessary object of inquiry in Christian ethics for the sake of the neighbor (Ramsey, *Basic Christian Ethics*, 116).

71 Ramsey, *Basic Christian Ethics*, 295.

72 Ramsey, "The Case of the Curious Exception," in *Norm and Context in Christian Ethics*, eds. Gene H. Outka and Paul Ramsey (New York: Charles Scribner's Sons, 1968), 73.

73 Ramsey, *Basic Christian Ethics*, 74.

74 Ramsey, *Basic Christian Ethics*, 75.

75 Ramsey, *Basic Christian Ethics*, 219.

76 Ramsey, *Basic Christian Ethics*, 217f.

77 Ramsey, "Liturgy and Ethics," 139-171.

in their entirety)."[78] The Eastern "liturgy for the sacrament of Christian marriage ... sets the wedding within the context of the movement of human generations depicted by realistic Biblical narrative,"[79] referring to "Abraham and Sarah, Isaac and Rebecca, Joseph and Asenath, Moses and Sepphora, Joachim and Anna, Zacharias and Elizabeth.[80] Within the liturgical context, moral habits are created, sustained, and reinforced. Liturgy acts as an agent in bringing what is a principle into the life of persons and a community. It aids the incarnation of that which is general through personhood into the area of practice.

3.3.2. In-Principled Love

It is remarkable that in a later publication Ramsey appears to move away from his earlier position set forth in *Basic Christian Ethics* and to move to a more normative ethic, in which he insists that 'love 'be inprincipled.'" [81] He argues that the "Christian life may ... take two forms: it may be productive of *acts only* or of *rules also*."[82] His reason for moving to this new position is his increasing awareness that many of his fellow representatives of contemporary

[78] Ramsey, "Liturgy and Ethics," 154.

[79] Ramsey, "Liturgy and Ethics," 157.

[80] Ramsey, "Liturgy and Ethics," 158.

[81] When in the 1960's "'situation ethics' threatened to overwhelm the capacity of theological ethics to give reasons for judgments apart from a vacuous appeal to love," Ramsey "responded with vigorous polemic" (Verhey, "Paul Ramsey (1913-1988)," 2). In 1965 Ramsey published a paper entitled *Deeds and Rules in Christian Ethics*, (*Scottish Journal of Theology Occasional Papers*, No 11. Edinburgh and London: Oliver and Boyd). It 1967 it was reprinted, and that same year Charles Scribner's Sons also published it as a book. This book actually is made up of an assortment of loosely related and overlapping essays. The final essay is a reprint of a satirical (and heavy-handed) "Letter to John of Patmos from a Proponent of 'the New Morality.'" It is "an imaginative representation of some of those circumstances and compulsions that have today invaded the mind of the church. Perhaps this chapter also has the virtue of treating the 'new morality' with the humor it, as a theory of ethics, so richly deserves," Ramsey, *Deeds and Rules in Christian Ethics*, 10.

[82] Ramsey, *Deeds and Rules in Christian Ethics*, 3. Edward LeRoy Long, Jr., commenting on Ramsey's *Deeds and Rules in Christian Ethics*, over against his *Basic Christian Ethics*, alerted to this new position of Ramsey. In "his *Basic Christian Ethics* code morality is criticized" whereas from then on he became "increasingly articulate about the importance of a more normative ethic--an ethic that finds guidance in agape beyond either the concept of duty in deontology or the pursuit of ideal goals in teleology" (*A Survey of Recent Christian Ethics*, 24-25, although in *Basic Christian Ethics* Ramsey had already indicated that Christian ethics is a deontological ethics, 115, and "neighbor love is ... obligatory," 116). "Ramsey's treatment indicates that he is moving from the deliberative stance to a more prescriptive one in order to underscore the role of the normative in Christian decision-making. Not that Ramsey excludes concern for circumstances--only the contention that circumstances by themselves provide the conditions for determining what love requires," *A Survey of Recent Christian Ethics*, 26.

Protestantism are moving more and more to relativism, and he is concerned to avoid this.[83] Christian ethics must be spared from subjectivism.[84]

Thus he takes the situationists[85] to task in his *Deeds and Rules in Christian Ethics*,[86] by pointing out that as much as they talk of freedom, the neighbor, and love-in-act-only, none of them can avoid, to one degree or another, generalizing from what love requires in a given situation to what it requires, as a rule, for similar situations.[87] In this publication Ramsey turns in particular to William K. Frankena[88] and John Rawls.[89] Their discussions have

[83] James M. Gustafson, in a footnote, comments: "A response to Christian relativism motivates much of Paul Ramsey's work," *Ethics from a Theocentric Perspective* I, 2.

[84] Verhey, Allen, "Paul Ramsey (1913-1988)," 2. In 1976 Ramsey wrote that he in 1967 "showed that agapism is productive of moral principles, covenants, and rules of practice; and that agapism need not exclude moral laws that are to be held exceptionless," Ramsey, "Some Rejoinders," in *The Journal of Religious Ethics* Vol. 4, Fall 1976, 191. According to him, "in and from love there are, or there may be, unbreakable rules, and the question to be relentlessly pressed is what these rules are," which are not to be found apart from love, Ramsey, *Deeds and Rules in Christian Ethics*, (1967), 35.

[85] John A. T. Robinson (*Honest to God*, London: S.C.M. Press, 1963) [Chapter III]; Paul Lehmann (*Ethics in a Christian Context*. New York and Evanston, Harper and Row Publishers, 1963) [Chapter IV]; and Joseph Fletcher, who professes a middle way between legalism and antinomianism (*Situation Ethics*, 1966) [Chapter VII].

[86] He devotes the most attention to Fletcher's situation ethics and attempts to totally demolish it. In a lengthy footnote, Ramsey observed that Fletcher committed "the 'naturalistic fallacy'" of having "derived the relativity of morals" (as contrasted with the pluralism of ethical behavior) "from anthropological and psychological evidence!", Ramsey, *Deeds and Rules*, 157.

[87] Ramsey, *Deeds and Rules*, 4-5. It is remarkable that Ramsey did not examine in this book his own position in *Basic Christian Ethics* as candidly and painstakingly for this deception as he did the writings of the three authors mentioned above. All he did was "freely concede" in his final footnote that in *Basic Christian Ethics* "*agape* ... was so analysed as to leave standing the assumption that this could itself come to full and faithful expression in acts only, and never in rules also," Ramsey, *Deeds and Rules*, 109-110.

[88] William K. Frankena, *Ethics* (Englewood Cliffs, NJ: Prentice-Hall, 1963); William K. Frankena, "Love and Principle in Christian Ethics," in *Faith and Philosophy*, ed. Alvin Plantinga (Grand Rapids: Eerdmans, 1964), 203-225.

[89] John Rawls, "Two Concepts of General Rules," in *Philosophical Review* 64 (1955), 2-32 (which he developed in detail into *A Theory of Justice* [Cambridge: Harvard University Press, 1971]). In April, 1965, Ramsey gave "the Presidential Address at the Annual Meeting of the American Theological Society," entitled, "Two Concepts of General Rules in Christian Ethics," in *Ethics* 76:3 (April 1966), 192-207. In it he dealt with Rawls's article "'Two Concepts of Rules.'" The importance and impact of John Rawls' article and book is pointed out in 5 articles on it in *Ethics* 85 (1974-1975): 1-74, by Stanley Bates of Middlebury College, "The Motivation to be Just" (1-17); Joe H. Hicks of Harvard Law School, "Philosophers' Contracts and the Law" (18-37); Andreas Eshete of Brown University, "Contractarianism and the Scope of Justice" (38-49); David L. Norton of University of Delaware, "Rawls's Theory of Justice: A 'Perfectionist' Rejoinder" (50-57); and by Oliver A. Johnson of University of California, Riverside, "The Kantian Interpretation" (58-66). Stanley Bates starts out by saying: "No other work of recent analytical philosophical history has had the immediate and widespread impact of John Rawls's *A Theory of Justice*, not only among philosophers and members of other academic disciplines, but also among a general public ... [in which he returns] to the great 'classical

helped him to see through various issues more clearly and direct him to clarify and correct his earlier position.

Thus he relies on the heuristic value of the rule-exception relations provided by Rawls, who distinguishes between a "summary rule" which is logically derivative from the acts that are independently justified by one's normative principle, and a "rule of practice," which is itself justified by one's principle, the acts being justified because they fall under the rule. In accordance with it, Ramsey insists that there are some unexceptionable moral rules on both the social level and the personal level. He proposes that an apparent "exception" to a general moral principle may be explicated as an actual application or fulfillment of the authentic meaning of that principle in a new form. This is apparently the case with regard to social practice-oriented rules but also with regard to some person-centered rules which are expressive of the demands of some covenant faithfulness to our neighbors. He accepts Rawls's suggestion that in some instances an ostensible "exception" to an established rule can be accepted if it really constitutes its own rule because it is a repeatable situation with right-making characteristics. Thus Ramsey provides justifications of ostensible expressions on the levels of both principles and rules.

From Frankena, Ramsey has learned that this distinction might also be applied to Christian love, if such love is indeed a third principle besides the principles of duty and utility that traditionally divide the moral philosophers. Frankena further suggests four possible positions for a Christian ethics that takes love as its only norm:

1) act-agapism (situation ethics--no rules at all; love decides what to do directly for every situation);
2) summary rule-agapism (a "modified" situation ethics--rules enter in, but only as summaries of acts that have been directly decided in accord with love; they serve only as guide-lines which in some situations may have to be ignored);
3) pure rule-agapism (rules indicate what love requires as a practice, and this precludes any consideration of what love might require in a particular situation); and
4) some combination of these three.

Ramsey favors the fourth position, for it seems "most in accord with the freedom of *agape* both to act through the firmest principles and to act if need be without them."[90] On the one hand, he does not have to abandon his original act-agapism entirely; on the other hand, he can move beyond it to a rule ethic--at

tradition..'" (1-2). Ramsey in "the Presidential Address" remarked that although Rawls' article "has become something of a classic in its own time," nevertheless "it has had almost no impact on Christian ethics, although its ... quite general ... allegations and demonstrations ... apply to the methods of Christian ethics as well as to any other," Ramsey, "Two Concepts of General Rules in Christian Ethics," 192.

[90] Ramsey, *Deeds and Rules in Christian Ethics*, 96. Cf. Ramsey, *Deeds and Rules in Christian Ethics*, 109.

least one of summary rules. For if a thoroughgoing act-agapism is inconsistent with a rule ethic of any kind, a "modified" version of it is not; indeed, summary rule-agapism is built upon act-agapism and can revert to it at any time.

But how can a summary rule-agapism be combined with a pure rule ethic? This question gives Ramsey some trouble, even to the point that he refuses to accept pure rule-agapism for what it is. He persists in this refusal even after admitting in his "Introduction" that his presentation was partially mistaken.[91] What he cannot accept is that, as Frankena formulated the view, "we may and sometimes must obey a rule in a particular situation even though the action it calls for is seen not to be what love itself would directly require." The whole point of a pure rule ethic is, however, that the principle (love) is to be related "directly" not to the act, but to the rule; the act in turn, then, is justified directly from the rule, in spite of the fact that when it is justified this way, it can on occasion be a different act than what love would directly require. In other words, love is precluded from thus directly requiring a certain act when it indirectly requires a different act because that act falls under the rule justified by love.

So on the one hand, Ramsey resists a pure rule ethic. On the other hand, he wants a pure rule ethic somewhere, for when he discusses Rawls' "rules of practice," he accepts them with their full force: "*Agape* justifies no exception within a practice."[92] Indeed, he regards Rawls' "rules of practice" as an important step "beyond" the pure rule ethic of Frankena; but that is only because he does not accept the latter for what it is.

That raises the question: How did such a discrepancy arise, especially since Frankena himself refers to Rawls' discussion as analogous to his own? Why does Ramsey even devote a separate chapter to Rawls when Frankena's analysis presupposes and incorporates that of Rawls? Apparently it has to do with the explicitly social-political context in which Rawls developed his concept.[93]

Thus Ramsey wants more than summary rules; and yet, when social ethics is not explicitly in view, he wants something less than a pure rule ethic. This is what leads him into what seems to be an effort to mark out a third concept of rules halfway between. This one he refers to as a concept of "general rules or principles or virtues or styles of life that embody love."[94]

The question may well be raised: does Ramsey by way of this multiplication of terms not confuse the rather precise and exclusive distinction between summary rules and pure ones? Is this effort also not strange, in view of an important suggestion Ramsey himself made, but failed to follow through?

---

[91] Ramsey, *Deeds and Rules in Christian Ethics*, 110-113.

[92] Ramsey, *Deeds and Rules in Christian Ethics*, 137.

[93] What Ramsey fails to note is that the difference between personal and social ethics does not in itself affect the difference between summary rule and pure rule ethics as logical types indicating two ways in which a normative principle can be related to rules.

[94] Ramsey, *Deeds and Rules in Christian Ethics*, 112, 129.

The suggestion he made was in connection with the central idea of combining the three views mentioned above:

> This final type of pure agapism arises from the fact that act-agapism may be believed to apply in certain kinds of particular cases or situations while rule-agapism applies to other kinds of situations or moral problems .... Summary rule-agapism may be believed to be the correct interpretation of certain principles of conduct, while pure rule-agapism is required for an adequate understanding of certain other principles.[95]

But if each type of rule is relevant to different types of situations or areas of life, is there then any need to "join the issue" between them, as Ramsey seeks to do? Is it then not sufficient to lay out with some care and detail just how and where love can enter into the formulation of each of the two kinds of rules? This Ramsey does not do, at least not to any significant extent.[96] He only goes as far as to say: "Someone *might* say ... that act-agapism, or its modification as summary rule-agapism, governs private morality, while pure rule-agapism to a very great extent governs public morality or social ethics."[97]

It is to be remembered that Ramsey was concerned with Christian ethics, not with natural law ethics. Furthermore, it is to be noticed that Ramsey's conception of "rule" is much more flexible than the ethical-theological conception of principle or precept. What can "the rule of love" be? Ramsey indicated that Christian love is lived and fulfilled in the Christian community. If the community is authentically Christian, certain principles or "rules" will emerge. The individual person does not solve his problems alone; the community will have given some expression of its moral belief and practice, and this is part of one's guidance. The word "part" is used, because situations arise in which the community does not offer a preformed decision. The point is that love is not merely what the individual person thinks it is, but what the Christian community thinks it is. But what if the community is not authentically or totally Christian? How does the Christian learn, for instance, that abortion cannot be a function of Christian love when his community fails to tell him? Ramsey did not answer this question in this book.

In "The Case of the Curious Exception," Ramsey, in opposition to many moral philosophers and theologians, argues that some moral rules should be held

---

[95] Ramsey, *Deeds and Rules in Christian Ethics*, 107. Here "pure agapism" indicates the position that *agape* is the only normative moral principle, and is not to be confused with pure *rule*-agapism, which indicates a position on how *love* can be related to rules.

[96] It would have been helpful, if he had spelled out the implications of this new stance for his earlier discussion in *Basic Christian Ethics*, where he vigorously opposed some other way of making important distinctions between kinds of laws.

[97] Ramsey, *Deeds and Rules in Christian Ethics*, 107.

to be significantly exceptionless.[98] This essay is an exercise in fundamental reasoning on the apparently technical issue of whether every conceivable rule must be assumed to have some conceivable "exception." But what is a "rule," and what is an "exception"?

Ramsey tirelessly works through the possibilities, the examples, the counter-examples. One case he refers to is the one in which "an inmate of a concentration camp ... [is] commanded by a sadistic camp guard to rape a woman inmate, under the threat that unless ... [he does] so he will kill her" (not him!). Would not this be a case of "justifiable" rape?[99]

In his response, Ramsey quotes J. G. Milhaven, S.J.: "'Even when extreme exceptions are conceivable, no sane man decides his actions ... on the basis of the remotely possible exception.'"[100] In support of his argument Ramsey mentions these three distinctively Christian considerations:

1) the Christian conviction that "there is another law in our members, and we can anticipate the consequences of this." This "is part of Christian theological normative metaethics," to point up "the fidelities to be done" and "to exhibit the fact that faithlessness in ourselves needs governing by ordinances ever to ensure that we keep covenant."[101]
2) "Christian normative ethics," flowing from God establishing "[h]is covenant with us and all mankind," in which "we are mainly concerned about the requirements of loyalty to covenants among men, about the meaning of God's ordinances and mandates, about the estates and moral relations among men" which "follow from His governing and righteous will," and "about steadfastness and faithfulness." From out of this concern "we can and may and must be enormously disinterested in any exception ...";[102]
3) "Christian hopes,"[103] that is, Ramsey defended exceptionless moral rules on the basis of the "conviction" that "the *ultimate* consequences cannot be such as to tender his (the Christian's) performance of fidelity obligations *wrong*."[104]

Ramsey's conclusion is that "it cannot be shown that Christians should never say Never."[105] Formally, this statement is a denial of Fletcher's pivotal assumption. If it cannot be shown that Christians should never say Never, then it

---

98 In *Norm and Context in Christian Ethics* (1968), 67-135. The background to Ramsey's essay was the question: If moral principles are absolute, how can there be any justifiable exceptions?

99 Ramsey, "The Case of the Curious Exception," in *Norm and Context in Christian Ethics* (1968), 127-128.

100 Ramsey, "The Case of the Curious Exception," 128.

101 Ramsey, "The Case of the Curious Exception," 118.

102 Ramsey, "The Case of the Curious Exception," 125.

103 Donald Evans, *Faith, Authenticity, and Morality* (Toronto: University of Toronto Press, 1980), 191.

104 Ramsey, "The Case of the Curious Exception," 133.

105 Ramsey, "The Case of the Curious Exception," 134.

is possible that in respect to some definite action, in some conceivable circumstances, they should say Never.

The same struggle of Ramsey noted above is evident also here. The tension between "summary rule-agapism" and "pure rule-agapism" is related to Ramsey's difficulty to leave love with a situational application or contain it in rules. This remains a problem for Ramsey. How does the principle of love relate to the reality of practice? Ramsey's use of natural law is part of this problem.

3.3.3. The Place of Natural Law

In the discussion above, attention was given to the principle of creation. Ramsey allowed creation to be a principle for Christian ethics, but only derivative from its main principle, namely Christian love.[106] It was indicated that, like Barth, Ramsey sees creation as "the external basis of the covenant, and the covenant is the internal basis of creation."[107]

To illustrate the relationship between love and natural law Ramsey also uses the typology of Egypt and Exodus. Using Eric Voegelin's book *Israel and Revelation* Ramsey establishes Egypt as the type of society governed by cosmological forms, i.e. natural law.[108] God's deliverance of Israel from Egypt in the Exodus was simultaneously a deliverance from the cosmological principle to the immediate intervention of God. This righteousness of God is redemptive instead of restrictive as Aristotelian justice is. This type of bondage to cosmological civilization recurs throughout Scripture in different forms, such as Baal worship where divine immanence is produced through fertility rites. The Exodus experience had set the people in covenant with the transcendent God, who delivered and gave a redemptive ethic.[109]

Over time Ramsey developed in his thinking on the place of natural law. This development was not as much a change in position as a refinement of position. Yet, this development in thinking on the place of natural law also suggests that Ramsey struggled with the applicability of principles in ethical practice. This became particularly evident when Ramsey began to immerse himself into particular ethical problems, especially that of the just war versus pacifism. It appears that when Ramsey approached the issues and problems of ethics, he found himself searching for means to bring the *agape* principle to the

---

[106] Ramsey, *Basic Christian Ethics*, 259.

[107] Ramsey, *Basic Christian Ethics*, 244. Cf. Karl Barth, *Church Dogmatics* III, 1(trans.A. T. MacKay *et al.*; eds. G. W. Bromiley and T. F. Torrance; Edinburgh: T. & T. Clark, 1961), sec. 41, 2, 3.

[108] *Israel and Revelation* is the first volume in Eric Voegelin's five volume work, entitled *Order and History* (Baton Rouge: Louisiana State University Press, 1956-1987). Voegelin's most well-known work has been in the area of the philosophy of politics and history. His theology has recently been examined by Michael P. Morissey, *Consciousness and Transcendence: The Theology of Eric Voegelin* (Notre Dame: University of Notre Dame Press, 1994).

[109] Ramsey, *Basic Christian Ethics*, 233-236.

level of practice. In his *War and the Christian Conscience* (1961), Ramsey suggests that the problem with Protestant ethics is that it has exchanged natural law for "contextualism."[110] In opposition to an ethics oriented to the situation, Ramsey reaches to the tradition of natural law for some compensatory guidance.

What does natural law have to offer for an ethics guided by the principle of Christian love? In his *Nine Modern Moralists* (1962) Ramsey labels his position that of "Christ transforming natural law."[111] The parallels with the position of H. Richard Niebuhr, often conveyed in the phrase "Christ transforming culture," should not be overlooked at this point.[112] With Niebuhr Ramsey shares a sympathetic view of the societal structures in place, or at least a non-oppositional view. As far as natural law is concerned Ramsey allows such a thing as "prudence which lives within reason and finds the fit embodiment for a man's sense of justice or injustice."[113]

The natural order is not the object of a Christian's unqualified allegiance. In the life of the Christian this natural prudence unites with the justice characteristic of love. *Agape* functions to transform natural law. Ramsey also uses the terminology of "infusion" of justice into natural law.[114]

The matter of "transformation" or "infusion" requires further definition. Ramsey recognizes the danger of a simple "synthesis" of church and culture. One form of this synthesis is the situation in which Christianity simply provides the motivation for action which is formulated on other than Christian ground. Against this Ramsey notes that *agape* is not only an inspiration but a "norm." Ramsey adds that this "norm" does not come in propositional form, but rather in the form of "a life and a relationship."[115] Another form of synthesis which Ramsey's "transformation" seeks to avoid is the merging of Christian message and culture to create an increasingly better world. Christianity is itself not a political structure and should not be collapsed with the state. *Agape* as an independent norm needs to transform the societal structures.

This does not yet answer the question as to the precise interaction of Christ and natural law. Ramsey himself writes: "The chief problem for Christian social ethics is how we are to understand the relation between the law of nature and the righteousness of the covenant."[116] As Long points out, this question is similar to Troeltsch's problem of how to relate the religious Jesus and a social

---

110 Ramsey, *War and the Christian Conscience: How Shall Modern War be Conducted Justly?* (Durham, N.C.: Duke University Press. Published for the Lilly Endowment Research Program in Christianity and Politics, 1961), 3.

111 Ramsey, *Nine Modern Moralists* (Englewood Cliffs, N.J.: Prentice-Hall, 1962), 4-5.

112 For a helpful comparison of the transformist position of H. Richard Niebuhr and that of Ramsey, see D. Stephen Long, *Tragedy, Tradition, Transformism: The Ethics of Paul Ramsey* (Boulder: Westview Press, 1993), esp. 77-94.

113 Ramsey, *Nine Modern Moralists*, 4-5.

114 Ramsey, *War and the Christian Conscience*, xxi.

115 Quoted in Long, *Tragedy, Tradition, Transformism*, 78.

116 Ramsey, *Nine Modern Moralists*, 181.

ethic.[117] With the help of the natural law theorist Jacques Maritain, Ramsey moves away from knowledge of natural law as a reflection on human nature in the abstract. Instead, natural law is ontologically intrinsic to every human being and epistemologically recognized in the actions of persons.[118] Ramsey therefore chooses to find his point of departure in epistemology rather than ontology. From actions one can induce inclinations and thus over time a tradition constructs itself which operates as a "pedagogue."[119]

In terms of the tension described above between principles and practice, Ramsey has found a solution in his use of natural law. For his emphasis on the inherence of natural law in persons and knowledge of natural law from actions of persons has caused him to focus on the practice and tradition of natural law. In order to get a better handle on this method, an analysis of the practice of ethical discourse, such as on the issue of the just war, is necessary.

One will recognize Ramsey's efforts to mediate between the principle or groundfloor of love and the practice of reality. It seems incongruent that Ramsey would gravitate towards natural law, but ignore and even reject all other codifications of the law, including the decalogue. He seems to see these codifications as returning people to the bondage of Egypt. He finds these codifications in Orthodox Judaism, fundamentalistic Protestantism, and absolutist Catholicism. While Ramsey rejects these codifications, one can perceive him searching for something to give form to the principle of love. When he does enlist natural law into his project, he is careful to emphasize the independence and dominance of love over any specifics. *Agape* remains for Ramsey the ground-floor of ethics. The ground for ethics is established in Christology and covenant.

3.3.4. Principled Interpretation as Idealistic Interpretation

The question deserves to be asked whether there is any idealistic import in Ramsey's use of the term "principle." Because the term is rather commonplace in contemporary Christian thought, the question might appear somewhat pedantic. If, however, there is evidence for adherence to idealism at the stage of Ramsey's dissertation and some sustained recognition of its contribution throughout his career, then the question will appear more legitimate.[120] If in idealism, reality and also ethics are fundamentally rooted in idea, in the mind, then this ethics must be articulated as an idea. The terms idea and principle are indeed interchangeable in Ramsey. Moreover, Ramsey frequently employs the term "duty" or "obligation" in relationship to his *agape* principle.[121] Ramsey is

[117] Long, *Tragedy, Tradition, Transformism*, 91-92.
[118] Ramsey, *Nine Modern Moralists*, 220.
[119] Ramsey, *Nine Modern Moralists*, 195. Cf. Long, *Tragedy, Tradition, Transformism*, 93-95.
[120] D. Stephen Long has given the best account of Ramsey's relationship to idealism in his *Tragedy, Tradition, Transformism*, 5-37.
[121] Ramsey, *Basic Christian Ethics*, 1, *et passim*.

convinced with idealism that neighbor-love is fundamentally deontological and not teleological.[122] Also, Ramsey begins his *Basic Christian Ethics* by grounding action upon knowledge: "[T]he student of Christian ethics can only know *that he knows* what the simplest true Christian vigorously 'doing the truth' knows already."[123] The conviction that action is rooted in knowledge is also the cause for a *basic* Christian ethics, a treatment of the fundamental theory, which lies as a basis for action. Ramsey writes: "Before there can be a Christian social ethic, understanding of the fundamental moral perspective of the Christian must be deepened and clarified."[124] But more important than any of these points are Ramsey's observations concerning "primitive ideas." Ramsey draws an analogy with logic or mathematics, which "begin with certain 'primitive ideas' whose meaning is either quite arbitrarily devised or presumed to be known already."[125] These primitive ideas belong to a different category than those derived from them, for their meaning is not based on anything beyond themselves. Their signification can only be assumed, either innately or attributively. Instead, these fundamental notions give definition to other points. Something similar holds true for "love" as a primitive idea. 1 Corinthians 13 should never be taken as a conglomeration of statements concerning love. This passage defines the meaning of love by pointing to Jesus Christ. Jesus Christ as the nature of divine love is the fundamental idea, knowledge of whom can only be assumed, not deductively established. Ramsey suggests that one put aside all previous notions of love, and substitute a blank, or the variable "x," or the unfamiliar Greek *agape* in order to experience its fundamental quality.[126] There is clearly idealistic import in the notion of principle in Ramsey and it is not coincidental that he emphasizes the "*thought* of the New Testament."[127]

One of the consequences of the idealistic import in Ramsey's use of the term "principle" is its reductionistic element. That all might derive from it and it not be deduced from anything, one must *reduce* all ideas to the fundamental one, namely, God's righteousness and love, or differently stated, "the reign of this righteousness in the Kingdom of God." Ramsey states: "Never imagine that you have rightly grasped a biblical ethical idea until you have succeeded in reducing it to a simple corollary of one or the other of these notions, or of the idea of covenant between God and man from which they both stem."[128] The question must be asked, what this reduction entails. Ramsey had to make room for other principles, such as creation, image of God, etc. Though one must acknowledge that he ever attempted to gather them under the notion of love, this was not always as evident as it was strained. Furthermore, Ramsey continued to

---

[122] Ramsey, *Basic Christian Ethics*, 115-116.
[123] Ramsey, *Basic Christian Ethics*, xi.
[124] Ramsey, *Basic Christian Ethics*, xii.
[125] Ramsey, *Basic Christian Ethics*, xv.
[126] Ramsey, *Basic Christian Ethics*, xvi.
[127] Ramsey, *Basic Christian Ethics*, xvii.
[128] Ramsey, *Basic Christian Ethics*, 2.

struggle with the applicability of a reduced idealistic notion. The second part of this chapter has traced that struggle, but its origin is undoubtedly an effect of the prior reduction.

It must be clarified that Ramsey's is not a pure idealism. Prevalent throughout Ramsey's thought is the idea of transformation, or as Stephen Long has designated it, "the conversionist motif" or "transformism."[129] H. Richard Niebuhr's notion of "Christ transforming culture," well-known from his book *Christ and Culture*, was part of a method which Niebuhr widely employed in his university lectures and elsewhere in his work.[130] Ramsey, his student, inherited this aspect of his method, and the notion of "transformation" would often inform his own work. For example, Ramsey would later speak of "Christ transforming natural law."[131] This suggests that perhaps Ramsey's relationship to idealism is that of Christ transforming idealism. Indeed, by making the demonstration of divine love in Christ to be the "primitive idea" or chief principle, Ramsey prioritizes Christ over concepts otherwise proposed by idealists, such as loyalty, duty, or even love on a human level. Christian love or divine righteousness assumes the place of prominence from which all other ideas derive their definition. Christian love transforms idealism.

It must also be remembered, however, that the whole motif of "transformism" is indebted to an idealist framework. The notion of an idea independent of various mundane forms, but adaptable to a multiplicity of contexts, and able to convert and transfigure other norms and forms, suits an idealist view of reality. *Agape* is an idea "not of this world" in the sense that "it was never drawn from the customary morality of any people and can never be identified with the structures of any particular civilization." Because it stands isolated and unmatched at the top, it "constitutes a standing judgment upon all human conduct and upon every human culture." Unlike Judaism and other religions, Christianity is not "a 'religious civilization,' it is rather a criticism of any civilization, religious or otherwise, and of any customary code of conduct, on behalf of the welfare of the neighbor, which all civilizations and codes are absolutely bound to serve in obedient love."[132] Philosophical ethics might answer the question, *what* is the good?, but Christian ethics answers the question, *whose* good? Christian love is of a different level, is the answer to a different question and is able to thus transform all other answers to the question what the good is by moving the philosophical value more towards the

---

[129] Long, *Tragedy, Tradition, Transformism*, 18 *et passim*. Long writes that "[a]ll of his [Ramsey's] work was an extension of Niebuhr's 'Christ transforming culture'" (190).

[130] Cf. Ramsey's own discussion of this motif in H. Richard Niebuhr: "H. Richard Niebuhr: Christ Transforming Relativism," *Nine Modern Moralists* (Englewood Cliffs, N.J.: Prentice-Hall, 1962), 186-223.

[131] Ramsey, *Nine Modern Moralists*, 4-5.

[132] Ramsey, *Basic Christian Ethics*, 44.

neighbor.[133] Ramsey illustrates this point by a reference to the philosophical school of hedonism:

> Christianity makes no essential attempt to transform a person who believes there are other goods besides pleasure. Its concern is to turn a hedonist who thinks only of *his own* pleasure into one who gives pleasure (the greatest good he knows) to his neighbors. When a person becomes a Christian he may also cease to be a hedonist and adopt some other theory of value, but he does not thereby become a better Christian. In fact it works the other way round: out of greater responsiveness to the entire range of his neighbor's need he may for the first time become sensitive to certain higher human values to which formerly, even in his own case, selfishness blinded him.[134]

The idea of Christian love becomes the idea which infuses into all other notions their fundamental significance. Ramsey's transformist ethic is expressed within an idealistic view of reality.

Of what consequence is this principled interpretation of Scripture, informed as it is by categories from idealistic philosophy? One can make at least three observations, which are implicit in the use of the important word "reduction," a term which Ramsey himself uses.[135] First, when one reduces something, whether it be narrative, or a variety of stipulations, it is always at the expense of something. How does one determine hermeneutically, how this process of reduction proceeds? Ramsey's approach to Scripture tends to be eclectic. Ramsey has chosen to delineate along the lines of the concept of *agape* love at the expense of moral codes, whether biblical or natural. Though there is precedence for this within the ethical disciplines, there is likewise resistance against this hierarchy.

Second, the idealistic concentration on mind and thought, on ideas and concepts, again prevalent as it is, has consequences for actions. For one, the interface with the particulars of actions becomes a continual problem. Though two persons could agree that love is indeed the chief principle for moral action, they might lend different forms to this principle in the realm of concrete action. Furthermore, there is a serious ambiguity with regard to other sources of moral wisdom, including philosophical positions. Ramsey might maintain that philosophical systems do not address the matter of "whose good" and that they are equal in their openness to a Christian orientation, but is it true that there is no competition between various philosophies and Christianity, for instance a naturalistic ethic or materialistic ethic? For instance, does not Ramsey's choice for deontology over teleology suggest that he finds the one more aligned to Christian content than the other?

---

[133] Ramsey, *Basic Christian Ethics*, 114-115.
[134] Ramsey, *Basic Christian Ethics*, 112-113.
[135] Ramsey, *Basic Christian Ethics*, 2.

Third, the process of reduction is done by the human mind in conversation with sources from the Christian tradition, such as Augustine and Luther, but also philosophical sources of existentialism and idealism. Unlike Gustafson, Ramsey does not in his *Basic Christian Ethics* explicitly advocate that the Christian community go and engage in this process. In this book he is laying a basis for this process. He takes upon himself the formulation of this basis and the attention to matters of social policy. Yet, towards the end of his career, his focus turned more to the church and the community as moral agents.[136] He became explicit about turning over to the community and the church the baton which he had held with such devotion and rigor in his life. But inherent in his emphasis on the process of reduction is the prominence attributed to the action of the community. This warrants a closer look at the role of community in Ramsey.

3.3.5. The Function of the Community

A focus on community takes a different place in Ramsey than in Gustafson and Verhey. For Ramsey, the church arose in the context of the prophetic voice of the church in the world. In 1967 Ramsey wrote *Who Speaks for the Church?*, in which he took the World Council of Churches to task on making policy pronouncements such as advocating withdrawal from Vietnam.[137] His stance is that the church should not argue in such particularity, for policy making is beyond the competency and the vocation of the church. The positive task of the church in this regard is to encourage its theologians to search out the principles behind political action and point out some directions on that level.[138]

In the year that he died (1988), Ramsey returned to the subject in his book *Speak Up For Just War or Pacifism* in the final chapter, entitled, "Speaking on Particulars for the Church to the Church and World."[139] Here he is less polemical regarding the issue of addressing the world as church than in his earlier publication. He is searching for

> some workable, practical Protestant analogue ... to the claim in Roman Catholic social encyclicals that the church's divine mission and mandate are to teach the entire moral law: both divine guidance for the Christian life distinctive to the faith community and the moral and political wisdom for Christian living that is also accessible and may be shared by all other reasonable creatures.[140]

---

[136] Cf. his *Speak Up for Just War or Pacifism: A Critique of the United Bishop's Pastoral Letter "In Defense of Creation"* (University Park/London: Pennsylvania State University Press, 1988).

[137] Ramsey, *Who Speaks for the Church? A Critique of the 1966 Geneva Conference on Church and Society* (Nashville: Abingdon Press, 1967).

[138] Ramsey, *Who Speaks for the Church?*, 45.

[139] Ramsey, *Speak Up For Just War*, 125-148.

[140] Ramsey, *Speak Up For Just War*, 133.

The recommendation which he makes is that "'different and critical opinions' [be] fully presented and given to the church" and then for the church "to locate a few forks in the road, selectively singled out because of their cruciality beyond which Christians and non-Christians alike are on their own, so to speak, and must rely on engagement in public discussion."[141]

The church thus has a mission for the world, also in its ethical address. Yet the agency of the church does not seem to receive systematic analysis, only incidental attention prompted by ecclesiastical statements with which Ramsey disagrees. One could perhaps explain this minimal attention in a couple of ways. First of all, together with the philosophical school of idealism, Ramsey assigns chief importance to the idea of *agape* love, which was more than a method, as theocentrism is for Gustafson. It has content; it is content. As described above, the struggle one is left with is finding a way to bring idea and practice together in which the content of the idea is not lost as in situationism, and its freedom and power is not forfeited in pure rule agapism or natural law ethics. Secondly, Ramsey is rather vigilant against situationism, and an emphasis on the community could corroborate the view that for particular situations, the communities must discern particular courses of action.

Notwithstanding the insignificance actually assigned to the agency of the community, it seems legitimate to ask whether Ramsey's method does not require more prominence for the agency of the individual person and community. For in his method he assigns weight to the process of drafting the first principle as well as the application of those principles. This is not simply the process of an action which any moral theory must deal with, but the actual generation of an ethic. He does acknowledge its place in the writings on the public speech of the church, which indicates the logical place which this notion must take in his model and simply his general disregard for the issue in favor of a focus on the relationship between the ideas and rules themselves. Another place where he acknowledges its place is in an unpublished review of Hauerwas' book, *Community of Character*. Here he notes that for Hauerwas, Scripture is "community dependent," while the community is "narrative dependent." He does not find this a problem, but instead calls it a "fruitful circularity."[142] This is one of the few places where Ramsey acknowledges the interdependence of Scripture on the community. Yet, if it is correct that Ramsey's method demands more prominence for the community than he in practice allots to it, then the collective aspect of American ethics does play a role for Ramsey, though admittedly more so implicitly than explicitly.

More broadly than just the agential aspect of the community, Ramsey is quite insistent upon the social and collective character of Christian ethics. There is no ground to reproach Ramsey for an individualistic ethic. His concern to supplement the notion of covenant to the idea of love in order to highlight its collective aspect is indicative. His concern for a public policy and not merely

[141] Ramsey, *Speak Up For Just War*, 138-140.
[142] Quoted in Long, *Tragedy, Tradition, and Transformism*, 135.

issues of micro-ethical importance illustrates this same concern. One wonders to what extent, Ramsey's respect for the school of philosophical idealism contributed to this attention to the community. One only needs to remember his concern to supplement the individualistic orientation of existentialism with the more social and communal orientation of idealism on the matter of original sin. One can conclude, therefore, that the collective aspect of American Protestant ethics has a follower in Ramsey, albeit not very explicitly so in its agential form.

3.3.6. Conclusion

Ramsey aligns himself with the rational strand in the history of American ethics through idealistic philosophy. His dissertation, a treatment of idealist anthropology, and his study with H. Richard Niebuhr led him on this track. One can use the affix "rational" in three qualified and related ways. The first is "rational" in the sense of working on the plane of ideas. Ramsey's ethics has a rational character owing to his use of the category of principle, idealistically defined. *Agape* is thus a chiefly deontological notion which stands in the place of and functions as "loyalty" did for Josiah Royce. The use of "rational" here must be qualified by the radically Christian character which Ramsey gives to the notion of *agape*. The second way in which Ramsey's ethic can be termed rational concerns the method by which he arrives at the principle. Though Ramsey carefully employs Scripture and the theological tradition flowing from Scripture, he is forced to reduce. He does so, for example, by setting the moral codes of Scripture in opposition to love, opting for the latter over and at the expense of the former. Thus Ramsey's method is rational not in the sense of opting for reason over revelation, but rationally opting within revelation for one reality over another. This is an important qualification. The third way in which Ramsey's ethic can be termed rational concerns a fundamental openness to any philosophy (hedonism, etc.) when controlled by *agape* and the particular openness to idealist philosophy, as illustrated above in the matter of the original sin. This use of the term "rational" must also be qualified, for the impression that Ramsey is arbitrary in his adoption of other sources would be incorrect. *Agape* permits an openness to reason and philosophical insights, for it is of a different level and can act transformatively.

Through the motif of "transformism" and extensive appeal to notions from Scripture, Ramsey is able to give quite a Christian content to Christian ethics. Different from Gustafson, he does not begin with experience, but rather with the idea of Christian love as it is reduced and constructed from Scripture, theology, and tradition.

It might be asked, what relationship of Ramsey's struggle to render love "inprincipled" has to the matter of the function of Scripture. The ambiguity which Ramsey felt regarding the freedom and concreteness of *agape* has arisen as a direct result of his use of Scripture in his construction of the *agape* principle. Since Ramsey went to work by reduction to arrive at a principle, and in the process disparaged the moral codes as they appear and are implemented within Scripture, he is left to construct the applications and the method of application in order to safe-guard against the situationism, which his position opens itself to when it remains unchecked. It is interesting to note that throughout his works, he is left to struggle with the absence of what he initially believed to stand in opposition to the *agape* principle. In this light, the place he allots to natural ethics is remarkable.

This discussion on the theory of Christian ethics has focused on Ramsey's efforts to define "principle" in a fashion which would suit the methodological requirements of bringing a concept such as Christian *agape* love to bear upon the practice of Christian ethics. In terms of the philosophical discussion of Frankena and Rawls on the nature of principles and rules, Ramsey recognizes the tension between summary rule agapism and pure rule agapism as that between practice and principles and is unable to go beyond restating the importance of inprincipled love.

In his work on natural law, Ramsey achieves some progress, particularly by viewing natural law not deductively, but as something ontologically in a person and epistemologically recognized in action. The focus for Ramsey is then action and practice. Yet, also in these instances, Christian love stands in a category of its own with the burden of transforming natural law. Thus for Ramsey there is only a place for natural law within the pre-existing and dominant framework of covenant and love. Ramsey works this out in some of his practical writings, for instance, on just war or care for the dying.[143]

3.4. The *Agape* Principle in the Practice of Christian Ethics

Besides his theoretical and systematic discussions, Ramsey has provided commentary on a range of practical issues. This segment of the discussion is focused on Ramsey's use of Scripture in the practice of ethics. The following areas will function as test-cases for the arguments which Ramsey has developed theoretically. In light of the discussion on natural law above, it seems logical to begin with Ramsey's discussion of the principle of agapism in light of traditions of just war and pacifism.

---

143 Cf. Charles Curran, "Paul Ramsey and Traditional Roman Catholic Natural Law Theory," in *Love and Society: Essays in the Ethics of Paul Ramsey*, eds. James T. Johnson and David H. Smith (Missoula: Scholars Press, 1974), 54 [art. 47-65].

3.4.1. The Case of Just War

Ramsey's writing on the matter of "War" is well-known and considered as a major contribution on the part of Ramsey.[144] Already in his first major work on war, in 1961, Ramsey insists that the proper procedure is to make love "in-principled."[145] The procedure is to find those moral prescriptions that specify the proper inferences from the law of love for the general problem areas of war. These principles in turn function as rules for conduct.

He argues that love "has to do not only with the motive of our actions, but also with our understanding of the content of the divine command."[146] At one point he, without divorcing Christian love from the moral law, insists that there is a selection among scriptural laws.[147] Some scriptural laws are "confirmed more than others, and at the same time, the law of love adduces or

---

[144] James T. Johnson argues that Ramsey's "writings on this subject constitute one of the most important thematic and substantive contributions of his thought," "Just War in the Thought of Paul Ramsey." There are particularly three major publications by Ramsey on war. 1) In 1961 Ramsey published *War and the Christian Conscience*. According to James T. Johnson, this is "a work that stands as a benchmark in the contemporary recovery and redefinition of just war theory," "Just War in the Thought of Paul Ramsey," *The Journal of Religious Ethics* 19 (1991), 185. It must be pointed up that already in 1950, in *Basic Christian Ethics*, Ramsey wrote about the use of force on pp. 166-184. 2) In 1968 he published *The Just War* (Scribner, 1968, 554 pp.), later published as *The Just War, Force and Political Responsibility* (University Press of America, 1983). In this book Ramsey brings together published and unpublished essays which he has written since his *War and the Christian Conscience*, 1961. Ramsey not only provides fundamental and historical ethical and theological justification of Christian participation in the use of military force and the conditions and limits of what he prefers to call "justified" war, but also moves on to apply it to a broad spectrum of problems relating to the responsible use of politico-military power in a nuclear age, coinciding with the escalation of the Vietnam War in those years and to specific topics, such as the problem of intervention. He also presents just war in the context of a theory of statecraft. Since the earlier publication, of *War and the Christian Conscience* in 1961, Ramsey continues to extend his analysis of the morality of war into new areas to discover whether ancient tests of "just conduct" in war could illuminate new situations. In this book he gives us an opportunity to see where he deepened and sometimes corrected his angle of vision on the morality of war, of deterrence and of insurgency warfare, and on political ethics and statecraft. 3) In 1988 he published *Speak Up For Just War Or Pacifism, A Critique of the United Methodist Bishops' Pastoral Letter "In Defense of Creation"* with an "Epilogue, A Pacifist Response to the Bishops," by Stanley Hauerwas. Stanley Hauerwas and D. Stephen Long insist that this work will be remembered chiefly for "his application of the just war theory to Protestant social ethics," "Forword" in Paul Ramsey's *Basic Christian Ethics* (Reprint, 1993), xiv.

[145] "...Christian morality may be described as 'faith effective through in-principled love,'" Ramsey, *War and the Christian Conscience*, 14.

[146] Ramsey, "War and the New Morality," in *The Reformed Journal* 18:2 (February 1968), 25-28, in response to an article by Dewey J. Hoitenga ("War and the New Morality," in *The Reformed Journal* 18:2, February 1968, 10-15), who advocates a full-blown pacifism foreign to his own (Reformed) tradition.

[147] Ramsey, "War and the New Morality," 26.

produces insight into the moral law that is not explicitly contained in Scripture."[148]

The procedure at work in all Christian ethics is "to search out the meaning and the content" of the "moral law with which it [love] is indissolubly joined."[149] Already in his introduction to *War and the Christian Conscience* he points up this procedure. He states that in working out the just war theory, the church fathers did not "'fall' from the original purity of Christian ethics," but were seeking to find what "responsible love and service of one's neighbors" required "in the texture of the common life."[150] The "limits placed on the just conduct of war," and the permission given for Christians to work within such limits, bears significant traces of the fact that the norm of Christian love, and not natural justice only, is still the main source both of what the Christian could and should do and of what he could and should never do in military action.[151] Love is the source of principles.

According to him, Jesus taught, and the early Christians believed, that violence as between individuals was always wrong and that a personal enemy should not be resisted.[152] Where groups were involved, however, the situation was different. Jesus Himself strenuously, and possibly at times violently, resisted the scribes and Pharisees and would presumably have resisted the robbers who molested the traveler on the road to Jericho (Luke 10:25-37).[153] In *War and the Christian Conscience* he approvingly refers to Ambrose of Milan, Augustine's mentor, who argued that a Christian when he himself is attacked may not defend himself by force, "'lest in defending his life he should stain his love toward his neighbor.'" But when the Christian on a lonely road comes upon another traveler being attacked injustly by a robber, it is his duty to defend his neighbor, using force if necessary. According to Ambrose, "'He who does not keep harm off a friend, if he can, is as much in fault as he who causes it.'" However, according to Ambrose, since the robber is also a neighbor for whom Christ died, the Christian may use violence only up to and including what is necessary to drive off or subdue the robber.[154] In *The Just War*, with a reference to the narrative of the Good Samaritan, Ramsey argues that the implication of this narrative is that a police force should "patrol along the road to Jericho" and keep people from being robbed.[155]

---

148 Ramsey, "War and the New Morality," 26, 27.

149 Ramsey, "War and the New Morality," 26.

150 Ramsey, *War and the Christian Conscience*, xvii.

151 Ramsey, *War and the Christian Conscience*, xviii.

152 In *War and the Christian Conscience* Ramsey even goes as far as insisting that the early Christians "were universally pacifists," xv. James T. Johnson rightly [so I believe] argues that Ramsey is wrong in this, *The Quest for Peace* (Princeton: Princeton University Press, 1987), chapter 1. Cf. Johnson, James Turner. "Just War in the Thought of Paul Ramsey," 186.

153 Ramsey, *Basic Christian Ethics*, 169-170.

154 Ramsey, *War and the Christian Conscience*, 37.

155 Ramsey, *The Just War*, 500.

According to Ramsey, therefore, the primary question for Christians is not whether to participate in war but how to act out of love toward the neighbor. If our neighbors are attacked injustly, love for them on the one hand requires that we use violent force to defend them, on the other hand love sets limits on the target of that force and its intensity.

It is therefore in these "multilateral relations"--relations in which one neighbor harms another neighbor, and a Christian comes upon them--that *agape* gives reasons for a qualified preferentialism. We are to give preference to the claims of the innocent needy rather than the neighbor who is attacking him, even if we are required to use violence to protect and care for our innocent neighbor.[156]

So to Ramsey, "obedient love" is an absolute demand when a person deals with one other person; when relations are multilateral, however, love makes justifiable demands which would be prohibited in person-to-person relations. Thus, whereas resistance to a threat upon one's own life is not justified, a participation in war is, and *everything turns upon the distinction between unilateral and multilateral relations*. Renouncing therefore self-defense as in itself always a bad motive, according to Ramsey, Christians may for the sake of others press for their own rights and if need be fight or even accept the office of public executioner.[157]

In accordance with what was written above, namely that Ramsey is strongly opposed to any teleology, he emphatically distances himself from those "Protestants in the modern period," who "seek to justify the doing of evil that good may come of it." His "'just war' theory defines right-doing that good may come of it, not wrong doing warranted by consequences expected to follow."[158]

According to Ramsey, this just war teaching is based on the "acceptance of the divine ordinance of preservation so that men might have by God's mercy a secure dwelling place in a fallen, disordered in-between time. The just war theory defines right doing that good may come upon the basis of natural justice and the law of nature .... It does this also on grounds established by Christian charity."[159]

In response to the question as to how we are "to think Christianly about politics and about the political use of violence on war," Ramsey argues that a Christian always must have "two things in mind, one positive, the other negative." The one thing is that he "will think politically in the light of Christ,"

---

156 Ramsey, *The Just War*, 143.

157 Cf. Ramsey, *Basic Christian Ethics* 188-190. Ramsey's constructive approach with regard to the almost-lost concept of vocation is noteworthy. He attempts to explore Luther's meaning of the *vocatio*, and to rediscover the dynamic by which the Christian man may transcend the inner "natural man"--who would have him draw his defences and live "within the dugout of his own rights"--and come to bear his vocational obligations, constrained by the love of Christ, *Basic Christian Ethics*, 190.

158 Ramsey, "War and the New Morality" [Response to Dewey J. Hoitenga], 27, 28.

159 Ramsey, "War and the New Morality," 28.

the other thing that "he will think politically in the light of the revealing shadow thrown by Christ over this fallen human existence."[160] From this perspective on Christian ethics, Ramsey argues that *agape* and violence are not always mutually exclusive, or to put it differently, he argues that one and the same *agape* can justify both pacifism and the acceptance of violence as a last resort in protecting the neighbor in need. *Agape* can take either fork in the road.[161] In "multilateral relations," when one comes upon a neighbor harming another neighbor, one encounters a conflict of duties, violence can be an expression of *agape*.

Christians, particularly after Constantine, began to catch on to the positive and negative line that is there. They saw that serving "the real needs of all the men for whom Christ died" demanded not only that they would personally witness to them but also that they would be "involved in maintaining the organized social and political life in which all men live"[162] which was "threatened by violence, by aggression, or tyranny." They saw in "love for their neighbors ... the grounds for admitting the legitimacy of the use of military force."[163] Although "the light of Christ" has confronted humankind, nevertheless humankind lives inevitably in the "shadows" cast by that light.[164]

It is also important to Ramsey[165] to realize that humankind's existence is "fallen."[166] Human loves tend to be "fratricidal"[167] as much as they try to be "brotherly." The "fratricidal love and brotherly love based on love of God are always commingled in human history. There is no heart, no people, and no public policy so redeemed or so clearly contrary to nature as to be without both."[168] Consequently, there is a radical discontinuity between true *iustitia* and the makeup of human regimes. It is important to see that "the gospel does not promise that we shall, within historical time, find a way to undo the consequences of the Fall."[169] The new situational moralists' attempt "to 'perfect the linkage between moral obligation and human happiness on earth by deriving

---

160 Ramsey, *The Just War: Force and Political Responsibility* (New York: Charles Scribner's Sons, 1968), Chapter 22, 497.

161 Ramsey, *The Just War: Force and Political Responsibility*, 501.

162 Ramsey, *War and Conscience*, xvi-xvii.

163 Ramsey, *The Just War*, 144.

164 Ramsey, *The Just War*, 497-498, 529; Ramsey, *War and Conscience*, 31.

165 Ramsey considers Augustine's just war idea foundational for a Christian perspective on the just war theory. He regards "love-transformed justice" to be the essence of Augustine's just war idea. To Augustine the basis for the just war theory lay not in mere self-preservation and not in natural justice, but rather in a combination of Christian love and natural justice. Ramsey also considers Augustine's understanding of humankind's existence as fallen foundational, *War and Conscience* , xviii-xix, 10.

166 Ramsey makes use here of Augustine's doctrine of "the divided will," Ramsey, *The Just War*, 497, 529, 530.

167 Derived from the Latin *frater*, a brother, and *caedere*, to kill.

168 Ramsey, *War and Conscience*, 30-31.

169 Agreeing with Hoitenga, Ramsey, "War and the New Morality," 26.

the former from the latter' is forever obstructed by the Fall." However, does that now imply that the Christian should "withdraw from the disordered historical existence"? Rather he should "acknowledge that this side of the resurrection the Christian is also implicated in this same disordered historical political existence." The Christian, "insofar as he is not fully perfect, himself also need[s] all the uses of the law, the restraint of the sin that remaineth in him, and the use of force"[170] on the basis of accepting "the divine ordinance of preservation so that men might have by God's mercy a secure dwelling place in a fallen, disordered in-between-time."[171]

The just war theory therefore, according to Ramsey, does not rest upon the idea of natural law, but rather upon the possibility of "right conduct" in war. Human beings are able to discern the content of Christian love in action.[172] In this Ramsey leans on Augustine's primary emphasis on the *ius in bello*, the right conduct of war and his distinction between "killing the unjust aggressor and killing the innocent,"[173] whereby Christian love permits lethal force directed toward an "unjust aggressor" and prohibits the same force directed against an innocent bystander.[174] In case noncombatants are harmed as a secondary effect of an attack directed primarily at combatants, such harm is regrettable and tragic, but it is not in and of itself "immoral." This is the "rule of double effect."[175] In dealing with the question of just cause, Ramsey again follows Augustine who insists that war is justifiably undertaken as an act of Christian love on behalf of the innocent fellow human beings who are suffering unduly.[176]

In the area of just conduct of war Ramsey finds in the principle of noncombatant immunity a clear guideline to Christian action. The primary manifestation of Christian love in all political endeavor is right conduct in relation to our fellow human beings. In the preparing for war, as well as in the waging of war, those who operate within the Christian tradition are obliged to direct their attack only against "the force which should be resisted." Christian love never allows us "to kill another man's children directly as a means of weakening his murderous intent."[177] "It is never right to do wrong that good may come of it."[178]

---

170 Ramsey, "War and the New Morality," 26.

171 Ramsey, "War and the New Morality," 28.

172 Ramsey, *War and Conscience* 32-33. James T. Johnson writes that "two themes central to Ramsey's understanding of just war theory" have been: "the centrality of Christian love as the core reference point and a conversionist understanding of history and of politics as a foundation for debate within the secular policy community," "Just War in the Thought of Paul Ramsey," 186.

173 Ramsey, *War and Conscience*, 36.

174 Ramsey, *War and Conscience*, 45, 59, 32.

175 Ramsey, *War and Conscience*, 50-51, 64; Ramsey, *The Just War*, 158.

176 Ramsey, *Just War*, 143; Ramsey, *War and Conscience*, 9-10.

177 Ramsey, *War and Conscience*, 11; cf. Ramsey, *War and Conscience*, xx.

178 Ramsey, *Just War*, 250.

Much of what Ramsey writes on war was written during the period in which Americans were preoccupied with a specific conflict, namely the Vietnam war. According to Ramsey, the U.S. waged the war in Vietnam with great restraint for limited ends and within the bounds of the morality of warfare. This is how he argues his case: The U.S. government carried on a counter*insurgency* and not a counter*society* operation. Ramsey insists that that is the "purpose of combat," namely, "to stop or incapacitate a combatant from doing what he is doing"; it is "not the killing"; therefore its conduct of the war has been just. He acknowledges that if the conflict had escalated, more and more women could have been killed and maimed. But that result would have to be blamed on the enemy, who had chosen the type of warfare and made hostages of many civilians. The intention of the U.S. was simply to get at the insurgents. Thus Ramsey justified the bombing of the North, for the "purpose and shape of these actions" to raise "the cost of the infiltration by Hanoi--not stopping it, but raising the cost in men and material of continuing it." It was to "prosecute the war against the infiltration, against the combatancy, against the manner in which North Vietnam has organized and disposed its energies and forces in this war."[179]

One of Ramsey's basic refrains is that contemporary ethicists have been so concerned with abstract notions of justice that they fail to recognize that some sort of concrete order is a condition of justice. In response to the quasi-revolutionary theologians who address themselves to the "new man" suddenly "come of age," Ramsey insists that modern man has in fact regressed to the illusions of past political utopians. He calls for the demythologization of politics and a return to an essentially Augustinian perspective. We live in "two cities," and not in the one world of the "city of man under construction." This puts politics in its place, and frees men for clear-sighted participation in it. Absolutely related to the Absolute, we should be content to be relatively involved in the relative.[180]

On the one hand, Ramsey sees the primarily Roman Catholic "natural law theory of the state." Its post-Augustinian formulations of just war theory have shifted "from voluntarism to rationalism in understanding the nature of political community" and have increasingly emphasized "the natural-law concept of justice in analysis of the cause that justifies participation in war." Indeed, "rules for the right conduct [have been] ... drawn up," but such rules have been "the weakest part of the traditional theory of the just war."[181] On the other hand, Ramsey sees the primarily Lutheran "analysis of the state as an 'order of necessity' (*Notverordnung*)."[182] Its post-Augustinian formulations of

179 Ramsey, *Just War*, 533. Cf. Ramsey, *Just War*, 502 .

180 Ramsey, *War and Conscience*, 180.

181 Ramsey, *War and Conscience*, 32-33.

182 "A proponent of natural law and human rights can so stress the common good which politics serves that the component of power seems lost from view; while a Lutheran can so stress the

just war theory in modern Protestant ethics have shifted to an ethic of political expediency. In concentrating its efforts on determinations of "the 'lesser evil' or perchance the 'greater good' among the supposed consequences of actions," it has "sought to find the path along which action should be directed in order to defend some sort of values at the end of the road toward which action reaches, yet never reaches."[183] It has become "a wholly teleological ethic--even a *wholly future-facing agape*-ethic." Yet such a morality "amounts to the suspension of a great part of morality." For if "no more can be said about the morality of action than can be derived backward from the future goal," then "ethics has already more than half-way vanished, i.e., it has become mere calculation of the means to projected ends."[184] Such an ethic therefore "produces some version of the opinion that the end justifies the means."[185]

According to Ramsey, the great benefit of a return to the Augustinian just war position is that such a position rightly focuses on the primacy of human will or love in politics and thus the ultimate significance of means in the problem of war. On the one hand, it accepts the reality of human sin, of "divided wills," and hence of the persistence of the power element in human political relations. According to this position, "[t]he use of power ... is of the *esse* of politics .... You never have politics without the use of power, possibly armed force."[186] Consequently, this position acknowledges forthrightly that war can be "a just resort of policy."[187] On the other hand, the Augustinian just war position insists also on the reality of a divine charity "in-forming" a fallen world. Beyond the *esse* of politics[188] it recognizes "the *bene esse*" of politics.[189] It therefore seeks to elevate the use of power by specifying limits to its use.

According to Ramsey, the truly Augustinian just-war position holds both the Roman Catholic and the Lutheran "divergent emphases ... together in balanced perspective."[190] It can take full account of the three realms of *ordo* ("the order of power"), *lex* ("the legal order"), and *iustitia* ("the regulative ideal of all political action"), aware of the lack of "entire congruency" among them but noting always their small "area of coincidence or overlap" and attempting, in love, to stay within the bounds of this small area.[191]

---

need for restraint of sin that he loses sight of justice and the other community values that also belong to the essence of political authority and the action of rulers," Ramsey, *Just War*, xiii.

183 Ramsey, *War and Conscience*, 3.

184 Ramsey, *War and Conscience*, 4-5.

185 Ramsey, *War and Conscience*, 8.

186 Ramsey, *Just War*, 5.

187 Ramsey, *Just War*, 79.

188 = "its act of being," Ramsey, *The Just War*, 5.

189 = "its proper act of being, or its act of being proper politics," *Just War*, 5.

190 Ramsey, *Just War*, xiii.

191 Ramsey, *Just War*, 12. Cf. Ramsey, *War and Conscience*, 13-14: "Those theologians who most stress the fact that Christian ethics is wholly predicated upon redemption or upon the Divine indicative, and who say that decisive action is made possible by virtue of *justification* in Christ and by God's *forgiveness*, are often precisely the thinkers who strip politics of norms and

Ramsey argues that this understanding of just war condemns most forcefully the only uses to his date of nuclear weapons--those on Hiroshima and Nagasaki. Already "the implied threat to use violent repression directly against civilians as a means of forcing a decision to surrender on the part of the Japanese military command would ... itself have been grossly immoral."[192] Ramsey refers at that point to the significance of the celebration of the Lord's Day for a Christian. "Because of the truth proclaimed and re-enacted on the Sabbath Day, because of the shedding abroad of God's love and justice among men, a Christian ... can only say that he is required to save the life." He may "never directly or intentionally bring about the death of any man not engaged or closely co-operating in the hostile force that he must and in justice should repel."[193] According to Ramsey, then, "*neither* deterrence *nor* warfare with these immoral means is or can be feasible."[194]

In another, equally important way, Ramsey's Augustinian theory clears the moral skies for "counter-force" nuclear strategy. To the extent that nuclear weapons remain counter-force in design, intention, and use, they fall decidedly within the bounds of just war theory. Love prohibits the direct killing of innocents, but it clearly permits war directed against the guilty. The advent and coming-of-age of nuclear weapons do not change the applicability of the "rule of double effect," nor the moral responsibility to fight wars on occasion. Also in the nuclear age "the question is not only the humanness or inhumanness of certain means of putting fighters out of the war, and those closely co-operating in the attacking force. The question is whether the 'target' has been so far enlarged as to obliterate the distinction between peoples and their government, between peoples and forces."[195]

Ramsey insists that a nuclear strategy based on counter-force tactics is not only the most moral response to a nuclear world, but is also the most rational deterrent. "War must be made morally possible ... for the deterrent that deters no one so much as ourselves." The nations will need some "alternative to peace until that day--which Christians know ... is an eschatological vision and not an event in time--on which men beat their swords into plows and their spears into pruning hooks."[196]

In short, a "'deter the war' capability depends on a 'fight the war' capability." If we do not have "the ability and willingness to fight the war, we cannot stop the relentless advance of an enemy."[197] The "threat of war can be

---

principles distinguishing between right and wrong action." Where "there is faith there is surely no need for the removal of the principles of civil righteousness ...." On the contrary, "the moral problem of war ... requires ... an *agape*-ethic precipitating some principled judgment about means that are permitted or prohibited."

[192] Ramsey, *War and Conscience*, 150.

[193] Ramsey, *War and Conscience*, 269-270.

[194] Ramsey, *War and Conscience*, 234.

[195] Ramsey, *War and Conscience*, 237.

[196] Ramsey, *War and Conscience*, 153.

[197] Ramsey, *War and Conscience*, 244.

used to deter war only if by 'war' something is meant that can be done, done politically as well as militarily."[198]

Ramsey argues that "[t]he crux (the cross, the crossroads) at which Christian pacifists and justifiable-war Christians part company is" their "respective accounts of the person and work of Jesus Christ as these bear on divergent understandings of discipleship."[199] For this he makes reference to "pacifists such as Yoder and Hauerwas," whose understanding he characterizes as "*Jesus*-centered"[200] rather than "*Christocentric*." To the Anabaptists of the sixteenth century discipleship "meant *participation* in his life," and the "'rule' of Christ" was Matthew 18:15-20, where Jesus tells His church, "to be a community in conversation about the meaning of discipleship, reproving, correcting, and disciplining one another."[201] In this way, "the church came to distinguish its way of dealing with conflict (with the 'ban' as last resort) in contrast to resort to the sword in civil community" and to insist that there "is no God-*given* order or ordinance outside the perfection of Christ." To be sure, there is "a providential process of *ordering* the world" for those not "schooled by Jesus," but with "Jesus at the center of the community's life, Christians are drawn off from 'the world.'"[202]

This separation from the world comes "from the unity" of these Christians "with Jesus." According to Yoder, "'[w]e are to be a part of what he is, and he is as he was. *We are to be in the world now what he was* according to the New Testament text.'" And reversely, "*Jesus did in the world what we are supposed to be doing in the world.*" The result of "this living unity with Jesus assumes the cast of 'realized eschatology' to be faithfully lived by a large empirical denomination, without taut tension with the Kingdom not yet a presence to the church."[203]

Likewise "unity with Jesus" is the "'foundation of the call for non-resistance.'" Again, the emphasis is particularly on "Jesus." Yoder acknowledges that it is possible to say "'unity with Christ.'" However, the Christ whom the 1527 Schleitheim formulation[204] "is talking about is not some cosmic figure, and not some present mystical guide alone, but the continuation in our experience, because we are a united body." That is the reason that

---

198 Ramsey, *War and Conscience*, 239.

199 Ramsey, *Speak Up For Just War*, Chapter 4 is a very lengthy chapter, entitled, "An Ecumenical Consultation," 79-123, in which Ramsey engages in an "ecumenical consultation" with John Howard Yoder, "widely recognized as the leading contemporary American exponent of Christian pacifism" from within the Mennonite tradition. Ramsey responds to Yoder's *When War Is Unjust, Being Honest in Just-War Thinking* (Minneapolis: Fortress, 1984).

200 Ramsey, *Speak Up For Just War*, 111. At this point he makes reference particularly to John H. Yoder, *Christian Attitudes to War, Peace and Revolution*, 165-200.

201 Ramsey, *Speak Up For Just War*, 111, 112.

202 Ramsey, *Speak Up For Just War*, 112.

203 Ramsey, *Speak Up For Just War*, 112.

204 This is a pre-Menno Simons document which Yoder makes use of (Ramsey, *Speak Up For Just War*, 111).

Ramsey calls this view "'*Jesu*centrism,'" which nevertheless is "a Christology among others."[205]

Ramsey underlines the need "to distinguish serious Christian pacifism based on the person and politics of Jesus from other 'exemplary' theories of the atonement, of the person and work of Christ, with which modern Christianity is awash." He warns that to "be persuaded by the pacifism of a Yoder ... without the Christology implied or unarticulated in it could be to do the right thing for the wrong reasons." The same thing can be said with regard to Yoder's view on the "imitation" of Jesus. Yoder tells us that Jesus' "nonresistance of evil" should be "our nonresisting love even of enemy-neighbors; his way of doing his Father's reconciliation, our reconciling spirit." Ramsey cautions at this very point. Jesus Christ's "incarnation, his life as the God-man among us, his suffering, his death, his resurrection were unique, never to be repeated."[206] Indeed, we are to follow Him, but "*from a distance*," so the Reformers said. "We are not to take up *his* cross, but *our* cross to follow him."[207]

Furthermore, according to Ramsey, if "the love of nonresistance" is not "purified of its twentieth-century alloy with 'non-violence,' the grounding of pacifism in its account of the person and work of Jesus Christ would have to be corrected back to a sort of *legalism*."[208] Over against this Ramsey calls for an awareness that there is "an enduring tension between loyalty to Christ and our responsibilities in a less than ideal world." We need to be aware that there is "a dialectic between the motif of withdrawal from the evil or the less than perfect structures of the world and the motif of shaping or reshaping society so as to maintain or better the human dwelling place." On the one hand, there "is movement toward perfection of discipleship, which entails (perhaps radical) withdrawal." On the other hand, "there is movement toward engagement, which entails selective (perhaps deep) involvement. Indeed, we are called to do both, to be in the world but not of it."[209]

Taking stock then of Ramsey's use of Scripture in these deliberations, one could make the following points:

1. Ramsey's argument concerning the practice of war is guided by the biblical principle of *agape*, which must be in-principled within the structures of society in order to achieve justice for communities. The emphasis on *agape* is also in this case decidedly set against natural law theory and situationism. *Agape* is the biblical mandate which must receive form and practice through a process of becoming "in-principled." This is an instance in which the biblical command takes "principled" form, incarnating itself in ever more concrete forms, gathered under the general and traditional phrase of "Just War."

---

[205] Ramsey, *Speak Up For Just War*, 112.
[206] Ramsey, *Speak Up For Just War*, 113.
[207] Ramsey, *Speak Up For Just War*, 113-114.
[208] Ramsey, *Speak Up For Just War*, 115.
[209] Ramsey, *Speak Up For Just War*, 142; cf. *Speak Up For Just War*, 123, last paragraph.

2. The example of Jesus enters the discussion through conversation particularly with the pacifists. On the one hand, the example of Jesus is authoritative, for Jesus' resistance against groups serves as a model. On the other hand, Ramsey draws the distinction in role between Jesus and us, Jesus' mission having been unique.
3. With Ramsey there is an acceptance of the role of structures and natural law transformed by love which the pacifists deny as being part of the gospel of Jesus. Ramsey expresses christological disagreement with Christian pacifist theory, which is focused on Jesus to the expense of an emphasis on Christ.

3.4.2. Abortion

It is remarkable that with regard to the debate on abortion Ramsey appeals particularly to the shape of biblical thought on abortion. In an article entitled "the Morality of Abortion,"[210] he starts out by making reference to a number of theories of when life begins, but then he emphatically spells out these theories are negligible from a truly religious point of view.[211] After all, the "value of a human life is ultimately grounded in the value God is placing on it."[212] Along these lines Ramsey makes reference to the doctrine of creation in the image of God. He also points to the concept of God's covenant with his people and all humans and the measure it sets for every human relation.[213]

Once one starts listening to biblical evidence, one sees that humans are distinct within creation. Ramsey also refers to the significance of the electing love expressed in Deuteronomy 7:7. The question is not when human life begins; rather the point is that "the Lord loved us even while we were yet microscopic and sent forth his call on us and brought forth from things that are not the things that are."[214]

Ramsey also refers to Jeremiah 1:5: "Before I formed thee in the belly I knew thee; and before thou camest forth out of the womb I sanctified thee; and I ordained thee ...." According to Ramsey, "anyone who has a glimmer of what it means to be a religious man, should be able to repeat" these words after Jeremiah.[215] Similarly he refers to Psalm 139:1,5,12b, 13-14. In verse 14 the psalmist sings: "Thou hast covered me in my mother's womb. I will praise thee; for I am fearfully and wonderfully made: marvelous are thy works: and that my soul knoweth right well." Ramsey commented: "Thus, every human being is a unique, unrepeatable opportunity to praise God." Man's "essence is his existence before God and to God, as it is from Him." Man's "dignity is 'an *alien*

210 Written originally in 1968, reprinted in *Abortion: The Moral Issues*, ed. Edward Batchelor (New York: Pilgrim Press, 1982), 73-91.
211 Ramsey, "The Morality of Abortion," 78.
212 Ramsey, "The Morality of Abortion," 79.
213 Ramsey, "The Morality of Abortion," 80.
214 Ramsey, "The Morality of Abortion," 80.
215 Ramsey, "The Morality of Abortion," 79.

dignity,' an evaluation that is not of him but placed upon him by divine decree."[216]

Furthermore, Ramsey makes reference to "the Exodus and the Genesis stories of creation,"[217] and particularly "the Nativity Stories." With regard to the latter, he points out: "Far more than any argument, it was surely the power of the Nativity Stories and their place in ritual and celebration and song that tempered the conscience of the West to its audacious effort to wipe out the practice of abortion and infanticide."[218]

Ramsey's use of Scripture is fundamental. It is also broad and theological. It makes direct references to the beginning of life (Jer 1:5; Ps 139:14), but not without theological and christological reflection. God's covenant and Christ's nativity also present an indictment against abortion.

Moreover, Ramsey makes clear that the principle of *agape* needs to be brought to bear upon the issue. In his *War and the Christian Conscience*, he registers his disagreement with the traditional Roman Catholic opposition to abortion on the basis of the view that intentional killing is always wrong, so also killing a fetus, even to save the life of the mother. Ramsey disagrees particularly for this reason, that the Roman Catholic position "in the matter of morality" fails to give any real role to *agape*. Ramsey emphasizes that "*agape* definitely does not justify every means, not even every indispensable means ... but surely every means to save life the only alternative to which is ... death ...."[219]

It is evident, then, that Ramsey considers the issue of abortion in the light of this *agape* ethic, treating others as persons as a requirement and expression of *agape* love.[220] Abortion can be an expression of *agape*, namely, in order to save the life of a non-visible fetus' mother. At this point Ramsey distinguishes between incapacitation and the direct killing of the fetus. In this case clearly the

---

216 Ramsey, "The Morality of Abortion," 80. From here on Ramsey goes on to indicate that these "biblical themes resound throughout Karl Barth's writings on respect for life and the protection of life" [referring to K. Barth's *Church Dogmatics*, III/4, sections 55-56]. He refers to Barth as "the greatest Protestant theologian of this generation," (80) to whom the word "respect" in the phrase "respect for life" means "to treat human life with 'holy awe.'" That meaning is "derived from the fact that whenever a man's life is in question, the primary affirmation to be made about it is that from all eternity God resolved not even to be God without this particular human life." It is not so that "a man must live and let live from some iron law of necessity," but rather that "because God has said 'Yes' to life, man's 'Yes' should echo His." Man "can and may live" because of "God's decree and election." Barth insisted that the "'unborn child is from the very first a child,'" although it "'is still developing'" and cannot live independently. "'But it is a man and not a thing, nor a mere part of the mother's body'" (81). Moreover, this "'child is a man for whose life the Son of God has died ....'" (82).

217 Ramsey, "Liturgy and Ethics," 161.

218 Ramsey, "Liturgy and Ethics," 162.

219 Ramsey, *War and the Christian Conscience* (1961), 186.

220 It is this same perspective on Christian ethics that is at work in Ramsey's position on war, namely, that as I indicated above, *agape* and violence are not always mutually exclusive. In "multilateral relations," when I come upon a neighbor harming another neighbor, I encounter a conflict of duties, violence can be an expression of *agape*.

intention of the abortion is not the killing of the fetus but rather the incapacitation of the fetus. The intention in this abortion is "stopping" the fetus' "lethal action upon its mother's life."[221]

According to Ramsey, the question may be raised: who qualifies as a bearer of the equal worth that persons have? Does a fetus so qualify? The question is not simply, "When does human life begin?" nor "When do we have to do with a fully actualized person?," but rather, "When does equally protectable human life begin?"[222]

Ramsey also gives attention to the question of abortion (as well as euthanasia) from the angle of the question, "When and on what basis is it justifiable to attack another person?" Ramsey responds: One must never intend (in a strict sense of the word) the death of another, even when striking him or her, but must always have as one's intention the prevention of some grave harm.[223] He discusses this thesis in detail in an article entitled "Incommensurability and Indeterminancy in Moral Choice" in *Doing Evil to Achieve Good: Moral Choice in Conflict Situations*.[224]

On the issue of abortion Ramsey displays a use of Scripture which is theological and christological. He begins with Scriptural data of creation and God's electing love and even with texts which speak to the issue of unborn life. Beyond this, the liturgical role of the nativity narratives is shown to be pertinent. This use of Scripture appears to be somewhat uncharacteristic of Ramsey on most other issues. But the more familiar emphasis on the *agape* principle is not absent, but in fact receives extensive application. It leads him to articulate the permissibility of abortion only in instances when death of the fetus would be the non-intended effect of doing the good of saving the life of the mother. Here the principled form of Scripture, namely, *agape*, functions in a way consonant with his theoretical proposals.

3.4.3. Genetic Control

On the issue of genetic control Ramsey also refers to the Bible. In response to H. J. Muller, who maintains that "according to the genetic apocalypse, there shall come a time when *there will be none like us to come after us*,"[225] Ramsey refers to "the Christian's Apocalypse," the Revelation of John and "the so called little apocalypse (Mark 13 and parallels)," which includes indeed "gruesome details about what will happen in the 'last days.'"

---

221 Ramsey, "Abortion: A Review Article," in *The Thomist* 37 (1973): 220.

222 Ramsey, "Abortion: A Review Article," 182.

223 Cf. Ramsey, "Liturgy and Ethics," 220.

224 In "Incommensurability and Indeterminancy in Moral Choice," Ramsey contends that "the rule of double effect, which is often supposed to be a program for reducing ambiguity in moral choice until there is none, has served rather to sustain acknowledgment of an actual ambiguity that characterizes much of our moral experience and many moral judgments," 69.

225 Ramsey, *Fabricated Man*, 25.

According to Ramsey, this "means that 'Christian hope into, and through, the future depends not at all on denying the number or seriousness of the accumulating lethal mutations which Muller finds to be the case ...."[226] He places genetics and Genesis next to each other. "Where genetics teaches us that we are made out of genes and unto genes return, Genesis teaches that we are made out of the dust of the ground and unto dust we and all our seed return" (Gen 2:19).[227] There is no need at all for Christians to "deny whatever account science may give him of ... this world, so long as science does not presume to turn itself into a theology by blitzing him into believing that it knows the one and only apocalypse."[228] But there is a difference between the Christian's knowledge of "gruesome details about what will happen in the 'last days'" and Muller's knowledge of mankind being "doomed unless positive steps are taken to regulate our genetic endowment." Whereas Muller, "when all hope is gone ... hopes on *in despair*," an "Abraham of genetic science if one should arise, would be one who, when all hope is gone, hopes on *in faith*, and who therefore need neither fear the problem nor trust the solution of it too much."[229]

From these biblical lines Ramsey argues that "anyone who is oriented upon the Christian *eschaton*" will have considerable room "for an 'ethics of means.'"[230] He will ask, What are right means? no less than he asks, What are the proper objectives? He will not overlook the wrongfulness of many actions in favor of good consequences. After all, in this temporal history Scripture nor sound reason promises success to mankind.[231]

Over against the geneticist's ethics "whose means are determined by the values of free will and thought," the ethics of one "who intends the world as a Christian" will emphasize that "man's dignity consists not only in thought or in his freedom" but in "more elements ... which are deserving of respect and should be withheld from human handling or trespass." Specifically in connection with genetic proposals, he will point out that "there are more ways to violate man-womanhood than to violate the *freedom* of the parties; and that something voluntarily adopted can still be wrong."[232]

When Ramsey writes on the ethics of genetic control, he repeatedly asserts the inseparability of these two spheres of procreation and marital love in human parenthood "as it came from the Creator," and we ought not to put asunder "what God joined together in creation,"[233] and therefore he rejects AID (donor insemination), cloning, and reproduction *in vitro*.

---

226 Ramsey, *Fabricated Man*, 26-27.
227 Ramsey, *Fabricated Man*, 27.
228 Ramsey, *Fabricated Man*, 27-28.
229 Ramsey, *Fabricated Man*, 29.
230 Ramsey, *Fabricated Man*, 29.
231 Ramsey, *Fabricated Man*, 30.
232 Ramsey, *Fabricated Man*, 31-32.
233 Ramsey, *Fabricated Man*, 124, 38.

According to Ramsey, the "anthropology that governs or is fostered by genetic science and technical genetic appliances" is an anthropology which is "profoundly antithetical" to the anthropology "in the Judeo-Christian tradition." The ethical premises "underlying the contemporary science of genetics" are "expressions of man's view of himself, his nature and being." It is here that "we must choose whom we shall serve."[234] The "biblical view of the life of this 'flesh'" is that "we are our bodies no less than we are our souls, minds or wills" and that to violate this flesh is to violate "man no less than to violate man's will or freedom," and this will show up in our ethical judgments. Over against this view there is the so-called scientific view with "an ethic which tries to base itself on the intentionality of the scientific mind alone" and which "nearly always regards mind or will or freedom ... as the only thing that can be violated in man." According to this so-called scientific ethic, "our bodies and our genes" essentially "are not part of that nature which has sanctity, which places moral claims upon us ...." Our bodies and our genes are "lower parts ... among the nonhuman world over which God gave man dominion." According to this so-called scientific ethic, "there is no reason why man should not become his own maker, the maker of all future generations, and the remaker of the nature of human parenthood."[235]

Ramsey maintains that pride is the great sin of human beings. They tend to claim too much for themselves and forget about their inherent limitations and sinfulness. Pride, or claiming too much power, is the root of all the evils in the world. The great human temptation is to play God. Ramsey sees many violations on the horizontal plane of human existence brought about by the new biology--coercive breeding or nonbreeding, injustices done to individuals or mishaps, the violation of the nature of human parenthood. In attempts of the new biology to fabricate human beings, to prevent aging, to make "'cybogs' (combining biology with cybernetics),"[236] to control intimate human moods and powers, he perceives the human desire to have limitless dominion over our lives--the fatal flaw of *hubris*, or the denial of our own creatureliness. He insists on the limitations of human wisdom as a guide for the rosy future portrayed by the messianic positivists. Human beings must be willing to accept our finitude and our limitations, to say nothing of our sinfulness.[237]

In sum, then, one can say that on the matter of genetic control, Scripture is brought to bear through the principles of creation and covenant. These principles serve as correctives or challenges to human impulses and ambitions. Inherent in the biblical account of creation is a realism about human potential.

---

234 Ramsey, *Fabricated Man*, 171.

235 Ramsey, *Fabricated Man*, 172.

236 Ramsey, *Fabricated Man*, 152.

237 Ramsey, *Fabricated Man*, 90-96, 151-160. In "Shall We Reproduce? II: Rejoinders and Future Forecast," in *Journal of the American Medical Association* 120 (12 June 1972), 1481, Ramsey argues that medicine exists to cure the medical ills of people but should not be used for nonmedical purposes or to fulfill people's wishes or desires.

The biblical coordination of love and procreation should not be loosened through genetic engineering. The biblical diagnosis of human pride must caution us against scientific arrogance. The biblical union of body, mind, and spirit ought not to be fragmented nor the body domesticated by the scientific mind. Furthermore, biblical eschatology is permeated with a hopefulness which guards against despair.

3.4.4. Euthanasia

The notion of covenant stands out in Ramsey's treatment of euthanasia, in which he accepts the moral difference between killing and allowing to die. He writes: "If the sting of death is sin, the sting of dying is solitude .... Desertion is more choking than death, and more feared. The chief problem of the dying is how not to die alone." Particularly with regard to the question, "How are we to regard irreversibly comatose individuals?," Ramsey argues:

> Patients are to be loved and cared for no matter who they are and no matter what their potential for higher values is, and certainly not on account of their responsiveness. Who they are, in Christian ethical perspective, is our neighbors. They do not become nearer neighbors because of any capacity they own, nor lesser neighbors because they lack some ability to prevail in their struggle for human fulfillment.[238]

At this point, Ramsey makes specific reference to a number of Scripture passages, the same passages he quotes with reference to his treatment of the issue of abortion, namely Jeremiah 1:5, Psalm 139:12b, 13, 14, and Deuteronomy 7:7, 8a. The difference is that here he adds these considerations: When the prophet Jeremiah writes these words, "he does not mean to start us on a search for the 'indicators of personhood' God was using or should have used before calling us by name. Neither did the psalmist" of Psalm 139. "No more did God," according to Deuteronomy 7:7, 8a, "at the outset of his Egyptian rescue operation, look around for 'indicators of peoplehood,' choosing only those best qualified for national existence."[239]

Moreover, although many of "God's life and death decisions are inscrutable to us ... there is no indication at all" that God's care for us depends on a number of functions or capacities in our personhood. On the contrary, "he has special care for the weak and the vulnerable among us earth people. He cares according to need, not according to capacity or merit."[240] The mandate

---

[238] Ramsey, *Ethics at the Edges of Life*, 226-227. According to Ramsey, the term "extraordinary" which is regularly used by those who wish to withhold treatment with the intention that the patient should die, is "leading us toward involuntary euthanasia," *Ethics at the Edges of Life*, 201. Cf. Ramsey's treatment of euthanasia, in *The Patient as Person* (1970).

[239] Ramsey, *Ethics at the Edges of Life*, 204-205.

[240] Ramsey, *Ethics at the Edges of Life*, 205.

"only to care, for the dying"[241] is justified first as "a medical-moral imperative," a faithfulness required of all men, not of Christians only.[242]

Second, Ramsey offers a distinctly Christian warrant for his prohibition of direct euthanasia. This warrant is the steadfast covenant love of God for man, which is the standard for the fidelity of man to man. "An attitude toward the dying premised upon mature and profoundly religious convictions will display an indefectable charity that never ceases to go about the business of caring for the dying neighbor."[243] After all, such convictions proceed from the faith-knowledge that the dying cannot pass beyond God's love and care. Only then will men have the courage to apply these limits to medical practice. Only "upon the basis of faith in God can there be a conscionable category of 'ceasing to oppose death,' making room for caring for the dying."[244]

Ramsey's ultimate ground for opposing euthanasia is therefore his ethics of covenantal fidelity, which calls for an ethics of "only caring for the dying" and defines the moral limits of the duty to heal and save the life of "all who bear a human countenance."[245] The imperative of this ethics is never to abandon care.[246] The general "rule" is that euthanasia is always to be prohibited as incompatible with the demand of covenant fidelity that we respect the lives of our fellow human beings. His ultimate justification for this rule is that to "'assist' the process of dying would itself be a sort of abandonment [of love and care]: an affirmative abandonment of the dying solely to God's care in separation from ours, a self-contradiction at the heart of Christian charity."[247]

According to Ramsey, there are two possible situations that constitute "exceptions" to our duty to care for the dying, namely, when the life of the dying person has passed beyond receptivity to our care and comfort, either through permanent unconsciousness or through extreme suffering. In such cases, the covenant and its responsibilities cease.[248] The cases Ramsey has in mind are "the cases of patients in deep and irreversible coma who can be and are maintained alive for many, many years,"[249] but who are "irretrievably inaccessible to human care." The duty to care for those people is suspended because of their inaccessibility to any form of care. When a patient is in this condition, the "crucial moral difference between omission and commission as a guide to faithful actions has utterly vanished."[250]

The second "exception" is that of the terminal patient, who is "undergoing deep and prolonged pain," and "who cannot be relieved by means

---

241 As distinct from either uselessly prolonging life or direct killing.

242 Ramsey, *The Patient as Person*, 134.

243 Ramsey, *The Patient as Person*, 153.

244 Ramsey, *The Patient as Person*, 156.

245 Ramsey, *The Patient as Person*, 134.

246 Ramsey, *The Patient as Person*, 153.

247 Ramsey, *The Patient as Person*, 160.

248 Ramsey, *The Patient as Person*, 160-164.

249 Ramsey, *The Patient as Person*, 162.

250 Ramsey, *The Patient as Person*, 161.

presently available to use to care for him and make him comfortable," who is also "beyond reach of the other ways in which company be kept with him and he be attended in his dying." This case is similar that of the prolonged comatose patient. For accomplishing or hastening his dying directly, one "can hardly hold men to be morally blameworthy."[251]

It is at the point at which such patients move beyond the reach of being given care and comfort and receiving it, that the distinction between killing and allowing to die disappears to Ramsey, and he allows for an "exception" to the general rule against euthanasia. He is not afraid of weakening the general rule prohibiting euthanasia as long as the exceptions to it within these "strict limits" are limited to those patients who are truly beyond the reach of human care and comfort.[252]

There are a number of questions that arise at this point. First, is this person dying? Second, what is the source of certainty that a person is beyond the reach of human care? Ramsey acknowledges that moralists cannot say whether there are such cases as he posited, for "this would be for physicians to say,"[253] but on what grounds would physicians make this judgment without the person who experienced care and now supposedly no longer does so? Ramsey admits that we should not lightly assume that the comatose patient is not aware of the sound of voices, the touch of a loved one's hand, etc. But what or who tells us whether our assumption is ill- or well-founded? Third, is Ramsey consistent in justifying his exceptions entirely with the theological warrant for his original rule? After all, he insists that the model for human covenant love is divine covenant love, which is steadfast, unending, and not dependent on a human response. Further, it is precisely on these grounds that he defends fetal life from attack. When life is most helpless, vulnerable, and unable to respond, it most demands our protection and care.[254]

Ramsey advocates a "medical indications policy" in order to determine when to initiate, discontinue, and withhold medical care. He vigorously rejects policy recommendations based on the patient's right to refuse treatment.[255] He regards it as essential to determine what treatment is medically indicated in the case of non-terminal patients, and whether any curative treatment is medically indicated in the case of the dying. This, he says, is an objective medical determination, albeit with margins of disagreement and error. It is not related to some idea in the doctor's mind of "standard medical care" or to any judgment about the worthwhileness of the patient's quality of life or his potential. It is simply: Can I offer treatment that will improve this patient's condition? If so, I should. If not, I should not, but rather I should let him die. In this case to let him die "is a justifiable, even commendable alternative *for the dying.*" If I do not let

---

[251] Ramsey, *The Patient as Person*, 163.
[252] Ramsey, *The Patient as Person*, 164.
[253] Ramsey, *The Patient as Person*, 161-162.
[254] Ramsey, *The Patient as Person*, 131, 161.
[255] Ramsey, *Ethics at the Edges*, chapter 4, "'Euthanasia' and Dying Well Enough," 145-188.

him die, I only prolong his dying, which does not benefit "unaware patients." Prolonging dying is beneficial to "the conscious ones only in special circumstances, such as affording them an opportunity to make a will or to have their last reconciliation with God or a family member." What is important to see is that "in his dying process" the person is "a valued patient-person (because of who he is, not his function or his prospective realizable potential)," and he "claims care and comfort and human company to the end."[256]

Ramsey maintains that for the non-dying also, there can be clinical judgments not to treat, but the decision is to be based on the belief that the treatment would be of no benefit, not on the view that the patient does not qualify for treatment. Although the question must be raised: what counts as "benefit," and how to react if burdens outweigh benefits?, the primary point is clear. We need to be alert to the situations in which "dying" and "non-dying" are terms relative to treatment. A person might not be "dying" if he had earlier been treated.

With reference to the criteria for selection, Ramsey suggests that the medical question is: Can I help, or only care? According to him, when sedative drugs are given, for instance, in order that a child will not seek food, we have a case of "active euthanasia but slow euthanasia."[257] The "benign neglect of defective infants" is a form of involuntary euthanasia. When a policy of non-treatment is entered into with the intention that the child should die, there is no significant distinction between allowing to die and causing death. "When care is not even attempted in the case of defective nondying infants, there is no morally significant distinction between action and abstention. Morally, what in this case is not done is the same as doing."[258] Then there is no more way of avoiding the charge of causing death and the related consequence that "medical care" then becomes "a function of inequities that exist at birth," which adds "injustice to injury and fate."[259]

Outside of the questions which can be raised with regard to consistency of application, it is clear that Ramsey employs the covenant principle to the matter of euthanasia. The fidelity which God demonstrates to us independent of certain criteria of response and life should be the standard for care to others. This again is an instance in which principles derived from Scripture serve to inform ethical practice rather than, for example, philosophical criteria concerning viability.

3.4.5. Conclusion

In the practice of Ramsey's Christian ethics, Scripture has a broad and theological role. There are times when direct references to Scripture are used

---

256 Ramsey, *Ethics at the Edges*, 178.
257 Ramsey, *Ethics at the Edges*, 197.
258 Ramsey, *Ethics at the Edges*, 195.
259 Ramsey, *Ethics at the Edges*, 202.

theologically and christologically. More important principles such as *agape* and covenant are used in order to provide guidance on issues. Natural law is called in to aid certain issues such as just war, but Ramsey is clear about how *agape* is to perform a transformative function and retains a normative character. The practice of Ramsey's Christian ethics also demonstrates how he struggles with the particular and concrete embodiment of the *agape* principle in practice. In the discussion of war, he emphasizes that love must have an in-principled character because of the nature of societal systems and the collective justice which it is able to achieve. In this particular case, the *agape*-principle of Scripture has been transformed into the *agape*-principle of theoretical ethics.

3.5. Summary and Evaluation

After his initial books on basic Christian ethics, Ramsey turned mostly to issues in political ethics and medical ethics. The former laid out the foundation of *agape* for ethical action. This foundation intends to be thoroughly Christocentric. It involves a love transforming, re-aligning and reshaping natural law. It is an *agape* which remains free and independent, not containing itself in codifications or social policies, but applying itself to the neighbor. Ramsey felt the tension of a situational application of this *agape* or some generalization in rules. He practiced a medium between these two approaches. When Ramsey moved on to more practical issues, some charged him that he no longer employed "the methodology of love transforming justice."[260]

According to E. Clinton Gardner, there has been "a shift from *agape* to 'covenant' in defining the primary norm of ethics," as a result of "Ramsey's continued effort to relate *agape* to the issues and problems of social ethics as well as his greater concern with continuity and stability in the moral life of individuals." But it is not a substantive change. It is only "a different way of expressing the claims which are embedded in neighbor-love." Already in his *Basic Christian Ethics*, Ramsey pictured "the notion of *agape*" as being "rooted ultimately in the idea of covenant."[261] Later on in *The Patient as Person*, he replaced *agape* with the concept of the covenant which "provides a stronger basis for affirming the claims of faithfulness and fidelity which are implicit in the practice of medicine as a profession." Moreover, "'covenant' provides a more precise model for reconciling the welfare of the individual with the welfare of society."[262]

What kind of rule-agapism (summary or pure) does a Christian social ethics require? Although a crucial question, Ramsey does not work out a very

---

260 Cf. Curran, "Paul Ramsey and Traditional Roman Catholic Natural Law Theory," in *Love and Society: Essays in the Ethics of Paul Ramsey* (1974), 55.

261 Cf. Ramsey, *Basic Christian Ethics*, 388.

262 Gardner, *Christocentrism in Christian Social Ethics*, 70-71.

complete answer. D. Stephen Long underlines that what Ramsey attempts to do in *Deeds and Rules in Christian Ethics* is "to salvage an agapeic ethic from Fletcher's consequentialist reasoning" and to reconsider "the freedom-legalistic dialectic." In reconsidering the latter, he "finds that principles do not inhibit freedom," but rather "provide resources for both moral and immoral action."[263] Moreover, he emphasizes that the "world in which we live is always already structured, i.e. it always comes with principles, rules and law that define who, what, and where we are."[264] He seems content to have opened up the possibilities for rules in all these areas. He appears to be, as he was at the end of his *Basic Christian Ethics*, still in search of a Christian social ethic. But he has made a significant discovery that Christian ethics has to make room not only for summary rules, but also for rules of practice, if it is to deal significantly with the social nature of man.

In his major works such as *Basic Christian Ethics* and *Deeds and Rules in Christian Ethics*, moral norms originate in covenant, both natural and revealed, and are discerned through the media of reasonable ethical perceptions and Scripture, respectively. To state it in oversimplified form, it is "faith effective through in-principled love." To state it in simplified form, Ramsey's position is that justice is the norm of the universal natural covenants among men; *agape* is the norm of the revealed Christian covenant. For the Christian, "love transforms justice," to use a phrase which is a keynote of Ramsey's Christian ethics. *Agape* should employ the policies of secular justice in its own service, fulfilling and transcending justice's demands in a dynamic relationship. As a Christian theologian, Ramsey wants to maintain the uniqueness and indispensability of *agape* as moral norm, while as an ethicist addressing persons of any or no religious persuasion on subjects of common interest, he wants to maintain the universality of standards of right conduct.

It has, however, been difficult to achieve a systematic balance between ethical distinctiveness and universality. In *The Patient as Person*, for instance, it is not entirely clear, precisely where the limits of moral norms drawn from natural covenants lie, how far the authority of norms drawn from revelation extends, or what the nature of the audience is to whom each is meant to appeal. This difficulty remains throughout Ramsey's writings, surely also in *Ethics at the Edges of Life: Medical and Legal Intersections*. Ramsey does not systematically relate two types of moral justification but presents them side by side. He seems to imply that the first should be sufficient to convince any reasonable person. He offers the second as an additional "interpretative principle" for Christians, which may not be without force for others.[265]

---

263 D. Stephen Long, *Tragedy, Tradition, Transformation: The Ethics of Paul Ramsey* (Boulder, CO: Westview Press, 1993), 105.

264 D. Stephen Long, *Tragedy, Tradition, Transformation: The Ethics of Paul Ramsey*, 106.

265 Cf. Charles E. Curran, *Politics, Medicine, and Christian Ethics: A Dialogue with Paul Ramsey* (Philadelphia: Fortress, 1973), 111.

The fact that Ramsey grounds ethics in theology is to be positively evaluated. Unlike Gustafson, his Christology is orthodox in the sense of acknowledging Christ to be both God and human. For the most part, Scripture is not subjected to philosophical hermeneutics as in Gustafson. Ramsey does employ various theological hermeneutics, concerning which questions can be raised, but he does not view Scripture as Troeltsch, Niebuhr, or Gustafson does.

At points, however, Ramsey interprets Scripture philosophically. His discussion of "original sin" is an example of a philosophical discussion of a biblical topic, which he regards as couched in myth. For the origin of sin in every man, he turns to Christian existentialism.[266] Aware of the radical individualism of Christian existentialism, Ramsey advocates that it be supplemented by the idealism of philosophers such as Jean Jacques Rousseau and Josiah Royce who gave a sharp analysis of the social occasion for sin, although they had an eye for the responsible nature of man's act. [267] Although he admits that the philosophical accounts do not attain to the theocentricity of the Genesis account[268] neither to the christocentricity of the New Testament, he does not point out how the philosophical accounts lack the aspect of the *revelation of sin* by the divine Word or in the divine law. The philosophical accounts do therefore not benefit the clear theocentric and thus also christocentric focus for ethics.

Concerning Ramsey's Christology, it could be asked whether it is sufficiently Trinitarian. Though Ramsey's Christology is articulated in the traditional terms of God-human and elaborated upon particularly in *kenotic* terms, the interrelationships between the persons of the Trinity are not kept in view. Thus the place of the Holy Spirit and his relationship to Christ is ignored. The result is that Ramsey has problems articulating the relationship between Christ and his followers. Ramsey's discussion is somewhat obscure here. In his *Basic Christian Ethics* he speaks of an encounter which produces in the believer greater humility and greater achievement.[269] Ramsey is not specific on this "encounter," nor on the role of faith. Would a greater understanding of Christology within the framework of the Trinity not give greater insight and depth here?

The second issue concerns the nature of *agape*. This chapter has noted that Ramsey himself has sensed the difficulty of having a deontology of love without rules of application. This was found to be one of the greatest tensions for Ramsey. He established as primary the freedom and independence of *agape* in contrast to the "Egypt" of various codes. If this is all that is said, then one would have a situational approach in the application of ethics, with which Ramsey is not content. In his *Basic Christian Ethics* Ramsey adopts an idealist

---

[266] Ramsey, *Basic Christian Ethics*, 306, 313.

[267] Ramsey, *Basic Christian Ethics*, 307, 313-315.

[268] Ramsey, *Basic Christian Ethics*, 294-295.

[269] Ramsey, *Basic Christian Ethics*, 200.

anthropology with some of its corollary social policies. But in his conclusion Ramsey warns that these social policies are in no wise fixed, but that *agape* stands above them all and can assert itself in opposition to social policies. Subsequently, in *Nine Modern Moralists* Ramsey allows some place for natural law and the exercise of prudence. In fact, Ramsey ascertains that this is the basis for many a decision which is ethically warranted. Yet, Ramsey also maintains that *agape* must transform and reshape this prudence of natural law to make it accord with the Christocentric *agape* he has laid as the groundfloor in ethics. In his *Deeds and Rules* Ramsey evidences the same tension of a situational application for love or the use of rules. He hovers between act-agapism, summary rule-agapism, and pure rule-agapism. Though he is not willing to commit to the pure rule-agapism, he does defend it to some extent: "The proponent of Christian situationist-ethics should no longer accuse the proponent of rule-agapism of being a legalist lacking in 'compassion' when he only believes that Christian compassion can and may and must embody itself in certain rules of action."[270]

The nature of the tension of Ramsey's *agape* ethic is evident. The question to be raised here is whether Ramsey could not have considered the view which holds love and codes together as Exodus and Deuteronomy appear to do. Ramsey calls all codes a form of "Egypt." Could the realization that God's Exodus led the people from bondage to Pharaoh to service *of God* not be of importance to Ramsey's tension? The relationship between love and the law will be raised in the final chapter of this writing, but suffice it to say, Ramsey has not duly considered the relationship between law and love in the Old Testament, or even in the New Testament.

This discussion of Ramsey has focused the issues pertaining to methodology in ethics. Ramsey's ethics are grounded in theology to a greater extent than Gustafson, and his theology is Christocentrically construed. Though selective, his use Scripture is substantial, particularly regarding concepts of covenant, righteousness, and love. Ramsey has not, however, theorized about his use of Scripture and the use of Scripture in ethics generally. Allen Verhey has focused on this matter to a greater extent, and to him we now turn.

---

270 Ramsey, *Deeds and Rules*, 4.

Chapter 4: Allen Verhey: The Use of Scripture in Moral Argument

4.1. Introduction

Allen D. Verhey was born on May 14, 1945. In 1966 he received a B.A. from Calvin College, in 1969 a B.D. from Calvin Theological Seminary, and in 1975 a Ph.D. from Yale University. He is married to Phyllis De Kruyter, with whom he is parent of three children. He is an ordained minister in the Christian Reformed Church.

Henry Stob was Verhey's professor in ethics at Calvin Theological Seminary. During his Ph.D. studies at Yale University James M. Gustafson was one of his teachers. Although he never had Paul Ramsey for classroom instruction, he acknowledges to have learned a great deal from him and considers him his teacher as well. In personal correspondence to the present author, he wrote that he thinks that Gustafson and Ramsey are "the two greatest American Christian theologians since the Niebuhrs."

As to his teaching experience, from 1970-1972 he was a Teaching Assistant at Yale Divinity School, from 1972-1975 Guest Lecturer in Christian Ethics at Calvin Theological Seminary, and from 1975 through 1992 he was Professor of Religion at Hope College, Holland, Michigan. In addition to this, he was in the summers of 1980, 1985 and 1987 a Visiting Lecturer at Fuller Theological Seminary Summer Program and in the winter of 1984 a Visiting Lecturer at Young Life Institute. In 1992 he moved to Houston, Texas, and became the Director of the Institute of Religion in Houston, Texas, which is part of the Texas Medical Center. Since then he has returned to Hope College, to be the Evert J. and Hattie E. Blekkink Professor of Religion and chair of the Department of Religion.

A focus on the use of Scripture in moral argument arises quite naturally from Verhey's writings. Verhey wrote his dissertation on Walter Rauschenbusch's use of Scripture in moral discourse.[1] In his dissertation Verhey laid the foundation for his own use of Scripture in moral discourse.

In 1984, Verhey published the book, entitled *The Great Reversal: Ethics and the New Testament*. In this book he deals at considerable length with the methodological issues involved in moving from the words of the New Testament to present day applications. He points out the acute hermeneutical difficulties involved in appropriating New Testament teachings for our guidance. He describes the varieties of ethical teaching in the New Testament and provides a

---

[1] Verhey, "The Use of Scripture in Moral Discourse: A Case Study of Walter Rauschenbusch," Ph.D. Diss., Yale University, 1975.

theoretical framework for debate about how to employ these texts in the actual doing of ethics. In a contemporaneous article, "The Use of the Scripture in Ethics," a subsequent dictionary article, "Bible in Christian Ethics," and a more recent dictionary article, "New Testament Ethics," Verhey summarizes his proposals.[2]

Another single publication of note is his *Living the Heidelberg*, a discussion of the Heidelberg Catechism with special attention to social and ethical dimensions of the Catechism.[3] Here a discussion of Scripture is refracted through theological and moral confessions. In various other publications Verhey elaborates his thinking on specific contemporary issues in Christian ethics along above-mentioned lines. In these publications, words such as community and narrative, disposition and virtue, also care and caution, stand out more and more. He deals with specific contemporary issues such as the doctor's oath,[4] abortion,[5] test-tube babies,[6] the morality of genetic engineering[7] as well as medical technology and care,[8] and health care amidst scarcity in resources.[9]

Also here the discussion in chapter 1 on the history of American Protestant ethics under the key phrases "practical," "collective," and "rational" is assumed. This chapter will closely examine the steps in Verhey's use of Scripture, both theoretically and practically. Verhey's relationship with Gustafson and Ramsey has been less that of a peer than that of a student. Through Gustafson and Ramsey and others the legacy of American Protestant ethics has been handed down to Verhey.

Another person from the history of American Protestant ethics, whose importance for understanding Verhey should not be underrated is Walter

---

[2] Verhey, "The Use of Scripture in Ethics," in *Readings in Moral Theology No. 4: The Use of Scripture in Moral Theology*, eds. Charles Curran and Richard McCormick, S.J. (New York: Paulist Press, 1984), 213-241; "Bible in Christian Ethics," in *Dictionary of Christian Ethics*, eds. James Childress and John Macquarrie (Rev. ed., Philadelphia: Westminster Press, 1986), 57-61; "New Testament Ethics," in *New Dictionary of Christian Ethics & Pastoral Theology*, eds. David J. Atkinson and David H. Field (Downers Grove: InterVarsity Press, 1995), 56-64.

[3] Verhey, *Living the Heidelberg: The Heidelberg Catechism and the Moral Life* (Grand Rapids: Christian Reformed Board of Publications, 1985), 124.

[4] Verhey, "The Doctor's Oath -- and a Christian Swearing It," in *On Moral Medicine: Theological Perspectives in Medical Ethics*, eds. Stephen E. Lammers and Allen Verhey (Grand Rapids; Eerdmans, 1987), 72-82.

[5] Verhey, *Living the Heidelberg*, 124.

[6] Verhey, "Test-tube babies," in *The Reformed Journal* 28 (Sept. 1978), 13; Verhey, "Again--*in vitro* Fertilization," in *The Reformed Journal* 29 (June 1979), 4; Verhey, "The Test-Tube Baby Boom: Technology and Parenting," in *The Banner*, 14 Nov. 1983, 9.

[7] Verhey, "The Morality of Genetic Engineering," in *Christian Scholar's Review* 14:2 (1985), 132; Verhey, "Genetic Control--On Celebration and Caution," in *The Banner*, 24 March 1986, 12-14.

[8] Verhey, "Medical Technology and Care: The Weakness of Power and the Power of Weakness," in *Reformed Review* 41:3 (Spring 1988), 189-199.

[9] Verhey, "Sanctity and Scarcity: The Makings of Tragedy," in *The Reformed Journal* 35 (Feb. 1985), 10-11.

Rauschenbusch. Through his study of Rauschenbusch, for his dissertation and otherwise, Verhey has learned to be attentive to the social emphases of the gospel. This is evident, for example, in his book entitled *Living the Heidelberg*. Furthermore, Verhey's own thinking with regard to Scripture has developed in dialogue with and to some extent under influence of Rauschenbusch.

Though the connections with H. Richard Niebuhr do not seem as explicit with Verhey as in the case of Gustafson and Ramsey, it would be mistaken to discount any relationship. In dealing with the questions which are appropriate to bring to Scripture, Verhey also points to the relevance of attention to the particulars of moral agency, as Niebuhr and others have done.[10] Verhey shares with Niebuhr an attention to the community where in dialogue with Scripture important grounds for moral action are found. In his treatment of the Heidelberg Catechism, Verhey gives some prominence to the term "radical monotheism," adopted from Niebuhr, as the consistent and thorough-going adherence to the one God, revealed in the Lord and Savior, Jesus Christ.[11] Finally, the language of ethics as "response" unites the two. Niebuhr's influence is undoubtedly refracted through students of Niebuhr, including Gustafson and Ramsey. Besides, some of the emphases which Niebuhr and Verhey have in common might have developed independently through the heritage of liberalism, the Social Gospel, and neo-orthodoxy.

The structure of this chapter largely parallels that of the previous chapters, discussing the place of Scripture as the ground for ethics and then the application of ethics in the thought of Verhey. Like Ramsey, Allen Verhey is committed to the Scriptures as the theological ground for Christian ethics. Yet, also Verhey explicitly qualifies this authority *hermeneutically*.

4.2. Hermeneutical Qualifications to the Authority of Scripture

The role of the Bible within Christian moral discernment and discourse is a given for Verhey. Tradition is responsible for the implementation of the Bible in ethics.[12] The Christian community has bequeathed to the believers of today the custom of turning to the Bible for answers to moral questions. The church turns to other sources alongside of the Bible, such as its wider theological tradition, as well as academic disciplines such as sociology and psychology. The Bible is then in the first instance, a source.[13] But it has also received the designation "canon" to indicate its character as standard. For both Catholics and Protestants, Scripture functions as a standard. The point of difference between the two traditions concerns the way in which Scripture authorizes. It is at the level of authorization, that is, how to move from Scripture to practice and how

[10] Verhey, *The Great Reversal*, 163.
[11] Verhey, *Living the Heidelberg* 15-20. Cf. esp. 19.
[12] Verhey, "The Use of Scripture in Moral Discourse," 3.
[13] Verhey, "The Use of Scripture in Moral Discourse," 4.

to imbue a certain course of action with authority, that Verhey's discussion takes place. Once Verhey has posited this, his real focus is on authorization, which qualifies the authority of Scripture in the process of application.

One should note that the authority of Scripture is set forth with a reference to the church and its tradition. Verhey acknowledges the status and function of Scripture by virtue of the prominence it receives in the church. In his dissertation, the primary reference to the church seems to be related to the use of a social scientific method.[14] Attention to the Bible is permitted by virtue of its use within the social institution of the church. But in his *The Great Reversal*, Verhey chooses the same startingpoint. One could compare the opening sentence: "By tradition and vocation Christian churches are communities of moral discourse and discernment."[15] In the process of discourse and discernment, the church has turned to among other things the New Testament. The term "vocation" supplements the weight of tradition, linking the practice of loyalty to God to the present.[16] This vantage-point yields to the church the primary ground within which the Scriptures manifest a certain function and role. The role of the Bible is thus presupposed by a reference to the context within which it has functioned and continues to function.

Since Verhey's focus is on the process of authorization, most of his discussion is devoted to qualifying the manner in which certain ethical decisions receive authority within the Christian community. Yet, authorization and authority are inseparable. Qualifications to authorization entail qualifications to authority. This will become clear in the course of the discussion of these qualifications, which could be gathered under the denominator "hermeneutical."

4.2.1. Levels of Authority

Verhey is concerned to interpret not only Scriptural moral teachings but also to consider the level of ethical authority that should be attributed to Scripture. Verhey has found in the writings of theorists Stephen Toulmin and Henry Aiken material to delineate the process of authorization, respectively in logic and moral discourse.[17] Toulmin sketches out the path of moral argument: A *claim* is made, founded upon certain *data*. It is possible that the inference from the data to the claim is challenged, in which case a *warrant*, an inference-license, is needed in order to sustain the logic. One must distinguish between kinds of warrants, for some function to establish the inference without

[14] Verhey, "The Use of Scripture in Moral Discourse," 3-4.

[15] Verhey, *The Great Reversal*, 1.

[16] Verhey, *The Great Reversal*, 2.

[17] Verhey, "The Use of Scripture in Moral Discourse," 13-18. Cf. Verhey, *The Great Reversal*, 156 note 9, 158 note 19. Verhey depends on Stephen Toulmin, *The Uses of Argument* (Cambridge: Cambridge University Press, 1958), particularly Chapter III, "The Layout of Arguments," 94-145 and Henry David Aiken, "Levels of Moral Discourse," *Reason and Conduct* (New York: Alfred A. Knopf, 1962), 65-87.

exception, others only provisionally. *Qualifiers* and *conditions of rebuttal* indicate the relative validity of the warrants. When warrants themselves are challenged, *backing* serves to uphold the warrants. One further distinction inherent in the above delineation is between *warrant-using* and *warrant-establishing* arguments. The former infers from data to claim *by means of* a warrant The latter describes the move from backing *to* warrant.

Henry D. Aiken's contribution is seen by Verhey in his delineation of the four levels of moral discourse: expressive, moral, ethical, and post-ethical.[18] The *expressive* level is the level at which sentiments or emotions are expressed, negative or positive. The *moral* level involves choices of conduct which need justification, either with factual data or moral regulations. The *ethical* level is enacted often upon conflict of rules, which leads to the questioning and re-evaluation of the moral regulations themselves. The post-ethical level surfaces the question of the need for and advantage of morality.

Verhey's chief use of Toulmin's categories of informal logic and Aiken's categories of moral discourse is to delineate the variety of authorization processes and to qualify the level at which Scripture functions. To complement these delineations concerning moral thought and language, Verhey distinguishes four questions concerning Scripture: 1) What is Scripture? 2) What questions are appropriate of Scripture? 3) What is the meaning of Scripture? 4) How does Scripture relate to other sources for morality?[19] Verhey's answers to these various questions will arise at various places in the subsequent discussion, but for now it is important simply to note that Verhey raises these questions on the basis of the delineations advocated by Toulmin and Aiken.

The function of these distinctions for Verhey is to determine that Scripture does not speaks with authority at every level of moral inquiry. Aiken's post-ethical question, "Why be moral?" is deemed appropriate to Scripture, as is Aiken's ethical level, where the question is, "What general principles are normative?" At the moral level, where concrete issues of conduct arise, Scripture does not speak with authority. Verhey states that "direct appeals to Scripture are not authorized with respect to questions and claims about what concretely we ought to do or to leave undone." To be sure, "we must ask what we ought to do, and we must answer that question in the light of the way the New Testament has formed and informed our moral identity and shaped and reformed our perspective, dispositions, intentions, and principles." However, we may not "simply lift a moral rule out of the New Testament as a moral rule for the contemporary church."[20] At the moral level, Scripture cannot be brought to bear in a direct way, but only "in ways mediated by its response to inquiries

---

[18] Verhey, "The Use of Scripture in Moral Discourse," 17-18. He refers to Henry David Aiken, "Levels of Moral Discourse," *Reason and Conduct* (New York: Alfred A. Knopf, 1962), 65-87.

[19] Verhey, "The Use of Scripture in Moral Discourse," 18-21.

[20] Verhey, "A Response to Douglas Schuurman," in *Calvin Theological Journal* 23:2 (November 1988), 234-235.

concerning our moral identity, our fundamental loyalty and perspective, and the dispositions and intentions which adhere in that identity."[21]

Verhey's tendency regarding method will be clear. From the side of moral discourse as well as from the side of Scripture, qualifications must be made. These questions arise out of the understanding of subject and object relationship, particularly as it concerns authoritative texts. Verhey mentions his indebtedness to Bultmann on this matter. Bultmann's emphasis on pre-understanding, which he gained from the epistemology of the existentialist school, argues that a presuppositionless approach to the text is impossible, and that presuppositions unavoidably condition the understanding of the text.[22] Bultmann himself asks the existential question of the text, and in this he is not followed by Verhey; nevertheless, his more general emphasis on presuppositions has found a strong following within biblical scholarship, including Verhey.

4.2.2. A Chalcedonian Hermeneutic

In response to the question, "What are these writings?," Verhey answers that the Bible is both Word of God and human words.[23] Verhey's view emerges from a correspondence with and indebtedness to Walter Rauschenbusch. For Rauschenbusch, the Bible derives its authority from its divine character.[24] Scripture is not the only item of revelation, for general revelation marks the starting-point for the development of religion and morality. But beyond general revelation, God is revealed by a special historical process, in two ways.[25] First, there is the combination of event and experience. God acts and a certain experience is evoked. This is an instance of primary revelation. Second, there is the accumulation of such instances into what becomes the Bible, secondary revelation. As secondary revelation it is meant to aid primary revelation: it is "helpful to the re-experiencing of actual revelation."[26] For interpretation it is

---

[21] Verhey, *The Great Reversal*, 59. This line of thinking is adopted in Verhey, with the Fellows of the Calvin Center for Christian Scholarship, *Christian Faith, Health, & Medical Practice* (Grand Rapids: Eerdmans, 1989), 19, Note 5.

[22] Cf. particularly Rudolf Bultmann, "Is Exegesis Without Presuppositions Possible?" in Schubert Ogden, ed., *Existence and Faith: Shorter Writings of Rudolf Bultmann* (New York: Meridian Books, 1960), 289-296. Verhey's acknowledgment of indebtedness to Bultmann appears in Verhey, "The Use of Scripture in Moral Discourse," 26, note 41; cf. Verhey, *The Great Reversal*, 160.

[23] Verhey, "Notes on a Controversy about the Bible," in *The Reformed Journal* 27 (May, 1977), 10. Cf. Verhey, "Bible in Christian Ethics," 58. Cf. Verhey, *The Great Reversal*, 177. Cf. Verhey, *The Practices of Piety and the Practice of Medicine: Prayer, Scripture, and Medical Ethics* [The Stob Lectures of Calvin College and Calvin Seminary] (Grand Rapids: Calvin College and Seminary, 1991), 34, 41.

[24] Verhey, "The Use of Scripture in Moral Discourse," 137.

[25] Verhey, "The Use of Scripture in Moral Discourse," 138.

[26] Verhey, "The Use of Scripture in Moral Discourse," 141.

important to realize that the Scriptures emerged as the product of primary revelations. This understanding legitimates the application of the so-called "development warrant," the "law of growth," whereby an individual's writing is the product of a community which is in development. The Scriptures are thus a human product and as such diverse and limited. But they are at the same time laden with potential, a part of the development which lends unity to revelation, undergirded as the process is by the Spirit of God.[27]

According to Verhey, liberalism's typical error has been to separate the divine and the human, while fundamentalism's typical error has been conflate the divine and the human in the Bible. Taking his cue from the Council of Chalcedon (A.D. 451) with respect to the two natures of Christ,[28] Verhey insists on applying this "Chalcedonian perspective" to Scripture.[29] The conjunction of divine and human in Scripture must be made without confusing or separating the two. The pertinence of these observations for ethics is that a simple equation of Christian ethics with biblical ethics is not appropriate, nor is the ignorance of the Bible or arbitrary selectivity within the Bible fitting.[30] Instead, a careful process of authorization which acknowledges the human and divine character of Scripture should mark the movement from the Bible to moral practice.

The character of a Chalcedonian hermeneutic emerges practically in a discussion of authorial intention. Verhey cites the examples of the *Haustafeln* and Matthew's teaching on divorce in this connection. The biblical statements should not be simply repeated and invested with authority for the Christian community of the present. Concerning Matthew's teaching of divorce, Verhey uses the characterization "time-bound and context-relative."[31] He proceeds to emphasize the intention behind these moral rules and advocates the appropriation of this intention. Verhey makes the parallel with reasoning as it takes place in the legal and moral disciplines, where statements must be made that cohere with the intention of a law or a principle. Verhey acknowledges the immense difficulty of discerning intention, but affirms its necessity.

Various questions arise at this point. Is Verhey implying that "the intention" is the divine aspect of the Scripture, since it transcends the time-bound expression? Why does he then speak of "Matthew's intention"? Or would he be unwilling to pin-point anything as divine since the human and the divine cannot be separated? If so, has not the recognition of something as "time-bound" already yielded a bifurcation in what should be indissolubly united? One wonders whether the Chalcedonian explication of the nature of the Scripture functions as a means to circumvent some aspect of biblical moral teaching. But

---

27 Verhey, "The Use of Scripture in Moral Discourse," 142-143.

28 Verhey, "Notes on a Controversy about the Bible," 10.

29 He makes use here of Wolfgang Schweitzer in his report to the World Council of Churches' Symposium on "the Biblical Authority for the Churches' Social and Political Message Today," Verhey, *The Great Reversal*, 156, 169-171.

30 Verhey, *The Great Reversal*, 181.

31 Verhey, *The Great Reversal*, 172-173.

this the Chalcedonian expression itself disavows, for it wishes neither "to merely repeat nor to flippantly disown" the words of Scripture. Another question is whether it is possible to simply repeat the words of Scripture. And how do persons know that they have not disowned the words of Scripture through relinquishing all but its intention? What criteria does one employ to discern what is "time-bound"? These are some questions in connection with Verhey's use of the Chalcedonian hermeneutic.

4.2.3. A Critical Hermeneutic

It is not an uncommon lament that few ethicists show that they have been well-trained as exegetes. With the fragmentation and specialization of the theological discipline, additional exertion must be made to stay abreast of the literature and developments in both ethics and exegesis. Verhey's *The Great Reversal* has not shunned the exegetical task, but managed it in an admirable way.[32] This suggests that Verhey is serious in his affirmation of the importance of examining the Scriptures. Despite what one might expect on the basis the qualifications to the authority of Scripture reviewed thus far, Verhey does not dispense with careful exegesis.

To ignore the implications of his method in exegesis, however, would entail disregarding some assumptions which have important consequences for the conclusions concerning biblical ethics. These methodological assumptions make some qualifications to the authority of Scripture and produce conclusions which in turn strengthen other qualifications to the authority of Scripture.

The first assumption Verhey makes, and concerning which he is explicit, is that the descriptive exegetical task is to examine the ethics of the New Testament developmentally, or in his own words, "as part of a developing tradition."[33] In this vein, there is, first of all, a quest for the origin or impulse of this moral tradition. Secondly, there is attention to the diversity which develops from this source. Thirdly, there is a focus on the background and matrix for the traditions. For instance, the ethic of Jesus is described in contrast to apocalyptic and rabbinical thought.

Related to the developmental project, is the second assumption, namely, that through form-critical, source-critical, and redaction-critical investigation, one can ascertain material which belong to the earliest strata of the Christian tradition. Though some avenues of "historical Jesus research" enable some reconstruction of Jesus's teaching, the New Testament is primarily categorized as a collection of documents of the early church.[34]

---

[32] Verhey is aware that this book seeks to combine both disciplines. He writes concerning the project: "Its greatest ambition is to bridge the gulfs that sometimes separate these disciplines [New Testament studies and Christian ethics] from each other and from the life of the Christian community," Verhey, *The Great Reversal*, 5.

[33] Verhey, *The Great Reversal*, 4.

[34] Verhey, *The Great Reversal*, 9.

The embrace of the historical method is not without implications. Verhey himself expresses ambivalence concerning its value:

> The historical method, profane though it is, is the only tool the historian has. With its more or less debatable conclusions, it is no substitute for faith; and neither is faith a substitute for it. Nevertheless, the rise of faith in this Jesus as the Christ, the beginning and continuation of a community which calls him Lord, is an historical datum with which any historical reconstruction of Jesus' life and moral teachings must cohere.[35]

The significance of this final sentence is somewhat obscure. For if the rise of the church's faith is an acceptable historical datum, then it would seem that its coherence with any historical reconstruction of Jesus could be plausible. The difficulty therefore seems to lie not first of all in the historical coordination of Jesus and the church, but the suitability of the historical method with the Scriptures as source.

Verhey's subsequent treatment of the writings, however, betrays little uneasiness over the suitability of the writings to historical inquiry. In terms of the discussion on the criteria for the veritable sayings of the historical Jesus, Verhey sees advantages in Käsemann's minimalist approach as well in Stauffer's maximalist approach, depending on whether the purpose is historical apologetic or ecclesiastical edification respectively.[36] For the purposes of his book, he employs the criterion of "multiple attestations" and the continuum from Judaism to Christianity, upon which Jesus functions as mid-point, an enterprise which Verhey associates with the work of Joachim Jeremias.[37]

It is in the midst of the discussion of Jesus' ethic that the phrase "the great reversal" (cf. the book's title) receives its significance. It denotes the transformation inaugurated in the present order. Jesus' message of the kingdom should be understood against the background of apocalyptic thought, though it does not coincide with apocalypticism. The ethic which Jesus advocates is an ethic of response to God's eschatological action, for which he is the agent. The "reversal" is this that the conventional order is radically confronted and its mores overturned.[38] A biblical term which Verhey gives some prominence in Christ's message is "repentance," which is the ethical coordinate to the action of reversal enacted by God. It involves a renunciation of "old securities" and

---

[35] Verhey, *The Great Reversal*, 11.

[36] Verhey, *The Great Reversal*, 10. Verhey refers to Ernst Käsemann's "The Problem of the Historical Jesus," in *Essays on New Testament Themes* (Naperville, Ill: A. R. Allenson, 1964), 15-47; and for Ethelbert Stauffer one could refer to *Jesus and His Story* (London: SCM; New York: Knopf, 1960).

[37] Verhey, *The Great Reversal*, 10. Verhey refers to Jeremias' *The Parables of Jesus* (Rev. Ed; New York: Scribners, 1967); *Jerusalem in the Time of Jesus* (Philadelphia: Fortress, 1969); *The Prayers of Jesus* (Philadelphia: Fortress, 1978).

[38] Verhey, *The Great Reversal*, 15-16.

"conventional values" and an openness to the reign of God and service to the neighbor.[39] This posture is evident in some of the concrete commands preserved in the tradition: "If any would be first, he must be last of all and servant of all" (Mark 9:35 and par.); "Be not anxious" (Matt. 6:25 and par.); "Sell all your possessions" (Luke 12:33 and par.); etc. But the ethic of Jesus is not the promulgation of "minimal standards" or of a political program, but "an ethic of response to the coming kingdom of God."[40]

This version of Jesus' message being that of eschatological import has been selectively constructed on the basis of particularly the synoptic tradition. Johannine material is largely passed over in this segment. Furthermore, much of the soteriological material in the gospel is disregarded, whether it be the Messianic passages or Christ's passion predictions. Instead, all the emphasis is on the eschatological. The historical method has determined some choices in the reconstruction of Jesus' ethic.

It is of course no surprise that Verhey's proposal concerning Jesus' ethic is in close proximity to what he himself suggests as an appropriate Christian ethic. For Verhey, biblical ethics provides an account of the work and will and way of the one God and evokes the creative and faithful response of those who would be God's people.[41] Naturally, Verhey looks at ethics in the light of the resurrection, a datum which confirms the eschatological import of the Christian ethic. Yet, the "original" Christian ethic, namely that of Jesus, remains determinative for Verhey and this ethic can be arrived at by means of the historical critical method.

The third point evident in Verhey's account of New Testament ethics concerns the subsequent tradition after Jesus. This part of the development of New Testament has a paradigmatic function for Christian ethics today, in three specific ways. First of all, the subsequent tradition articulated an ethic which remained consonant with Jesus' ethic. Verhey makes the point that the preservation of Jesus' ethic in collections, oral traditions, and finally the gospels, did not intend to preserve facts or teachings, but "to reorient personal and communal life toward Jesus as the Christ."[42] A selection of quotes will serve to illustrate: "Mark's ethic of watchful discipleship provided no code, but ... provided a moral posture."[43] "The ethic of Matthew is no calculating works-righteousness; it is rather a response to Jesus' announcement of the kingdom and his summons to a surpassing righteousness."[44] Luke's "inalienably religious approach to morality is content to proceed by way of narrative, to retell Jesus'

---

39 Verhey, *The Great Reversal*, 16.

40 Verhey, *The Great Reversal*, 21. Cf. Verhey, *The Great Reversal*, 21-33.

41 Verhey, "Biblical Ethics," in *From Christ to the World: Introductory Readings in Christian Ethics*, eds. Wayne G. Boulton, Thomas D. Kennedy, and Allen Verhey (Grand Rapids: Eerdmans, 1994), 17.

42 Verhey, *The Great Reversal*, 35. Cf. Verhey, *The Great Reversal*, 51, 70, 81 *et passim*.

43 Verhey, *The Great Reversal*, 80.

44 Verhey, *The Great Reversal*, 92.

story. Those who make the story their own will be shaped and formed by it."[45] Paul's ethic is summarized in the phrase "[d]iscernment as personal and historical response to what God has done, is doing, and will do in Christ."[46] The duties listed in the epistle of Hebrews are "paradigms of the response of gratitude and praise that keeping covenant requires."[47]

Connected to this fact that these ethics are fundamentally consonant with Christ's ethic of response, is the apparent reality that the many writings articulated this fundamental ethic diversely within the context of different communities. According to Verhey, tradition is all about "continuity and change." The New Testament authors "utilized their traditions that were at once faithful to the Christian tradition and creatively responding to new situations, interpreting tradition and appropriating it with new understanding and power in new situations."[48] Verhey wishes to make clear that this will sometimes be done at the expense of repeating biblical rules. For instance, Verhey states that Matthew's treatment of divorce "is neither to be repeated as a moral rule or *Halakoth* governing judgments about divorce today, nor is it simply to be disowned."[49] At this point Verhey introduces the notion of interpreting the Bible according to its intention.[50] He advocates that we discern the intention of "Matthew's time-bound and context-relative words." We must then come to "share his intention" and "apply it in ways and words bound to our time."[51] We must exchange Matthew's time-boundness for our own time-boundness but retain and share his intention. Matthew's process of ethical discernment is paradigmatic for us and his moral intention normative.

Finally, the various ethics of the New Testament are paradigmatic in the sense that they show how moral wisdom from other sources can be adapted and modified within the Christian community. Verhey cites instances in the Pauline letters, e.g., when he transforms a Stoic ethic of contentment by an emphasis on the cross and resurrection of Christ (cf. Phil 4:11-13), or the various so-called

[45] Verhey, *The Great Reversal*, 96.
[46] Verhey, *The Great Reversal*, 107.
[47] Verhey, *The Great Reversal*, 132.
[48] Verhey, *The Great Reversal*, 171.
[49] Verhey, *The Great Reversal*, 172.
[50] In a recent article, in which he draws together many of the lines of his earlier publications, Verhey accepts some criticism that has been directed to him at this point. "I would no longer (as in *The Great Reversal*, 172-174) make knowledge of the 'author's intention' necessary for interpretation." However, "I would still argue that attention to an author's actions in forming a text can make us more aware that it remains the author's text and willing to recognize the potential value to interpretation of what can be known about the author's intention. Moreover, even if we are not able to know confidently an author's subjective intention, consideration of what an author *did* in forming a text can make a modest but important contribution to interpretation and to the assessment of performance," "Scripture and Ethics: Practices, Performances, and Prescriptions," in *Christian Ethics: Problems and Prospects* [Essays in honor of James Gustafson], eds. Lisa Sowle Cahill and James F. Childress (Cleveland: The Pilgrim Press, 1996), 42, note 38.
[51] Verhey, *The Great Reversal*, 173.

Haustafeln (Col 3:18-4:1., Eph 5:21-6:9; 1 Tim 2:8-15, etc.) in which the standard emphasis on submission is modified by reciprocity and mutuality.[52] Verhey talks about the "redemptive transformation of natural morality."[53]

The matter of divorce might show the implications of Verhey's approach. In his article "Divorce and the New Testament,"[54] Verhey's argument is as follows: Verhey surveys the New Testament on divorce and concludes that each of these Bible writers was "influenced by" his "own situation and audience." But through each of them the word of God comes to us. Each of them discerned the will of God for his communities in "loyalty to the risen Lord and in commitment to the moral value entailed by that loyalty." That is also how we are to "rethink divorce cases out of that same loyalty to the risen Lord, in terms of that same regard for his invitation to live marriage on the basis of his grace, and recognizing that the powers of evil have not yet laid down their arms and admitted defeat." Today God does not give us "specific legal requirements." Instead, He calls us to exercise sexuality "in the context of a commitment to total communion, and to exercise it 'sacramentally' with the relation of Christ to his church as the model with God as the third partner." We are to protect and honor marriage, "as a part of his intention for creation." We are to protect, honor, love and cherish marriage partners, and we are always to consider divorce as "an evil." Yet, sometimes divorce is "necessary 'between the times' for the protection and honoring of marriage itself or of one of the partners in marriage." Just as killing sometimes, in a just war, is allowable with fear and trembling, "so divorce may sometimes be permissibly done accompanied by mourning and repentance."[55] Verhey's argument moves from the diversity within the New Testament to an ethic of response. The New Testament functions paradigmatically.

To summarize this section, Verhey's approach in *The Great Reversal* is critical, constructing a developmental scheme of ethics within the New Testament, from the original ethic of Jesus, along a trajectory through the early church. Primacy resides with Jesus' eschatological ethic of response, but the later tradition exemplifies the diverse yet coherent application of this ethic. His *critical* hermeneutic leads Verhey to a fundamentally *paradigmatic* hermeneutic.

4.2.4. A Resurrection Hermeneutic

It is important to see that the recognition of the diversity within Scripture raises a hermeneutical question for Verhey. The diversity within Scripture is such that one cannot speak of a unitary, monolithic ethic within the New

---

[52] Verhey, *The Great Reversal*, 110-111, 67-69

[53] Verhey, *The Great Reversal*, 71.

[54] The article appeared in two segments in *The Reformed Journal* 26 (May-June 1976), 17-19; (July-August 1976), 28-31.

[55] Verhey, "Divorce and the New Testament" II, 29-30.

Testament.[56] The diversity is the result of the human hands which composed the documents. The task to discern the convergence of the various ethics is left to the heirs of the Christian tradition.[57]

According to Verhey, the resurrection of Jesus is to function as the hermeneutical key that unlocks the significance of the New Testament for us.[58] New Testament ethics is an ethics of a common "loyalty to God who raised Jesus from the dead."[59] Verhey makes clear that we cannot rightly remember Jesus if we ignore his death. Without due recognition of Christ's death, our resurrection risks turning into triumphalism. Faith in the resurrection must be complemented by a remembrance of Christ as the "*wounded* healer," who still after the resurrection retained his wounds.[60]

The resurrection of Christ as the hermeneutical key for understanding Scripture is crucial at every point. One could refer to Christ's command in Luke 6:27-28: "Love your enemies ... bless those who curse you, pray for those who abuse you." This command does not cohere with some eternal code but rather with a story whose plot "climaxes in the resurrection of Jesus Christ."[61]

Verhey arrives at the importance of the resurrection on the basis of the weight the New Testament itself gives to it. In the New Testament, it does not merely function as one doctrine among many, or simply a claim concerning a historical fact, but is portrayed as an event which unlocks the meaning and significance of God's work in the world.[62] It inaugurates the eschatological reign of God. But it also affirms the cause of creation and providence and could therefore be called protological: it is God's fulfillment of the covenant. Furthermore, the resurrection of Christ gives a foundation to God as Sanctifier. For the resurrection of Christ has established him as Lord, and if he is Lord, then the orientation of life should be towards this resurrected one.[63]

The question might be asked how this confession qualifies the use of Scripture in moral ethics. Verhey states its effect succinctly: "If, and only if, the movement from Scripture to moral claims today is coherent with the message that God has already made his eschatological power and purpose felt in the resurrection, is the use of Scripture authorized."[64] The confession of the resurrection governs all appropriations of morality from the New Testament. To use a hierarchical image, one could speak of the hegemony of the confession of the resurrection over all moral statements in the New Testament, lending and refusing authorization depending on its coherence to the resurrection. Or to use

---

[56] Verhey, *The Great Reversal*, 73.
[57] Verhey, *The Great Reversal*, 74, 152.
[58] Verhey, *The Great Reversal*, 5, 73-74.
[59] Verhey, *The Great Reversal*, 2.
[60] Verhey, *The Practices of Piety*, 59. Cf. Verhey, "Medical Technology and Care," 189-199.
[61] Verhey, *The Great Reversal*, 54.
[62] Verhey, *The Great Reversal*, 182.
[63] Verhey, *The Great Reversal*, 183.
[64] Verhey, *The Great Reversal*, 183.

a more dynamic image, other data from the New Testament must pass through the "prism of the resurrection," which will lend unmistakable color and impression to the other indicators of morality.

It is evident how Verhey attributes to the confession of the resurrection the place of a fundamental qualifier of Christian morality. The qualifications which it yields are theological, for all other references must be theologically related to the resurrection, but also hermeneutical, for all other indicators must be accepted, rejected, and interpreted through the confession of the resurrection.

4.2.5. A Response Hermeneutic

Verhey refers to the commandments of the Decalogue as "permissions."[65] Likewise, Verhey emphatically describes the ethics of the New Testament in terms of "response" to the Gospel, and not in terms of imperatives, expressed or implied in various passages.[66] However, that is not to say that Verhey describes "the developing tradition" of the New Testament "as consistently moving away from regulations" or "adverse to the formulation of rules." Rather he claims that "the history of the moral tradition which begins with Jesus and reaches climactic and canonical expression in the New Testament ... is not adequately or accurately described as a collection of rules or as a developing code."[67] Clearly, there are sayings in that New Testament tradition "that provide for community regulation and thus must be considered 'law' in the new community,"[68] but they are "rules that are formulated and reformulated in ways that are faithful to the memory of Jesus and creatively responsive to new situations."[69] So "not ... all law is bad." But "in order to answer appropriately and sufficiently the contemporary questions of conduct," we may not "directly" appeal to "the concrete rules of Scripture, including those of the New Testament."[70]

Verhey maintains that "the early churches" did not merely "passively" receive the words and deeds of Jesus but rather "creatively shaped and modified his words and deeds to address new situations they encountered."[71] Verhey regards the fundamental ethic of Jesus to be "response to the apocalyptic action of God," who in Jesus makes felt the "great reversal" of the kingdom. Moreover, the "great reversal of the kingdom brings a transformation of values." Verhey is interested to see how the New Testament enables the Christian community to develop moral discernment.[72]

---

[65] Verhey, *Living the Heidelberg*, 101-110, 117-137; cf. esp. 101.
[66] Verhey, *The Great Reversal*, 15.
[67] Verhey, "A Response to Douglas Schuurman," 233.
[68] Verhey, *The Great Reversal*, 44.
[69] Verhey, "A Response to Douglas Schuurman," 233.
[70] Verhey, "A Response to Douglas Schuurman," 236.
[71] Verhey, *The Great Reversal*, 51.
[72] Verhey, *The Great Reversal*, 15.

So Verhey advocates a hermeneutic which requires the use of Scripture in a way coherent with its own intention. Christian moral identity should be thought of in terms of response, perspectives, dispositions, and principles, but not in terms of fixed moral rules. This is a manner consistent with the eschatological message of Christ crucified and risen, and the Biblical notion of justice. This response hermeneutic is relevant enough, that "[i]f a moral claim, even one purportedly based on Scripture, is inconsistent with justice, it should not be allowed to stand, and if an authorization for the use of Scripture warrants claims that are inconsistent with justice, it should not be allowed to stand."[73]

Verhey admits that his method does not provide a recipe for making decisions on the basis of Scripture. "It has formulated no neat and tidy Christian ethic that may be identified as *the* New Testament ethic."[74] What is required for proposing particular "authorizations for the use of Scripture in ethics" is "good argumentation," but not only "at the end of an argument as much as in the midst of life, where an experience of the authority of Scripture can make Scripture vivid and alive and can illuminate and unify the moral life in particular ways."[75]

4.2.6. A Social Hermeneutic

Verhey follows Rauschenbusch's recommendations to the Christian community to accept a particular use of Scripture for moral discourse.[76] Rauschenbusch understands Scripture as a response to the social question. According to him, "the message of Scripture is the spiritual concern for sound personality and righteous social relations."[77] Verhey shorthands this as the "exegetical conscience warrant."[78] According to Rauschenbusch, there are three ways of gaining knowledge concerning the social aspect of the gospel. First, there is the "'divine instinct for righteousness within us that acts as a guide'"; second, "there is 'the historical experience of mankind'"; third, "there is Jesus and his message."[79]

Verhey follows these recommendations of Rauschenbusch to the Christian community to accept this particular social use of Scripture for moral discourse. This is evident particularly in his interpretation of the Heidelberg Catechism.[80] Scripture addresses our social consciences and our social situation by always considering us "related both to God and our neighbors" and teaching

---

[73] Verhey, *The Great Reversal*, 193.
[74] Verhey, *The Great Reversal*, 196.
[75] Verhey, *The Great Reversal*, 158.
[76] Verhey, "The Use of Scripture in Moral Discourse," 9-10.
[77] Verhey, "The Use of Scripture in Moral Discourse," 36-37.
[78] Verhey, "The Use of Scripture in Moral Discourse," 46. Verhey's reason for this shorthand is: 1) "Exegetical conscience" "is Rauschenbusch's own shorthand for the social interest"; 2) the "'pre-understanding' out of which the social question is addressed to scripture is itself authentic understanding and capable of discriminating the will of God," 61, Note 19.
[79] Verhey, "The Use of Scripture in Moral Discourse," 51-52.
[80] Verhey, *Living the Heidelberg*.

us to "see our neighbors as persons related to both God and ourselves."[81] Verhey's discussion on the union with Christ as it is raised in the Catechism (Questions and Answers 32, 43, 45, 53, 54, 55, 61, 64) might serve to illustrate this.[82] He concentrates on the moral significance of our participation in Christ. Being in Christ is "the foundation of a substantial ... social posture." Using some of the phrases of Question and Answer 89, Verhey states that "[s]haring in Christ's death is 'to be genuinely sorry for [racism], to hate [exploitation] more and more, and to run away from [injustice].'" To participate in Christ is "to 'delight to do every kind of good [including social, political, and economic good] as God wants us to.'" To be sure, "the way of righteousness ... is not merely social righteousness, but it surely includes social righteousness."[83]

Likewise, with reference to being a living member of the church of Christ, Verhey focuses on the social implications. Being a living member of the church makes us "uneasy about the remnants of social and ethnic homogeneity in our denomination" and rather welcome, be one with, serve and enrich "those quite unlike us ... the black, the poor, the hungry, the women among us."[84]

With regard to the sacraments and the exercise of discipline in church, Verhey traces the same sort of implications. When we biblically understand baptism "as baptism into Christ," then we realize that it "speaks to us about our day-to-day affairs, about the way we treat our wives or husbands, children and/or parents, employers or employees, and all the other people with whom we live ...."[85] He quotes Gustavo Guttierrez and the apostle Paul with regard to the Lord's Supper and states that when we celebrate the Lord's Supper "without communion, without fellowship, without seeking justice or correcting oppression, without defending the poor or pleading for the powerless," we "partake in an 'unworthy manner.'" Similarly, with reference to church discipline, he insists that the "scope of church discipline is social and political because our participation in Christ is social and political."[86] Mutual "admonition" concerns not only "marital and family problems" but also "business policies, mortgage policies, political life, and race relations."[87]

---

[81] Verhey, *Living the Heidelberg*, 7. Cf. the Heidelberg Catechism's "interest in the social morality of the sixteenth century" for instance in "Q 110 with its reference to merchandising, counterfeiting, and usury."

[82] Verhey, *Living the Heidelberg*, Chapter 7, entitled "membership in Christ," Questions and Answers 32-90 of the Heidelberg Catechism. According to Verhey, the Heidelberg Catechism in its emphasis on union with Christ follows Paul and Calvin, who do not "treat our union with Christ as 'mystical union,'" in the sense of "participation in Christ's being" but rather "as an active union," in the sense of "participation in Christ's work ... our conformity to his righteousness," Verhey, *Living the Heidelberg*, 84.

[83] Verhey, *Living the Heidelberg*, 86.

[84] Verhey, *Living the Heidelberg*, 89.

[85] Verhey, *Living the Heidelberg*, 91.

[86] Verhey, *Living the Heidelberg*, 92.

[87] Verhey, *Living the Heidelberg*, 93.

Verhey's implementation of the "Exegetical Conscience Warrant" is clearly evident in his discussion of the Decalogue. With reference to the first commandment, he refers to the realism of the "conflict between God and the gods." That conflict has to do "with such mundane and 'secular' things as farming and fertility, international politics and defense, justice for the poor and powerless, and community for different races."[88]

In the second commandment God announces that He will not permit us to use Him "for our success in battle or in business, in politics or in sex. He is the Lord, and his lordship includes our battles and our business, our politics and our sex."[89] Likewise with reference to the fourth commandment, Verhey points out the social implications. Our "permission to celebrate the Lord's day is at the same time our permission to side with the poor, to seek their rest and well-being to prevent them from being exploited and used."[90]

When Verhey turns to the second table of the law, to "what we owe our neighbor,"[91] the same concern is evident. When dealing with the eighth commandment, Verhey concentrates on some social implications of this commandment. "God's grace permits and enables us to live the new life--also economically." He forbids "greed because he permits us to live in his grace and for his glory also in the economic dimensions of our life."[92] God's righteousness "frees us from greed, from the assumptions that 'more is better,' that 'more will provide security and happiness.'"[93] The "social implications of loving our neighbor in the economy" are with regard to 1) employment, that we try "to secure a job for everyone who is able to hold a job and seeking employment"; 2) housing, that we strive "for decent housing for all"; 3) health care, that we work toward "adequate health care for all."[94] Similar lines could be drawn on the basis of the Lord's Prayer, but the above should suffice to illustrate. The social hermeneutic seeks to foreground the social element in the biblical presentation of Christ's ministry, the ethics of permission on the basis of the Decalogue, and other data emerging from Scripture.

4.2.7. Dialogue with Other Sources

Verhey considers the question as to the relevance of other sources. According to him, at "the level of moral rules, where the question is, what should I do?, the answer is ordinarily arrived at by an analysis of the facts and by application of the community's rules." At this level "both the natural sciences and the human sciences ... play an important and often critical role." It

[88] Verhey, *Living the Heidelberg*, 103.
[89] Verhey, *Living the Heidelberg*, 106.
[90] Verhey, *Living the Heidelberg*, 110.
[91] Verhey, *Living the Heidelberg*, 118.
[92] Verhey, *Living the Heidelberg*, 132.
[93] Verhey, *Living the Heidelberg*, 133.
[94] Verhey, *Living the Heidelberg*, 134.

"may be appropriate to argue that some models of scientific analysis are more coherent than others for a perspective on persons and their societies formed and informed by the New Testament." The various scientific models may well be "weighed against the Christian vision." In this way the New Testament "can provide the last word about whether and how a particular scientific model can be used with Christian integrity as well as scientific integrity. Changes in the model or in the analysis, however, must be argued on scientific grounds, not on biblical grounds."[95]

At the same time Verhey points out that the various rules of any particular community "are not unchallengeable. To challenge" them, however, "is to enter the ethical-principle level." It is at this level that "the New Testament provides the critical source within the Christian community for evaluation, criticism, and change of the rules, but other sources are relevant too."[96] As "Christian moralists and communities," we "must be constantly open to the ... other 'authorities,'" that is, "to the analysis, criticism, and reformation that might come from the community, the tradition, new experience, and the reason as well as scripture itself."[97] They "must not reject natural morality nor allow it the 'last word.'"[98]

Paul also used the "natural" moral wisdom of the pagans, although Verhey admits that it was not normative to him.[99] Nevertheless, "the new discernment" that Paul writes about in Romans 12 does not "abandon the rule and moral wisdom it finds around it." Rather love's discernment "makes use of other sources, especially the teachings of Jesus, the Church's catechetical tradition, the Jewish law, and 'natural' moral standards."[100] As far as James' sources for the paraenesis are concerned, there are "echoes ... of instructions and metaphors in Jesus' sayings, Hellenistic Judaism, and Stoicism." What James does is "simply" utilize "traditional paraenesis ... for the sake of moral persuasiveness, not for the sake of providing specifically Christian admonitions or motives." James' morality is "commonplace," although he "gives it an eschatological urgency and stringency."[101] II Peter clearly makes use of "key virtues in Greek morality for centuries" to describe the Christian life, although "Peter certainly does not forget the basis of such a life in the gift of God." Nevertheless "the notes of progress and achievement in virtuous character are

---

[95] Verhey, *The Great Reversal*, 187-188.
[96] Verhey, *The Great Reversal*, 188.
[97] Verhey, "The Use of Scripture in Moral Discourse," 222.
[98] Verhey, "The Use of Scripture in Ethics," in *Religious Studies Review*, Jan. 1978, 35.
[99] Verhey, *The Great Reversal*, 110-111.
[100] Verhey, *The Great Reversal*, 108-109.
[101] Verhey, *The Great Reversal*, 136.

surely more Greek than Pauline."[102] Nevertheless the "last word about whether to follow a particular community's rules belongs--in principle--to Scripture."[103]

By this last statement, however, Verhey does not mean to authorize "the movement from Scripture to moral claims about rules." Rather, what he means is that Scripture enables and requires "Christians to have a loyalty and identity, perspective, dispositions, intentions, and principles that govern their character and conduct. They must act in ways that have integrity with their story, that are truthful to the affirmation that God raised Jesus from the dead."[104]

Verhey argues that the New Testament does not necessarily disown "as sources of moral wisdom" those other sources such as the "moral identities that are inherited along with memberships in other communities." Rather, Christians are to bring them "under the critical and reconstructible lordship of Jesus Christ." Christians are to "develop a relationship toward them appropriate to their relationship to God the sanctified and to the Jesus whom he raised."[105] Under the lordship of Jesus Christ, "injustice has no place," and we are called to "face and meet the exacting and discomforting challenges of social righteousness."[106]

Verhey also considers the question of the relationship of moral philosophy as a relevant source to Scripture, which he acknowledges to be "a complex enterprise." He centers in on moral philosophy's concern to define, defend, and apply certain fundamental principles, which "functions as an important source at the ethical-principle-level and ... as a partner-in-dialogue with Scripture concerning what rules ought to be obeyed and why." He makes a couple of general observations. First, according to Verhey, "neo-orthodoxy's 'theological veto' on natural morality and moral philosophy" is a position which is "an inappropriate response not only to humans but to their creator and sustainer, the very God who raised Jesus from the dead and is their sanctified." It is also an inappropriate response to "the New Testament itself, where the natural morality and the ethical theory of the first century were clearly not summarily dismissed."[107]

A good example of this is the Christian adoption of the Hippocratic Oath from the Pythagoreans. According to Verhey in an article on the physician's oath, the oath is "an example of the moral significance of a natural piety ... of

---

[102] Verhey, *The Great Reversal*, 141.

[103] Verhey, *The Great Reversal*, 141. Cf. Verhey, with the Fellows of the Calvin Center for Christian Scholarship [Hessel Bouma III, Douglas Diekema, Edward Langerak, Theodore Rottman], *Christian Faith, Health, & Medical Practice*, 19, Note 5.

[104] Verhey, *The Great Reversal*, 188.

[105] Verhey, *The Great Reversal*, 189.

[106] Verhey, *Living the Heidelberg*, 13. Verhey refers to the Holy Spirit as the One through Whom we "'share in Christ and all his blessings.'" What the Spirit brings into our lives is "nothing other than the reality of Jesus Christ and his lordship ...," Verhey, *Living the Heidelberg*, 87

[107] Verhey, *The Great Reversal*, 191.

what Calvin would call a *sensus divinitatis*."[108] The physicians acknowledged "a sense of responsibility to the inscrutable power who stands behind the gifts and the order and who judges the fault."[109] The fact that Christianity adopted this oath and adapted it demonstrates that Christian ethics "selects and assimilates the 'natural' moral wisdom around it in terms of its own truthfulness and in terms of its integrity with the Christian vision."

Verhey summarizes his own position on the relationship of Christian ethics to moral philosophy eloquently:

> The one who bears toward us the relationship of sanctifier in Scripture is the very one who created the world and preserves it, restraining the effects of sin on the meaning and value he built into the world by his law. That law is knowable apart from Scripture, confirmed and critically reconstructed by Scripture, but also capable of providing a minimal but critical standard for testing claims based on Scripture and authorizations for the use of Scripture. Natural morality and the normative ethics that articulate it and defend it are valued partners-in-dialogue with Scripture at this level. Such a dialogue will be a complex undertaking: on the one hand, it will protect the independence and autonomy of moral philosophy and its project of articulating and defending principles that hold on the basis of reason alone, independent of the character, identity, and roles of persons; on the other hand, it will be committed to the critical reconstruction of those principles in view of the cosmic sovereignty of the Creator and Preserver who raised Jesus from the dead and who bears toward us in Scripture the relationship of the sanctifier.[110]

4.2.8. Conclusion

Each of the above observations encapsulates a qualification to the authority of Scripture in the process of authorization which takes place in moral discourse. Whether it be the theological observation that Scripture has both a divine and a human character to it or the epistomological decision to foreground the social character of morality, the focus on authorization has served to substantially qualify the authority of Scripture. There are sources external to Scripture which are drawn into dialogue with Scripture; there is the element of the resurrection which is raised to a hegemonic level; there is the posture of response which properly fits the New Testament depiction of ethics better than that of proposition. All in all, as much authority as one might invest in the Scriptures, the process of authorization presupposed in the above qualifications

---

108 Verhey, "The Doctor's Oath--and a Christian Swearing it," in *On Moral Medicine: Theological Perspectives in Medical Ethics*, eds. Stephen Lammers and Allen D. Verhey (Grand Rapids: Eerdmans, 1986), 77-78.

109 Verhey, "The Doctor's Oath--and a Christian Swearing it," 78.

110 Verhey, *The Great Reversal*, 193-194.

consigns at least a segment of the authority to the process, often termed dialogue, in which Scripture is hermeneutically engaged and put into relation to the moral matter.

The crucial step in Verhey's proposal is the concentration on authorization as opposed to authority. Authorization looks to the process of infusing authority into a particular course of action. Since authority resides in the process, the ingredients of this process must share authority among them, and the particular interaction of these ingredients will determine the resolved course of action. One wonders to what extent it is not a shift of authority which has taken place, but a lacuna of authority which has developed. Only an examination of Verhey's further proposal and the practice of this proposal which will be able to test this.

4.3. Reading Scripture Hermeneutically in the Christian Community

The above section has examined one side of Verhey's proposal concerning the relationship of Scripture to ethics, namely, his qualifications to the use of Scripture. This section seeks to address another side, namely, his proposal for the actual implementation of Scripture. The demarcation between the two sides is somewhat arbitrary and artificial, since each qualification has both a negative and positive side. The division, however, seeks to illumine the nature of the qualifications as a sort of "prolegomena" to the actual constructive proposal. The qualifications do not prohibit, but permit, further elaboration and positive construction. This implementation of the Scriptures has as a common theme the context of the Christian community.

4.3.1. Moral Discourse in Community

Verhey underlines the role of the Christian Church as a community of moral discourse and discernment. As members of the church we are living in this "unique community of moral discourse by our radical loyalty to the God who raised Jesus from the dead." At the same time we "live in other communities with values and loyalties: professional societies, labor unions, suburbs, political associations, the country." But all our other values and loyalties must be subjected to the lordship of Jesus Christ.[111] The "authority of scripture calls us again and again to listen reverently to the whole canon in the midst of the whole believing community."[112] We learn and test discernment "in the community gathered around the scripture." It "involves the diversity of gifts present in the congregation."[113] Moral discourse "can and should" take such

[111] Verhey, *Living the Heidelberg*, 95.

[112] Verhey, "Bible in Christian Ethics," 61.

[113] Verhey, *The Practices of Piety*, 49.

forms as dialogue after the sermon, "study groups, task forces"—all within the framework "of our active union with Christ"—and invite "the contributions and gifts of economists and laborers, of moralists and mothers, of employers and managers."[114] All "are gifted with their own experience, and each is gifted with the Spirit that brings to remembrance (John 14:26)," although it is not a perfect situation here yet, for there is spiritual blindness and corruption.[115]

The diversity which exists within the body of Christ is reason for dialogue. Precisely in this dialogue, the Spirit exercises guidance for the community. The church gathers around the Word and knows itself in subjection to the Lord of the church, in whose resurrection lies the source of its existence and loyalty.

Here Verhey is elaborating upon the moral dimension of ecclesiology. The moral dimension is not its sole dimension, for the Church is also a liturgical, pastoral, and pedagogical community.[116] But at least one aspect of the life of the Christian community is to "guide men's lives and to have their lives guided, to teach and to learn holiness."[117] Verhey expresses his indebtedness to James M. Gustafson for this emphasis on the Christian community.[118]

It is important to note that Verhey's constructive work begins here. This is true in the presentation.[119] But this is true also methodologically. As noted above, the references to the Bible only continue to hold within the context of the Christian community. That is a matter of tradition, but also of vocation. The church has traditionally been a gathering for moral discourse. The church is continually called to exercise its loyalty to Christ in this way.

What is the relationship between the tradition of moral discourse and the vocation to moral discourse? Verhey sees the two interacting in a circular fashion: there is loyalty to tradition and the call for loyalty arises from tradition. The corollary is true as well: tradition is born out of and continues because of a sense of loyalty.[120]

It is not unimportant that the prominence of the Christian community is pointed up in a dissertation in which the Social Gospel and Rauschenbusch's views on the function of Scripture are at the center of attention. For the Social Gospel, the collective nature of the Christian faith was of paramount importance, which included the social dimension of the interpretation of Scripture. This will be discussed at greater length in what follows on the matter of the "exegetical conscience warrant"; it is sufficient to note here that the

---

114 Verhey, *Living the Heidelberg*, 96, 134.

115 Verhey, *The Practices of Piety*, 49. Cf. Verhey, with the Fellows of the Calvin Center for Christian Scholarship, *Christian Faith, Health, & Medical Practice*, 25-26, 67-68.

116 Verhey, *Living the Heidelberg*, 93-94.

117 Verhey, "The Use of Scripture in Moral Discourse," 1-2.

118 Verhey, "The Use of Scripture in Moral Discourse," 22, note 2. He refers to Gustafson's *The Church as Moral Decision-Maker* (Philadelphia: Pilgrim Press, 1970).

119 Cf. Verhey, "The Use of Scripture in Moral Discourse," 1; Verhey, *The Great Reversal*, 1; Verhey, *Living the Heidelberg*, 93-97.

120 Verhey, "The Use of Scripture in Moral Discourse," 3.

legacy of the collective character of American ethics has reached Verhey refracted through the Social Gospel movement. For Verhey, the collective character has become the primary emphasis and framework within which Scripture and its interpretation receive their place.

4.3.2. Scripture's Authority Experienced in Community

Besides the datum of the community, Verhey raises the datum of experience to a level of prominence in his discussion on the function of Scripture in moral discourse. Verhey has opted to deal with the matter of authorization rather than authority. Authorization involves the experience of authority.[121] For Rauschenbusch, this experience was the encounter with the social ills in urban America. The experience of the authority of Scripture is the final claim in the authorization of Scripture. Past all the logic of warrants and backings (Toulmin's categories) is the experience itself, "the limit of arguments," in Verhey's words. Any argument which might be made beyond this, is what Verhey terms "self-authenticating": it asserts itself and establishes itself by reference to itself. Basically, it pragmatically seeks to reproduce itself in the experience of others.[122]

It is important that Verhey determines experience to be the final court of appeal in authorization. His focus on authorization has led him to consign authority to the "experience of authority." The use the term experience here is, in the first instance, philosophically determined. The categories of Toulmin, as applied to the moral argumentation of Rauschenbusch, have led Verhey to attribute prime authority to the experience of authority. This reference to "experience" also suits to the hermeneutical theory of existentialists like Bultmann, to whom Verhey earlier referred on the matter of inherent subjectivity in interpretation.[123] As a philosophical category, experience has the sense here of those cognitions subjectively obtained by perception and encounter with alterity. As in the case of the Christian community as social organism above,[124] these experiences can be discussed by the social scientific method. Their causal connection to Scriptural interpretation can be traced and maintained and attributed significance. As a philosophical category, it belongs to the rational character of American ethics, introduced in the Enlightenment, and in theology through liberalism. It is employed by Verhey as the basis of Scriptural interpretation. Though Verhey prefers the language of dialogue between Scripture, experience, reason, and other sources, ultimately experience is the ground and determinant of one's use of Scripture in the moral discussion.

121 Verhey, "The Use of Scripture in Moral Discourse," 222. Verhey states: "The experience of the authority of scripture in the context of one's own moral life and struggles is vitally important to the authorizations for the use of scripture."
122 Verhey, "The Use of Scripture in Moral Discourse," 222.
123 Verhey, "The Use of Scripture in Moral Discourse," 26, note 41.
124 Cf. sub 4.2. "Hermeneutical Qualifications to the Authority of Scripture."

This is established by the assertion that the "experience of the authority of scripture in the interpreter's moral life establishes the limit of arguments where the claims are authorizations for moving from scripture to moral claims."[125]

In light of these observations on the role and function of experience, Verhey has two recommendations: 1) That tentativeness characterize all moral claims in the acknowledgment that "moral claims on the basis of biblical data or with biblical backing" are "nevertheless the work of human minds."[126] 2) That sloth or skepticism not paralyze the moral discussion because of the realism of subjectivity. Verhey qualifies what he has said up till now:

> The important priority belongs not to experience in and of itself, not to pure subjectivity, but to the experience of the authority of scripture. The meanings that become subjective, that become, that is, internalized and vital[,] are understood as the meanings of the Bible. The Bible--along with the creeds, symbols, and liturgies--exists objectively, independently. It can exist without being understood (or believed).[127]

Verhey is not withdrawing what he has said about experience. Instead, he restricts valid experiences to those of the authority of Scripture. Nevertheless, the ground lies in the subjective. Verhey adds that the Bible exists as an objective entity. The connection of this addition to the preceding is unclear. Does this statement seek to speak in favor of realism in the sense that the Bible as a book objectively exists, as do other books? The import of that sense would not be clear. Does Verhey mean that the Bible asserts its own authority? That would seem entirely impertinent to the previous discussion which concentrated on authorizations which communities give to Scripture. And yet, it appears that Verhey wishes to affirm precisely that, independently of and alongside the bulk of the discussion. For he continues by saying that this realization "frees the scripture to address different people and different cultures. It frees the Scripture to account for, purify and intensify, and multiply a great variety of memorable, decisive, and unifying experiences, not perfectly, but confidently and faithfully." Scripture is here portrayed as an agent which functions to perform its own work. This portrait is discrete from what has been pictured throughout the dissertation in terms of authorization. And yet even this statement puts

[125] Verhey, "The Use of Scripture in Moral Discourse," 223.

[126] Verhey, "The Use of Scripture in Moral Discourse," 223.

[127] Verhey, "The Use of Scripture in Moral Discourse," 224. For Verhey's discussion of "Rauschenbusch's experience of the authority of scripture in his own moral life" as having an important priority in the formation and recommendation of his use of scripture, cf. Verhey, "The Use of Scripture in Moral Discourse," 203-213. For Verhey's discussion of Carl F. H. Henry's "experience of the authority of scripture in his own life," cf. Verhey, "The Use of Scripture in Moral Discourse," 260-261. Verhey's criticism with reference to Henry's experience of the authority of scripture in his own life, is that his "own experience of the authority of scripture governs the selection of biblical data," Verhey, "The Use of Scripture in Moral Discourse," 268.

human realization in the potential situation of achieving this effect: "For this being understood by subjects, being experienced in the context of other experiences, frees the scripture to address...." [128] Essentially, this statement is setting forth human realization as liberator of the Scriptures.

Yet, Verhey ends with the affirmation that Scripture is authoritative. Philosophically, this is perhaps a "self-involving" position, but Verhey subscribes to it. It is similar to his affirmation that the use of Scripture is not simply a tradition of the Christian church, but a vocation as well.[129] But Verhey only makes this affirmation in the context of the Christian community, which theologically provides the primary framework and the referent for the Scriptures. At the same time, the datum of experience is philosophically the final ground and determinant for the Scriptures.

4.3.3. Narrative Ethics in Community

Following Hauerwas, Verhey underlines the importance of learning "the practice of reading scripture ... in Christian community." It is important to make a certain past one's own as "constitutive of identity and determinative for discernment." It is important to learn "to remember," for it is in "memory" that "one finds an identity."[130] This remembering in Christian community involves "story telling." In this way "a new generation remembers and owns the story as their story and God as their God." For the Christian community to "remember ... the stories of God's glories" and his "works of power and grace" means to "live them, to shape one's life and character and conduct into something fitting to them." For instance, in the Christian community the story of the Good Samaritan functions to test the faithfulness of the character and conduct of Christians.[131] Thus, to remember Jesus takes the shape of discipleship and obedience.[132] In the way of listening "reverently to the whole canon in the midst of the whole believing community ... perhaps the God who ... in scripture and the community ... bears toward us ... the relation of sanctifier may cleanse and renew our use of the Bible in Christian ethics."[133]

The stories of Jesus' healing "point to the victory over Satan and his hosts" and disclose "'God's cause,'" which is "'life, not death; health, not sickness.'" That "'cause is assured ... in the resurrection.'" Through these stories "physicians and nurses may think of their profession as ... a 'holy'

---

128 Verhey, "The Use of Scripture in Moral Discourse," 224.

129 Verhey, "The Use of Scripture in Moral Discourse," 1-2.

130 Verhey, *The Practices of Piety*, 42-43.

131 Verhey, "The Good Samaritan and Scarce Medical Resources," *Christian Scholar's Review* Vol. 23:3 (1994), 360.

132 Verhey, *The Practices of Piety* , 44.

133 Verhey, "Bible in Christian Ethics," 61.

calling, and of themselves as 'disciples of the saving Christ.'"[134] The story in Mark 5 of Jesus healing the strong man, who was demon-possessed, had no control of himself, and was isolated, "separated from community, alienated from the very ones who would help if they could," is the story of Jesus restoring him to "self-control (Mk. 5:15) and to community" (Mk. 5:19). In this light, "a scripture-formed medical practice must use" medical knowledge to explain what is happening in and to their patients "'in ways that ... honor God and serve God's cause, including not only life and health but also the integrity of patients and their community with those who are well.'" As to how this relates to the power of medicine "'to prolong a person's dying,'" or to "'rob the dying of their dignity and separate the dying from the companionship of family and friends,'"[135] Verhey insists that "'a scripture-formed medicine must acknowledge that the moral limits to its powers come long before the technological limits to its powers.'"[136]

Verhey is tapping into some of the insights which have been developed by narrative theologians such as Hans Frei and narrative ethicists such as Stanley Hauerwas. After the collapse of some of the biblical theology schools of the mid-twentieth century with their emphasis on salvation history, the emphasis on narrative increased.[137] For ethics, the connections between narrative and community, and narrative and obedience are important.[138] Verhey makes the link between narrative and obedience through memory: remembering creates narratives as well as prompts obedience.[139] For example, to remember the exodus from Egypt involves releasing one's own servant from servitude. God's action is not simply paradigmatic for our action; instead, narrative Molds character and conduct flows out of that. There is a certain dynamism about narrative to bring into being, to engender both identity and action. Its workings are not clearly traceable, but its effects are seen. In Verhey's description, as in most discussions of narrative of this sort, a certain automatism is assumed as part of the mechanisms of narrative.

---

[134] Verhey, *The Practices of Piety*, 55. "Double quotation marks" are used in this paragraph around the quotes in view of Verhey's reference to Robert Coles' *Harvard Diary: Reflections on the Sacred and the Profane* (New York: Crossroad Publishing Company, 1990.

[135] Verhey, *The Practices of Piety*, 56.

[136] Verhey, *The Practices of Piety*, 57.

[137] Cf. Hans Frei, *The Eclipse of Biblical Narrative* (New Haven, Conn.: Yale University Press, 1974); also James Barr, "Story and History in Biblical Theology," in *Journal of Religion* 56:1 (Jan. 1976), 1-17.

[138] One could refer to many of Stanley Hauerwas' publications. Representative is his *A Community of Character: Toward a Constructive Christian Social Ethic* (South Bend: Notre Dame University Press, 1981).

[139] Verhey, *The Practices of Piety*, 44.

With regard to Verhey's use of narrative ethics, through the influence of men such as Stanley Hauerwas, Verhey has been moving more and more into the direction of narrative ethics.[140] The intriguing thing is that this may well be indirectly through Julian Hartt's influence, although Verhey makes no reference to him. Jonathan R. Wilson[141] points out that one "of the lesser known sources" of Hauerwas'[142] use of narrative[143] "is the thought of Julian Hartt."[144] Hartt "argues that 'story [is] the art of historical truth.'" It is his "conviction that the Gospel is a 'reality-intending' story." The "Gospel is not about a non-existent world dreamed up by its storytellers" but rather "about events that its storytellers believed happened," and "many today believe that the reality intended by the story continues today as an everlasting actuality." According to Hartt, the "'New Testament faith is not just a story'" that must be "'understood but, above all, appropriated,'" which "'requires ... a strenuous effort.'" According to Jonathan R. Wilson, it is precisely at this point that "Hartt's influence on Hauerwas' use of narrative takes place." Through Hartt's influence,[145] Hauerwas's use of narrative "seems expressed less in terms of biblical hermeneutics and more in terms of Christian convictions about history and reality and how to make a case for those convictions."[146] Hauerwas' turn to narrative "is rooted in the conviction that re-presenting the Gospel story and delineating its import through 'theological ethics' is precisely the way to engage the contest for truth and make the case for Christian convictions."[147] With regard to Verhey, however, it must be noted not only that he does make reference to Hans Frei, but also that his use of narrative is expressed in terms of biblical hermeneutics

---

[140] Cf. also Verhey, *The Practices of Piety*, 69, note 58: For "the notion of remembrance as 'the good' of reading scripture (and for much besides), I am indebted to Stanley Hauerwas." In conversation with the present author, Verhey has explicitly indicated as much.

[141] Jonathan R. Wilson, who wrote his Ph.D. dissertation at Duke University on: "By the Logic of the Gospel: Julian Hartt's Theology of Culture," points out how "Hartt gave Hauerwas the foundations and basic direction of his theological project," "From Theology of Culture to Theological Ethics: The Hartt-Hauerwas Connection," in *Journal of Religion and Ethics* 23.1, Spring 1995, 149.

[142] Stanley Hauerwas expresses his indebtedness to Hartt at various points in his books, such as *The Peaceable Kingdom*, xx.

[143] While Jonathan R. Wilson acknowledges the rightness of Hauerwas' "claim" that "'the central focus of his position'" is not "'his emphasis on narrative,'" he does insist that "narrative is an important concept for Hauerwas," "From Theology of Culture to Theological Ethics: The Hartt-Hauerwas Connection," 157.

[144] Hartt distances himself from Hegel, "by disqualifying a priori rejections of metaphysical theories of history, and by criticizing *heilsgeschichte* theology." Over against Hegel's system, Hartt "adduces the cosmological Christ of Colossians." With reference to "*heilsgeschichte* theology, Hartt acknowledges the primacy of the revelation of Jesus Christ but argues against absolutizing that history to the exclusion of other avenues of historical knowledge," "From Theology of Culture to Theological Ethics: The Hartt-Hauerwas Connection," 158.

[145] Jonathan R. Wilson argues that Hauerwas "in his method ... is much closer to Hartt" than to H. Richard Niebuhr. He and Hans Frei "are well-known Yale sources of 'narrative' in theology." Hauerwas' "turn to ... narrative is not rooted in a historical relativism that is confessionalist ... in its method," "From Theology of Culture to Theological Ethics: The Hartt-Hauerwas Connection," 159-160.

[146] Hartt's theology is reflected in Hauerwas' work in two ways. First, like Hartt, Hauerwas roots "the story not in unavoidable demands of our culture or in a foundational account of the nature of human experience but in the very nature of the Gospel." Second, like Hartt, Hauerwas sees "that simply telling and retelling the story is not enough—one must also say what the story is about, how to act upon the story, and how the Gospel competes with other stories," "From Theology of Culture to Theological Ethics: The Hartt-Hauerwas Connection," 160.

[147] Wilson, "From Theology of Culture to Theological Ethics: The Hartt-Hauerwas Connection," 160.

but then expressed in the process of authorization, which qualifies the authority of Scripture in the process of application, as we have noted.

If one may register a question at this point in the discussion, then it seems appropriate to ask why narrative is emphasized to the exclusion of didactic or sapiential elements of the Scripture. It would seem that this exclusionary emphasis is arbitrary and artificial. Does narrative shape character separate from moral stipulations?

4.3.4. Reading Scripture as a Practice

Verhey calls for the practice of reading Scripture in Christian community in such a way that we "construe God's relation to scripture and ... us through scripture as 'sanctifier.'" This is an extension of what Verhey has said concerning the dynamic of narrative. Reading Scripture becomes a medium of sanctification. This emphasis is intended to complement the emphasis of Scripture as a medium of revelation. The latter by itself has a tendency to turn too doctrinal and sterile.[148]

To assist this process, Verhey proposes three sets of virtues for the practice of reading Scripture. The first pair is holiness and sanctification. Holiness concerns the manner of approach to Scripture. Scripture has been set apart and so our going to Scripture must also be consecrated. With a reference to sanctification, Verhey has in view the opposite direction, namely that the reading of the Scriptures will consecrate the totality of life. Verhey is describing here the double-action to the Scripture and from the Scripture. This re-articulates the idea that Scripture is a medium of sanctification. In the process of treating Scripture as holy and being open to its sanctifying effect, the practice of Scripture works to renew. Approach and effect are held together in relationship.[149]

The second pair of virtues is fidelity and creativity, which have to do with the way the past is treated. Here Verhey uses these terms as poles within which a balance must be found. An exclusive concern for fidelity with regard to the past and the Scriptures leads to archivism and anachronism. Pure creativity loses continuity with tradition and promotes theological "amnesia." Verhey advocates a balance in which fidelity modifies creativity and vice versa.[150]

The third pair of virtues for reading Scripture is discipline and discernment. Discipline in reading Scripture is the willingness to submit to change in matters in which Scripture challenges us.[151] Discernment in reading Scripture is the virtue that sees how to direct the segments of our lives towards

---

[148] Verhey, *The Practices of Piety*, 45.
[149] Verhey, *The Practice of Piety*, 45.
[150] Verhey, *The Practices of Piety*, 45-47; 70, Note 64.
[151] Verhey, *The Practice of Piety*, 47-48.

the totality which lies in Scripture.[152] Discernment is not simply the application of general rules to particular situations, but a process in which individual and communal identity and conduct are brought into close relationship before the narrative of God's actions. The individual and the community ask who they are and what they must do of the Scriptures. Discernment is also exercised in conversation with others and other sources. Thereby we are sometimes better able to discern what suits better with Scripture.[153]

Under this heading of reading Scripture in practice, Verhey has not offered something novel to his own program. The prominence of the community is also here evident. There where the Christian community enacts these virtues, God acts as sanctifier of the community through Scripture. There is some more attention to the narrative aspect of Scripture and its mechanisms in appropriation. In fact, one might say that the operations of narrative have provided an analogy for how Scripture in general works upon the community. In the dialogue with Scripture, how does Scripture exercise its voice? In the process of our exercise of the virtues of holiness and sanctification, fidelity and creativity, discipline and discernment, Scripture has effect.

It is fitting also to signal the prominence given to the place of virtues. Verhey in his ethical thinking has come to put more and more emphasis on virtue and shifted the focus from conduct to character. In an article which he wrote together with Stanley Hauerwas, he proposes that the attention should shift "from what acts we are ready to permit to what sort of people we would be and become, from rules to virtues." For example, he mentions the virtue of chastity. By speaking of it this way, the issue is no longer whether intercourse is permitted prior to or outside of marriage. "The issue is whether the narrative we provide for ourselves sexually forms a character ready to sustain the common history God may call us to develop with another." The point is that "rules and prohibitions can leave us just as unchaste and lustful as ever, even if we never violate them." A "good character, a virtuous character, can usually do the right thing without having to think about it very much." [154]

The shift to an emphasis on virtues thus influences the very practice of reading Scripture. The cultivation of virtues is not solely the result of reading Scripture. The relationship between virtue and Scripture is more mutual, more circular. The cultivation of virtues are seen as instrumental in the appropriation of the Scriptures to the moral life.

---

152 For defining discernment, Verhey makes reference to the work of James Gustafson, "Moral Discernment in the Christian Life," *Norm and Context in Christian Ethics*, ed. Gene H. Outka and Paul Ramsey, 17-36.

153 Verhey, *The Practices of Piety*, 47-51.

154 Verhey and Stanley Hauerwas, "From Conduct to Character--A Guide to Sexual Adventure," in *The Reformed Journal* (Nov. 1986), 12-16 [quotes from 16].

4.3.5. The Kingdom of God

The Kingdom of God is crucial for moral discernment in the proposals of Verhey. This biblical concept combines the collective and social aspect of Christianity in a way which Verhey finds useful. As to what the message of the Bible is, in his dissertation Verhey seems to favor Walter Rauschenbusch's emphasis on understanding Jesus "as one who comes announcing the kingdom of God as an ideal social order." He authorizes "the use of scripture in moral argument ... if and only if it is consistent with the social ideals of the kingdom."[155] Verhey makes clear that to Walter Rauschenbusch the Kingdom of God is the "'marrow of the gospel.'"[156] It is interesting to see how Verhey evaluates Rauschenbusch's defense of this claim, particularly Rauschenbusch's use of "arguments from scriptural data which use the 'developmental warrant' and the 'exegetical warrant.'"[157]

The "developmental warrant" has a number of elements. First, only if "the scriptures are understood in their relation to their historical setting as a development of their social past and as intending to move toward a certain goal," then they are properly approached.[158] This has a Christological aspect, for Scripture must be related to Jesus, who is called "the hinge on which the testaments turn: before him everything was in development toward him, after him everything was a developing interpretation of him." The "developmental warrant" authorizes the Christocentric interpretation of the whole of the Scriptures.[159]

Secondly, the "developmental warrant" determines the selection of data for understanding Jesus' ministry. Jesus must likewise be understood as a point in a social development with a past and with a goal.[160] Jesus opposed the social structures around him, and proclaimed a kingdom that was inclusive and democratic, both spiritual and moral, which had already come and which was developing into its own fullness.[161]

---

155 Verhey, "Bible in Christian Ethics," 60.

156 Verhey, "The Use of Scripture in Moral Discourse," 95. In view of this, Rauschenbusch "demands that theology" give "the doctrine of the Kingdom of God a central place and revise all other doctrines so that they will articulate organically with it," 124, Note 9.

157 Verhey, "The Use of Scripture in Moral Discourse," 96.

158 Verhey, "The Use of Scripture in Moral Discourse," 97.

159 Verhey, "The Use of Scripture in Moral Discourse," 98.

160 Verhey, "The Use of Scripture in Moral Discourse," 98-99.

161 Verhey, "The Use of Scripture in Moral Discourse," 104. As to how Jesus interpreted his own death, Rauschenbusch states that Jesus "ranged his sufferings in line with those of the prophets," Verhey, "The Use of Scripture in Moral Discourse," 127, Note 52. Jesus was sad due to "'the consciousness that his purpose for his nation had failed.'" Jesus' death on "the cross was not the intention from the beginning. Indeed it was not the result of the will of God but rather of the willful rejection of that will by men. The cross, however, was turned to good." It was when Jesus "'saw ... death impending, he accepted the law of vicarious suffering as part of the method of redemption.'" It turned out that "God's purposes were stronger than the social sin that crucified him. The greatest evil was turned to the greatest good, and his life and message

The evolutionary presuppositions are clear in both aspects of the "developmental warrant." In the first, Christ is the center and essence of the whole development. In the second, Christ is subject also to the process of development, part of a particular time and culture. It is the message of the kingdom which rises to the surface as the essence of Christianity. One can therefore describe the "developmental warrant" as the hermeneutical lens which acts as a magnifying glass to concentrate the rays of Scripture into the force which burns into human history the message and the reality of the kingdom.

As noted above,[162] beyond the "developmental warrant," Verhey pinpoints the existence and function of the so-called "exegetical conscience warrant" in the work of Rauschenbusch. He criticizes others for having used Scripture for their ecclesiastical and dogmatic purposes or for the purpose of nurturing their "mystical piety." Their interests have blinded them to the message of Scripture.[163] The "exegetical conscience warrant" means that one then properly understands Scripture, when it is viewed as a response to the social questions.[164] Rauschenbusch uses the "exegetical conscience warrant" to allow him

> to move from his Biblical data to his claim that the real message and call of scripture is that "every man must have a conscious determination to help in his own place to work out a righteous social order for and with God." The message of scripture is an ethical message: the future hope is ... a moral ideal that calls for social action.[165]

The "exegetical conscience warrant" is the hermeneutical avenue whereby the social content of Scripture is prioritized. Verhey pin-points the circularity of this argument, but finds it not "viciously circular." The "exegetical conscience" is rooted in the fact that humans are social beings and it gradually forms over time. Verhey concludes that the "'developmental warrant'" and the "'exegetical warrant' operating in concert" authorize the "movement in argument from scriptural data to the claim that the Kingdom of God is the message of scripture."[166]

It is particularly in his *Living the Heidelberg* that Verhey reflects the influence of Rauschenbusch. The conclusion to the book provides as well an illustration of this social emphasis on the kingdom. Verhey titles his discussion of the Lord's Prayer and the Heidelberg Catechism's comments on its parts "Prayers for a Social Awakening," after the subtitle of a book by

---

were given their greatest power by his death," Verhey, "The Use of Scripture in Moral Discourse," 106-107.

[162] See sections 4.2.6 and 4.3.1.

[163] Verhey, "The Use of Scripture in Moral Discourse," 108.

[164] Verhey, "The Use of Scripture in Moral Discourse," 110.

[165] Verhey, "The Use of Scripture in Moral Discourse," 111.

[166] Verhey, "The Use of Scripture in Moral Discourse," 112.

Rauschenbusch.[167] Each petition is elaborated upon in at least two ways: 1) with a strong conviction that the petitions are aimed at social realities; and 2) with a urgent sense that the social effects of the gospel which manifest themselves in our realities are nurtured and expand and extend to fullness in the future. The first conviction parallels, of course, the "exegetical conscience warrant," seeing Scripture as a response to a social question. The second sense parallels the "developmental warrant," relating the historical circumstances of society to the reality of the kingdom which is gradually forming in the world. For example, the address "our Father" is exegeted and elaborated as follows:

> We come to you, together with all your children, united to them by the grace of your creation and redemption ... Remind us that we invoke as Father him who judges impartially (1 Pet. 1:17) ... And help us strive to be a community "renewed more and more after God's image" (Q & A 115). [168]

The petition "Thy kingdom come" is expounded in part as follows: "Destroy the terrible powers of institutionalized oppression and covetousness. Destroy racism and injustice. Destroy corruption and inequity. ... Wherever there is social evil, makes us tools of your righteousness."[169] More examples could be cited, but these suffice to indicate prominence of the datum of the kingdom with at its background the social and developmental qualifications.

It should be signaled that this treatment of kingdom identifies the social community as the primary locus of ethical amelioration. It had been noted above that Verhey assigns to the community a large agential role in the interpretation of Scripture. In addition, this discussion of the kingdom has shown the community to be the primary locus of ethical change. This aspect coincides or is aligned with the collective aspect of ethics as it emerged within American ethics through Puritanism. The development of this collective character through the industrialization in the late 19th and early 20th century and the Social Gospel movement has given it a different flavor. The Puritans came to a new continent in order to reconstruct a new godly society, "a city on a hill." By the 20th century, the collective character has become more polemical, having recognized the structural evil imbedded in society. The emphasis on the community as the locus of ethical change is now more than reconstructionist, and more transformist, emphasizing the negative aspect of ridding a society of its ills and transforming itself and re-constituting itself with new habits.

---

[167] Verhey, *Living the Heidelberg*, 152. The title of the book by Rauschenbusch is: *For God and the People: Prayers for the Social Awakening* (Boston: Pilgrim, 1910).
[168] Verhey, *Living the Heidelberg*, 149.
[169] Verhey, *Living the Heidelberg*, 150.

4.3.6. Enacting Scripture in Practice

In various publications Verhey further works out his thinking along the above-mentioned hermeneutic, in which Scripture is normative for Christian ethics but not "ethically prescriptive," and in which words such as community and narrative, disposition and virtue, also of care and caution, stand out more and more at many a corner.

4.3.6.1. The "Pro-life Permission"

With reference to the sixth commandment as the "pro-life permission" in the Decalogue, Verhey writes that, although "we must receive human physical life as God's gift" and acknowledge it as "valuable" and "protect it," we should be careful not to regard "human physical life" of "absolute value." After all, only "God is of absolute value ... and commands our absolute loyalty." Our approach to the issues of capital punishment, euthanasia, and abortion should be similar to the "just war" tradition. We are "to be faithful to God's pro-life permission within the ambiguities and realities of our world and our history" and be careful not to "permit the crusader mentality in war ... and the abortionist mentality."[170]

With regard to the ruling of the Supreme Court of the United States in *Roe v. Wade*,[171] Verhey insists that the pro-life permission calls us not merely "'to outlaw abortion'" but "'to outlove it,'"[172] which is "a 'more excellent way' to oppose the outcome of *Roe v. Wade.*" Moreover, he argues that for Christians "the moral status of the fetus is tied not to genetic uniqueness and completeness but to the sovereign grace of God." We should not concentrate on the question, "'When does life really begin?' but, 'Who is life's true sovereign?,'" or "'Whom shall we trust?' and 'In whom shall we hope?'"[173]

We who live a world "marked and marred by tragedy" but believe that God reigns and therefore hope, should receive "life, even the prenatal beginnings of it ... as a gift from God's gracious and nurturing hand." However, because we "acknowledge tragedy," we may "acknowledge as well that sometimes abortion may mournfully, repentantly, tearfully, be indicated."[174]

With reference to the question of the beginning of life, Verhey suggests that the question should not be, "when does personhood begin?" but rather: "what is the quality of life at its beginning?"[175] It is remarkable that he does not

[170] Verhey, *Living the Heidelberg*, 124-125.

[171] It stated that "state laws prohibiting abortion before a fetus is viable were unconstitutional."

[172] Verhey, *Living the Heidelberg*, 126. Verhey quotes a friend of his, Helen John, who "once said, 'It's not enough to outlaw abortion; you have to outlove it.'"

[173] Verhey, *Living the Heidelberg*, 126-127. Verhey quotes Stanley Hauerwas, *A Community of Character*.

[174] Verhey, *Living the Heidelberg*, 127.

[175] Verhey, with the Fellows of the Calvin Center for Christian Scholarship, *Christian Faith, Health, & Medical Practice*, 34-48. Although this part of this book cannot be considered as

consider biblical texts such as Psalm 139:15-16, Jeremiah 1:5 to be settling "the issue for all Bible-believing Christians." Judges 13:7 "implies that God knew and called Manoah's son Samson even before he was conceived." However, this does not imply "that the sperm and unfertilized egg which later united to produce the promised child already had the moral status of persons."[176] In a footnote he underlines his "reservations," as indicated already on pp. 18-19, about using a proof-text approach to the Bible's message. With reference to Exodus 21:22-23, he states that it "is doubtful" that "these passages should be the basis of moral or legal policy today." He says the same with reference to Numbers 5, "which some interpret as calling for abortion in cases of infidelity."[177]

He argues that the quality of human life at its beginning is one of "potentiality." At conception and somewhere into its later development, the embryo is to be interpreted by "the potentiality principle." This "'potentiality' position attributes moral and theological status to the fetus from conception, but it does not argue that the fetus is an actual person from conception." If, "in the normal course of its development, a being *will become* an imager of God, then by virtue of this potential it already deserves some of the reverence due imagers of God."[178] He is critical of abortion "being used as a means of birth control and as a matter of convenience, not as a necessity," for "it devalues human beings who are in the process of becoming persons and it violates or at least fails to live up to the responsibilities of covenantal fellowship."[179] However, he also uses this principle to argue that abortions should not be "made illegal, at least not during the first trimester," for "they do not constitute murder,"[180] although this principle "does imply that killing unborn human beings is an extremely serious moral and religious matter."[181]

Thus, this principle of potentiality, on the one hand, gives a significant status to a fetus. On the other hand, it does not give it the status of being an

---

only the work and thought of Verhey, nevertheless because of his explicit involvement and his consensus with the other authors, it can be included (cf. Verhey, with the Fellows of the Calvin Center for Christian Scholarship, *Christian Faith, Health, & Medical Practice*, xiii).

176 Verhey, with the Fellows of the Calvin Center for Christian Scholarship, *Christian Faith, Health, & Medical Practice*, 37.

177 Verhey, with the Fellows of the Calvin Center for Christian Scholarship, *Christian Faith, Health, & Medical Practice*, 37-38, Note 11.

178 Verhey, with the Fellows of the Calvin Center for Christian Scholarship, *Christian Faith, Health, & Medical Practice*, 45.

179 Verhey, with the Fellows of the Calvin Center for Christian Scholarship, *Christian Faith, Health, & Medical Practice*, 228.

180 Verhey, with the Fellows of the Calvin Center for Christian Scholarship, *Christian Faith, Health, & Medical Practice*, 228.

181 Verhey, with the Fellows of the Calvin Center for Christian Scholarship, *Christian Faith, Health, & Medical Practice*, 208.

actual person. Thus, when confronted with certain "hard cases,"[182] an induced abortion is "an acceptable alternative."[183] In cases of those pregnancies arising from rape, he "would cooperate with abortions and, at least in the cases of some young teenagers, recommend them." He also "would sadly but strongly recommend abortion when a woman's carrying a fetus is a serious and undeniable threat to her life," because he does "not believe God desires the probable sacrifice of a covenant member (especially one with many relationships and responsibilities) as the means of welcoming another being into the covenant."[184] Moreover, he "would recommend abortion on genetic grounds in those cases in which the fetus is not a potential person because deformities prevent it from coming even close to having God-imaging capacities." Thus, he "would recommend abortion for anencephaly, a condition that causes the lack of a brain." He would "recommend abortion in those rare cases in which life would inevitably be short and subjectively indistinguishable from torture."[185]

4.3.6.2. Genetic Control

With regard to "Genetic Control," Verhey writes a word of caution. Over against the public's enthusiasm over "successful genetic therapy," the church must "say, soberly, 'All flesh is as grass'; all our genes direct us to our death; we cannot create or sustain ourselves; we are dependent—in our strength as well as in our weakness—on God." Before Him we need to exercise our responsibility. If "we simply celebrate genetic control itself--as if now we can even master human nature--we will have lost our capacity to direct and limit this new power to therapy."[186]

For that matter, also therapy "requires control." It is to be directed "to the good of health, to the goal of healing genetic disease." But even at this point "there is still some cause to worry." He considers the "meaning of genetic therapy" to be "dangerously slippery precisely because the meaning of genetic disease is dangerously slippery." After all, "'disease and health' involve evaluation as well as description."[187]

---

182 Cf. Verhey, with the Fellows of the Calvin Center for Christian Scholarship, *Christian Faith, Health, & Medical Practice*, 226, 228.

183 Verhey, with the Fellows of the Calvin Center for Christian Scholarship, *Christian Faith, Health, & Medical Practice*, 208. Verhey and the other authors add that the "hard cases" which they describe "probably represent only a small percent of current abortions," Verhey, with the Fellows of the Calvin Center for Christian Scholarship, *Christian Faith, Health, & Medical Practice*, 228.

184 Verhey, with the Fellows of the Calvin Center for Christian Scholarship, *Christian Faith, Health, & Medical Practice*, 226.

185 Verhey, with the Fellows of the Calvin Center for Christian Scholarship, *Christian Faith, Health, & Medical Practice*, 227.

186 Verhey and Hessel Bouma III, "Genetic Control--On Celebration and Caution" (1986), 13.

187 Verhey, "Genetic Control--On Celebration and Caution," 13.

It is remarkable that Verhey writes at this point that it is "crucial for the church to hear again God's word to Paul, 'My grace is sufficient for you, for my power is made perfect in weakness'" (2 Cor 12:9). The emphasis is on grace being the context of God's word. The grace of God enables and permits us to live as genuine and faithful humans, as God gives and claims them. By our "dispositions and attitude and actions of ordinary men and women shaped by the gift and claim of God," we are to form and inform those around us. Verhey suggests that the "faithful recognition that God's power does not despise weakness may keep us from calling diseased any who do not meet our standards." Indeed, "God's cause, signaled in the healing miracles of Jesus and in his resurrection, includes life and its flourishing in health." But we must know that "as we wait for God's final triumph, God's power is revealed decisively in one who was despised and rejected, 'smitten of God, and afflicted.'" Verhey refers to what Christ will tell us at "that final triumph (and last judgment)." He "will tell us that we met him in the sick and in the weak, in 'the least,' as the world counts greatness." We will "see even the diseased not just as genetic accidents but as Christ's presence among us." To be sure, "God calls us ... to heal and to help." But He also calls us "to care for those we cannot cure and to love those who do not meet our standards." We need to realize that "the fundamental problems are not genetic and that the fundamental remedies are not found in genetic manipulation." Verhey suggests that our "delight in God's cause will involve us in efforts to change social values and social prejudices," but at the same time "to discern whether it is God's cause or a social prejudice calling us to change the genetic structure of a child." We should not "nurture a disposition to bear our children or to treat them as though they can be spared from suffering and death." No, "we will not and may not choose suffering or death for our children," but rather "care for children as a way of demonstrating our confidence in God rather than in human technology."[188]

The practice of Verhey's ethical thinking has been considered by focusing on the social emphasis in his treatment of the Decalogue and his discussion of some specific moral issues. Since the "permissions" of the Decalogue determine our relationship to God and other humans in this world, its primary dimension is social. Also the individual petitions of the Lord's Prayer nurture social disposition in the reality and expectation of God's kingdom. With regard to the issues of abortion and genetic control, Verhey asks the ethical questions of Scripture and seeks to construct a response consonant with the intention of Scripture.

[188] Verhey, "Genetic Control--On Celebration and Caution," 13-14.

4.4. Summary and Evaluation

Verhey is explicit about his commitment to the Scriptures as the theological ground for Christian ethics. Scripture needs to be read in the believing community and thus an ethic needs to be formed and formulated. In his *The Great Reversal* Verhey surveys the ethics of the New Testament in its unity and diversity. In his *Living the Heidelberg* Verhey discusses the theological ground for ethics in the Heidelberg Catechism, emphasizing its social importance, for instance in the Decalogue. The Catechism is an example of the product of a community reflecting on Scripture for their ethic. Verhey proposes the same activity for our time.

Once Verhey has made his claim, however, he must explicate hermeneutical issues on how to approach the text. Obviously, a fundamentalist hermeneutic of reading the words of Scripture as the words of God will not suffice. The Scriptures are both divine and human, and these strands, as in Christology in Chalcedonian fashion, can neither be confused nor separated. Thus the question remains: what is the word of God? There are various ways in which Verhey proceeds. First of all, Scripture speaks to ethical and post-ethical questions, but not directly to moral questions, the relatively unambiguous questions of duty. Secondly, the resurrection of Christ provides the hermeneutical key to understand Scripture and all its segments. Thirdly, the commands of Scripture are to be regarded not so much as *commands* for us as human *responses* to God's actions. Fourthly, following Rauschenbusch, Verhey implements something called "the exegetical conscience warrant," which has Scripture responding to social questions. Fifthly, Verhey points to the diverse ethics of the New Testament, unified as a covenantal ethics of response. Sixthly, other sources of ethics such as natural law can serve as useful means of creating a dialogue with Scripture. Each of these matters should in turn or together influence one's posture to Scripture as an authority. One could say that Verhey *hermeneutically* qualifies the authority of Scripture in ethical matters. Verhey's conclusion is that Scripture is "normative" but not "ethically-prescriptive" for Christian ethics. The influence of Walter Rauschenbusch is evident at a number of these points.

Verhey's insistence that the Bible is authoritative for the Christian moral life is a welcome thing to the present author. The church, the believing community, has no moral identity apart from the Bible. Verhey maintains that the Bible is the primary and final norm for the Christian life, and shares the Reformation's insistence that the Scripture is the rule for faith and practice, while it is to bear on the concrete decisions of Christians. Verhey wishes to stand in line with Calvin, who also acknowledged the authority of Scripture but refused to apply the biblical rule against interest "literally," and also in line with the Belgic Confession of Faith in that it distinguishes between "temporary" and "perpetual" obligations.

Secondly, Verhey's insistence that one must be careful about how one uses Scripture is equally valuable. Verhey writes that "Christian ethicists must become more self-conscious about the level of moral discourse at which they use scripture as data or backing and how they authorize the movement in argument from scripture to claim."[189] To say that the Bible is authoritative for moral discernment is not yet to say what authority the Bible provides and how the Bible functions as a norm. We must distinguish between "authority" and "authorization" and reflect on the authorizations for moving from Scripture to moral claims. Appreciation can be expressed for Verhey's insistence that "the problem of distinguishing temporary from perpetual obligations is a good deal more difficult than" Christian ethicists observe.[190]

Verhey justly insists that the "Bible claims our loyalty to God, gives us a community and history, and requires integrity with that identity in our dispositions and intentions."[191] The question "'Why be moral?' is appropriate to scripture," and that "scripture also speaks with authority at the 'ethical principle' level, where the question is, 'What general principles are normative?'" All these matters are valid and essential points for Christian ethics.

The questions to be posed to Verhey touch upon the categories of the "rational," the "collective," and the "practical," introduced in chapter 1. The utilization of the potentiality principle in *Christian Faith, Health, & Medical Practice* relates to the matter of the "rational." Is the concept of potentiality of personhood not largely philosophical and separate from the biblical concept of the image of God? Indicative of this is already the fact that few biblical texts are employed in elaboration. But the use of the word "potentiality" itself raises questions. Henry Stob prefers the phrase "in process becoming" to "potential" to apply to sperm and egg before conception.[192] In Note 20 on p. 46 of *Christian Faith, Health & Medical Practice* the authors make reference to Henry Stob, whose discussion of abortion in *Ethical Reflections* chapter 21 they otherwise follow. But they fail to counter Stob's point of allowing the term "potential human" to apply to sperm and egg before conception, although they do use it that way on p. 218.[193] Is not the Biblical teaching that the human being is created in the image of God, whereas this philosophical concept suggests that a human being must meet some minimal criteria to be considered the image of God, such as the capacity of "self-consciousness," the capacity "for choosing how to choose" and "the responsibility to exercise it in the way that our good and wise creator intended, and consciousness of this responsibility" as "the

---

189 Verhey, "The Use of Scripture in Moral Discourse," 280.

190 Verhey, "The Use of Scripture in Moral Discourse," 286, Note 25.

191 Verhey, "Bible in Christian Ethics," 58-59.

192 Stob, *Ethical Reflections: Essays on Moral Themes* (Grand Rapids: Eerdmans, 1978), 230.

193 Stob, *Ethical Reflections: Essays on Moral Themes*, 230.

foundation of our moral sense"?[194] This is one point of contact with the rational aspect of American Protestant ethics.

Verhey's focus on the economic, political and social implications of doctrine touches upon the "collective" and "practical" aspects. Verhey is correct in pointing up the fact that many of the social implications in the Heidelberg Catechism are perhaps neglected to a large extent. But does not Verhey in turn ignore the promiment personal posture of the Catechism? Indeed the Heidelberg Catechism is not individualistic, neither collectivistic. As K. Exalto also has correctly has underlined, there is the proper balance of the personal "I" and the collective "we" in the Heidelberg Catechism. It is not only "I" and "me." Neither is it only "we" and "us." It is both "I" and "we."[195]

A related issue is the tension between accepting what Scripture says about the social order, and ignoring what Scripture prescribes about the individual. This concerns Rauschenbusch's "exegetical conscience warrant," which Verhey implicitly follows in especially *Living the Heidelberg*. This approach asks of Scripture the social questions and finds particularly Jesus promoting a reform of the social order. These prescriptions are accepted in a way in which individual prescriptions are not. There seems to be some inconsistency here. To what extent does the "exegetical conscience warrant" constitute a pragmatic hermeneutic?

Some questions are raised by Verhey's inference from the diversity within Scripture that it cannot provide rules on a moral level for the church of the present raises. This inference is clear, for example, in the following quote: "Biblical ethics does not provide us an autonomous and timeless and coherent set of rules; it provides an account of the work and will and way of the one God and evokes the creative and faithful response of those who would be God's people."[196] Even if one were to give credence to the first part of the sentence, it does not necessarily follow that the Bible only reveals the actions of God, which in turn evoke a response from God's people in every generation. In fact, Verhey includes the terms "will and way" of God in his enumeration of what the Bible (or biblical ethics) supplies. Thus it is not entirely clear why one should move from the diversity of Scripture to the inference that rules cannot be applied. For that matter, one could say that there is a diversity of works of God revealed in the Bible, which should not connote that the work of God cannot be applied to the present. Moreover, what is the character of that diversity? Is there nothing within Scripture which can lend coherence to the diversity? This question addresses the inferences made on the basis of alleged diversity within Scripture.

---

[194] Verhey, with the Fellows of the Calvin Center for Christian Scholarship, *Christian Faith, Health, & Medical Practice*, 32. That, by the way, eliminates whole segments of humanity from the category of image-bearer.

[195] Exalto, *De Enige Troost: Inleiding tot de Heidelbergse Catechismus* (Kampen: Kok, n.d.), 105.

[196] Verhey, "Biblical Ethics," 17.

Other qualifications of the authority of Scripture belong to an emphasis on the rational. Though it is quite correct to distinguish between affirming the authority of Scripture and prescribing how the Bible is to be used, it can be asked whether Verhey limits the authority of Scripture with philosophy. That is suggested when he insists that there are three levels of moral reasoning: the "moral-rule" level (at which we ask: "What ought I to do?"), the "ethical-principle" level (which provides "basic ethical principles" but not specific rules), and the "post-ethical level" (at which we ask the question, "But why should I be moral at all?"), but he contends that the Scriptures function normatively for us only at the "ethical-principle" level and at the "post-ethical level," but that it is "inappropriate ... to inquire of Scripture at the 'moral-rule' level."[197] He considers it wrong to "ask the New Testament" what to decide or how to judge "in a particular concrete case and to expect it to reply with an authoritative prescription" at this "moral-rule" level. The difficulty here is that this easily leads to a dismissal of moral rules in Scripture which did bind the readers of the first century but, according to Verhey, not us. It seems that Verhey does not have safeguards to prevent the erosion of a Scriptural ethic.[198] The real danger for Verhey is that this hermeneutical qualification of the authority of Scripture becomes a philosophically created distance from the authority of Scripture, leaving a gap which must inevitably be filled with traditions and opinions. The reader must note that this is not something the present author is accusing Verhey of; it is just something against which, given the circumstances, there are only few safeguards.

In reality, Verhey sets in place only one safeguard against relativism by suggesting that the construction of moral rules must be the experience of the Christian community, rather than that of the individual. But how can this be effective in cases where whole communities and churches depart from the Scriptures and from the Christian faith?

It seems that Verhey does not wish to become too bound to certain aspects of Scripture, but wishes rather to emphasize the freedom of the believing community from the law. This freedom is elaborated in a philosophical way, namely the freedom from authority. Is this, however, the biblical understanding of freedom? The question is whether the Bible gives an understanding of its own authority for matters of life and practice which will inhibit the erosion of its authority. This matter will be pursued in the following chapter. There the

---

197 Verhey, *The Great Reversal*, 176-177.

198 Cf. David Clowney, "The Use of the Bible in Ethics," in *Inerrancy and Hermeneutic*, ed. Harvey M. Conn (Grand Rapids: Baker, 1988), 223, Note 12. Cf. also Paul Jin-Yaun Jaw, "The Roles of Jesus Christ in the Ethics of James M. Gustafson," 2,3, Note 3: "I do not intend to distinguish in this work the levels of moral discourse as suggested by Henry David Aiken. For the primary thrust of this work is ... the content of moral discourse as it relates to Jesus Christ." With reference to Verhey, he writes: "These four levels of discourse may be distinguished in methodological study. In practical moral reasoning, however, the lines are not as clearly drawn. It is my assumption that Jesus Christ is related to all levels of moral discourse."

question will be: What is a proper view of Scripture for ethics which will allow for interpretation without depriving its authority? For instance, a Trinitarian understanding of the word, the relationship between Word and Spirit, and the place of the law need elaboration.

Chapter 5: Reason, Community, and Practice: A Reformed Critique and Proposal

5.1. Introduction

This chapter aims, firstly, at a critique of the respective theological configurations of Gustafson, Ramsey, and Verhey at those points raised throughout the previous chapters. Here the topics provide the primary ordering scheme while the individual positions are secondary. Thus, the categories which emerged from the preceding chapters -- reason, community, and practice -- provide the points of cross section. In practice, this means that the questions raised of the authors in the previous chapters are gathered into constellations and articulated as a problem, to which the respective answers of the authors are delineated as proposals. The critique is cast in the form of a response in which the issues imbedded in the topic are indicated, the implications of the proposals reviewed, and the positions interrogated for their legitimacy.

The second aim of the chapter is to suggest a corresponding proposal for a Reformed basis to theocentric ethics. This proposal is interwoven throughout the critique of the authors, and together these constitute a response to the authors. In line with the critique, this proposal organizes itself according to the topics of "reason," "community," and "practice." It must be noted that the corresponding dogmatic *loci*, revelation, church, and the Christian life are at issue.

This chapter aims at the proposal that a proper view of the Reformed tenets of revelation, the church, and the place of the law, implies a biblical and truly theocentric option. It is not a non-theological approach of Gustafson, Ramsey, and Verhey which leads them to a rational approach. Rather it is the misconstrual of aspects of the theological tradition which opens them up to a rational approach.

It is no accident that the two theologians other than Gustafson, Ramsey, and Verhey whose names are most prominent throughout this chapter are Calvin and H. Richard Niebuhr. As to Niebuhr, his significance as a representative of the school of transcendence within the immanence of modernity, is pronounced. The proposals on the recent American Protestant scene have been greatly indebted to H. Richard Niebuhr. As to Calvin, he is a highly suitable spokesperson for the Reformed tradition. His adroitness in delineating theology biblically is still a convenient source and a model for theology and ethics even centuries later.

The order of the topics reason, community, and practice is not unimportant. The previous chapters have demonstrated that the priority of the moment of reason in the methodological argument of the authors is under discussion. This is, of course, not to say that the basis of ethics for each of the authors is reason. Instead, reason is a fundamentally qualifying element in the program of the authors. Historically, the influence of the Enlightenment and its effects upon religion have cultivated a climate in which the role of revelation in theology and ethics has been fundamentally conditioned by reason. As a result, the Christian character of ethics was ostensibly in danger of being eroded. To thwart such erosion, the appeal to the Christian community was engaged. The configuration of practice in the ethics of the authors under discussion has also attended the ascendancy of reason. The distinctives of this argument will be elaborated upon throughout this chapter, but the deliberateness of this arrangement is surfaced at this point.

5.2. Reason

5.2.1. Problem

A number of questions posed in the previous three chapters gather themselves around the topic of the role of reason in the construction of ethics. It should be noted that in this context the term "reason" is intended to include "experience." This section is not differentiating rationalism from empiricism, but grouping them together as they both take their point of departure in the human subject and human cognitive ability. Of Gustafson it was asked whether he has not relayed the center of gravity for moral decision within experience. It was pointed out that Gustafson's commitment to a Troeltschian view of knowledge and religion determines his view of revelation. In this connection it was asked whether Gustafson's proposed dialogue between experience and "a discernment of divine governance" does not render anthropocentrism inevitable. It was also asked whether Gustafson's concept of both "piety" and "faith" is not influenced by such an rationalistic startingpoint.

Of Ramsey it was asked whether his principalist ethics do not ultimately involve reason at the groundfloor of Christian ethics. Likewise, it was asked whether Ramsey's use for natural law and idealism, and his advocacy for the exercise of prudence does not promote a certain rationalism.

Of Verhey it was asked whether his distinctions and prescriptions regarding the levels of reasoning does not create a rationally qualified use of Scripture. Likewise, are not Verhey's conclusions regarding the diversity of Scripture rationally grounded? Finally, is not Verhey's use of the potentiality concept in the debate on the beginning of life not characteristic of a significant use of reason?

These questions must be understood against the background of the Enlightenment and liberalism. In his Gifford Lectures, the Oxford professor

Basil Mitchell contrasts the secular and religious basis for morality.[1] The secular option has been that of rational humanism, romantic humanism, and liberal humanism, types which Mitchell has selected to cover the range of Enlightenment ethics. Of rational humanism he writes that it reduced reason to scientific method and hailed its competence to construct a universal ethic. Kant proved to be the "turning-point," when following Hume he rejected the competence of metaphysical reasoning towards proof of the existence of God. Morality was free from religion and in his own words "by virtue of pure practical reason it is self-sufficient." Mitchell points out the inconsistency of Kant when he then reintroduces an appeal to nature in his conception of the categorical imperative. Yet since reason has been deemed to be "without content," in the categorical imperative it is "purely regulative." Mitchell observes that "here reason is at once at its least substantial and most authoritative." The effect of Kant has been to make the individuals creators of their own morality. Mitchell delineates this effect as "romantic humanism," both an heir and a reaction to Kant's rationalism.[2] Its values are spontaneity, creativity, and individuality. Liberal humanism is a hybrid of the two former types in maintaining that there is a minimum social morality acceptable to all, beyond which, however, one can choose. Yet, each type makes its argument substantially independently from religion.

Marking the end of historicism, Ernst Troeltsch already heralded a place for religion, of which humans who are sensitive to its echo in their soul see a new phase. The aim of action should be "a personhood filled with the import of eternity." The goals are transcendent and can only be found in the "sphere of the divine." Here with Troeltsch, the last great theorist for the historicist school, the era of transcendence breaks through. It would develop in many forms and many ways.[3]

The term "neo-orthodox" is as ambiguous as the movement was, for in many cases the debt to liberalism was as great as its reaction to it. This is particularly clear in the work of H. Richard Niebuhr, who pointed to Troeltsch

---

[1] Basil Mitchell, *Morality: Religious and Secular: The Dilemma of the Traditional Conscience* (Oxford: Clarendon Press, 1980). A similar contrast is made between Enlightenment ethics and Aristotelean ethics by Alasdair MacIntyre, *After Virtue: A Study in Moral Theory*, 2nd ed. (Notre Dame, Indiana: University of Notre Dame, 1984).

[2] Mitchell, *Morality: Religious and Secular: The Dilemma of the Traditional Conscience*, 27-29.

[3] Stanley J. Grenz and Roger E. Olson, *20th-Century Theology: God and the World in a Transitional Age* (Downer's Grove: Intervarsity Press, 1992), 63-112. Besides connecting Transcendence and Neo-orthodoxy, this book characterizes neo-orthodoxy as "The Revolt against Immanence." A standard study on the development of Troeltsch's thought is J. Klapwijk's *Tussen Historisme en Relativisme: Een studie over the dynamiek van het historisme en de wijsgerige ontwikkelingsgang van Ernst Troeltsch* (Assen: Van Gorcum, 1970).

and Barth as his main mentors.[4] Moreover, many quite different theologians are gathered under the umbrella of neo-orthodoxy, such as Barth, Bultmann, Tillich, and the Niebuhrs. H. Richard Niebuhr moved within the circles of the neo-orthodox, and though he expressed reservations about some of its forms, he was comfortable aligning himself with other aspects of it.[5]

Against this background, the question is whether reason has a place on the groundfloor of Christian moral decision making. The role of reason comes into stark relief when it is brought into relationship with revelation. Does reason stand alongside of revelation as a source of Christian ethics? Does reason envelop the discussion of the role of revelation as a source of Christian ethics? In what ways can reason function to qualify the concept of revelation? In what ways can reason operate to qualify the function of revelation? Since they determine the very basis of ethics, these are important questions. The preceding chapters have made arguments as to how reason functions in relationship to revelation for the authors in question. At this point, the opinions are gathered together and responded to in detail.

5.2.2. Proposals

5.2.2.1. Gustafson and Verhey

On the matter of the relationship of reason to revelation, Gustafson and Verhey move on the same plain. For that reason they are grouped together in their proposed solution to the problem of revelation and reason. This is not to insinuate that there are no theoretical or practical differences between the two. Their differences precisely surface in a comparison. Yet, both have been influenced by H. Richard Niebuhr, Verhey undoubtedly in part through Gustafson. To understand Gustafson and Verhey on reason, one must first turn to Niebuhr. Two problems surrounding Scripture have been most prominent for the authors under discussion: 1) the possibility of revelation in history; and 2) the diversity of Scripture. Both problems, or at least the recognition of them, are to some extent the legacy of the Enlightenment, and so belong under the heading of Scripture and reason.

---

[4] H. Richard Niebuhr, *The Meaning of Revelation* (New York: MacMillan, 1941), x. Cf. van den Berg, "Tussen Troeltsch en Barth." On Niebuhr's theological background, cf. Hans W. Frei, "Niebuhr's Theological Background," in *Faith and Ethics: The Theology of H. Richard Niebuhr*, ed. Paul Ramsey (New York: Harper & Brothers, 1957), 3-64.

[5] Jon Diefenthaler describes Niebuhr's ambivalence during his traffic in "the orbit of 'neo-orthodoxy,'" in *H. Richard Niebuhr: A Lifetime of Reflections on the Church and the World* (Macon, GA: Mercer University Press, 1986), 32-33.

5.2.2.1.1. *Revelation in History*

H. Richard Niebuhr's *The Meaning of Revelation* is illustrative of neo-orthodoxy's recognition of the problem of Scripture.[6] First, Niebuhr's work acknowledges with historicism that spatial and temporal relativity encloses all our knowing. Second, it seeks to describe the significance and operation of revelation *within that relativity*. Third, Scripture in its generation was subject to the same laws of historicity and relativity as all our knowing. Fourth, Scripture in its reception is subject to the same laws of historicity and relativity as all our knowing. Fifth, revelation cannot simply be Scripture, but only Scripture read from the point of view of church history and within community. Sixth, revelation cannot be known from its operations but from its effects. Seventh, the effects, faith and community, fundamentally determine knowledge concerning its operation. Eighth, in the midst of historical relativity, a reality can be postulated called revelation which impinges upon the relativity.

Niebuhr's proposals are recognized by especially Gustafson and Verhey. On the resemblance of Gustafson and Verhey to Niebuhr's theory of revelation, one could make the following points. First, historical relativity is present in the generation of Scripture. Gustafson finds Scripture to be recordings by the ancients of experiences of God bearing down on their lives. Drawing upon critical study of Scripture, Verhey speaks of the historical particularity of the writers, whose moral discernment is above all paradigmatic for Christians today. Second, historical relativity is present in the reception of Scripture. Gustafson maintains that experience is "an indispensable aspect of both how it [revelation] is known and what is known through it." Verhey agrees with Bultmann that presuppositions fundamentally determine the results of exegesis and Verhey's emphasis on hermeneutics and the levels of authority (the kinds of questions) proceeds on the basis of that warrant.[7] Third, one can affirm the communication of revelation, albeit qualified by relativity. In his Reality-Morality disjunction, Gustafson acknowledges that Scripture does mediate some revelation of reality. It reveals the living God as the one who bears down upon us and in relationship to whom the totality of our life needs to be ordered. The precise articulation of that revelation and the morality prescribed in it belongs to its historical and relative provenance. Verhey's Chalcedonian hermeneutic is a doctrinal portrayal of revelation within relativity, for the coordination of the divine and human in Scripture affirms the presence of revelation, albeit within the constraints of human articulation. Fourth, the reality of revelation can be gauged from its effects. Gustafson points to the "pervasive significance" of the Bible in the Western world. For Verhey, the rise of the church's faith is the historical datum with which any depiction of the ministry of Jesus must cohere. Fifth, the effects of faith and community are determinative for the understanding of revelation. In both Gustafson and Verhey the community is given prominent agential status in

---

[6] Niebuhr, *The Meaning of Revelation*. (New York: MacMillan, 1941).

[7] Verhey's acknowledgment of indebtedness to Bultmann appears in "The Use of Scripture in Moral Discourse," 26, note 41; cf. Verhey, *The Great Reversal*, 160.

reflecting upon the message and significance of Scripture for the moral life. *The movement in these five points could be characterized as "reason seeking community."*

The close alignment of Gustafson and Verhey must be qualified. Verhey himself has critiqued Gustafson's program by pointing to its lack of attention to categorical prohibitions and "the spectacles" of the Scriptures, an emphasis which is otherwise quite generally characteristic of the Reformed tradition.[8] There is in Verhey also a quantitative difference of attention to the Scriptures, both in the theory and practice of ethics. It can even be said that this quantitative difference has a qualitative effect, as is visible in their respective discussions of suicide. It must be noted that this qualitative difference is then chiefly rooted in the quantitative difference of attention to the Scriptures, for essentially their method is upon the same line, as has been demonstrated immediately above. The distance between Gustafson and Verhey might be practically considerable, but methodologically their programs operate upon similar assumptions. Verhey's criticism of Gustafson that he has neglected to give significant attention to "the spectacles" of Scripture is by itself somewhat deceptive, because for Verhey certain hermeneutical "spectacles" are affixed to qualify one's vision through the spectacles of the Scriptures. The focus on authorization in Scripture in Verhey is not unconnected to the matter of the authority of Scripture and most certainly has consequences for the latter.

5.2.2.1.2. *Diversity of Scripture*

A problem more internal to Scripture has been created by the emphasis on the diversity within Scripture. The historical-critical method has produced a fragmented or piecemeal view of the Bible. Now, over the course of the past two centuries, various proposals have been made on how to still retain some sort of unified view of Scripture, whether with notions of progressive revelation, redemptive history, or concepts such as Covenant or Word.[9] Bultmann's famous *Sachkritik* proposed a method in which what was written was critiqued by that "to which it referred."[10] Since Bultmann, other methods have developed which seek less to unify the diversity as to select within the diversity. Generally, however, there is an increased emphasis on the agency of the interpreter in constructing theology from a variety, even a polarity, of traditions.

Thus to Gustafson, it is important to "acknowledge changes in religious ideas in the Bible itself."[11] Gustafson points out that within the New Testament texts there are several Christologies. He takes the liberty to build his Christology

---

[8] Verhey, "On James M. Gustafson: Can Medical Ethics Be Christian?" *Second Opinion* 7 (March 1988), 122-123.

[9] Cf. e.g., John Goldingay, *Theological Diversity and the Authority of the Old Testament* (Grand Rapids: Eerdmans, 1987).

[10] Cf. Goldingay, *Theological Diversity*, 166-121.

[11] Gustafson, *Theocentric Perspective* I, 138.

selectively. He prefers a Christology based mainly on the narratives in the synoptic gospels. To explain this preference he simply cites his appreciation for narrative and his suspicion of a pre-existent Christ, as described in Colossians and Ephesians.[12] Recent theological developments have made it more difficult to view the teachings of Jesus as normative for Christians.[13] The radical question that "form-critical scholars" have raised "of whether or not verifiable historical authenticity could be a ground for the authority of much that was attributed to Jesus by the nonscientific writers of the Gospel narratives," have made or kept the ethicists uncertain. After all, if "the so-called teachings of Jesus" are "not the words or teachings of Jesus himself ... what reliance and authority" can they carry?[14]

It is important to see that the recognition of the diversity within Scripture raises a hermeneutical question for Verhey. The diversity within Scripture is such that one cannot speak of a unitary, monolithic ethic within the New Testament.[15] The diversity is the result of the human hands which composed the documents. The task to discern the convergence of the various ethics is left to the heirs of the Christian tradition.[16] The diversity of Scripture impels Verhey to turn to philosophical hermeneutics to solve the internal dilemmas which Scripture poses.

5.2.2.1.3. *Philosophy*

The emphasis on hermeneutics in Gustafson and Verhey is largely to be aligned with philosophical hermeneutics as it has been developed in the existentialist school of this century. Some clarification of the term "philosophy" is necessary. Of course, there is a long history to the use of philosophical concepts in ethics, particularly in Roman Catholic ethics.[17] The relation of these concepts to divine revelation is crucial.[18] The thorough-going independence from or even opposition to revelation entails that the Christian character of ethics is forfeited.

An example of a reliance upon a philosophical concept in the construction in ethics is Verhey's use of potentiality in the matter of abortion. In *Christian Faith, Health, & Medical Practice* there is an extensive discussion of

[12] Gustafson, *Theocentric Perspective* I, 275. Cf. also his footnote 65.
[13] Gustafson, *Christ and the Moral Life*, 149.
[14] Gustafson, *Christ and the Moral Life*, 192-193.
[15] Verhey, *The Great Reversal*, 73.
[16] Verhey, *The Great Reversal*, 74, 152.
[17] Cf. Alasdair MacIntyre, *A Study in Moral Theology*.
[18] Cf. W. H. Velema, *Oriëntatie in de Christelijke Ethiek*, 27-28. Cf. H. Stob, "On taking too much philosophy," *Theological Reflections*, 70: "The Christian cannot, without ceasing to be himself, adopt non-Christian principles of explanation."

the concept of "potentiality,"[19] with reference to the question of the beginning of life. The argument is that the question should not be, "when does personhood begin?" but rather "what is the quality of life at its beginning?" The authors argue that the quality of human life at its beginning is one of "potentiality." At conception and somewhere into its later development, the embryo is to be interpreted by "the potentiality principle." This "'potentiality' position attributes moral and theological status to the fetus from conception," but it does not regard the fetus "an actual person from conception." If "in the normal course of its development," the fetus "*will become* an imager of God, then by virtue of this potential it already deserves some of the reverence due imagers of God."[20] This principle of potentiality, on the one hand, gives a significant status to a fetus. On the other hand, it does not give it the status of being an actual person. Thus, when confronted with certain "hard cases,"[21] an induced abortion is considered "an acceptable alternative."[22]

This approach is decidedly philosophical. It is remarkable that biblical texts are mentioned to point up some difficulties that are not thoroughly discussed. It seems that the biblical teaching that humankind is created in the image of God has been replaced by the philosophical concept that persons must meet some minimal criteria to be considered the image of God, such as the capacity of "self-consciousness," the capacity "for choosing how to choose," and "the responsibility to exercise it in the way that our good and wise creator intended"; to this the authors add that "consciousness of this responsibility is the foundation of our moral sense."[23] That is due to the fact that, although at an early point in chapter 2 a number of biblical data about the image of God is presented in general, the starting point is not taken in Scripture for pointing up that a fetus is a person from conception.[24]

5.2.2.1.4. *Philosophical Hermeneutics*

Hermeneutics as such need not be a purely philosophical activity. Traditionally, theological hermeneutics has been a indispensable aspect of

---

[19] Verhey with the Fellows of the Calvin Center for Christian Scholarship, *Christian Faith, Health, and Medical Practice* (Grand Rapids: Eerdmans, 1989), chapter 2, the section, entitled "Imaging God: Beginnings," 34-48.

[20] Verhey with the Fellows of the Calvin Center for Christian Scholarship, *Christian Faith, Health, and Medical Practice*, 45.

[21] Cf. Verhey with the Fellows of the Calvin Center for Christian Scholarship, *Christian Faith, Health, and Medical Practice*, 226, 228.

[22] Verhey with the Fellows of the Calvin Center for Christian Scholarship, *Christian Faith, Health, and Medical Practice*, 208.

[23] Verhey with the Fellows of the Calvin Center for Christian Scholarship, *Christian Faith, Health, and Medical Practice*, 32.

[24] The authors do express respect for such an approach, *Christian Faith, Health, and Medical Practice*, 37.

biblical interpretation.[25] One meets this even in Verhey, when, for example, he speaks of "a hermeneutic of the resurrection." According to Verhey, the resurrection of Jesus is to function as the hermeneutical key that unlocks the significance of the New Testament for us.[26] Yet, even here, the function of this theological hermeneutic is used philosophically, for it is subservient to his emphasis on "authorization." Verhey writes: "If, and only if, the movement from Scripture to moral claims today is coherent with the message that God has already made his eschatological power and purpose felt in the resurrection, is the use of Scripture authorized."[27]

This shift in hermeneutics from a theological to a philosophical orientation has developed largely in the existentialist school of this century. A standard treatment of hermeneutics as it was developed in this school is given in *The Two Horizons* by Anthony Thiselton. Thiselton gives specific examples of Bultmann's interpretation of biblical passages and points out how Bultmann's pre-understanding affects his interpretation of the biblical text. According to Thiselton, Bultmann's approach to the hermeneutical problem was well established before his encounter with Heidegger. The various elements of his thought, such as the main outlines of his program of demythologization, the radical dualism between "this world" and "the Beyond," his exegetical skepticism and its legitimization by means of the doctrine of justification by grace came before Bultmann first encountered Heidegger, from the complex and distillate of his Lutheranism, Neo-Kantian dualistic world view, the influence of Hermann, Dilthey, Kähler, Wrede, and many others. "*What makes Bultmann foreclose in advance certain possibilities of interpretation is not his hermeneutical theory as such, but the theological response which he makes to the legacy of Neo-Kantian thought.*"[28] Thiselton concludes that the introduction of philosophical considerations into the hermeneutical debate, far from leading to a one-sided or distorted interpretation of the New Testament, will provide the interpreter with a broader pre-understanding in relation to which the text may speak more closely in its own right.

It has been noted that Verhey expresses his indebtedness to Bultmann's emphasis on pre-understanding.[29] Though he does not cite Bultmann, Gustafson

---

[25] Cf. J. van Bruggen, "The Authority of Scripture as a Presupposition in Reformed Theology," in *The Vitality of Reformed Theology: Proceedings of the International Congress June 20-24th 1994, Noordwijkerhout, The Netherlands*, eds. J. M. Batteau, J. W. Maris, K. Veling (Kampen: Kok, 1994), 84-98.

[26] Verhey, *The Great Reversal*, 5, 181-183.

[27] Verhey, *The Great Reversal*, 183.

[28] Anthony C. Thiselton, *The Two Horizons: New Testament Hermeneutics and Philosophical Description with Special Reference to Heidegger, Bultmann, Gadamer, and Wittgenstein* (Grand Rapids: Eerdmans, 1980), 284.

[29] Chapter 4 above, section 4.2.1. Cf. particularly Rudolf Bultmann, "Is Exegesis Without Presuppositions Possible?", in *Existence and Faith: Shorter Writings of Rudolf Bultmann*, ed. Schubert Ogden (New York: Meridian Books, 1960), 289-296. For Verhey's acknowledgment

shares a similar conviction, namely, that experience is one's only access to revelation.[30] Thiselton phrases it concisely: the interpreter of Scripture cannot but address Scripture in terms of some pre-understanding. However, he is not therefore at the mercy of his present cultural framework, for "there is an ongoing process of dialogue with the text in which the text itself progressively corrects and reshapes the interpreter's own questions and assumptions."[31] In his *New Horizons in Hermeneutics* (1992), Thiselton builds on the philosophical foundations laid in *The Two Horizons* and argues that hermeneutics needs to provide the "metacritical" grounds upon which readers' interpretative interests can be transformed in conformity with the "foundation reality" of the cross.[32]

The larger issue at stake here is the relationship between revelation and experience. The Enlightenment has led humans to be more preoccupied with experience. With Descartes, the fascination was with humans as thinking subjects. With Kant, human subjectivity was engaged to even a larger degree in the category of practical reason. Practical reason could postulate God for the benefit of morality and thus the focus on the human subject and his experience has fully replaced the real need for revelation.[33]

Although neo-orthodoxy attempted to turn away from those consequences, its failure to relinquish these Enlightenment presuppositions left it in the same predicament. Thiselton's work makes evident how in the existential tradition of the twentieth century the emphasis on hermeneutics has been the means to retain the primacy of experience over Scripture. It is even claimed that this is an inevitable reality.

5.2.2.2. Ramsey

The chapter on Ramsey has discussed how Ramsey's idealism manifests itself in the use of the categories of "principle" and "transformation," as well as his making "common cause" with philosophical idealism. He illustrates this cooperation in his treatment of original sin. Idealism shines through particularly in the way Ramsey treats certain portions of Scripture which he determines to be "mythical."

What consequence does this collaboration with idealism have in the ethical work of Ramsey? First, it involves reason in a significant way in the *construction* of the ground for ethics. For when one reduces something, whether

---

of indebtedness to Bultmann, cf. Verhey, "The Use of Scripture in Moral Discourse," 26, note 41; cf. Verhey, *Great Reversal*, 160.

30 Gustafson, *Theocentric Perspective* I, 148.

31 Anthony C. Thiselton, *Two Horizons*, 439.

32 Anthony C. Thiselton, *New Horizons in Hermeneutics: The Theory and Practice of Transforming Biblical Reading* (Chicago: University of Chicago Press, 1992), 604-619.

33 On the relationship between Descartes and Kant and the significance of the subject cf. H. G. Geertsema, *Van Boven naar Voren: wijsgerige achtergronden en problemen van het theologische denken over geschiedenis bij Jürgen Moltmann* (Kampen: Kok, 1980), 221-245.

it be narrative, or a variety of stipulations, it is always at the expense of something. How does one determine hermeneutically, how this process of reduction proceeds? Ramsey's approach to Scripture tends to be eclectic. For example, Ramsey thinks that Matthew's presentation of the law is "not to be trusted."[34] Ramsey has chosen to delineate along the lines of the concept of *agape* love at the expense of moral codes, whether biblical or natural. There is therefore a selective aspect to Ramsey's principled interpretation of Scripture. Reason has a role in determining the ground of ethics.

Second, the idealistic concentration on mind and thought, on ideas and concepts, again prevalent as it is, involves reason in a significant way in the process of the *application* of ethics. For one, with an idealistic principle, the interface with the particulars of actions remains a continual problem. Reason occupies a significant role in the application of a principle to concrete problems. When Ramsey sensed the problem himself he chose to give greater place to rules. With a mere principle, however, the application of ethics is left largely to the orientation which reason gives to the principle.

Finally, Ramsey leaves considerable place to reason in his openness to the inherent neutrality of philosophical ethics. Ramsey might maintain that philosophical systems do not address the matter of "whose good" and that they are equal in their openness to a Christian orientation. But is it true that there is no competition between Christianity and the various philosophies,[35] for instance a naturalistic ethic or materialistic ethic? For instance, does not Ramsey's choice for deontology over teleology suggest that he finds the one more aligned to Christian content than the other? Thus, is it not conceivable that the orientation of the philosophies will leave a considerable stamp?

In these three ways, Ramsey gives considerable place to reason in the formulation of a ground of ethics. It is true that Ramsey does not explicitly prioritize experience over the Scriptures; yet, within his treatment of the Scriptures, the formulation which he gives to the ground of ethics allows reason to operate in ways that fundamentally determine the ground and application of ethics. Reason occupies a place within the very ground and formulation of ethics.

In his letter to Gustafson, Ramsey points up that Gustafson's ethics remains "strangely anthropocentric" because of the subordination of Scripture and tradition to philosophy and experience. This claim is similar to that of Verhey's that Gustafson largely ignores the "spectacles" of Scripture. Ramsey contrasts Gustafson's method with his own approach, which claims Christ as foundation and the Bible as source and authority for Christian ethics. Gustafson has in turn written that the stark contrast that some (including Ramsey) wish to draw between those who emphasize "principles" in ethics and those who

---

[34] Ramsey, *Basic Christian Ethics*, 64.

[35] It is important to see that philosophy "is never neutral." It always and inescapably "has a religious root." The important thing is that it completely submit to the Word, H. Stob, "On taking too much philosophy," *Theological Reflections*, 67.

emphasize "context" or "situation" is misinformed.[36] Gustafson concludes that "contextualists find some moral principles or generalizations that give guidance to existential decisions, and that defenders of principles find some ways to proceed from generalizations to particular situations."[37] Gustafson analyzes Ramsey on this score and notes how Ramsey's principled approach does not fundamentally set him in a separate camp from those with a more context-oriented approach. First of all, Ramsey has to move from principles to the particulars of a moral problem, such as modern weapons in just war. Secondly, Ramsey turns to both philosophical (natural law) and theological (*agape*) authorizations for his principles. Thirdly, Ramsey opens himself to the reality of love manifest in the life of a person beyond its identity as a principle. Gustafson concludes therefore: "If he [Ramsey] were to be more completely systematic than he has been ... He would move not only from principles toward the historical situation and the theological affirmations, as he does, but also to a view of human moral life in faith."[38] Gustafson is noting that Ramsey's rhetoric does not wholly accord with his practice and *vice versa*. Gustafson does not point to the idealist background to this problem, but notes its actuality in Ramsey's own work.

What is at issue in Ramsey's use of principles? The authority of the Word has been traded for the authority of a principle with all its rational associations. Ethics then rests upon the reduced and generalized nature of a principle. Owing to this reduced and generalized character, the principle requires supplementary supports in its application to existential practice, whether they be considerations from philosophy or reason, which in the end share as the foundation upon which ethics is based. The issue then is that of the relationship between reason and revelation. Should reason function in an equal and competitive relation to revelation? With Gustafson and Verhey, the rational datum of experience, whether in its hermeneutical form or not, stands in a competitive relationship with revelation, an assumption which is explicitly acknowledged by them. With Ramsey, it is reason that stands in a competitive relationship with revelation, though this is never explicitly stated.

5.2.2.3. Conclusion

Through philosophical hermeneutics, a concentration on experience, and the use of "principlism," philosophy has been used alongside of, in front of, upon, and in distillation of Scripture. Reason has been introduced as a means to

---

36 Gustafson, "Context Versus Principles: A Misplaced Debate in Christian Ethics,"in *New Theology No. 3*, eds. Martin E. Marty and Dean G. Peerman (New York: MacMillan, 1966), 69-102.

37 Gustafson, "Context Versus Principles: A Misplaced Debate in Christian Ethics," 89.

38 Gustafson, "Context Versus Principles: A Misplaced Debate in Christian Ethics," 89-92. Elsewhere Gustafson writes that he finds Ramsey's practical ethics "quite rationalistic": "A Response to Critics," in *The Journal of Religious Ethics* 13 (Fall 1985), 207 [185-209].

solve the problem of Scripture. The crucial role of reason changes the configuration of a Christian and Scriptural ethic. It is revealing that Verhey and Ramsey question Gustafson's theocentrism, whereas Gustafson finds at least Ramsey on the same line or "in the same camp" as those with a more contextual approach. There seems to be a realization by Ramsey and Verhey of the erosion of a theocentric and Scriptural ethic in Gustafson. One must be cautious to generalize, and therefore it is more helpful to put the authors at various points on the same line, the line of the enlistment of reason to surmount the neo-orthodox problem of Scripture.

5.2.3. Response

5.2.3.1. Configuration of the Reformed Tradition

Gustafson, Ramsey, and Verhey each make an appeal to the Reformed tradition. Ramsey insists on drawing on the theological tradition, especially its Pauline-Augustinian strain, and the Reformational strain which lies in its extension.[39] Verhey expresses commitment to the Reformation's celebration of the grace of God in Jesus Christ the Lord, both as the mercy of God and the will of God for human lives--both as grace and claim.[40] He has written a commentary on the Heidelberg Catechism, of which he writes that it "always portrays God's grace as engendering and shaping the Christian life." Verhey appreciatively mentions that the Heidelberg Catechism takes after "its spiritual father, John Calvin,"[41] and above all after Scripture.[42]

Gustafson is perhaps most explicit about his alignment with the Reformed tradition.[43] He is particular about situating himself within a tradition, since it functions to ground and direct him. Gustafson's selectiveness within the Reformed tradition, however, has far-reaching effects. For example, with regard to Calvin's theology Gustafson acknowledges that he has "left out the redemptive work of Christ, so central to Calvin's theology."[44]

The charge that Gustafson, Ramsey, and Verhey avoid being theological cannot stand. At issue is rather 1) their configuration of the Reformed tradition, and 2) the function and effects of this configuration. It is the misconstrual of aspects of the theological tradition which opens them up to a rational approach.

The reader must understand that the assumption is not that the historic Reformed tradition is sacrosanct. Instead, it too must be examined for its consonance with Scripture and its advantage for Christian ethics. Throughout this chapter Calvin will often be taken as representative spokesperson for

---

[39] He even calls his *Basic Christian Ethics* "an essay in the Christocentric ethics of the Reformation" (*Basic Christian Ethics*, xiv).

[40] Verhey, *Living the Heidelberg*, 64.

[41] Verhey, *Living the Heidelberg*, 5.

[42] Verhey, *Living the Heidelberg*, 6.

[43] Gustafson, *Theocentric Perspective* I, 163-164.

[44] Gustafson, *Theocentric Perspective* I, 167.

Reformed tradition. This is both due to his adroitness in delineating theology biblically, but also for convenience's sake, since one could not possibly do justice to the full range and development of Reformed theology within this context.

5.2.3.2. The Knowledge of God and Revelation

The term "revelation" is meant as the theological counter-part to "reason." The coordination of "knowledge of God" and "revelation" echoes, of course, Calvin's *Institutes*. The phrase "knowledge of God" assumes humanity as the subject, whereas the phrase "revelation" assumes God as subject. The preceding chapters have raised the question, whether in their approach to Scripture, Gustafson, Ramsey, and Verhey have not elevated reason to a competitive level with revelation. The approach of this section is to assert the absolute primacy of revelation for the knowledge of God. A discussion of the relationship of piety and revelation forms an appropriate point of departure. For Gustafson, the reference to piety fundamentally determines his theological method. This might seem to lie in close proximity to Calvin; however, Gustafson has a radically different understanding of the nature of piety.

5.2.3.3. Piety and Revelation

5.2.3.3.1. *Gustafson*

Gustafson calls for piety to form the intention to relate all things in ways appropriate to their relation to God.[45] His approach to ethics is an unabashedly confessional approach, necessitated by his understanding of the relationship between theology and ethics. Yet, he brings his own nuances to the concept of piety. Gustafson defends his use of the term "piety" instead of "faith." In theological parlance, "faith" is often contrasted with reason, though, according to Gustafson, "this dichotomy is wrong in part because of the experiential basis of all our knowledge."[46] Gustafson therefore prefers the term "piety" as more inclusive. Experience is primary for Gustafson, and thus "the affection of piety" is most properly "an assumption in theology."[47] Theology can then be understood as the "construal" of these experiences, experience always remaining the point of departure.

This is a particular formulation of the conviction that faith is fundamental in one's approach in theology and ethics. Piety denotes that religious subjectivity rooted in the experience of the power of God. Piety is synonymous with "the feeling of absolute dependence on God," or "the sense of God bearing down upon us." It is therefore theocentric in orientation. It is only Christocentric in the sense that Christ most eminently incarnated this experience of absolute

[45] Gustafson, *Theocentric Perspective* I, 158, 227; Gustafson, *Theocentric Perspective* II, 146, 227.

[46] Gustafson, *Theocentric Perspective* I, 201-202.

[47] Gustafson, *Theocentric Perspective* I, 61.

dependence. Christ's experience is related to general human experience paradigmatically. Scripture functions similarly, for it records "experiences of absolute dependence on the deity." The origin of this sense of piety is shrouded in mystery. It appears fundamental to human experience, as Calvin noted concerning the "*sensus divinitatis.*" But these experiences are prompted "through the particular objects, events, and powers that sustain us, threaten our interests, create conditions for human action, or evoke awe and respect."[48] These experiences can take on specifically natural, historical, cultural, social, and individual forms. For example, nature in the form of earthquakes, disease, or fertility, evokes piety. Or history in the form of wars, change of political systems, etc. stimulates a sense of dependence.[49] Gustafson's fondness for Schleiermacher is visible in his elaboration upon piety.[50]

What is theology then, if "piety" is a "sense of absolute dependence," which arises quite generally? Gustafson writes: "Theology primarily is an activity of the practical reason." Gustafson affirms that it is more than "a linguistic-intellectual activity," but it is first of all that. What it is "more" is not a "believing activity," but a "practical" one. This practical character means that "it is testable in part by its consequences for those whose lives are informed by it." The criteria for these tests are the adequacy and coherence with which it reflects the variegated and mysterious experiences of the deity.[51] One might ask how this "practical" character exceeds its "rational" character, except in the sense that it does not remain in the world of ideas. "Reason" is then not employed in contrast to "piety," but in distinction to "practice." The question remains: what does piety entail for theological activity?

"Piety" in this sense is reduced to "rational subjectivity," which is free from true theocentricity. In fact, theocentricity here simply constitutes an emphasis on the transcendence of God as it is conjectured from the immanence of human subjectivity.

5.2.3.3.2. *Exegetical Lines*

In response to Gustafson, it must be noted that his concept of piety diverges from the biblical concept of piety. Scripture never speaks about humanity in general, but always about persons in concrete relationship to God, that is, as they are created in the image of God--as they know God (Jer 31:34), walk with God (Gen 5:24; 6:9; Deut 10:12), and listen to God's voice (Gen 6:22; Deut 6:4; 9:1; 1 Sam 3:10). The Scriptures also reveal the brokenness of

---

[48] Gustafson, *Theocentric Perspective* I, 209.

[49] Gustafson, *Theocentric Perspective* I, 209-225.

[50] Gustafson, *Theocentric Perspective* I, 176-178. Cf. the discussion in the chapter on Gustafson, section 2.3.2.2.

[51] Gustafson, *Theocentric Perspective* I, 158-159.

this relationship as a result of sin[52] -- creatures alienated from God, wandering about in exile, without fellowship with God, listening to the voice of the evil one and the voice of their own passions (Eph 2:1; Rom 3:11, 12). Scripture speaks of Christ coming into this world to restore the broken communion with God.[53] Christology is at the basis of true piety. Christ also actively fulfilled all piety (Matt 3:17; 17:5; 1 Cor 1:30; 2 Pet 1:17).[54] Piety has a Christological thrust.[55]

The Holy Spirit propels true piety. The works of piety are called the fruit of the Spirit (Gal 5:22; cf. Rom 8:23). The Spirit leads the believer to exercise piety in prayer (Eph 6:18). Piety is undergirded and motivated pneumatologically.

Scripture also indicates the theocentric nature of piety. It speaks of the people of God walking with Him (e.g., Gen 5:22). God is so much a part of their ordinary lives that the divine presence (e.g. Ps 91:1; Acts 4:13), assistance (e.g. Pss 121:2, 124:8; 146:5), and guidance of God (e.g. Ps 25:4f.) are at the center of their lives. They know and have fellowship with God, who for Christ's sake is the God of mercy and strength (e.g. John 17:24; 1 Thess 5:10; 1 John 1:7). By faith they look to God's promises and his requirements (Gen 17:1; Heb 11:13-16).

An emphasis on piety in this way is necessary.[56] A theocentric, christocentric, and pneumatological perspective on ethics calls for piety, indeed.[57] According to Scripture, true religion means knowing God individually

---

[52] Cf. Ford Lewis Battles, "True Piety According to Calvin," in *Readings in Calvin's Theology*, ed. Donald K. McKim (Grand Rapids: Baker, 1984), 197.

[53] Cf. 1 Thessalonians 5:10; John 17:24; Revelation 21:3.

[54] Cf. H. Vreekamp, *De Vreze des Heren: Een oorsprongswoord in de systematische theologie*, Th.D. diss, Rijksuniversiteit, Utrecht (Epe, 1982), 52, 169. Vreekamp interprets the fear of the Lord in connection with the Name of Jesus Christ in a threefold way: (1) the fulfilment of this fear by Christ as Mediator in His incarnation, death and resurrection (57-66); (2) the revealing of this fear by Christ Who now wants to be our Redeemer, as the Judge to come (86-96); (3) the veiling of this fear in the living relation with Christ in the present between His Ascension and Second Coming (114-124).

[55] Cf. Battles, "True Piety," 196, 198, 201-202. There is in *pietas* the notion of "filial obedience" on the part of us as "adopted children of God the Father, adopted brothers and sisters of Christ the Son," Battles, "True Piety," 198.

[56] A biblical theological treatment of piety can be found in B. J. Oosterhoff and W. Steenbergen, *Vroomheid in het Oude en Nieuwe Testament* (Apeldoornse Studies 7; Kampen: Kok, 1974). Oosterhoff makes clear that piety in the O. T. is the believing response to and reflection on God's Word as the proclamation of God's revelation in creation and history (7). Steenbergen brings out that piety in the N.T. is characterized particularly by its faith relation to Christ as the One Who is the Pious One and in Whom God has come to save in His cross and resurrection, and through Whose Word and Spirit the believers in principle here learn to live in imitation of Christ (30-32, 43-45).

[57] Cf. Sinclair B. Ferguson, *John Owen on the Christian Life* (Edinburgh: The Banner of Truth Trust, 1987).

and personally.[58] Moreover, to know God involves a particular involvement on our part. In 1 Chronicles 28:9 David addresses Solomon: "If thou seek him, he will be found of thee." Proverbs 2:2-5 establishes this as well: "If thou ... incline thine ear to wisdom, and apply thine heart to understanding; yea, if thou criest after knowledge, and liftest up thy voice for understanding ... then shalt thou understand the fear of the Lord, and find the knowledge of God." The terms "fear of the Lord"[59] and "knowledge of God" contain the essence of biblical piety.[60]

In Scripture revelation is the necessary coordinate to piety. In fact, Scripture not only portrays true piety, but also teaches true piety. This is evident not only in books such as Deuteronomy, the teaching book in the Old Testament *par excellence*. The remarkable passage in Proverbs 30:2-6, the words of Agur, contrasts human ignorance of God with the revelation of the word of God. Only through the revelation of the Word can knowledge of the Holy One be obtained. Verhey has argued a similar point with Gustafson. He observes that for the call to piety to be meaningful, there must be some means of revelation.[61]

---

[58] Cf. 1 Chronicles 28:9, David's address to Solomon: "Know thou the God of thy Father." Cf. also 1 Samuel 3:7, where it is stated that Samuel "did not yet know the Lord," as later he did.

[59] The filial fear of God in the Old Testament contains the two elements of feeling dependent on and devoted to God, which are interwoven. Sometimes the feeling of dependence is stronger than that of devotion, but the sense of distance is never removed: Cf. B. J. Oosterhoff, *De Vreze des Heren in het Oude Testament*, Th.D. Diss., Rijksuniversiteit, Utrecht. (Utrecht: Kemink en Zoon, 1949), 124-125. It is important to note that the fear of God is not merely a response to the exaltedness of God but also to the holiness of God. God has made known His will in a constant law to man, demands obedience and in wrath will punish man for disobedience. Through this there is a moral character to the fear of the Lord, which brings about a sense of guilt over against God's moral holiness ["...De vrees voor God richt zich in het O.T. maar niet slechts op een verheven God, maar ook op een zedelijk God, die Zijn wil in een constante wet aan de mens heeft kenbaar gemaakt en op straffe van Zijn schrikkelijke toorns, waardoor de mens vergaat, van hem gehoorzaamheid verlangt. Hierdoor krijgt de vreze des HEREN een zedelijk karakter en wordt ze tot schuldbesef van de mens tegenover Jahwe's zedelijke heiligheid"] (126). Cf. H. Vreekamp, *De Vreze des Heren: Een oorsprongswoord in de systematische theologie*, 123.

[60] "The fear of the Lord in the Old Testament is ... the subjective response of man to the objective revelation of God" ["...De vreze des HEREN in het O.T. ...(is) steeds...de subjectieve beantwoording van de mens aan de objectieve openbaring Gods"], B. J. Oosterhoff, *De Vreze des Heren in het Oude Testament*, 110. Cf. B. J. Oosterhoff in B. J. Oosterhoff and W. Steenbergen, *Vroomheid in het Oude en Nieuwe Testament*, 7.

[61] Cf. Verhey, "On James M. Gustafson: Can Medical Ethics Be Christian?", in *Second Opinion* 7 (March 1988), 111.

5.2.3.3.3. *Calvin*

The first book of Calvin's *Institutes* contains a classic demonstration of the necessity of revelation for piety.[62] The term *cognitio Dei* announces the theme of the first two books of the *Institutes*. As indicated in the exegetical lines drawn above, the term is decidedly biblical. It attests to the importance of theology as a "theology of the word."[63] It is true that Calvin brings *pietas* in relation with the knowledge of God the Creator.[64] Nevertheless, he clearly states that this is a hypothetical knowledge: "I speak only of the primal and simple knowledge to which the very order of nature would have led us if Adam had remained upright. In this ruin of mankind no one now experiences God either as Father or as Author of salvation, or favorable in any way, until Christ the Mediator comes forward to reconcile him to us."[65] Warfield paraphrases Calvin: "If man were not a sinner, indeed, such would be the result: men, knowing God, would turn to Him in confidence and commit themselves without reserve to His care."[66] Dowey also points to Book II, 6, 1, where Calvin gives his "short, final verdict" of the *cognitio Dei creatoris*: "Therefore, since we are fallen from life to death, all that knowledge of God the Creator of which we have discoursed would be useless unless it were succeeded by faith exhibiting God to us as the

[62] John Calvin, *Institutes*, I,6. Cf. the standard treatment of this aspect of Calvin's thought in Edward A. Dowey, Jr., *The Knowledge of God in Calvin's Theology* (New York: Columbia University Press, 1952). Dowey's work has been criticized by T. H. L. Parker ("Book Review: E. A. Dowey, *The Knowledge of God in Calvin's Theology*," in *Evangelical Quarterly* 26 [1954], 225-229; cf. B. B. Warfield, *Calvin's Doctrine of the Knowledge of God* [Rev. ed.; Grand Rapids: Eerdmans, 1959], 117-125) on two points: 1) the validity of the two-fold knowledge of God as the ordering device for the *Institutes*, and 2) on the point of "inexcusibility." In the preface of the 1964 edition of his book, Dowey responds briefly to these criticisms. What follows circumvents the actual debate and is not dependent upon either position. Also significant is Benjamin Warfield, "Calvin's Doctrine of the Knowledge of God," in *Calvin and Augustine*, ed. Samuel G. Craig (Philadelphia: Presbyterian and Reformed 1956), 29-130. Cf. W. Balke, "Apologetiek bij Calvijn?", *Omgang met de Reformatoren* (Kampen: De Groot Goudriaan, 1992), 139-144; and W. Balke, "Het Woord van God en de Ervaring volgens Calvijn," *Omgang met de Reformatoren* (Kampen: De Groot Goudriaan, 1992), 191-202. For a standard and substantive treatment of the relationship with Christ in Calvin, cf. W. Kolfhaus, *Christusgemeinschaft bei Johannes Calvin* (Neukirchen: Krs. Moer, 1939); also the incisive article by W. van 't Spijker, "'Extra Nos' en 'In Nobis' bij Calvijn in pneumatologisch licht," in *Theologia Reformata* 31 (1988), 271-291.

[63] Dowey, *Knowledge of God*, 3.

[64] Calvin, *Institutes*, I,2,1.

[65] Calvin, *Institutes*, I,2,1. Cf. W. van 't Spijker, "Calvijn tussen Reformatie en Orthodoxie," *Geest, Woord en Kerk: Opstellen over de geschiedenis van het gereformeerd protestantisme* (Kampen: Kok, 1991): Calvin's distinction of a "duplex cognitio" does not imply two sorts of knowledge; "it is merely an ordering scheme which led Calvin to distinguish the first and second articles" ["het is slechts het ordeningsprincipe, dat Calvijn er toe bracht om het eerste artikel van het tweede te onderscheiden"] (148).

[66] Warfield, "Knowledge of God," 37-38.

Father in Christ."[67] God can be known only by way of the Scriptures, which reveal God in Christ. Christ is the Incarnate Word, who reveals the Father. Revelation is indissolubly linked to piety, for it evokes piety.[68] Calvin writes: "...[T]he pious mind does not dream up for itself any god it pleases, but contemplates the one and only true God. And it does not attach to him whatever it pleases, but is content to hold him to be as he manifests himself."[69]

That Calvin builds his discussion around the *duplex cognitio domini* is remarkable. W. van 't Spijker observes that the uniqueness of Calvin's theological "system" is that he uses the theme of the knowledge of God both as the actual object and as an ordering principle. As with Luther, Zwingli, Bucer, and others, the object God and man is used as a "*modus docendi*," or as a "*modus loquendi.*"[70] What Calvin was able to keep conjoined in the *duplex cognitio domini*, became detached in orthodoxy and pietism. For Calvin, theology was always *coram Deo*, and the object of theology was always united with the center of his theology, the *unio cum Christo*.[71]

Dowey points to the significance of this emphasis in place of speculation concerning the being of God. He writes: "Calvin is here a kind of Kant, an epistemologist not a metaphysician, with reference to both God and the world."[72] Since Calvin's discussion speaks to epistemology, it is pertinent to any discussion of reason and revelation as a ground for ethics. According to Calvin, special revelation is necessary because of the dullness of our minds.[73] Natural revelation does not suffice for knowledge of God, neither as a basis for ethics. In an analogous way, reason does not suffice for ethics, since our minds and consciences are subject to insipidity.

Morality must be returned to the framework of theology, namely, the speech about God which is a response of faith. Then ethics is placed in its proper framework, and reason can then also appropriately be employed, since

---

67 Dowey, *Knowledge of God*, 45. Dowey makes the astute observation: "Yet, while this background is a frame of reference and a presupposition of the redemptive revelation--it is not even known apart from the redemptive revelation which Calvin has yet to discuss. Thus, from another point of view the redemptive revelation is actually the presupposition of the knowledge of the Creator which in Calvin's treatment precedes it" (Dowey, *Knowledge of God*, 46).

68 Cf. Battles, "True Piety According to Calvin," 193.

69 Calvin, *Institutes*, I,2,2.

70 "Calvijn tussen Reformatie en Orthodoxie," 146.

71 W. van 't Spijker, "Calvijn tussen Reformatie en Orthodoxie," 149; W. van 't Spijker, "'Extra Nos' en 'In Nobis' bij Calvijn in pneumatologisch licht," 271-291 [esp. 290]. W. Balke concurs: "Calvijn interesseert zich niet voor een abstracte godskennis op grond van filosofische argumentatie. Het gaat hem om de kennis van de levende God, om de verborgen omgang met Hem. Deze kennis brengt ons ertoe dat wij God liefhebben en eren en Hem voor al Zijn weldaden danken" [Calvin is not interested in an abstract knowledge of God on the basis of philosophical argumentation but rather in the knowledge of the living God, the secret (intimate) communion with Him. This knowledge causes us to love and honor God and thank Him for all His benefits.] ("Apologetiek bij Calvijn?" in *Omgang met de Reformatoren*, 143).

72 Dowey, *Knowledge of God*, 8.

73 Calvin, *Institutes*, I,4,1.

loving God--part of our moral response--also occurs through the mind. The reliance on natural ethics, typical of Roman Catholic ethics, can only be beneficial when it is in this framework. Here natural ethics is illuminated and redeemed by the Word of God, written and Incarnate.

As an independent entity, philosophy stands antithetical to revelation and is confounded thereby. Calvin writes: "The Scriptural teaching concerning God's infinite and spiritual essence ought to be enough, not only to banish popular delusions, but also to refute the subtleties of secular philosophy."[74]

Calvin rightly emphasizes the accommodated nature of all knowledge of God: "For who even of slight intelligence does not understand that, as nurses commonly do with infants, God is wont in a measure to 'lisp' in speaking to us?"[75] Dowey calls the concept of accommodation "the horizon of Calvin's theology."[76] Accommodation does not imply the obscurity of revelation, but precisely the comprehensibility thereof. To again cite Dowey: "Calvin never for a moment doubts the objective clarity of God's revelation, whether in creation or in Scripture."[77] The perspicuity of Scripture is not absolute, but it is sufficient.[78]

Recently, a dissertation from the hand of J. de Jong has treated the subject of accommodation as a theme in Schilder's theology of revelation.[79] Schilder's thoughts are seen to be in line with Calvin. Calvin has a broader understanding of the term, employing it generally to characterize divine actions. Schilder reserves the idea of accommodation to Scripture, God's speaking to humankind. De Jong calls this difference between Calvin and Schilder "marginal."[80] Accommodation does not detract from the perspicuity of divine revelation, but precisely supports it.[81] De Jong advocates that the use of accommodation be maintained in the theology of revelation, though never isolated from other principles, such as the inspiration of Scripture, and exegeting it according to the *analogia fidei*. Such a view of accommodation should motivate to careful exegesis rather than the rationalistic rejection of Scripture, as has been customary since the *Aufklärung*.[82]

---

74 Calvin, *Institutes*, I,13,1.

75 Calvin, *Institutes*, I,13,1. Cf. J. van Genderen, in J. van Genderen and W. H. Velema, *Beknopte gereformeerde dogmatiek* (Kampen: Kok, 1992), 41, 80; J. de Jong, *Accommodatio Dei: A Theme in K. Schilder's Theology of Revelation*, Th.D. diss. Theologische Universiteit, Kampen (Kampen: Mondiss, 1990), 35-43.

76 Dowey, *Knowledge of God*, 17.

77 Dowey, *Knowledge of God*, 32. De Jong in connection with revelation shows that God's accommodation to our understanding does not make God's revelation uncertain. Rather, it is God's way of giving us sure knowledge of Him and things divine, *Accommodatio Dei*, 40-43, 192-194.

78 Dowey, *Knowledge of God*, 37.

79 De Jong, *Accommodatio Dei: A Theme in K. Schilder's Theology of Revelation.*

80 De Jong, *Accommodatio Dei*, 269.

81 De Jong, *Accommodatio Dei*, 40-43.

82 De Jong, *Accommodatio Dei*, 268, 277.

5.2.3.4. The Noetic Effect of Sin

It has been suggested that for Calvin the clarity of revelation, whether general or redemptive, is paramount. That there is obscurity with reference to revelation is to be attributed to "the noetic effect of sin."[83] That humans fail to contemplate God or forge a twisted concept of God is owing to human "stupidity."[84] The phrase "if Adam remained upright"[85] verbalizes the *irrealis* of the unimpeded knowledge of God. This is true also with regard to what is considered the difficulty and obscurity of Scripture.[86] Over against this, Calvin asserts the inspiration of the Scriptures and the internal witness of the Spirit in the believer. Scripture is self-authenticating, but it is so to those who are fitted by the Spirit to see this authentication.[87]

It is remarkable and regrettable that in their theories Gustafson, Ramsey, and Verhey do not acknowledge the noetic consequences of sin. For then the epistemological could be soteriologically grounded and defined. To say this [whatever] is not at the neglect of creation. For though theologically creation is primary, the proper knowledge thereof can only be gained in redemption. For in this proper knowledge, creation then again obtains its primary place. This is a point, where a proper theological configuration detains the rationalization of the matter. Calvin provides an excellent model of this in his *Institutes*. *In contrast to the rational solution to a rationally determined problem of Scripture, Calvin gives a theological solution to the problem of the human understanding.*

5.2.3.5. Philosophical Hermeneutics and the Law of God

Thiselton has been cited to represent the view that it is an inevitable reality that experience has primacy over Scripture. Thiselton, along with Gustafson and Verhey, emphasizes the need for hermeneutics. This emphasis on hermeneutics is the transposed problem of epistemology, known from ancient philosophy. How does understanding arise and how does an individual understand meaning? Neither in mathematics, nor in social sciences, nor theology can anything be said without at least one postulate. George Steiner has pointed to this in his *Real Presences*.[88] Even Descartes postulates that the universe was made by God in a way so not as not deceive humans. Kant assumes a basic harmony between matters of perception and understanding.

---

[83] Dowey uses this term to characterize Calvin's doctrine of the obscurity of our knowledge. Cf. Dowey, *Knowledge of God*, 32.

[84] Calvin, *Institutes*, I,5,11; cf. I,4,1; I,4,4; I,5,14; I,5,12; I,6,2; I,6,4.

[85] Calvin, *Institutes*, I,2,1.

[86] Cf. Dowey, *Knowledge of God*, 32, where Dowey quotes on this matter from Calvin's Commentaries.

[87] Dowey, *Knowledge of God*, 108.

[88] George Steiner, *Real Presences* (Chicago: University of Chicago Press, 1989).

There is no reflection on reality which does not make one *a priori.*[89] In light of this, Steiner goes on to wager the reality of presence, and the experience of meaning, the meaning of meaning.[90] A negation of the understanding of text by posing the questions of hermeneutics cannot be allowed to create a distance of unknowability between the reader and text. Existentialism has occupied itself with experience and the human subjectivity in a way that it has made the understanding of the biblical text to be on uncertain ground. However, existentialism resists not saying anything. For Thiselton even admits that the reader is not at the mercy of agnosticism. The confrontation with the text will bring understanding. One could ask, how far one advances with raising these hermeneutical questions, while in the end still embracing some form of knowability.

The issue of hermeneutics in modern ethics runs deeper, however. By claiming the hermeneutical distance between the text and praxis, many authors have disregarded certain elements of the Scriptures. Hermeneutics is used as a rationale for neglect of certain biblical motifs. Here experience has taken precedence over revelation and has been used to judge revelation. The problem here is that experience and revelation are defined separately from what God's revelation says. The Scriptures speak about the self-revelation of God as something that comes to us, manifesting God's deliverance in Christ, and so establishing communion.[91] Experience flows from revelation, but only in the way of faith.[92] This faith is the coordination of the *fides qua* and the *fides quae*. This is the biblical understanding of the order of revelation and experience. The order is revelation and then through faith experience. These are all held together in the work of the Triune God.[93]

It often goes unmentioned that what is presently designated as "hermeneutics" is a matter upon which the divine law of the Scriptures has some bearing. An aspect of the knowledge of God which is quite prominent in Calvin, but otherwise generally neglected, is the role of the law in the knowledge of God. The commandments are raised early on in the *Institutes* as part of the obedience, which alongside of worship, is "pure and real religion: faith so joined with an earnest fear of God that this fear also embraces willing reverence, and carries with it such legitimate worship as is prescribed in the law."[94] Obedience to the commandments is therefore the *telos* of the knowledge of God.

---

[89] Steiner, *Real Presences*, 213-214.

[90] Steiner, *Real Presences*, 214.

[91] J. van Genderen, "Openbaring en Ervaring," *Naar de Norm van het Woord* (Kampen: Kok, 1993), 146.

[92] Cf. H. Stob, "The Doctrine of Revelation in St. Paul," *Theological Reflections*, 161: "Unless the Spirit accompany the Word there can be no belief. To enable a man to grasp the truths conveyed to his mind by revelation a power of recipiency must be divinely imparted."

[93] Van Genderen, "Openbaring en Ervaring," 146-147, 150.

[94] Calvin, *Institutes*, I,2,2. In the same section, Calvin writes: "Because it acknowledges him as Lord and Father, the pious mind also deems it meet and right to observe his authority in all things, reverence his majesty, take care to advance his glory, and obey his commandments."

The *telos*, however, functions not only as *telos*; it is part of the revelation requisite for the knowledge of God. This is very masterfully outlined by Calvin when he describes the necessity of Scripture: "[T]he law ... was especially committed to Moses and all the prophets to teach the way of reconciliation between God and men, whence also Paul calls 'Christ the end of the law' [Rom 10:4]."[95] The evangelical purpose of the law is set upfront. But the law first finds a place extensively with regard to our knowledge of God the Creator. True worship is taught in the first table of the Decalogue, while charity is taught in the second.[96] Calvin's discussion of God the Creator, that is, his divine attributes, the Trinity, and providence, is prefaced by the declaration of the unity of God and the stupidity of idolatry, concepts clearly comprising the first two commandments.[97] Here Calvin furnishes the law with a function before he delineates the functions of the law.[98] The function it has here corresponds roughly with what are delimited as the first and third uses of the law.

5.2.3.5.1. *The Law and Knowledge of Sin*

The Law functions, first of all, as a mirror to disclose human sinfulness.[99] Calvin refers to passages such as Rom 3:19 and 7:7 to establish this point.[100] The Heidelberg Catechism concisely declares that persons know their misery "out of the law of God," "taught by Christ."[101] In the introduction to his exposition of Psalm 51, Luther clearly distinguishes between a theological insight and philosophical insights in anthropology. Persons do not come to know themselves as sinners through "natural powers."[102] Knowing oneself as a sinner

---

95 Calvin, *Institutes*, I,6,2. In a treatment of Romans 10:4, W. H. Velema (*Wet en Evangelie* [Kampen: Kok, 1987]) argues in line with Calvin that Christ and the law are intimately related ["alles met elkaar te maken hebben"]. The Law has received its fulfillment in Christ. "Precisely by bearing its curse He has confirmed its validity. On the other hand, He has terminated its enslaving and condemning dominion" ["Juist door haar vloek te ondergaan heeft Hij haar geldigheid bevestigd. Anderzijds heeft Hij haar knechtende en veroordelende heerschappij ten einde gebracht."] (85).

96 Dowey, *Knowledge of God*, 31.

97 Calvin, *Institutes*, I,10-18.

98 Calvin, *Institutes*, II,7,6-13.

99 Cf. John Hesselink, *Calvin's Concept of the Law* (Princeton Theological Monograph Series, Dikran Y. Hadidian gen. ed. Allison Park: Pickwick Publications, 1992), 219-236.

100 Calvin, *Institutes*, II,7,6-9.

101 Lord's Day 2, Q & A 3-4.

102 "Der Grund aber für eine so grosse Blindheit und Unwissenheit liegt darin, dass die wahre Erkenntnis dieser hohen Artikel [i.e., the knowledge of sin] nicht von der Erkenntnis und Weisheit der menschlichen Vernunft abhängt oder dass ich so rede, bei uns Zuhause geboren wird, in unseren Herzen; nein, sie wird von dem Himmel herab offenbart und gegeben" (M. Luther, *Der 51. Psalm: Ein Grundkurs des christlichen Glaubens* [München: Claudius, 1983], 12). The ground however for such a great blindness and ignorance lies in the fact that the true knowledge of this exalted article [i.e., the knowledge of sin] does not depend on the knowledge

is a faith-knowledge. The Holy Spirit teaches persons that they are sinners, exiles, rebels, and fugitives from God. Romans 3:20 declares: "For by the law is the knowledge of sin."

One's misery is not known merely from self-analysis, history, conscience, nor from experience, but rather from the law of God. Taught by Christ the law functions epistemologically in two ways. Firstly, it manifests the fallen state of our being. Secondly, it declares our natural way of knowing as insolvent. The second point is implicated in the first and inferred from it. Since the data of our natural knowledge are erroneous, the natural capabilities must be defective. A third implication is that the law taught by Christ imputes a new epistemology to a person to discern the very deficiency of the fallen epistemology. These three points are all contained simply in Paul's declaration: "I had not known sin, but by the law" (Rom 7:7). Thus Calvin can say: "Thus man, schooled in the law, sloughs off the arrogance that previously blinded him."[103]

The law functions epistemologically. It is regrettable that neither Gustafson, Verhey, or Ramsey choose this theological avenue to show the inadequacy of human knowledge. Instead, the problem is projected upon the workings of revelation.

5.2.3.5.2. *The Law as a Reflection of God*

The law reaches back before sin, however. Genesis 2:16 states that "the Lord God *commanded* the man." This indicates that the law serves a function beyond the revelation of sin. God's command to Adam is to be seen as an extension of the reality that both he and the woman were created in the image and likeness of God (Gen 1:26-27). The mandate flowing from the reality of being an image-bearer is that humanity would act, think, plan, and speak as the image of God (Gen 1:28-30). God is said to have "sanctified the seventh day" (Gen 2:3), the implication being that as God rested, so the image-bearer would rest. This implication is made explicit in Exodus 20:9-11. The mandate continues and is qualified in Gen 2:15-17, as well as 2:19, and 24. In all things humanity was to continue as those who bore the image and likeness of God.

Two conclusions can be drawn from these exegetical lines. Firstly, the law is connected to the reality of humanity being the image-bearers of God. The law of God is an expression of his own being and character. The law of God is not some arbitrary code which God somehow invented, but instead the law is a transcript of the purity and the holiness of God himself, as he intends for and

---

and wisdom of human reason, nor is such speech in our hearts; instead, it is revealed and given from heaven.

103 Calvin, *Institutes*, II,7,6.

has given to humanity.[104] Secondly, the law lays out the path for image-bearers to be what they are. The reality of being an image-bearer does not remain an objective reality without coming to subjective expression. It comes to subjective expression in the path of divine commandments. A life in accordance with the divine mandate subjectively actualizes the reality of the imager-bearer.

This notion that the law is the reflection of God can be seen at work elsewhere in the Scriptures. E. W. Nicholson calls attention to the fact that in Deuteronomy 5:24 "Yahweh's direct proclamation of the Decalogue at Horeb is seen as the manifestation of his glory and his greatness."[105] The law of God is an expression of His own being and character. Along the same lines, in Romans 7:12 Paul writes: "The Law is holy, and the commandment is holy, just and good." The law shares the attributes of God, since it is the expression of what God is.

If the law is a reflection of God's being, then the law promulgates the knowledge of God. This would be the force and content of the term "reflection." There are various aspects to this promulgation. These can be illustrated most clearly with reference to Calvin. When Calvin turns to the knowledge of God the Creator from Scripture, he turns first to the law.[106] The law, in the first instance, reveals the name of God (Ex 20:1). Within the context of the giving of the law, Moses declares the attributes which are announced by the name of God (Ex 24:6-7). Calvin contrasts the attributes of "eternity" and "self-existence" inherent in the name and those "by which he is shown to us not as he is in himself, but as he is toward us."[107] Calvin points out that both the creation and the prophets declare the same attributes; his starting-point is, nevertheless, the law.

Calvin then moves from the attributes of God to speaking about the unity of God. Here he begins with a demonstration how the heathen language of "God" is inconsistent with a multiplicity of gods.[108] But then he turns to the first and second commandments (Ex 20:3-4) to propound the unity and formlessness of God.[109] This is the preface to a discussion about the Trinity, creation, and providence. The preface serves to set direction for speaking of God (theology) and worship of God (theolatry). In this context, the law serves two purposes: first, through the law God "binds believers to himself to be their sole lawgiver";

---

[104] Cf. John Murray, "The Nature of Sin," *Collected Writings* II, 78: The law of God is "not the law of cosmos, nor the law of reason," but rather it is "the expression or transcript of his moral perfection for the regulation of thought and life consonant with his perfection."

[105] E. W. Nicholson, "The Decalogue as the Direct Address of God," in *Vetus Testamentum* 27 (1977), 425.

[106] Cf. Dowey, *The Knowledge of God*, 225: "The concept of law here is seen to belong to the revelation of God the creator ...."

[107] Calvin, *Institutes*, I,10,1.

[108] Calvin, *Institutes*, I,10,2.

[109] Calvin, *Institutes*, I,11,1.

second, God "prescribes a rule whereby he is to be duly honored according to his own will."[110]

The first point conflates two separate points. One can isolate them as follows: first, the law shows God to be the lawgiver; second, through the law God binds believers to himself. It could be asked, how God binds believers to himself through the law. Calvin answers this negatively: by the law "a bridle has been imposed upon men, to prevent their sinking into vicious rites."[111] Human error constitutes a separation from God and decline into fiction, or fictitiousness. Positively stated, a proximity to God is cultivated and maintained by the law in divine hands. One could perhaps paraphrase by noting that concurrence with and obedience to the law constitutes a recognition of God's being in faith.

It must be registered that throughout this treatment of the knowledge of God the Creator, as Calvin is wont to do, the law is not to be understood negatively but positively as well. Here Calvin practices what he later will explicate, namely, that the interpretation of the law should include "an argument on the other side, in this manner: if this pleases God, the opposite displeases him; if this displeases, the opposite pleases him; if he commands this, he forbids the opposite; if he forbids this, he enjoins the opposite."[112] Thus the corollary to the first prohibition is the commandment to have only one God. The corollary to the second prohibition is the commandment that everything proper to his divinity be rendered unto him alone. The law functions then epistemologically to reveal God.

So far, the discussion has been on the law as it functions in Book I of the *Institutes*. In Book II, the primacy of the law in the discussion is not only more definite, but also more categorical. The references are less oblique, and are arranged in distinct categories. Book II intersects the theological line from Sin to Christ with the biblical line from the Fall of Adam to the work of Christ.[113] The law is given its redemptive-historical place, but also a prominent theological place. That is to say, the breadth of the law spanning the years from Moses to Christ is combined with the depth of the law in its functions (3) and its commandments (10).[114]

One cannot say that essentially, the law is attributed different places in Book I and Book II. Calvin's own cross-reference is already demonstrative of this.[115] Likewise, the fundamental interconnection of the knowledge of God as Creator and Redeemer for Calvin establishes this.

---

110 Calvin, *Institutes*, I,12,1.

111 Calvin, *Institutes*, I,12,1.

112 Calvin, *Institutes*, II,8,8.

113 Cf. Hesselink, *Calvin's Concept of the Law*, 7-12.

114 Calvin, *Institutes*, I, 6-11.

115 Calvin, *Institutes*, I,12,1: "As for the law, since its use and purpose are manifold, I will discuss it in its own place. I now touch merely on this point, that by it a bridle has been imposed upon men, to prevent their sinking into vicious rites."

5.2.3.5.3. *Conclusion*

The law of God must be duly considered in order to achieve the proper theological understanding for ethics. It must be understood against the background of the noetic effects of sin. Since the problem of human understanding is owing to human understanding, and not revelation, the solution cannot derive from human understanding in the form of philosophy; instead, the solution must come apart from human reasoning. The divine disclosure in the Word, inclusive of the law, brings knowledge of God to persons otherwise wandering in ignorance. Firstly, in Christ the law functions epistemologically to reveal sin. It unveils the reality of our sin, the natural defect of our epistemology, and grants us a new epistemology to discern these things. Secondly, being a reflection of God, the law in the hands of Christ functions to reveal God. This is clear, firstly, from the connection between persons as "image-bearers of God" and the moral law; secondly, from the connection between the attributes of God and the attributes of the law; thirdly, from the connection between the name and law of God; and fourthly, from the connection between the individual commandments and the being of God, e.g. the unity and formless of God. All this is taught in and through Christ. Epistemology cannot be separated from soteriology. Its self-authenticating force is perceived through the witness of the Spirit.

5.2.3.6. Faith and Reason

The nature of revelation has been delineated in its relationship to the knowledge of God. At this point, it is important to clarify this relationship with a focus on the relationship of faith and reason. For Calvin rational speculation was equated with the activity of the Scholastics, and termed "the science of the wind."[116] Yet, since Calvin, Enlightenment ethics sought to eliminate faith as a category and subject everything to the criticisms of reason. The world was seen as a mechanistic universe and scientific reasoning was applied to all areas of reality. This is sufficiently obvious and needs no substantiation.[117] It should be noted that the neo-orthodox project during the first half of the twentieth century precisely heralded the return of faith to the exercises of theology and ethics. H. Richard Niebuhr, for one, spoke of faith as the inevitable disposition of theology: "theology must attend to the God of faith if it is to understand faith no less than it must attend to faith in God if it would understand God. Faith is at least as much an unavoidable counterpart of the presence of God as sense experience is an unavoidable counterpart of the presence of natural entities or

[116] Dowey, *Knowledge of God*, 27.

[117] Cf. e.g. Diogenes Allen, *Christian Belief in a Postmodern World: The Full Wealth of Conviction* (Louisville: Westminster/John Knox, 1989), 36-49.

powers."[118] Faith and reason are not mutually exclusive, as reason and sense experience are not mutually exclusive, Niebuhr maintains. The point is, that neo-orthodoxy is not embarrassed about the fundamental role of faith in theology and by implication in ethics.

5.2.3.6.1. *Fides Qua et Fides Quae*

The question is, however, what the nature of this faith is. Traditionally, the two aspects of faith, the act of faith and the content of faith, have been distinguished respectively by the terms *fides qua* and *fides quae*. In Gustafson, faith is subjectivity, which aims toward a divine being from out of what is naturally available to human experience. Reason is not detached from this subjectivity, but part of it. In fact, one could say that reason has assumed chief place in the construction of morality, for "experience" is a rational datum which in theological construal is given priority. With other words, what Gustafson chooses for experience as the starting-point of theological reflection is a choice indebted to and determined by reason. But reason remains laden with subjectivity. One may conclude, therefore, that in Gustafson the traditional term "faith" becomes the cipher of subjectivity. Theology remains a rational activity, but faith lends it its inevitably subjective character. For Gustafson, the *fides qua* has swallowed the *fides quae*.

Allen Verhey points to the nature of Gustafson's nuance to faith with the comment: "God must be knowable to some measure for piety to exist."[119] This comment introduces a difference between Gustafson and Verhey on the matter of faith. In Gustafson faith is not related to revelation, except if one were to call "the sense of the deity bearing down upon us" in experience "revelation." For Gustafson, Christ and the Scriptures are examples for theocentric piety, but not sources of revelation, except in the sense that as part of tradition, the Scriptures yield perimeters and resources within which theological construal takes place. For Verhey, the emphasis on revelation is still crucial. Verhey's criticism of Gustafson's neglect of the "spectacles" of Scripture was noted above.[120] Verhey often refers to "the loyalty to Christ" and "faith in Christ's resurrection" as the source and ground of ethical reflection.

In Ramsey and Verhey, faith is discussed less as an epistemological phenomenon than a soteriological phenomenon.[121] Yet as such, faith is the basis of ethical deliberation, in Ramsey particularly as it relates to love, and in Verhey as it relates to Christ and His resurrection. Epistemologically, faith is implicit in the confessional character of their approaches, but it is not

---

[118] H. Richard Niebuhr, *Radical Monotheism*, 12. On Niebuhr's conception to faith, cf. Hans Frei, "The Theology of H. Richard Niebuhr," 68-87.

[119] Verhey, "On James M. Gustafson: Can Medical Ethics Be Christian?", 111.

[120] Verhey, "On James M. Gustafson: Can Medical Ethics Be Christian?", 123.

[121] Ramsey, *Basic Christian Ethics*, 133-152; Verhey, *Living the Heidelberg*, 15-17; Verhey, *The Great Reversal*, 11, 181-183.

fundamentally related to Scripture, either causally or teleologically. That is, "faith seeking understanding" is not explicitly related to Scripture either in the sense that the Word gives rise to faith, or in the sense that faith looks to the Word for direction. It must be understood, that Ramsey and Verhey would not deny either some causal or teleological relationship of faith to the Word, and in fact, the confessional character of their proposals implies this. In their approaches, Scripture most definitely retains a certain role, as elaborately demonstrated above.

On the other hand, however, it can be said also here that Ramsey and Verhey's approaches manifest a connection between faith and the Word that is either philosophically or hermeneutically, and fundamentally rationally qualified. This has been argued above detached from an explicit reference to faith. All the ways in which this happens need not be reiterated, but it needs to be stated here that this qualification is a qualification of the source and orientation of faith. One could perhaps characterize their position as *fides qua* in conjunction with a qualified *fides quae*. Faith hereby stands to a greater or lesser extent in a competitive relationship with reason.

The relationship of faith and reason in Ramsey and Verhey is distinct from that in Gustafson. For the latter, faith is a subjective cipher which envelops rational discernment. Gustafson wants to deny the competition between faith and reason, for all forms of thinking are enveloped by subjectivity. Yet, the question must be raised whether in its effects faith and reason are not competitively related for Gustafson. For if he wishes to achieve theocentricity in ethical discourse, but the fundamental nature of rational and linguistic construal is subjective and necessarily anthropocentric, so that circularity is necessitated, then it might be asked whether his definition of faith and reason do not lead to competitive objectives. At any rate, it appears that each of their approaches, though explicitly distinct on the matter of faith and reason, implicitly arrives at a method in which the relationship between faith and reason is competitive in character.

Neo-orthodoxy revived the positive use of faith within the discipline of ethics by creating room for confessional and theological ethics. Yet, the return to revelation, at least in the work of H. Richard Niebuhr and his heirs, Gustafson, Ramsey, and Verhey, was not free from its rational appropriation by theological liberalism. As a result, faith and reason have been engaged in a competitive relationship and the singular normativity of the Scriptures suffered loss.

5.2.3.6.2. *Faith and Reason of Different Orders*

A clear alternative to this competitive relationship has been suggested by Blaise Pascal in his *Pensées*.[122] Our existence takes place on three levels: the

[122] Blaise Pascal, *Pensées*, ed. Louis Lafuma, trans. John Warrington (London: J. M. Dent and Sons, 1973). A good treatment of these matters of Pascal is in Diogenes Allen, *Three Outsiders:*

body, reason, and the heart. Each level has its own faculty (the senses, the mind, and the will). The levels are not connected in the sense that the one follows naturally on the other. Pascal says: "One cannot obtain one little thought from all bodies together. That is impossible; thought belongs to a different order. One cannot produce a feeling of true charity from all bodies and minds. That is impossible; charity belongs to a different and supernatural order."[123] The chief exercise of the heart (or will) is love. Enlightenment philosophy has assumed by reason alone to be able to speak of matters of the heart. However, only when the heart has responded to God's goodness by faith, can reason be properly employed. Without faith, reason can only arrive at the possibility of God and revelation, but cannot establish the content.[124]

W. Aalders says it succinctly: "Between Plato and Pascal lies the metanoia."[125] He explains: "It is not the human organ of cognition which as such receives wisdom; instead, the organ of cognition, which is the heart, experiences the metanoia. Knowledge is also intricately connected to the self-communication of God; only thus can there be knowledge. Knowledge does not rest upon itself, but receives ever anew from the reality of revelation."[126]

The important thing to note in the context of this discussion of revelation and reason is that the heart must be directed to the Word of God in order to thus be taught. Pascal writes: "Humble yourself, helpless reason; be silent, foolish nature; understand that man is infinitely beyond the comprehension of man, and learn from your Master your true condition, of which you are ignorant. Listen to God."[127]

Aalders frames his discussion of this point with a reference to the Barth--Brunner debate on the question of nature and grace. Pascal's anthropology rejects any reconciliation of nature and grace. Consequently, his apologetic

---

Søren Kierkegaard, Blaise Pascal, and Simone Weil (Cambridge, MA: Cowley, 1983). In his dissertation on Blaise Pascal, W. Aalders (*Pascal als Apologetisch Prediker*, Ph.D. diss. [Van Gorcum's Theologische Bibliotheek 12; Assen: Van Gorcum, 1941]) contrasts Pascal's method with a rationalization of faith ("rationaliseering van het geloof"), and characterizes *Les Pensées* as "een apologetische opzet, die zeer sterk verwant is aan de nieuw-testamentische, apologetische prediking" [an apologetic design which is strongly related to the New Testament, apologetic preaching] (27).

123 Pascal, *Pensées*, 169. Aalders explains: "Pascal verbreekt hier in principe den band tusschen de Renaissance en het Evangelie, tussen Plato en den Bijbel" [Pascal in principle breaks here the relationship between the Renaissance and the Gospel, between Plato and the Bible], *Pascal als Apologetisch Prediker*, 85.

124 This is worked out along the lines of the traditional proofs for the existence of God by Diogenes Allen, *Christian Belief in a Postmodern World.*

125 Aalders, *Pascal als Apologetisch Prediker*, 36: "Tussen Plato en Pascal ligt de metanoia."

126 Aalders, *Pascal als Apologetisch Prediker*, 89: "Niet het kennisorgaan in den mensch als zoodanig ontvangt wijsheid, maar het kennisorgaan, dat het hart is, gaat door de metanoia heen. Ook is de kennis volstrekt gebonden aan de Zelfmededeeling Gods; pas zoo is er sprake van kennen. De kennis is niet een in zichzelf rustend systeem, maar een steeds weer ontvangen vanuit de werkelijkheid der openbaring."

127 Pascal, *Pensées*, 65.

method fails to find any sounding-board in human nature. Instead, he emphasizes human responsibility, namely, the existential-dynamic character of faith, which cannot be aligned with reason, but is evoked by the gospel of God's condescension in love. Aalders writes: "The nature of grace, belonging to the gospel as condescension, is not deterministic nor causal, but creates a real personal communion, which takes hold of the free will of a person."[128] According to Aalders, Pascal answers both Barth's concern against natural theology, and Brunner's concern that human responsibility be engaged.[129]

Notwithstanding, the primary note of Pascal remains that since the book of nature, which includes reason, cannot attain unto the content of the things of God, the book of Scripture alone can aid the understanding of spiritual matters.

5.2.3.6.3. *Fides Quaerens Intellectum*

The preceding raises the question whether any positive role for reason should be acknowledged. This cannot be the place for a detailed discussion of the role of reason in ethics and dogmatics. The focus has been on disputing the competition of faith and reason and establishing their disparity. The phrase *fides quaerens intellectum* points to the fundamental order of the two. Reason should not act of its own accord.

Why use reason at all? The grounds for the use of reason parallel the grounds for the existence of theology as a whole, such as the apologetic and confessional grounds. G. C. Stead has written an essay entitled "How Theologians Reason."[130] He takes into account that theology is rooted in Scripture and that Scripture does theology. Tradition, such as Nicea or Athanasius, has made pronouncements in order to continue to accord with the given revelation. Diogenes Allen, a noted proponent of Pascal's concept of the three orders, also acknowledges the need for the use of reason in "theological screening": "Historical study may help in determining in some cases what is and what is not orthodox."[131] This is not inconsistent with the argument that faith does not rest upon reason. As Allen observes, "One who is in the faith will in consistency with his commitment accept results of a study which shows that something is or is not in line with the given revelation."[132] One should note that faith responds to God's revelation of himself. Reason is an instrument in determining what in doctrine, practice, and liturgy accords with this revelation.

---

[128] Aalders, *Pascal als Apologetisch Prediker*, 165: "De aard van de genade, van het Evangelie als condescendentie, is geen deterministische, geen causale, maar een werkelijk persoonlijke gemeenschap scheppende, die den vrijen wil van den mensch opeischt."

[129] Aalders, *Pascal als Apologetisch Prediker*, 110-111, 122-123, 164.

[130] G. C. Stead, "How Theologians Reason," in *Faith and Logic: Oxford Essays in Philosophical Theology*, ed. Basil Mitchell (London: George Allen & Unwin), 108-131.

[131] Diogenes Allen, *The Reasonableness of Faith: A Philosophical Essay on the Grounds for Religious Beliefs* (Washingon: Corpus Books, 1968), 77.

[132] Allen, *The Reasonableness of Faith*, 77.

J. W. Maris has named various grounds for the use of reason in theology. Firstly, he observes that the very fact that God has given the ability to think warrants the use of reason.[133] This is an appeal to the Scriptural datum of creation in *imago Dei.* Secondly, he mentions the Scriptural directive to love God with all one's mind. This is an ethical ground, namely, the divine command. In the New Testament it is expressed in terms of "taking every thought captive to the obedience of Christ" (2 Cor 10:5).[134] Thirdly, one could point to the liturgical ground, since Scripture calls for "reasonable service" (Rom 12:1).[135] In worship, the human mind must be employed in a sanctified way.[136] Fourthly, one could mention the oratorical ground. Maris points out that theology is in need of prayer.[137] One could also speak of the fact that prayer, the chief exercise of faith, involves the mind. Paul writes: "What is it then? I will pray with the spirit, and I will pray with the understanding also" (1 Cor 14:15).[138]

Each of these grounds are motivated by faith, including the first. To act in accord with the image of God after the effects of sin, persons must be renewed in the image of Christ through faith (Rom 8:29; 2 Cor 4:4; Col 3:10). Whatever is not of faith is sin (Rom 14:23). This underscores the framework of faith in which reason has its place. As Maris writes: "The human ratio meanwhile does not have its own territorial claims over against the revelation of God. Anselmus' adagium [adage] 'fides quaerens intellectum' has its legitimacy, but that can never lead to some model by which faith is indebted to intellect for its own existence. Revelation appeals to intellect. Human intellect can never try revelation."[139]

5.2.3.6.4. *Levels of Reasoning*

How is this use of reason as an instrument different from Verhey's use of the various levels of reasoning? Verhey insists that various "warrants" are needed for moving in argument from the Bible to contemporary moral claims. He distinguishes three levels of moral reasoning: the "moral-rule" level (at

---

[133] J. W. Maris, "The Vitality of Reformed Dogmatics Challenged," in *The Vitality of Reformed Theology: Proceedings of the International Theological Congress, June 20-24th 1994, Noordwijkerhout, The Netherlands*, eds. J. M. Batteau, J. W. Maris, K. Veling (Kampen: Kok, 1994), 59.

[134] Maris, "The Vitality of Reformed Dogmatics Challenged," 61.

[135] Maris, "The Vitality of Reformed Dogmatics Challenged," 54.

[136] John Murray, *The Epistle to the Romans* II. (The New International Commentary of the New Testament) (Grand Rapids: Eerdmans, 1965), 112.

[137] Maris, "The Vitality of Reformed Dogmatics Challenged," 61-62.

[138] Leon Morris, *The First Epistle of Paul to the Corinthians*. (Tyndale New Testament Commentaries) (Grand Rapids: Eerdmans, 1958), 194-195. Cf. John Calvin, *Commentary on the Epistles of Paul the Apostle to the Corinthians*. Vol. I. (Trans. by Rev. John Pringle. Grand Rapids: Eerdmans, 1948), 447.

[139] Maris, "The Vitality of Reformed Dogmatics Challenged," 59.

which we ask: "What ought I to do?"), the "ethical-principle" level (which provides "basic ethical principles" but not specific rules), and the "post-ethical level" (at which we ask the question, "But why should I be moral at all?"). His contention is that the Scriptures function normatively for us only at the "ethical-principle" level and at the "post-ethical level," but that it is "inappropriate ... to inquire of Scripture at the "moral-rule" level.[140] He considers it wrong to "ask the New Testament" what to decide or how to judge "in a particular concrete case and to expect it to reply with an authoritative prescription" at this "moral-rule" level.

In critique of this argument, the following could be noted: 1) These differentiations are not theologically developed. Verhey bases himself on the theory of Aiken and Toulmin. On the surface, the classical distinction between the moral, ceremonial, and political law of the Old Testament might seem to be similar to Verhey's delineations. Yet, these delineations are theologically developed and are arguably arising from within Scripture itself. The differentiation between "moral," "ethical," and "post-ethical" is imposed upon Scripture. 2) The distinction between "moral" and "ethical" is unclear. It is not clear where the "moral" would end and the "ethical" begin. For instance, is the command "When thou goest out to battle against your enemies, and seest horses, and chariots, and a people more than thou, be not afraid of them" (Deut 20:1), moral or ethical? This seems more abstract than, for instance, a later command: "When thou shalt besiege a city a long time, in making war against it to take it, thou shalt not destroy the trees thereof by forcing an axe against them" (Deut 20:19). What are the criteria for differentiation? 3) Verhey seems to say that there is either an appropriateness in the cases of ethical and post-ethical levels or an inappropriateness in the cases of the moral level. There would seem to be other gradations of appropriation than mere appropriateness or inappropriateness. 4) Are there not aspects of even the post-ethical which are not simply "literally" transposable to today? For instance, the child's question "What is the meaning of the testimonies, and the statutes, and the judgments?" is a question at the post-ethical level, i.e., "Why be moral at all?" The answer is: "We were Pharaoh's bondmen in Egypt; and the LORD brought us out of Egypt with a mighty hand" (Deut 6:19-25). This post-ethical statement is not "transferable" to today without certain appropriate adjustments. 5) The function of this differentiation, i.e. selective appropriation, is foreign to Scripture. In fact, Scripture often introduces the "post-ethical" (if one follows Verhey's terminology) in order to legitimate the moral and the ethical (Deut 7:1-11). Or it functions in the ethical to justify the moral (e.g., Deut 6:5-9). The "post-ethical" is never cited in order to dispose of the "moral." E.g., when Jesus speaks on divorce, he does not make an appeal to the "post-ethical" in order to "deduce" the moral (Matt 19:9).

---

140 Verhey, *The Great Reversal*, 176-177.

It is true that there is a certain progression in the revelation of morality within the Scriptures, but the coherence between the moral, ethical, and post-ethical is never disintegrated. The difficulty with Verhey on this score is not that there is a measure of appropriation of Scripture. The problem is rather, how that appropriation is configured. Is it delineated through philosophical categories, which leave the Christian community to elaborate specifics from principles? This philosophical differentiation assigns a decisive role to human experience. Paul, however, writes in 1 Cor. 14:37: "If any man think himself to be a prophet, or spiritual, let him acknowledge that the things that I write to you are the commandments of the Lord."

5.3. Community

5.3.1. Problem

A number of questions raised in the previous three chapters gather themselves around the role of the church in the construction of ethics. It was asked whether Gustafson displaces the authority for the moral life from God and his Word to the human community and their experience. It was asked whether Verhey's insistence that the Christian community respond creatively to the diversity within Scripture could stem the tide of pragmatism. Besides this dynamic, there is the question to Verhey regarding the emphasis on the social within Scripture over against the individual.

The positions of these authors must be viewed against the American theological background. The emergence of a collective character in the seventeenth century has its roots in the Puritan idea of a national covenant which prompted the establishment and maintenance of a godly community. Within this community the private and public spheres were strongly interdependent, in that personal and social morality were seen as extensions of each other. With the social gospel of the late nineteenth century, the practical and rational elements had begun to ingrain themselves in American society and theology, so that the collective character of the social gospel should be understood as fundamentally modified by the motifs of pragmatism and rationalism. During the twentieth century, the social gospel was sublimated in the influential ethic of responsibility of H. Richard Niebuhr. Here ethics is seen as response and responsibility within the context of the community.

Against this background, the question has arisen concerning the agency of the community. What function does the church have in the construction of norms? Does the church share the ground of the norm of the church? The nature of the role of the church comes into stark relief when the relationship of Scripture and church is brought into view. What is the agency of the church with regard to Scripture? Does Scripture exercise formative agency upon the church? Do church and Scripture define one another? Is there a primacy of the one over the other, or is their relationship to be conceived as symbiotic, one of mutual dependence?

5.3.2. Proposals

Besides considering the proposals of Gustafson, Ramsey, and Verhey, it is helpful to add the proposals of H. R. Niebuhr and Stanley Hauerwas. Niebuhr's influence upon the American theological tradition generally, and upon Gustafson, Ramsey, and Verhey specifically is conspicuous. Hauerwas' position has become prominent within the last two decades, and has influenced Verhey. Hauerwas' view leads into a discussion of the theological position of Anabaptism on the nature of the church.

5.3.2.1. H. Richard Niebuhr

Niebuhr's article entitled "The Norm of the Church" articulates a view of the role of the community which has been significant in American theological circles within the past fifty years.[141] What provides the norm for the church, so that the church can be truly the church? According to Niebuhr, the church is not in the first place a "religious" community, but a "moral" society. It must, of course, be a moral society which has Christ as its central moral norm. This is not limited to the institution in which religious worship takes place, for if families, schools, and unions pursue the question what Christ demands of them, then they are the church.[142]

How does this norm receive content in the life of the church? Niebuhr answers this question by pointing to the church itself: "This purely formal definition of the church's norm needs, of course, to be developed by the church in order that it may have specific knowledge of the nature and character of the one to whom it belongs."[143] The church thus plays an agential role in the explication of what its norm is. As such, it has become the elongation of that norm. Niebuhr writes: The "clarification of the mind of Christ and of the mind of the church, which with and in Christ legislates for and to itself, is a constant process going on throughout the life of the church."[144] The genitive in the title "The Norm of the Church" is not simply an objective genitive, but a subjective genitive as well. The church is part of its own norm.

How do the Scriptures play a role in this? The person of Christ may never be substituted by certain propositions. Yet, in order to know the mind of Christ, the church makes study of the Scriptures. Through its study of the

---

[141] H. Richard Niebuhr, "The Norm of the Church," *The Journal of Religious Thought* 4 (1946-1947), 5-15.

[142] Niebuhr, "The Norm of the Church," 10.

[143] Niebuhr, "The Norm of the Church," 10.

[144] Niebuhr, "The Norm of the Church," 10.

Scriptures the church can explicate its faith and continue the norming activity, which is ever in process.[145]

Moreover, the element of community supplies the religious or subjective element without which the rational appropriation of Scripture might be devoid of confessional significance. To use the terminology of H. Richard Niebuhr: closing the norming circle by involving the church in the norming process, guarantees the existence of a norm. Without the involvement of the church, the norm would remain ethereal and unformed. The church is then the *sine qua non* for the existence of normative activity. It is pivotal and primary and without it the confessional character of ethics is forfeited.

5.3.2.2. Verhey

Allen Verhey has expressed indebtedness to Hauerwas on the connection of narrative and community.[146] The narrative ethics of Stanley Hauerwas has also assigned to the community an important norming role.[147] In reference to the term "the authority of Scripture," Hauerwas argues that authority needs a community. Scripture exercises authority upon the church in a formative manner, in the process of Christians remembering the narrative of God's actions.[148] Scriptural authority is therefore, according to Hauerwas, in practice mediated through the community.

Through the appropriation of narrative, the community is brought to obedience. But Verhey has also elaborated upon the function of the community apart from the emphasis on narrative. Verhey begins his dissertation with a reference to the authority of the Scriptures within the church by virtue of tradition and vocation. Tradition is responsible for the implementation of the Bible in ethics.[149] The Christian community has bequeathed to the believers of today the custom of turning to the Bible for answers to moral questions. The authority of Scripture is set forth with a reference to the church and its tradition. Verhey acknowledges the status and function of Scripture by virtue of the prominence it receives in the church. In his book *The Great Reversal*, Verhey chooses the same starting-point.[150] The role of the Bible is thus presupposed by a reference to the context within which it has functioned and continues to

---

[145] Niebuhr, "The Norm of the Church," 10-11.

[146] Verhey, *The Practice of Piety*, 42.

[147] Cf. Hauerwas' *A Community of Character: Toward a Constructive Christian Social Ethic* (Notre Dame: University of Notre Dame Press, 1981) and *Vision and Virtue* (Notre Dame: University of Notre Dame Press, 1974). A representative piece of his on this subject is "The Moral Authority of Scripture: The Politics and Ethics of Remembering," in *Interpretation* 34 (1980), 356-370. Reprinted in *Moral Theology No. 4: The Use of Scripture in Moral Theology*, eds. Charles E. Curran and Richard A. McCormick, (New York: Paulist Press, 1984), 242-275.

[148] Hauerwas, "The Moral Authority of Scripture," 361-365.

[149] Verhey, "The Use of Scripture in Moral Discourse," 3.

[150] Verhey, *The Great Reversal*, 1.

function. Furthermore, the ethic of response which Verhey advocates in *The Great Reversal* is that of a posture which the moral community takes and in which it with discernment engages the tradition to authorize certain courses of action.[151]

That Verhey raises the issue of the authority of Scripture within the context of the church's tradition and vocation and thus within the perimeters of the church's function places him in the same camp as Hauerwas on this matter.[152] His focus on authorization by the church instead of the authority of the Scriptures is related to this. That at one point he explicitly says that Scripture exists independently and objectively, would appear to be inconsistent with the more pervasive notion that experience qualifies and determines the authority of Scripture.[153]

5.3.2.3. Gustafson

Verhey expresses indebtedness to James Gustafson for the emphasis on the community.[154] Gustafson's view of the place of the community in the appropriation of Scripture can be stated succinctly in his own words: "the sustaining of a theological interpretation of man must take place in the context of a religious community, with its first-order religious language, its liturgies and symbols, and its procedures for transmitting a heritage."[155] Scripture functions here on the same level as tradition within the community, which is able to actualize the impact of Scripture within.

More explicitly than even Hauerwas, Gustafson makes the authority of Scripture ecclesiologically dependent. Gustafson says that what "gives the scriptures some authority for us is ... that the perceptions of the meaning of God's presence recorded there are to some extent confirmed in our current experience in the Christian and wider community."[156] Here Gustafson surfaces the connection between the norming function of the church and its rational coordinate. The subjective experience of the church is what provides the resonance, which assigns Scripture its authority in ethical discourse.

5.3.2.4. Ramsey

As noted in the discussion on Ramsey, he is nowhere explicit about the authority of the community as effecting or realizing the norm of Scripture. The only instance where it is explicit is when he discusses Hauerwas' thesis

---

[151] Verhey, *The Great Reversal*, 177, 180-181.

[152] Verhey, "The Use of Scripture in Moral Discourse," 3; Verhey, *The Great Reversal*, 1-2.

[153] Verhey, "The Use of Scripture in Moral Discourse," 224.

[154] Verhey, "The Use of Scripture in Moral Discourse," 22, note 2. He refers to Gustafson's *The Church as Moral Decision-Maker* (Philadelphia: Pilgrim Press, 1970).

[155] Gustafson, *Theocentric Perspective* I, 318.

[156] Gustafson, *Can Ethics Be Christian?*, 161.

regarding the interdependence of narrative and community and terms it a "fruitful circularity."[157] It was asked in the discussion of Ramsey whether Ramsey's method does in fact allot a norming function to moral agents, either individuals or communities. It appears that throughout his work, Ramsey simply exercised that norming function rather than theorized about the agency of the community. Yet, this authority is implied in the place allotted to rational discernment in the process of formulating a principle, "in-principlization," as well as application.

It appears that whether it be coordinated with an emphasis on narrative or principles, or simply a social scientific or experiential method, the authority of the Scriptures is made ecclesiologically contingent. The church actualizes or realizes the authority of Scripture in a process of discernment or dialogue. Using the terms of H. Richard Niebuhr, one might say that the church is part of the norm of church.

5.3.2.5. Anabaptism

It is interesting that Hauerwas ascribes the idea of the norming influence of community to the Free (Anabaptist) Church. According to Hauerwas, it discerned the significance of the spiritual community appropriating Scripture, in contrast to the "extreme" (Lutheran and Calvinists) Protestants insisting on the objective authority resting in Scripture.[158] Hauerwas is drawing upon the work of John Howard Yoder, who finds in the experience of the Free Church (the Anabaptists) during the Reformation a "procedure for doing practical moral reasoning."[159] Yoder builds on Matt 18:15,18 ("Whatever you bind on earth ... etc.") and states: "A transcendent moral ratification is claimed for the decisions made in the conversation of two or three or more, in a context of forgiveness and in the juridical form of listening to several witnesses."[160] The Anabaptist community could fulfill this more closely than the other communities of the Reformation, since it did not align itself with the civil powers of the state. Yoder elaborates on the components of this practical moral reasoning, but the focus is on the action of the community.

In an essay entitled "The Hermeneutics of the Anabaptists," Yoder refers to the "rule of Paul" (1 Cor 14:29), interpreted by various leaders of the Reformation as calling for debates within the context of the church.[161] The church would be called upon to decide who had spoken most in accord with

---

157 Quoted in Long, *Tragedy, Tradition, and Transformism*, 135.

158 Hauerwas, "The Moral Authority of Scripture," 357-358.

159 John Howard Yoder, *The Priestly Kingdom: Social Ethics as Gospel* (Notre Dame: University of Notre Dame Press, 1984), 27.

160 Yoder, *The Priestly Kingdom: Social Ethics as Gospel*, 27.

161 Yoder, "The Hermeneutics of the Anabaptists," in *Essays on Biblical Interpretation: Anabaptist-Mennonite Perspectives*, ed. Willard M. Swartley (Text-Reader Series 1; Elkhart, IN; Institute of Mennonite Studies, 1984), 11-28.

Scripture. Yoder notes that this "was a common conviction in the circles where Anabaptism came into being, and continued to be upheld by them when the official Reformation leaders had abandoned it."[162]

The emphasis on the importance of the community for interpretation is not only made in the Free Church tradition, but also very insistently in the Roman Catholic tradition. The "Dogmatic Constitution on Divine Revelation" (*Dei Verbum*) of the Vatican II council reaffirmed the belief that "the task of giving an authentic interpretation of the Word of God, whether in its written form or in the form of Tradition, has been entrusted to the living teaching office of the Church alone."[163] This quotation illustrates, first of all, the coordination of Scripture and the tradition of the church, and secondly, the authority of the *magisterium* to determine the interpretation of Scripture. The nature, extent, and interpretation of the Scriptures are established by and with reference to the church.

In a recent, more popular work, Hauerwas draws upon the Catholic position to argue that a serious commitment to the life of the church is needed for proper interpretation.[164] Hauerwas has herewith brought the Catholic and Anabaptist positions on the same line. The differences between the positions should, of course, not be lost from view. In the one case, there is the *magisterium*, in the other local gatherings; for the Catholics, there is the weight of tradition, for the Anabaptists, the threat of tradition. For the Anabaptists the life of Jesus was a hermeneutical key and among the Anabaptists there were also spiritualists. It would seem that the process which Hauerwas and others envision for the contemporary church is more in line with the Anabaptist tradition, since democracy would appear more attractive than hierarchy. Yet, Hauerwas' association of both the Anabaptist and the Catholic positions with one another does reveal a similarity on the point of defining interpretation with a strong reference to the community.

Gustafson, Ramsey, and Verhey have nowhere explicitly expressed debt to the Anabaptist or Catholic tradition on the matter of reading in community. Yet, both Gustafson and Verhey have expressed reservations about the use of the term *sola scriptura*. Since the roots of the term are so closely aligned with the Reformation, it would seem that their position is in fact a matter of dogmatic heritage. Gustafson explicitly rejects the term for two reasons: first, he sees the value of other sources, and second, a process of dialectic between different

---

162 Yoder, "The Hermeneutics of the Anabaptists," 21.

163 The document "The Dogmatic Constitution on Divine Revelation" is reproduced in English translation in A. Robert and A. Feuillet, *Interpreting the Scriptures* (trans. by Patrick W. Skehan *et al.*; New York: Desclee, 1969), 212-224 [quote taken from 217].

164 Hauerwas, *Unleashing the Scripture: Freeing the Bible from Captivity to America* (Nashville: Abingdon, 1993). Cf. esp. the chapter entitled "Stanley Fish, the Pope, and the Bible."

sources takes place in the Christian community.[165] Verhey calls the term "methodologically deceptive."[166] Hereby he means that everyone implements logical "warrants" in their authorizations of Scripture and therefore one cannot use Scripture alone. Elsewhere he writes that the rejection of natural and philosophical ethics involves inconsistency. Besides, "the dismissal of arguments based on reason alone is an *argumentum ad hominem* on the scale of an *argumentum ad humanum.*"[167]

The rejection of the term *sola scriptura* by Gustafson and Verhey is a corollary to their emphasis on the role of reason and experience in the construction of ethics. It is also agreeable to the social scientific method which is more comfortable with an acknowledgment of the institution within which the Bible has a place rather than the authority of Scripture which is without analogy within the social scientific worldview. The rational approach to Scripture engenders a competitive relationship between reason and revelation which is in turn checked, delineated, and qualified by the church.

The competition between reason and revelation and the resultant hegemony of reason has harnessed the coordinate of community into the norming process. It might be asked whether one can isolate reason as the chief actor in the enlistment of the community and practice. In response, one can point out that Gustafson and Verhey find the *sola Scriptura* principle untenable not because of the inevitability of the interpretive agency of the community, but because of the alleged interpretive priority of reason. The interpretive agency of the community is a solution to retain the distinctiveness of theocentric or Christian ethics. In other words, Gustafson and Verhey describe the role of reason, whereas they prescribe the role of the community. The former is considered inevitable, the latter desirable. The former is the indicative, the latter the imperative. This is delineated in two ways. Firstly, since reason co-exists with revelation competitively, the community is needed to arbitrate or at least to provide the delineations along which action can be decided. Secondly, since revelation can only be brought to bear upon the practice of ethics in rationally modified categories, practice in the form of the issues themselves must determine much of the character of the moral response. Reason, community, and practice coexist in a constellation in which reason has empowered the community and practice as constituents in ethics, and the community and practice rely on reason to justify their role in ethics.

---

[165] Gustafson, "The Place of Scripture in Christian Ethics: A Methodological Study," *Theology and Christian Ethics* (Philadelphia: United Church Press, A Pilgrim Press Book, 1974), 140-141.

[166] Verhey, "The Use of Scripture in Moral Discourse," 283.

[167] Verhey, "Bible in Christian Ethics," 60.

5.3.3. Response

The difficulty of this position that the church authorizes the interpretation of Scripture is evident in the article by Niebuhr, referred to above.[168] One is left with the question: if the church defines the authorization of Scripture, what is it then that defines the church? The answer to this question determines the nature and extent of the church. The question could be answered broadly with a reference to Jesus Christ, as Niebuhr also does. Yet, the question as to the recognition of that body whose norm is Christ remains. The problem is the move from the invisible to the visible. Niebuhr senses this and deals with marks of the church at the end of his article. He proposes the following fallible signs: first, the church is marked by praise of Christ and dependence upon the Father. Second, the presence of Scripture and order are signs of the church. Finally, acts of charity mark the presence of the church.[169]

The second of these marks introduces two of the marks associated with the church in Reformed thought.[170] Niebuhr simply mentions them and the difficulty and fallibility of their application. This hesitancy regarding these criteria is telling, for Niebuhr cannot escape fundamental circularity. For if the church is part of the norm for the interpretation of Scripture and the discernment of the mind of Christ, then it is circular to say that the presence of Scripture is at the same time a mark of the church.

It is therefore important to affirm that the church is called into existence and normed by the Word. When this is confessed, then the faithful attendance to the Word will be a mark of the true church, for the church depends for its existence on the Word. To that end the church has received and receives Scripture from the Lord of the church, Christ himself. W. van 't Spijker calls for a congregational ethic which causes us to understand how individually and collectively we ought to walk in this world. The church is the place where the concrete questions of every day are considered in the communion of saints in the light of the commandments and the gospel.[171] But there is then no room for

---

[168] H. Richard Niebuhr, "The Norm of the Church."

[169] Niebuhr, "The Norm of the Church," 12-15.

[170] Cf. J. van Genderen, "De kenmerken van de kerk," in *De Kerk: Wezen, weg en werk van de kerk naar reformatische opvatting*, eds. W. van 't Spijker *et al*; Kampen: De Groot Goudriaan, 1990), 283-397. Cf. The Belgic Confession of Faith, art. 29.

[171] W. van 't Spijker, *Gereformeerden en Dopers: Gesprek onderweg* (Reformatie Reeks; Kampen: Kok, 1986), 119: "Waarom zouden we niet spreken van de noodzakelijkheid van een gemeente-ethiek, die ons doet verstaan, hoe wij gezamenlijk, maar ook ieder op eigen plaats zullen wandelen in de wereld." The church is the place where the "concrete vragen van alledag in de gemeenschap der heiligen worden afgewogen in het licht van de geboden en van het evangelie." Cf. W. H. Velema, *Het Spreken en het Preken van de Kerk* (Apeldoornse Studies 23), 45-46. J. I. Packer writes: Although personally studying Scripture is important, "Scripture shows that the main means of learning from God is to hear his message preached and to involve oneself in the ... interchanges of church fellowship, both institutional and informal ... in exploring the content of Holy Scripture" (J. I. Packer, *Truth & Power: The Place of Scripture in the Christian Life*, [Harold Shaw Publishers, Wheaton, Illinois], 150-151). Cf. also J. W.

the phrase "the norm of the church" (Niebuhr) as a subjective genitive but only as an objective genitive, for which the subject is the Word of Christ.

This affirmation is consistent with the nature of faith outlined above, for faith assumes the posture of teachability. Faith is the only proper response to the claims of the Word. The church is only called to reason upon the basis of that faith evoked by the Word. The Word does not depend on the church for the demonstration of its power. The church is a demonstration of the power of the Word. The church must always be normed by the power of the Word.

5.4. Practice

5.4.1. Problem

A number of questions raised in the previous three chapters gather themselves around the role of practice in the construction of ethics. It was asked whether Gustafson avoided pragmatism and achieved theocentricity or whether his appeal to theocentricity was in fact pragmatic. His discourse is replete with references to the human good, which he defines socially rather than individually. Is Gustafson not simply more oriented towards the totality and extensiveness of the human world, but yet on a pragmatic line? Ramsey himself struggled with the question whether the principle of *agape* is sufficient to avoid the pragmatism of situation ethics. In this connection it was asked whether Ramsey has duly considered the relationship between law and love in Scripture. It was asked of Verhey whether the "exegetical conscience warrant" which asks social questions of Scripture and finds it promoting social reform is not a pragmatic hermeneutic. In addition, is the emphasis on the community enough of a safe-guard against pragmatism? What if the community operates pragmatically?

The question of this section centers on the terms practice and pragmatism. The introduction sketched the shift from an emphasis on moral practice in the eighteenth century to the pragmatism of the nineteenth century. By the time of the 19th century awakening, New England theology had paved the way for a voluntarism which became widely practiced in revivals and thus ingrained in the churches and society. This voluntarism accomplished the shift from the practical to the pragmatic. The enormous emphasis placed on social reform grew out of this spirit of the practical, and the transformation of religion into movements such as the social gospel was not a far step. In the meantime, philosophies of pragmatism, promoted by William James and John Dewey,

Jonker, "Reformed Theology and the Identity of the Christian Congregation," in *The Vitality of Reformed Theology: Proceedings of the International Theological Congress, June 20-24th 1994, Noordwijkerhout, The Netherlands*, eds. J. M. Batteau, J. W. Maris, K. Veling (Kampen: Kok, 1994), 99-126. B. J. Oosterhoff makes clear that in the OT, piety can only be experienced and expressed in community with others (in B. J. Oosterhoff and W. Steenbergen, *Vroomheid in het Oude en Nieuwe Testament*, 16-18).

gained their following within the American academy and the effect on both private and public spheres was pronounced.

In his book *The Politics of Jesus*, John Howard Yoder makes the point that as mainstream ethical consensus seeks to bridge the gap from revelation to the present, only a "certain very moderate amount of freight can be carried across this bridge: perhaps a concept of absolute love or humility or faith or freedom. But the substance of ethics must be reconstructed on our side of the bridge."[172] This is a very astute analysis of much of contemporary ethics. It also applies to the authors under discussion.

Each of the authors under investigation has published significantly in the theoretical area of ethics, each has also devoted many publications to the issues. Much of the agenda is set by developments in technology, and the various innovations and capabilities demand particular attention. Perhaps most of all, it has been Ramsey who after his major theoretical works, *Basic Christian Ethics*, *Deeds and Rules*, and *Nine Modern Moralists*, allowed his focus to be guided by the issues.

As such, attention to issues does not have to be an expression of pragmatism. Pragmatism enters in when the discussion of the issue and the conclusions reached on the issue are guided primarily by the issues themselves and the ends which can be achieved by them. The "practical" and the "pragmatic" are not synonymous, and lie at some distance from each other. However, the shift between them is subtle and one needs to be vigilant.

The fundamental question in this section, then, is: What can guarantee the absence of pragmatism? The relationship of practice and Scripture is at the heart of the matter. How much of Scripture can be brought to the practice of Christian ethics? Or in the words of Yoder, "how much must be reconstructed on this side of the bridge?"

5.4.2. Proposals

5.4.2.1. Gustafson

For Gustafson it is basically the idea of theocentrism which is carried over into the practice of Christian ethics. The content of this idea of theocentrism is heavily dependent upon scientific analysis and a very eclectic appropriation of theology. Theocentrism aims at ordering all things in relation to God. Theocentrism involves a sense of dependence upon God, namely, God bearing down upon one. Moral discussion therefore seeks to order life in accordance with divine governance. As for the relationship of theocentrism to Scripture, Gustafson himself explicates that the idea of theocentrism "has a strong biblical base in the creation narratives, in some of the Psalms, in the Wisdom literature, and in some aspects of the New Testament."[173] But it appears

[172] John Howard Yoder, *The Politics of Jesus* (Grand Rapids: Eerdmans, 1972), 19.

[173] Gustafson, *Theocentric Perspective* II, 86.

from the construction of this idea, that it has occurred without fundamental attention to Scripture and has been to some extent recognized within parts of Scripture. In the practice of ethics then, it is true that "the substance of ethics must be reconstructed on our side of the bridge." For Gustafson, that is a dialogical process comprising a reflection on social, cultural, and individual situations. Gustafson terms this process of reconstruction "discernment." The question is, how much of the choices is determined by the issues?

5.4.2.2. Ramsey

For Ramsey, the freight carried across the bridge is indeed a principle, namely that of *agape* or covenant. In the practice of ethics, Scripture is also brought to bear in other ways as well. But Ramsey is himself explicit about the difficulty of determining a course of action which is discernibly consistent with the principle. A survey of the positions which Ramsey advocates on issues suggests that Ramsey's practice is perhaps better than his theory, in the sense that often he advocates a point of view significantly informed by Scripture. His method, however, does not seem to guarantee that. The mere delineation of a principle from Scripture does not guarantee that ethics will not be determined by the issue or the situation. Gustafson has made the point against Ramsey that an ethics based on principles and one based on the context are not necessarily radically opposed.[174] What is needed is more than a principle.

5.4.2.3. Verhey

In the case of Verhey, Scripture as it is read by the believing community is what will guarantee that the practice of ethics will not slip into pragmatism. Once Verhey has made this claim, he substantively qualifies what a hermeneutical approach to Scripture involves. Scripture addresses ethical and post-ethical questions, but not moral questions. Scripture must be interpreted through the hermeneutical key of the resurrection. Scripture's movement from the indicative to the imperative is paradigmatic rather than prescriptive. Verhey has raised Scripture as the important datum in the construction of ethics. Yet its function is qualified hermeneutically, and the exercise of its authority is dependent upon the discernment of the community. These theoretical qualifications leave one wondering whether the authority of Scripture has been eroded so much that it cannot restrain the tide of pragmatism. One must acknowledge that Verhey's practice of ethics is more significantly informed by Scripture than his method seems to warrant. Methodologically, the question remains whether Verhey's method can guarantee that it is not the issues which guide and determine the ethics, but rather Scripture as the source of Christian faith.

---

174 Gustafson, "Context Versus Principles: A Misplaced Debate in Christian Ethics," 69-102.

5.4.3. Response

Conceiving of the question in terms of "freight across the bridge," it is important to carefully consider the theological abstractions and deductions made within Scripture. In this vein, the question has been asked regarding Ramsey whether his Christology is sufficiently Trinitarian. Likewise, has Ramsey properly conceived of the relationship between Christ and the law? Furthermore, does the moral law receive a proper place in the ground of Christian ethics in Gustafson, Ramsey, and Verhey? These questions are not detached from issues of pragmatism. A proper configuration of these theological concepts is of the essence for preventing pragmatism. For example, Ramsey's misunderstanding of the relationship between Christ and the law, leaves him to assert Christ solely in an antithetical relationship to the law. As a result, the *agape* principle he distills from Scripture is devoid of concrete shape in the practice of moral life, and he is forced to look to alternatively natural law or idealistic philosophy to supplement his principle.

5.4.3.1. Christ and the Father

In contrast to Gustafson, for whom Christ is essentially an example of theocentric piety, Ramsey articulates Christology in the traditional terms of divine-human and elaborates particularly in *kenotic* terms. Nevertheless, Ramsey does not adequately keep the interrelationships between the persons of the Trinity in view. This results in a narrow Christology. The relationship of Christ to the Father is not configured with an emphasis on the active and passive obedience of Christ. Thereby, Christ's relationship to the law is not properly kept in view.

Certain exegetical lines from Scripture will indicate the intricate connections between Christ and his Father and the benefits of recognizing these connections. One can point, first of all, to Christ's ministry. Jesus is referred to as "the Lord's Christ" (Luke 2:26). At his baptism he states his purpose as the fulfillment of all righteousness (Matt 3:15). There the Father responds by declaring that he is well-pleased in his Son (Matt 3:17). It is his atoning death and his fulfilling of all righteousness that actually secured for sinners the blessings of a new relationship with God.

Secondly, one can refer to Christ's connection to the word of his Father. Jesus was fully aware of his unique union with the Father (John 5:19; 17:5). It is remarkable how Jesus, while setting his personal authority against the rabbinical interpretation ("but I say to you"; Matt 23), made clear how he bowed to the word of his Father. It is evident in a passage such as John 12:48-50: "I have not spoken of Myself; but the Father who sent me, he gave me a commandment, what I should say, and what I should speak" (verse 49).

Thirdly, in his cross and resurrection, the relationship between Father and Son is indicated. In his address to his Father on the cross he made clear that he consciously suffered as the Son of the Father, bearing the sin of many (Isa 53:12; Luke 23:34, 46). Scripture at the same time makes clear that the Father in the resurrection of his Son set his seal of approval on all his Son said and did (Matt 28:18; Col 1:18-20), also in terms of his passive and active obedience (Phil 2:8-11; Rom 5:19).

A recognition of this relationship of Christ with the Father holds Christ's relationship to the law in view. The ministry of the Son is commissioned by the Father and approved by the Father. The words of the Son are of the Father and point to the Father. The implication is that the God of the Old Testament is not to be treated separate or detached from the God of the New Testament. This also holds true for the validity of the law of the Old Testament.

This stands in contrast to Ramsey's exclusive focus on the teachings of Jesus summed up in the phrase, "Jesus overcomes the law."[175] Consequently, Matthew 5:17-20 has to be eliminated. According to Ramsey, these words "are either not the original words of Jesus or else they are sorely in need of a loose interpretation, an interpretation not encouraged by reference to such details as the 'iota' and the 'dot.'" Ramsey understands "Christ fulfilling the law" to mean that "the Jewish religious heritage was 'finished' by Jesus Christ. Jesus completes in such fashion as entirely to annul the law."[176]

If, however, Christ's relationship with the Father is understood from out of the exegetical lines above, Matt 5:17-20 will be viewed differently. It will be read in relationship with the phrase "to fulfill all righteousness" (Matt 3:15). There appears to be some dispute regarding Matt 5:17-20 whether this fulfillment primarily concerning Christ's teaching or his existence.[177] Since it is in the context of the Sermon on the Mount, where Jesus chiefly acts as the divine teacher, the fulfillment of the law would appear to have reference to his teaching. Yet, for Christ, "the existential" and "the doctrinal" were never unrelated.[178] Moreover, in verse 19, Jesus harmonizes doctrine and life in the statement: "Whosoever therefore shall break one of these least commandments, and shall teach men so, he shall be called the least in the kingdom of heaven: but whosoever shall do and teach them, the same shall be called great in the kingdom of heaven."

---

175 Ramsey, *Basic Christian Ethics*, 54-74.

176 Ramsey, *Basic Christian Ethics*, 54.

177 Cf. W. H. Velema, *Wet en Evangelie* (Kampen: Kok, 1987), 82-83. Cf. W. H. Velema, *Het Spreken en het Preken van de Kerk*, (Apeldoornse Studies 23), 45.

178 W. H. Velema, *Wet en Evangelie* (Kampen: Kok, 1987), 82-83. Cf. Vern Sheridan Poythress, *The Shadow of Christ in the Law of Moses* (Brentwood: Wolgemuth & Hyatt, 1991), 264-268: "Jesus in His person and His ministry brings to realization and fulfillment the whole warp and woof of Old Testament revelation, including the revelation of the law. The whole law points to Him, and its purposes find their realization in Him..." (268).

As far as the significance of the term "fulfillment" is concerned, it is important to note that Jesus does not merely confirm or establish the law against Pharisaic distortions. He does not simply reiterate the law but rather brings "the purposes of the law into realization. The law is to be written on the hearts of His disciples (see Jer 31:31-34). Jesus does not assert merely a static continuation of the force of the law, but rather a dynamic advance—in fact, the definitive fulfillment."[179] Jesus "came to realize the full measure of the intent and purpose of the law and the prophets. He came to complete, to consummate, to bring to full fruition and perfect fulfillment the law and the prophets."[180]

To ignore the relationship of Christ with the Father is to distort the relationship of Christ to the law, and to disjoin the Old Testament from the New. It is also to forfeit the structure of the biblical ethic, namely the law, and in the case of Ramsey, be left with principles. The Trinitarian framework for Christology is then important for ethics.

5.4.3.2. Christ and the Spirit

In Ramsey's Christology, the place of the Holy Spirit and his relationship to Christ is also ignored. The result is that Ramsey has problems articulating the relationship between Christ and his followers, also for ethics. In his *Basic Christian Ethics*, Ramsey speaks of an encounter which produces in the believer greater humility and greater achievement.[181] Ramsey is not specific on this "encounter," nor on the role of faith. Likewise with regard to the relation between Christ and the Spirit, some exegetical lines will indicate the indissoluble connections between Christ and the Spirit and the benefits of recognizing these connections. Firstly, again at Christ's baptism, the heavens were opened to him and he saw the Holy Spirit descending on him. He had already been conceived by the Holy Spirit (Matt 1:20; Luke 1:35) and had not been without the Holy Spirit during the first 30 years of his life, but at the start of his public ministry he was equipped with the Holy Spirit in order to be the Redeemer of his people (Luke 4:18-19). He descends on Jesus in order to enable him to perform his work of redemption. In Hebrews 9:14 we read that Christ "through the eternal Spirit offered himself without spot to God."

Secondly, as Christ did not speak of himself, so the Spirit of the Father and of the Son, guiding the followers of Christ into all truth, does not speak of himself but rather what he hears. Christ says: "...He shall receive of Mine, and shall show it to you" (John 16:14). Christ points to the relationship to the Father, when he adds: "All things that the Father has are Mine: therefore said I, that he shall take of Mine, and shall show it to you" (John 16:15).

The close connection of Christ and Spirit in the ministry of Christ and in the word of Christ has a soteriological thrust with ethical implications. The

---

179 Vern Poythress, *The Shadow of Christ*, 265.

180 John Murray, *Principles of Conduct: Aspects of Biblical Ethics*, 150.

181 Ramsey, *Basic Christian Ethics*, 200.

exalted Christ works and abides in us through his Word and Spirit. This involves two things with reference to the law in the life of the believer.[182]

Firstly, because of what Christ has done in bearing the condemnation of the law for us, soteriologically, Christ's Word and Spirit give persons power to know the glory of Christ. This glory was also present in the law but then it brought condemnation and death. Through the work of the Spirit, this glory is the redeeming and transforming glory in the face of Jesus Christ (cf. 2 Cor 3:3-4; 6; 9-11). From this soteriological ministry upon the tablets of the heart flows forth the ethical: a renunciation of dishonesty, craftiness, and deceit (2 Cor 4:1-4), in accordance with the law.

Secondly, the law was given for life but brought death for men instead (Rom 7:10), because it could not make alive (Gal 3:21). Soteriologically speaking, Jesus Christ as the life-giving Spirit (1 Cor 15:45) gives to believers the Spirit of life (Rom 8:2). This is so because Christ is the One in whom promise and law, which in the Old Testament dispensation were "earlier" and "later" by some 430 years, are now made one in Jesus Christ.

This soteriological union of promise and law has the ethical implication that the one who walks by the Spirit fulfills the righteousness of the law (Rom 8:4). This involves the same love--which is the fruit of the Spirit (Gal 5:22) and which is the fulfillment of the law (5:14)--which led Christ to suffer under the law for us (Gal 4:4). We no longer live and suffer under law, since "we are not under the law, but under grace" (Rom 6:14), but love--the love wherewith we have been loved--does call us to "suffer with him: that we may be also glorified with him" (Rom 8:17).

It is, however, also true that those who are led by the Spirit are not "under the law" (Gal 5:18). Hence, Paul's position seems to be that Christians who thus walk by the Spirit are not under the law. Yet they are not without law. For in walking according to the Spirit, the Spirit of righteousness is fulfilled in them.

To recognize the relationship between Christ and the Spirit along the exegetical lines outlined above, sustains the validity of the law for the believer as well as honors Christ's crucial fulfillment of the law. It establishes the connection between Christ and the believer, which in Ramsey is understood only vaguely as "an encounter." Ramsey has to content himself with principles which by their very nature struggle against concretization.

Christology is very essential for Christian ethics. But so is pneumatology, for there needs to be a living union with Christ, which is effected through the Holy Spirit. The Holy Spirit effects this union by working "in us a living *faith*" through the Word of promise. This faith is a bond, "made and maintained by the

[182] H. Stob, *Ethical Reflections*, 50-61. Cf. Ford Lewis Battles, "True Piety According to Calvin," 196-201.

Holy Spirit Himself."[183] Ethics needs a christological basis and the pneumatological application or apprehension (e.g. Rom. 8:1-11).[184]

5.4.3.3. The Law-Structure of a Scriptural Ethic

The effects of this narrow Christology show themselves in Ramsey's ethics in a neglect of the law, Christ's fulfillment thereof, and the benefit of Christ's fulfillment for the believer. It is the conviction of the present author that the dilemma which is so aptly characterized by Yoder in the terms of "freight across the bridge" is in part due to the lack of understanding regarding the function and significance of the structure of ethics in the Scripture. Words such as love, covenant, justice, compassion, etc. can all be found within Scripture and give expression to Scriptural realities. However, the actual framework or structure which these realities take is indicated by that element termed "law."

This is of relevance to the matter of the practice of ethics, for if Scripture can lend the categories or the configuration for a Christian ethic, then the need to reconstruct the largest part of ethics on "our side of the bridge" is lessened. Careful attention to the structure for ethics provided in that component of the Scriptures termed "law" can reduce the threat of pragmatism, that is, simply being directed by the issues themselves and their consequences.

The Ten Commandments specify the various areas in which the divine command comes. For example, the eighth commandment concerns matters of property and ownership. The ninth commandment concerns matters of language, court justice, and truth. Moreover, they either positively or negatively point in the direction which God's command takes. For example, the seventh commandment indicates negatively that the boundaries of marriage should not be infringed upon. Positively, it implies that the command of God is in favor of fidelity and mutuality. Furthermore, the commandments delineate areas in which the morality of the rest of the Bible is appropriately suited, substantiating or elaborating upon a certain commandment either through narrative, wisdom, or apocalyptic. For example, the narrative of Naboth's vineyard (1 Kgs 21) could be cited as a commentary upon the sixth, eighth, and tenth commandment. Wisdom's treatment of wayward persons (Prov 7) could be classified as

---

[183] H. Stob, *Ethical Reflections*, 56-57.

[184] Cf. J. P. Versteeg, *Christus en de Geest: een exegetisch onderzoek naar de verhouding van de opgestane Christus en de Geest van God volgens de brieven van Paulus*, Th.D. diss. Free University, Amsterdam, (Kampen: Kok, 1971), 338-380. Versteeg agrees with A. J. Bandstra (*The Law and the Elements of the World: An Exegetical Study in Aspects of Paul's Teaching*. Th.D. diss. Free University, Amsterdam. Kampen: Kok, 1964, 148): "In the Spirit, the 'law of God' in which the 'I' delighted, has become a reality in the Christian walk of life." "This law of the Spirit lies in line with the promise of Jeremiah 31:31-34. ...There where the freedom through the Spirit is known, there the law is interpreted from out of Christ," ["Deze wet van de Geest ligt in het verlengde van de belofte van Jer. 31,31-34." "...Waar de vrijheid door de Geest gekend wordt, (daar wordt) de wet vanuit Christus geïnterpreteerd"], Versteeg, *Christus en De Geest*, 345-346.

teaching concerning the seventh commandment. Thus the Decalogue provides a structure for Christian ethics.

The Ten Commandments lie at the heart of all Christian decision making and action. These Ten Commandments reflect God[185] and "correspond to the way we are made. They even correspond to creation,"[186] although creation has come under curse, but Christ's work of redemption concerns also this creation. The law is the Torah, which includes both the story of redemption and the demand accompanying it. This Torah is spelled out in both Testaments (by Moses and the prophets under the Old Testament, and by Christ and his apostles under the New Testament[187]). Its purpose is that persons might lovingly obey and obediently love him in accordance with his will.[188] Faith is crucial (Rom 14:23), for faith is obedience. Christian obedience means imitating God (Matt 5:48) in holiness and Christ in humility and love. It springs from gratitude for

---

185 Cf. J. Murray, "The Christian Ethic," *Collected Writings of John Murray* I, 176. Cf. J. Murray, "The Sanctity of the Moral Law," *Collected Writings of John Murray* I, 196. Cf. J. Murray, "The Nature of Sin," *Collected Writings of John Murray* II, 78. H. Stob points out that what distinguishes God, "as Christians know him," from "the gods of the philosophers is ... that he ... is not an object that is searched out, but a subject that invades ...." It is God "revealed ... who is the true and only principle of all good behavior ...." According to Scripture, "morality is grounded in the character, the acts, the purposes, and the instructions of the God of revelation. It is upon this God, the God spoken of in the Bible and professed in the Christian Church, that the Christian ethicist attempts to build his ethics and establish all practice. This is his ultimate principle," *Ethical Reflections*, 39.

186 Oliver Barclay, "The Nature of Christian Morality," in *Readings in Christian Ethics*: Volume 1: *Theory and Method*, eds. David K. Clark and Robert V. Rakestraw (Grand Rapids: Baker, 1994), 44.

187 Cf. Matthew 5:19-20; Romans 13:8-10; 1 Corinthians 6:9-11; 1 Corinthians 8. Cf. James 2:8-12. Cf. Gottlob Schrenk, "εντολη," *Theological Dictionary of the NT* II, eds. Gerhard Kittel and Gerhard Friedrich, trans. by Geoffrey W. Bromiley (Grand Rapids: Eerdmans Publishing Company, 1968), 548. Cf. W. H. Velema, "De liefde is de vervulling van de wet," in *Uw knecht hoort: Theologische opstellen aangeboden aan W. Kremer, J. van Genderen, B. J. Oosterhoff*, eds. J. Kruis, J. Plantinga, W. van 't Spijker, J. P. Versteeg (Amsterdam: Ton Bolland, 1979), 114. Cf. I. Howard Marshall, "Using the Bible in Ethics," *Essays in Evangelical Social Ethics*, ed. David F. Wright (Cape Town: Oxford University Press, 1981), 52.

188 Donald G. Bloesch, *Freedom for Obedience: Evangelical Ethics for Contemporary Times* (San Francisco: Harper and Row, 1987), also insists that Christian morality is a morality of obedience to the divine command. According to him, this obedience is guided by the example of Christ. My problem with his position is that he does not regard the Decalogue as "the absolute or irreducible criterion." He regards the Ten Commandments and the Sermon on the Mount as "relative criteria that nevertheless by the Spirit participate in the Absolute." According to him, the "absolute criterion is the unity of the law and the gospel in the divine commandment as it is applied to a particular situation." What these "relative criteria do" is "direct us to the Absolute--God's self-revelation in the Christ of biblical history," 7. He regards the divine command as specific, direct, spontaneous and free. This is in essence still a neo-orthodox position, although Bloesch differs from the neo-orthodox theologians in that he affirms a positive role for casuistry in Christian ethics, in view of his conviction that the Spirit gives the Bible a vital role in the revelation of a divine command, applying biblical commands to concrete situations.

grace received. The law is fulfilled by Christ (Matt 5:17).[189] The law is full of Christ and calls for Christ.[190] We cannot understand the law apart from Jesus Christ, for he has given its right interpretation. Apart from Christ, we cannot speak about the validity of the law for them who have been justified by faith. "Christ is the *telos* of the law for righteousness to every one that believeth" (Rom 10:4).[191] The law remains God's law, and therefore is "holy, just, good and spiritual" (Rom 7:12,13) for the Israelite as well for the Gentile (1 Cor 9:19-21).[192] It is the dignity of the Christian life to keep the divine law[193] with a glad and cordial obedience, for Christ's sake. By faith, in love, God's law is obediently observed. The church hopes for the day when the Savior will receive it and acknowledge his own work in it: "Well done, good and faithful servant" (Matt 25:23).

In a similar vein, Paul focuses on the moral agent's identity rather than activity (Rom 12). Like Jesus, Paul is concerned to portray a distinctively Christian character. Ethics is ultimately an outflow of one's being, that is, being in proper relationship with God and one's neighbor and the place and task on the earth. For Paul, the resurrection of Jesus Christ imparts a powerful and dynamic quality for the life of a Christian (Rom 6:4-5).[194] And precisely because Christian conversion means a radical transformation, much of Paul's moral teaching is in the indicative mode rather than in the imperative mode.[195] The events of the Pentecost further give Paul the confidence that the ideal of Christ can actually be realized, through the power and the grace of the Holy Spirit.

The distinctive biblical teaching of a life in imitation of Christ[196] deals with the moral agent himself. It challenges the moral agent with the ideal of the highest moral standard: the obedience of Christ. This concern with the character of the moral agent is ultimately what counts in the process of moral reasoning, because what we do ultimately depends upon who we are.[197] This emphasis on the personal dimension is not absent, even in the Old Testament. One of its

---

[189] Cf. W. H. Velema, *Geroepen tot heilig leven* (Kampen: Kok, 1985), 102, 97, 99. Cf. H. N. Ridderbos, *Paulus: ontwerp van zijn theologie* (Kampen: Kok, 1966), 315-316.

[190] Cf. W. H. Velema, *Wet en Evangelie*, 85. Cf. Guthrie, *New Testament Theology* (Downers Grove: InterVarsity, 1981), 677.

[191] Cf. W. H. Velema, *Wet en Evangelie*, 85. Cf. A. J. Bandstra, *The Law and the Elements of the World: An Exegetical Study in Aspects of Paul's Teaching*, Th.D. Diss. Free University, Amsterdam (Kampen: Kok, 1964), 101-106; 183ff. Cf. N. T. Wright, *The Climax of the Covenant: Christ and the Law in Pauline Theology* (Minneapolis: Fortress, 1991), 241.

[192] Cf. W. H. Velema, *Geroepen tot heilig leven*, 105-106.

[193] Cf. H. N. Ridderbos, *Paulus: ontwerp van zijn theologie*, 240.

[194] Cf. J. Murray, *The Epistle to the Romans* I (The New International Commentary of the New Testament), 229.

[195] Cf. H. N. Ridderbos, *Paulus: ontwerp van zijn theologie*, 279-284. Cf. L. Floor, "Die indikatief en die imperatief in die prediking," in *Theologia Reformata* 17 (March 1974), 24-27.

[196] Cf. John 13:34; Ephesians 4:32; 5:1; Colossians 3:13 1 Peter 2:21. Cf. W. H. Velema, *Geroepen tot heilig leven*, 119-125. Cf. J. I. Packer, *Our Lord's Understanding of the Law of God*. Dr. G. Campbell Morgan Memorial Lecture (Glasgow: Pickering and Inglis, nd.), 9, 10.

[197] Cf. J. I. Packer, *Our Lord's Understanding of the Law of God*, 11.

fundamental teachings is that the Israelites are called to be God's people. God presents his character and gracious activities toward Israel as a model for them to emulate in their relationships with others. For "the God who brought you out of the land of Egypt" acts as moral shorthand to instruct and to inspire. Likewise in the New Testament Jesus becomes the perfect model of humankind, calling his disciples to a life of imitation. " ... Be perfect therefore, even as your Father Who is in heaven is perfect" (Matt 5:48). Jesus provides the fullness and the richness of what God intends humanity to be: the image of God.[198] For this reason the essence of Jesus' moral teaching is neither merely a totally inflexible allegiance to the God-given laws as rules, nor a calculating assessment of neighborable consequences. Instead the Incarnate God challenges disciples to be faithful co-workers in service of the Kingdom of God. Jesus furnishes a multitude of both positive and negative examples of obedience, often challenging rather than commanding.[199]

We can also say that what the Lord promises and calls for is obedience to revelation. There is the normative Law of the Ten Commandments in the framework of the Gospel of Christ. Moreover, there is the existential or personal dimension, the moral agent himself. The coordination of the normative and the existential provides ethics with a structure and standard to guard against pragmatism.

5.4.3.4. An Illustration - Physician-Assisted Suicide

To illustrate how the structure of the Scriptural ethic operates in contrast to pragmatism, a brief comparison of H. Kuitert's proposal concerning assisted suicide and some biblical lines on the matter seems fruitful. The extreme character of Kuitert's proposal renders it a good candidate to bring the issues into sharp relief. It should be remembered that both Ramsey and Verhey oppose assistance in suicide.[200] Gustafson has written that "suicide" under certain circumstance is to be considered "morally justifiable."[201] Yet he never speaks about assisting in suicide as legitimate. The Dutch ethicist H. Kuitert has argued that in view of the fact that the right to autonomy includes the right to suicide, as long as practicing that right does not harm others, it is morally permissible to assist some one in suicide at his request, under certain conditions.[202] Someone

---

[198] Cf. Klaus Bockmuehl, "The Ten Commandments: Are They Still Valid?", in *Crux*, 15:4 (December 1979), 24.

[199] Cf. J. I. Packer, *Our Lord's Understanding of the Law of God*, 11.

[200] Ramsey, *Ethics at the Edges of life*, 322; Verhey, "Luther's 'Freedom of a Christian' and a Patient's Autonomy," in *Bioethics and the Future of Medicine: A Christian Appraisal*, eds. John F. Kilner, Nigel M. de S. Cameron and David L. Schiedemayer (Grand Rapids, Michigan: William B Eerdmans Publishing Company, 1995), 82.

[201] Gustafson, *Theocentric Perspective* II, 215.

[202] H. M. Kuitert, *Suïcide: wat is er tegen? zelfdoding in moreel perspektief* (3rd ed.; Baarn: Ten Have, 1994).

who assists in suicide should consider all of the following criteria: the unbearability and the constancy of the pain, the absence of external pressure and the awareness of options, the involvement of a physician and the consideration of the person's family.[203] For Kuitert the Bible is important for its narrative, but not for its morality.[204] Turning to Christian doctrine, Kuitert finds the unique responsibility of humans over against God as Creator and Redeemer to be an important consideration against suicide. Nevertheless, according to Kuitert, this does not imply an unconditional "No" to suicide. Kuitert regards suicide as a calamity but stipulates that this is not moral judgment. He insists on peeling off the moral skin off the classical argument against suicide. Suicide is not a crime of the "suicide"[205] against himself, but rather a calamity that he brings on himself. We do not say to him: "You may not do this, for it is morally wrong"; rather we say: "do yourself no harm" (cf. Acts 16:28).[206]

Kuitert's extreme position illustrates the dynamics of pragmatism well. Firstly, human autonomy is here the only norm but it constitutes no more than a reflex of individual pragmatism. The moral considerations for the assistant in suicide create some space for moral caution. The controls of this caution are conceivably within the reach of the individual to manipulate. More significant than the pragmatism it embraces, is the pragmatism it fosters. As Verhey points out, by regarding assisted suicide as an option, the options are increased but also one option is effectively eliminated, namely the option of "staying alive without having to justify one's existence." We must realize that by morally maximizing freedom and so socially making assisted suicide legal we are in essence asking any one who is weak and sick to provide grounds for them to continue to exist. Verhey prefers to keep the option of being weak and ill without having to "justify one's existence ... for it fits the story of life as a gift, as a given."[207] Kuitert's position fosters a culture of pragmatism.

Over against the proclivity to pragmatism, the structure of Scripture produces a theocentric alternative. The command "not to kill" (Ex 20:13; Deut 5:17) delineates the space, points the direction, and indicates the force of revelation on the matter of life and death. One cannot and should not take the commands on their own. Each is intertwined with all the others. On the matter of assisted suicide this is clear especially of the fifth, eighth, and tenth commandments (according to the Reformed count). But all the rest impinge on the issue as well. Yet, in this case, the sixth commandment is clearly the primary referent.

The immediate space of the sixth commandment is that of life and death. The direction of the commandment is in favor of the preservation of life. The

---

[203] Kuitert, *Suïcide: wat is er tegen? zelfdoding in moreel perspektief*, 220-222.

[204] Kuitert, *Suïcide: wat is er tegen? zelfdoding in moreel perspektief*, 137.

[205] Kuitert uses the term "suïcidant", which in English is "suicide" and refers to the person who intentionally takes his own life. The context as well as the article differentiates between the two.

[206] Kuitert, *Suïcide: wat is er tegen? zelfdoding in moreel perspektief*, 169-173.

[207] Verhey, "Luther's 'Freedom of a Christian' and a Patient's Autonomy," 89-91.

force of the commandment is against death. This would clearly include the preservation of one's own life, and the corresponding prohibition of its destruction.

The commandments are framed in such a way that ethical material from throughout the Scriptures can appropriately stand in its extension. Scripture pictures the reality of the Sovereign Lord over all of creation and from whom all value and meaning flow. The world we live in is a world under God. Scripture pictures all that is as having value and meaning as a gift and favor from God. For this reason value and meaning are not intrinsic to any person or thing as such, but neither is the reality of living in this world devoid of meaning and value. Rather, these are bestowed upon all creatures by God as his gift. Because of this, God calls upon society and each member of society to recognize him and his Word and to recognize the value and meaning which God has given to each of his creatures. In view of this view of a cosmos under God, we are not in a position to argue intrinsic rights, such as for instance, the right to self-determination. Rather we must emphasize human life as valued by God.

Scripture describes life as a gift from God. That is clearly taught already in the first pages of Scripture. God did not need human life, for he in himself is life. God has been pleased to create human life, outside of himself. Though human life is entirely in dependence upon him, God gave it a measure of freedom. Beyond the comprehension of the finite mind is the confession that with God is the fountain of life (Psalm 36:9). Life is a divine gift from beginning to end.

A few points can be inferred. Firstly, neither to ourselves nor to others do we give life. Parents are the instrument, but not the source of the life of their children. Secondly, we may not do as we seem fit either with our life or with the lives of others. Thirdly, there is an collective and individual aspect to life. On the one hand, God has construed life collectively. On the other hand, persons received life individually.

Furthermore, Scripture indicates that life is a divine favor. With sin, the creature deprived the Creator of honor, while also dispossessing himself of life. God has intervened and promised life anew. Eve is called "the mother of all living" (Gen 3:20). From her the Son of God was born in due time. He, however, had to lay down His life. Through Him God has given man favor to live for Him and one another.

Scripture also speaks about sickness. Hezekiah's sickness can be referred to as an illustration. One day he "was sick unto death," which is tantamount to saying that his life was ebbing away (Isa 38:1). In Isa 38:11 he is aware of and expresses the implication of death. "I shall not see the Lord, even the Lord in the land of the living; I shall behold man no more with the inhabitants of the world." Here is indicated that life is more than just breathing, eating and drinking, working and relaxing, being awake and asleep; more than thinking and having pleasure. Life is living in the fellowship with the Lord on this earth and in the companionship of others. That is the biblical meaning of life here on the earth, as a favor of the Lord.

On his sickbed Hezekiah learned to see the high value of life as a gift from God but also as a favor from the Lord. His reference in verse 17 to his sins suggests that God not only faced him with death but also with his sins. Then he called upon the Lord, and his prayer was heard by God. Another 15 years of life was granted to him as a gift and favor of the Lord, purchased later by Jesus Christ on the cross, who was forsaken of God and humanity.

Scripture also describes life as a calling of the Lord that we are to respect, a life in which we are to live in loving obedience and obedient love to the Lord and His Word, also his commandments (Matt 22:37-40). Then when we become ill unto death and are no longer to occupy what we and others consider to be a significant role in society, we must realize that we as human beings are more important than our work, more important than any contribution we can make to society. The Lord God considers our life here as his gift and favor, even when it seems there is no more significance to our life.

Scripture does not suggest anywhere that suffering might justify the taking of human life.[208] We know that Job in his suffering did long for death, but he expressed it to God. He did not think of taking his own life (Job 3, 6, 7, 14). In 2 Corinthians 1:4 Paul blesses God for comforting "us in all our tribulation, that we may be able to comfort those who are in any trouble, by the comfort wherewith we ourselves are comforted of God." He goes on to write about "the sufferings of Christ" abounding in us, "that our consolation also abounds by Christ" (verse 5). In these passages "the Bible seems to define a way of life in suffering." Over against the "secular standards of love and mercy," which value medicine not only to fight suffering but also to help die by suicide, Scripture indeed teaches that God gives us medicine to combat suffering but prohibits taking one's life (Ex 20:13; Rom 13:9). According to Scripture, "we may never take our lives, even at death's door,"[209] but we must learn to come to terms with this encounter with suffering in a Christian way.

Scripture exposes death as an enemy (1 Cor 15:26). It speaks about death as painful, as associated with suffering of both body and soul (Ps 55:4,5; Ps 90:6,7; Heb 2:15). Death severs ties of love that are precious. It breaks the heart and burdens the spirit. We may well try to dismiss it from our mind, thinking that life must go on. But when death involves ourselves and those we love, we feel pain; we struggle with agony. It hurts, and we weep (Job 19; Isa 38:14). And it comes to all of us, to rich and poor, strong and weak, old and young. Its advance may be delayed, but its arrival is sure. Nigel M. de S. Cameron reminds of the "old Christian image" of death as that of the "waters of the Jordan, to be crossed at last as we finally reach the Promised Land." Although Scripture "tells

---

208 Dewey J. Hoitenga, Jr., "Death's Door," in *The Banner*, 25 January 1993, 10.

209 Dewey J. Hoitenga, Jr., "Death's Door," 11. Dewey J. Hoitenga, Jr. does not use this phrase, "According to Scripture" but rather: "God seems to tell us clearly...." Hoitenga rejects "active euthanasia."

us that the riverbed dried up for the Israelites (Josh. 3) ... the image of crossing" the cold waters of that "river is still a potent image." After all, death is the wages of sin (Rom 6:23). Though resurrection "hope shines into the night ..., on this side of death the darkness lingers."[210]

When we consider this, it is an anomaly to speak about "a right to die with dignity." Hoitenga rightly points out that much of this idea of "a right to die with dignity ... springs from the secular humanitarianism of our society." According to Scripture, "there is no dignity at all in death or dying. Jesus neither sought death as a right nor asked for" dying with dignity. That Christ refused an offer of pain relief (Matt 27:34), is to be understood against the background of his unique, mediatorial work, "choosing to endure with full consciousness the sufferings appointed for him" (Mark 10:38; 14:36).[211] His death reminds us that death and dying are still terrible, unnatural things that God requires of us.

Nevertheless Scripture also says that "Jesus Christ...has abolished death...." (2 Tim 1:10). Persons still die, but Jesus Christ has broken the power of death by destroying its finality. Death is a painful experience; but that pain is bearable with the remembrance that in Christ the penalty has been paid, the price has been paid, and the sting has been removed (1 Cor 15:55-56.). On account of Christ's death, for believers death is "not a satisfaction for ... sins, but only an abolishing of sin, and a passage into eternal life,"[212] the gateway to heaven. The keys of death are in the hands of the Lord of life. When believers fall asleep in their Savior, they are delivered once and for all from sin's grasp, Satan's power, and death's claim (John 11:25-26). Thus we face it not in fear but in faith, for "we are more than conquerors" in Jesus Christ (Rom 8:37). There is the comfort of the Lord's abiding presence, as Psalm 23 describes it. We enter into the dark valley of pain and trial, remembering God's gracious promise, "I will not leave you nor forsake you" (Heb 13:5). The words, "Thou art with me" (Ps 23:4), express not only divine companionship but also divine compassion. The Good Shepherd loves and cares for me, his sheep. "Death is both our enemy and friend. This paradox of death, like the paradox of suffering, no Christian can escape. Nor should we want to."[213] Those who believe in Jesus know even that one day their "broken mortal bodies shall be raised up like ... [Christ's] glorious body"[214] (Job 19:25-27; 1 Cor 15:53-57).

Reference needs to be made to the role of faith. By faith we become partakers of Christ and all His benefits.[215] Moreover, the comfort which is to be

---

210 Nigel M. de S. Cameron, "Living Wills and the Will to Live," in *Christianity Today*, 6 April 1992, 22-23.

211 William L. Lane, *Commentary on the Gospel of Mark* (The New International Commentary of the New Testament), 564.

212 Heidelberg Catechism, Lord's Day 16, Answer 42.

213 Dewey J. Hoitenga, Jr., "Death's Door," 11.

214 Nigel M. de S. Cameron, *The New Medicine: The Revolution in Technology and Ethics* (London: Hodder & Stoughton, 1991), 37.

215 Cf. John 1: 12, 13; Heidelberg Catechism, Lord's Day 7, Answer 20.

obtained by the knowledge of God's providence is a comfort which is obtained only by faith. It is by faith that we can also live and overcome the world.[216] It is by faith that we can fulfill whatever God's purposes are for us--subdue kingdoms, work righteousness.[217] But it is also by faith that we can suffer, endure the things that come at us. The grace of faith is just as powerful and victorious if we have to suffer. We will be sustained.[218]

W. H. Velema, in his *Oriëntatie in de christelijke ethiek*, has pointed out that when we use the word and concept "tragic" or "tragedy,"[219] we actually in a given situation remove from a person his responsibility and regard him as a prey of his circumstances. It is not a biblical concept. Rather it originates with the Greeks who see man as being subject to fate. Moreover, the concept of fate originates with the concept of more than one god who do not live in harmony with each other and under whose conflicts and strifes man lives as a victim.[220]

This comparison of some lines from the structure of a Scriptural ethic with Kuitert's autonomous position, shows the effect of attention to the category and force of law in revelation. Whether the commandment is viewed as a spring-head of a multitude of different lines, or as a magnet attracting an array of ethical directions, the commandment lends a unity and direction regarding the matter of assisted suicide. In conversation with the moral direction throughout the Scriptures, the commandment weaves a web of theocentricity. It yields the categories and energies for an ethical response to the issue of assisted suicide and minimizes the threat of a pragmatism which reaches for criteria within the issue and its consequences.

5.5. Retrospect

5.5.1. Scripture and Ethics

This final chapter has intentionally shifted to theological categories and made use of exegetical lines. This chapter has assumed that *proper* theological and exegetical delineations are fundamental to ethics. It appears that improper or

---

216 Cf. 1 John 5:4.

217 Cf. the first part of Hebrews 11.

218 Cf. Hebrews 11:32-38.

219 Gustafson uses this terminology at various points. So does Verhey, "Sanctity and Scarcity: The Makings of Tragedy (Reflections on a Crisis in Medicine)," in *The Reformed Journal*, Feb. 1985, 10-14. Cf. Verhey, "The Good Samaritan and Scarce Medical Resources," in *Christian Scholar's Review* 23:3 (1994), 363.

220 W. H. Velema, *Oriëntatie in de Christelijke Ethiek*, 106. W. H. Velema also suggests that the ethical problem of *collisio officiorum* is related to this concept of tragedy. This is evident in Gustafson. He acknowledges the tragedy and does not see a *collisio officiorum*. It is needful wish to insist that evil remains evil, even when, "being the lesser evil", it appears the right thing to do. We shall do the evil with a heavy heart, and seek God's cleansing of our conscience for having done it, through Jesus Christ, W. H. Velema, *Oriëntatie in de Christelijke Ethiek*, 101-108.

unbalanced theological emphases leave the door open for the crisis of authority within theocentric ethics. The forces of reason, community, and practice were found to be crucial in American Protestant ethics, and the analyses of the authors in the preceding chapters fell into these categories. In Gustafson, Ramsey, and Verhey, to varying degrees, the "rational" has harnessed the "collective" and the "practical" as constituents in ethics. Conversely, the "collective" and the "practical" have depended upon the "rational" for legitimation.

Philosophical approaches to ethics often retort to theological approaches, that they make philosophical choices, but leave them unacknowledged.[221] This chapter has sought to demonstrate that philosophical choices are by necessity theological choices, but often unacknowledged. For instance, the problematizing of Scripture is a theological choice. The utilization of the concept of "potentiality" on the issue of abortion is a theological choice. The openness to the "rational" is not owing to the non-theological approach, but rather to the miscontrual of theology at various points.

The following could be noted in terms of compact summary:

-Revelation and the Knowledge of God:
The key to the proper relationship between philosophy and theology lies contained in the recognition of the proper relation of faith and reason, the proper balance and interrelation of the *fides qua* and the *fides quae*, and the necessity of revelation for the knowledge of God owing to the noetic effects of sin. Epistemology is to be defined and grounded by soteriology.

-The Scriptural Norm and the Church:
The relation of the Scripture and the church is seen aright when the church is viewed as the assembly of true Christian believers (Belgic Confession of Faith, Article 27). The church is called into existence and normed by the Scriptures. When this is confessed, then the faithful attendance to the Scriptures will be a mark of the true church, for the church depends for its existence on the Scriptures. To that end the church has received and receives the Scriptures from the Lord of the church, Christ himself.

-The Law and the Christian Life:
Within the assembly of those who exercise faith, the ground for the Christian life is Christ viewed within a Trinitarian framework. Christ's fulfillment of the law, and the benefit for the believer must be kept in view. Careful attention to the structure for ethics provided in that component of the Scriptures termed "law" can reduce the threat of pragmatism, that is, simply being directed by the issues themselves and their consequences.

---

[221] Cf. Thiselton, *The Two Horizons*, 448.

5.5.2. Law

In this chapter, the law has been extensively featured. Firstly, it has been argued that the law has a prominent place in revelation and thus is instrumental in the knowledge of God. A classical function of the law is its role in the knowledge of sin. The law can also be seen as a reflection of God. The law in the hand of Christ (H.C., L.D. 2) functions then epistemologically to reveal God. The law of God is part of the theological alternative to the function of philosophy in Gustafson, Ramsey, and Verhey. Secondly, the law as it has been fulfilled by Christ functions ethically in the life of the church. The law furnishes the categories or the configuration for a Christian ethic. Consequently, the need to reconstruct the largest part of ethics on "our side of the bridge" is lessened.

When the law has been treated in Christian theology, it has often received a place in relationship to practice. Related to this, and symptomatic thereof, is the emphasis on the commandments with more seemingly more "tangible" content, broadly coinciding with the second table of the law. This is, however, a misrepresentation of the commandments and of ethics generally. The commandments concern not only practice, but also the mind and the heart (Matt 22:36, Mark 12:30). In fact, it is dangerous to separate the noetic and the practical, the epistemological and the ethical. The commandments instruct the mind, heart, and hand to act in coherent and total obedience to God. This seems to be at least one aspect of the force of the bipartite *Shema* (Deut 6:4-5): since God is one (v. 4), our whole being ought to be oriented to God alone (v. 5). A separation of the noetic and the practical is liable to break the whole commitment to God required by the law, from the first commandment to the last.

Classical theology has regularly concentrated the epistemological function of the law in its first usage, namely the conviction of sin. The third use of the law, as in Calvin,[222] ought, however, to carry its share of the epistemological weight. In both cases, the ethical and epistemological must be thoroughly united.

The massive attraction of many theologians and ethicists, including Gustafson and Verhey, to philosophical hermeneutics would be curtailed if the proper epistemological function of the law were recognized. Such recognition would also lessen the reliance on principles with their idealistic baggage, as in the case of Ramsey.

5.5.3. Theocentricity

It might seem conceptually inconsistent to insist that theocentricity is not established by a simple focus on God. The nature of theocentricity and the manner of obtaining it might appear needlessly compounded: definition and

222 Calvin, *Institutes* II,7,12.

method appear so disjunctive. The chief determinant for this disjunction is the noetic effect of sin. Philosophically speaking, without this postulate, Gustafson's project would achieve what it aims for. With this postulate, a simple reconstruction of theocentricity is impossible without revelation and without Christ. The relationship of reason and revelation parallels that of general and special revelation. For that reason, Calvin's argument in the *Institutes* is so relevant to the discussion. A proper view of revelation and its function is the *sine qua non* for theocentricity. The datum of revelation itself must be taken seriously.

The corollary to this is that the content of revelation must be taken seriously. True theocentricity can only thus be achieved. For example, a mere focus on God or on Christ will not suffice to guarantee theocentricity. This can be seen in Ramsey's neglect of the Trinitarian framework for Christology, or in Yoder's "Jesu-centrism." A broad emphasis on the Trinity and its interrelationships alone can ensure theocentricity. This has been characteristic within the Reformed tradition, and particularly in Calvin. W. H. Velema has typified Calvin's ethics as "theocentric, christological and pneumatological." Christ is the foundation of the Christian life in Trinitarian relationship.[223]

The contours of this theocentricity are as follows. Firstly, God is in the center in Calvin's dogmatics and ethics. That is, everything is derived from God and is to be directed to God. By virtue of creation we come from God, and--more profoundly so--by virtue of redemption we belong to him, insofar as we believe in him. For that reason we ought to direct our life to him. We are not our own, we are God's.[224] Secondly, Christ's work is the foundation of his ethics. Mindful of the connection between Christ's person and work, W. H. Velema points up that, according to Calvin, Christ is the foundation of the Christian life, and with that he is the foundation of justification and sanctification, which are applied to us through the Spirit.[225] Thirdly, the Holy Spirit is the bond that unites us to Christ, kindles in our hearts love to God and love to our neighbor, and burns out the sinful passions.[226] In view of the fact that these three aspects are interrelated, it is important to see that which makes the theocentric perspective theocentric is precisely the christological basis and the pneumatological application or apprehension.

Finally, a proper recognition of the place of the law is as well necessary for theocentricity. This is, however, on a different level than the Trinitarian emphasis, for the law is not to be classified in the same way. It is rather an aspect of the revelation of the Trinity. As was argued concerning Christology, that a full view of the relationship of Christ to the Father illumines the role of the law in Christ's work, and a full view of the relationship of Christ to the

---

[223] W. H. Velema, "Ethiek bij Calvijn," in *Reformatorische Stemmen verleden en heden* (Apeldoorn: Willem de Zwijgerstichting, 1989), 200.
[224] Velema, "Ethiek bij Calvijn," 198. Cf. Calvin, *Institutes*, I,7,1.
[225] Velema, "Ethiek bij Calvijn," 199.
[226] Velema, "Ethiek bij Calvijn," 199-200.

Spirit illumines the role of the law in the believer, so the law is an aspect of the relationship of each of the persons to the Trinity. The implication is that the law is important in the relation of each person of the Trinity to humanity in its collective and individual aspects.

Moreover, the law is a significant portion of revelation itself, sometimes being used as a synonym for it (cf. Pss 19; 119). And revelation from God to the corrupted mind singularly effects any knowledge of God. Finally, the law in its details focuses the mind, heart, and being upon God and God alone. Each of the commandments possesses a theocentric orientation and enforces a theocentric orientation.

Summary

Theological Ethics and Holy Scripture: The Use Of Scripture in the Works of James M. Gustafson, R. Paul Ramsey, and Allen D. Verhey

The subject matter of this dissertation is the role of Scripture in theological ethics. The specific inquiry is after the level at which and the manner in which Scripture informs ethics. The issue is broached by way of the work of James M. Gustafson, R. Paul Ramsey, and Allen D. Verhey, three representative ethicists on the recent American Protestant scene. The perimeters of inquiry are thus delimited according to the American context and Protestant affiliation of the authors. The discussion of Gustafson, Ramsey, and Verhey reveals the guiding components of the question as to the role of Scripture in ethics, namely, the role of reason, the character of the community, and the place of practice.

I. Introduction: Historical background and contemporary context

Chapter 1 provides a historical background and contemporary context for the issue of the role of Scripture in ethics within the American Protestant scene. The distinctly American character can be discerned in a focus on the practice of ethics and the impetus to collectively and individually conform to a social standard. These three elements, the practical, the collective, and the rational, can be traced historically for their emergence and development. Puritanism, the Enlightenment, and the Great Awakening were the primary shapers of these aspects and their force in ethics. Yet they did not find a wholly developed fusion till Walter Rauschenbusch and the Social Gospel. During the course of the twentieth century, the theological momentum shifted to so-called Neo-orthodoxy, in America associated chiefly with Reinhold and H. Richard Niebuhr. H. Richard Niebuhr, long time professor at Yale University, combined an emphasis on the transcendence of God and the relativity of human understanding. He blended the collective, rational, and practical by putting forward the community's discernment as the determining context for ethical decisions. All graduates of Yale University, Gustafson, Ramsey, and somewhat later Verhey, have worked in the wake of and under the influence of H. Richard Niebuhr.

The contours of the role of Scripture in the recent ethical discussion have been set by this preceding history. The prominence of the datum of experience draws upon the rational strand in American ethical thought. The role of the Christian community is stressed as the framework within which Scripture has and receives authority. The aspect identified as "collective" in the discussion above has been raised to the prominent level of the determinative context in which and through which Scripture receives authority. The rational and the collective aspects make the term "dialogue" popular.

II. James M. Gustafson: The use of Scripture in theocentric ethics

Chapter 2 examines the function of Scripture in the work of James Gustafson. Gustafson can be best placed at the cusp of the neo-orthodoxy and modernism. In his work, the subject of Scripture and its authority is raised in three settings: 1) in polemical discussion with fundamentalists on authority; 2) in sympathetic discussion as an example of the development of religious tradition; 3) in amenable discussion on the source of Christian theology. In each instance, Gustafson's discussion of Scripture is highly qualifying in nature. These qualifications can be grouped together under four distinct, though related, tenets. 1) The Experience-Revelation disjunction: The experiential nature of the construction and reception of knowledge renders the normativity of Scripture indelibly subjective. 2) The Reality-Morality disjunction: Scripture does not reveal morality, but rather the gospel reality, to which the law morality is then a response to be constructed by the community. 3) The Christ-Bible disjunction: Faith is in Christ and not in the Bible. 4) The Character-Norm disjunction: Biblical teachings are not easily applicable as norms, but seem to inform Christian character. Each of these points is a manifestation of a rational qualification of the normativity of Scripture and a transfer of authority to the community.

Gustafson's actual employment of Scripture comes to the fore in his theocentric program for ethics. Theocentrism is defined as the aim to order all things in relation to God. Anthropocentrism, its opposite, orients itself towards the mere well-being of humans and is evident in outright pragmatism, but also in theologies which hinge simply on human salvation. Experience is necessarily the point of departure, which for the Christian is best characterized by piety, the sense of dependence upon the sovereign governance of God. Ethics is then a dialogical process with reflection upon social, cultural, and individual situations with a discernment of divine government. Gustafson does not advocate casuistry, but a dialogism in which Scripture is a source much like tradition. Scripture, then, occupies a role at at least four levels: 1) in the definition of theocentrism, in that the Scripture provides an impulse for monotheistic theism; 2) in the shaping of tradition, which has a voice in the dialogue of discernment; 3) as a distinct voice in the discernment process as a deposit of construed experience; and 4) as it portrays Christ as the incarnation of dependence upon God, such as in the Synoptics.

Theology and ethics belong to second order reflection upon experience. Gustafson does theology within the Reformed tradition in dialogue with the data from natural sciences. Gustafson acknowledges his distinct preference for the Reformed tradition, three aspects in particular: 1) the pronounced sense of the otherness of God; 2) the profound exercise and valuation of piety; and 3) a distinct conviction to relate all things to the powerful Other. Gustafson's construal of the Reformed tradition is selective and revisionist. The importance for Gustafson of aligning himself with a tradition could be seen as part of his method and his point of departure for ethics. One could conclude that Gustafson's preference for the Reformed tradition provides him with 1) the "soil" on which he is able to "cultivate" his discussion, and 2) the warrants for certain theological and ethical choices.

Experience being his starting-point, Gustafson moves in close proximity to Schleiermacher, understanding God as the power who bears down upon us and Christ as the incarnation of theocentric piety. Gustafson's anthropology emphasizes the dependencies and interdependencies of human life, his soteriology the enlargement of vision and valuation. The Christian life is an extension of this correction of vision and being, and morality is discerned in rational and reflective activity within community. Ethics is interdependent upon theology, for theocentric piety, which is exercised in theology, impacts the life of individuals and communities. From Troeltsch and others, Gustafson has learned to view everything within the confines of sociological and historical knowledge. The locus of ethical decision-making is the Christian community, as it discerns, in part on the basis of Scripture, what is the proper theocentric response.

III. R. Paul Ramsey: The Use of Scripture in Christian ethics

Chapter 3 examines the function of Scripture in the work of Paul Ramsey. Ramsey belonged to the neo-orthodoxy of the mid-century, somewhere on an axis between Barth and Reinhold Niebuhr. In Paul Ramsey's ethical thought there is less a direct urge to create a distance between Scripture and moral action, as with Gustafson. Ramsey turns to Scripture without much explanation. He calls the Bible the traditional source of ethics in the Hebrew-Christian tradition. The essential character of the Bible for ethics is grounded in the connection between God and Christian ethics.

Meanwhile, a certain distance is evident in the desire to construct a single unifying principle with which to meet the issues of Christian practice. The distance which Ramsey creates between Scripture and Christian ethics is a principled distance. The similarities in situations call for principles of action. He seeks a middle way between pure situationalism and those who propose only rules with no attention to the situation.

The agape principle as it is taught in the Bible and manifested in Christ is the highest embodiment of the Christian moral practice. The lacuna created by the absence of immediate biblical authority is filled by a christocentric understanding of love. Ramsey does not leave behind the remainder of the Bible once he has arrived at the person of Christ. The totality of the Bible helps him get the full significance of Christ in view.

The term "principle" has two senses. The first sense is that of coherent simplicity in the form of an idea which carries the potential of being brought into relation with other matters enabling a certain method of appropriation. The second sense is that of a singular notion which stands in an antithetical relationship of infinite quality to that which has the potential of being pluralized and set in opposition to the singular notion. The first is prioritizing, the second dialectic. The two senses are dependent upon one another. As Ramsey "distills" the principle of "love" from the Scriptures, he finds it in an antithetical relationship to natural and human codifications.

Ramsey's discussion assumes some of the results of historical criticism of the Bible and its rationalistic heritage, such as the supposed presence of myth in Scripture. This gives occasion to philosophical elaboration, idealist, and existentialist, on biblical themes, such as sin.

Later on Ramsey appears to move to a more normative ethic, in which he insists that love be "inprincipled." He argues that the Christian life may be productive of rules as well as mere acts. Thus he takes the situationists to task by pointing to the inevitability of generalizing from the particular to the general. On the one hand, Ramsey does not have to abandon his original act-agapism entirely; on the other hand, he moves beyond it to a rule ethic--at least one of summary rules. A similar development can be traced in Ramsey's increased recognition for the place of natural law, particularly for the issue of just war. He labels his position "Christ transforming natural law" by analogy with Niebuhr's adage "Christ transforming culture."

Ramsey had earlier interacted with idealism in his dissertation. Later his concentration on principles would suit an idealist view of reality. Though Ramsey prioritizes Christ over concepts otherwise proposed by idealists, even the motif of "transformism" is indebted to an idealist framework. The consequences of a principled interpretation of Scripture are at least three: 1) reductionism and the risk of eclecticism; 2) an idealistic concentration on mind and thought; 3) a greater focus on the moral agency of the community.

Ramsey aligns himself with the rational strand in the history of American ethics in two ways. 1) He is "rational" in the sense of working on the plane of ideas. Ramsey's method is rational not in the sense of opting for reason over revelation, but rationally opting within revelation for one reality over another. This is an important qualification. 2) His ethic can be termed rational because of a qualified openness to any philosophy.

In the practice of Ramsey's Christian ethics, direct references to Scripture are used theologically and christologically. Important biblical principles such as righteousness and covenant are used in order to provide guidance on issues. Natural law is called in to aid certain issues such as just war, but Ramsey is clear about how agape is to perform a transformative function and retains a normative character. The practice of Ramsey's Christian ethics also demonstrates how he struggles with the particular and concrete embodiment of the agape principle in practice.

IV. Allen D. Verhey: The use of Scripture in moral argument

Chapter 4 examines the role of Scripture in the work of Allen D. Verhey. Verhey's work suggests influences from Dutch Reformed orthodoxy, American evangelicalism, Rauschenbusch, and neo-orthodoxy. The role of the Bible within Christian moral discernment and discourse is a given for Verhey. Tradition is responsible for the implementation of the Bible in ethics, as both source and standard. This vantage-point yields to the church the primary ground within which the Scriptures manifest a certain function and role. The role of the Bible is thus presupposed by a reference to the context within which it has functioned and continues to function.

It is at the level of authorization, that is, how to move from Scripture to practice and how to imbue a certain course of action with authority, that Verhey's discussion takes place. At this level of authorization, Verhey makes at least seven hermeneutical qualifications to Scripture. 1) Verhey has found in the writings of theorists Stephen Toulmin and Henry Aiken material to delineate the process of authorization, respectively in logic and moral discourse. Which questions are appropriate to Scripture? This point arises out of the understanding of subject and object relationship, particularly as it concerns authoritative texts. Verhey mentions his indebtedness to Bultmann on this matter. 2) Taking his cue from the Council of Chalcedon, Verhey insists that the conjunction of divine and human in Scripture must be made without confusing or separating the two. A careful process of authorization which acknowledges the human and divine character of Scripture should mark the movement from the Bible to moral practice. 3) Verhey's approach is critical, constructing a developmental scheme of ethics within the New Testament, from the original ethic of Jesus, along a trajectory through the early church. Primacy resides with Jesus' eschatological ethic of response, but the later tradition exemplifies the diverse yet coherent application of this ethic. His critical hermeneutic leads Verhey to a fundamentally paradigmatic hermeneutic. 4) According to Verhey, the resurrection of Jesus is to function as the hermeneutical key that unlocks the significance of the New Testament for us. This confession entails that only then is the use of Scripture authorized if it coheres with the message of God's power in the resurrection of Jesus. 5) Christian moral identity should be thought of in terms of response, perspectives, dispositions, and principles, but not in terms of fixed moral rules. This response hermeneutic is so dominant that any moral rule must cohere with the biblical notion of justice. 6) Verhey follows the recommendations of Rauschenbusch to the Christian community to accept a particular social use of Scripture for moral discourse. Verhey shorthands this as the "exegetical conscience warrant." Verhey's implementation of the "Exegetical Conscience Warrant" is clearly evident in his discussion of the Decalogue. The social hermeneutic seeks to foreground the social element in the biblical presentation of Christ's ministry, the ethics of permission on the basis of the Decalogue, and other data emerging from Scripture. 7) Verhey considers the question as to the relevance of other sources. Christians are to bring them captive to the obedience of Jesus Christ (cf. 2 Cor 10:5).

Verhey underlines the role of the Christian Church as a community of moral discourse and discernment. The diversity which exists within the body of Christ is reason for dialogue. Precisely in this dialogue, the Spirit exercises guidance for the community. The church gathers around the Word and knows itself in subjection to the Lord of the church, in whose resurrection lies the source of its existence and loyalty. Here Verhey is elaborating upon the moral dimension of ecclesiology. For Verhey, the collective character has become the primary emphasis and framework within which Scripture and its interpretation receive their place.

Besides the datum of the community, Verhey raises the datum of experience to a level of prominence in his discussion on the function of Scripture in moral discourse. It is important that Verhey determines experience to be the final court of appeal in authorization. His focus on authorization has led him to consign authority to the "experience of authority."

Verhey calls for the practice of reading Scripture in Christian community in such a way that reading Scripture becomes a medium of sanctification. In the process of our exercise of the virtues of holiness and sanctification, fidelity and creativity, discipline and discernment, Scripture has effect. Since the 'permissions' of the Decalogue determine our relationship to God and other humans in this world, its primary dimension is social. Also the individual petitions of the Lord's Prayer nurture social disposition in the reality and expectation of God's kingdom. With regard to the issues of abortion, and genetic control, Verhey asks the ethical questions of Scripture and seeks to construct a response consonant with the intention of Scripture.

V. Reason, Community, and Practice: A Reformed critique and proposal

Chapter 5 is a theological-ethical critique of Gustafson, Ramsey, and Verhey's work, and a corresponding proposal interwoven throughout this critique. This chapter organizes itself according to the three topics of 'reason,' 'community,' and 'practice.' It must be noted that the corresponding dogmatic loci, revelation, church, and sanctification are at issue.

1. The role of reason comes into stark relief when it is brought into relationship with revelation. Does reason stand alongside of revelation as a source of Christian ethics? Two problems surrounding Scripture have been most prominent for especially Gustafson and Verhey: 1) the possibility of revelation in history; and 2) the diversity of Scripture. In Ramsey, they have been 1) the reducibility of Scripture to a principle, and 2) the interaction with existentialist and idealist philosophy. Through the influence of philosophical hermeneutics reason has become an important means to solve the problem of Scripture. The crucial role of reason changes the configuration of a Christian and Scriptural ethic.

SUMMARY

In the Reformed tradition, which all three of the authors appeal to in differing ways, the knowledge of God is the appropriate dogmatic category to bring the relationship of reason and revelation into focus. Gustafson brings in the idea of piety as the religious subjectivity from which the linguistic-intellectual and practical activity of theology can be done. This entails, however, that theocentricity is simply an emphasis on the transcendence of God as it is conjectured from human subjectivity.

Scripture, on the other hand, portrays revelation as the necessary coordinate to piety. Similarly, in Calvin, revelation is indissolubly linked to piety, for it is precisely through revelation that God evokes piety. Special revelation is necessary because of the dullness of our minds. Morality must be returned to the framework of theology, namely, the speech about God which is a response of faith. Then ethics is placed in its proper framework, and reason can then also appropriately be employed, since loving God--part of our moral response--also occurs through the mind. Calvin rightly emphasizes the accommodated nature of all knowledge of God. Accommodation does not imply the obscurity of revelation, but precisely the comprehensibility thereof. The obscurity with reference to revelation is to be attributed to 'the noetic effect of sin.' Consequently, the epistemological can be soteriologically grounded and defined. In contrast to the rational solution to a rationally determined problem of Scripture, Calvin gives a theological solution to the problem of the human understanding.

This emphasis on hermeneutics iimplies a transposition of the problem of cpistcmology, known from ancient philosophy. Existentialism has occupied itself with experience and the human subjectivity in a way that it has made the understanding of the biblical text to be on uncertain ground. Hermeneutics is used as a rationale for neglect of certain biblical motifs. Here experience has taken precedence over revelation, instead of flowing from revelation, in the way of faith.

The law of God must be duly considered in order to achieve the proper theological understanding for ethics. Since the fall, it can no longer be understood apart from the acknowledgment of the noetic effects of sin. Since the problem of human understanding is owing to human understanding, and not revelation, the solution cannot derive from human understanding in the form of philosophy; instead, the solution must come from beyond to human reasoning. The divine disclosure in the Word, inclusive of the law, brings knowledge of God to persons otherwise wandering in ignorance. The law functions epistemologically, in Christ first of all, to reveal sin. It unveils the reality of our sin, the natural defect of our epistemology, and grants us a new epistemology to discern these things. Secondly, being a reflection of God, the law in the hands of Christ functions to reveal God. This is clear 1) from the connection between persons as 'image-bearers of God' and the moral law; 2) from the connection between the attributes of God and the attributes of the law; 3) from the connection between the name and law of God; and 4) from the connection between the individual commandments and the being of God, e.g. the unity and formlessness of God. All this is taught in and through Christ. Epistemology cannot be separated from soteriology. Its self-authenticating force is perceived through the witness of the Spirit in the exercise of faith.

Neo-orthodoxy revived the positive use of faith within the discipline of ethics by creating room for confessional and theological ethics. Yet, the return to revelation, at least in the work of H. Richard Niebuhr and his heirs, Gustafson, Ramsey, and Verhey, was not free from its rational appropriation by theological liberalism. As a result, faith and reason have been engaged in a competitive relationship and the singular normativity of the Scriptures has suffered loss.

Blaise Pascal has suggested an alternative to this competitive relationship of faith and reason. Faith and reason belong to distinct levels of being, respectively, the mind and the will. Enlightenment philosophy has assumed by reason alone to be able to speak of matters of the heart. At the level of the will, where the heart is most central, faith responds to the goodness of God. The phrase fides quaerens intellectum points to the fundamental order of the two. Reason should not act of its own accord. In theology, reason serves for the purpose of theological screening. In Scripture the place of reason is indicated by the framework of the human as image of God, to which are added ethical, liturgical and oratorical grounds. Verhey's 'levels of reasoning' approach permits too much competition between reason and faith, by trading theological appropriation for philosophical appropriation.

2. The competition between reason and revelation and the resultant hegemony of reason has harnessed the coordinate of community into the norming process. If the church defines the authorization of Scripture, what is it then that defines the church? At issue is the relationship between Word and church as it was debated during the Reformation. It is therefore important to affirm that the church is called into existence and normed by the Word. This affirmation is consistent with the nature of faith outlined above, for faith assumes the posture of teachability.

3. In the constellation of reason, community, and practice, configured in the works of Gustafson, Ramsey, and Verhey, the relationship of practice and Scripture comes at the heart of the matter. How much of Scripture can be brought to the practice of Christian ethics? A proper configuration of theological concepts is of the essence for preventing pragmatism, particularly regarding the law and gospel. Thus to ignore the relationship of Christ with the Father is to distort the relationship of Christ to the law, and to disjoin the Old Testament from the New. It is also to forfeit the structure of the biblical ethic, namely the law, and in the case of Ramsey, be left with principles. Furthermore, to recognize the relationship between Christ and the Spirit sustains the validity of the law for the believer and in that way honors Christ's crucial fulfillment of the law. The Ten Commandments provide a structure for Christian ethics and lie at the heart of all Christian decision making and action. This is of relevance to

the matter of the practice of ethics, for if Scripture can lend the categories or the configuration for a Christian ethic, then the need to reconstruct the largest part of ethics on 'our side of the bridge' is lessened. The law must never be bracketed from the place it receives in the canon.

A comparison of some lines from the structure of a Scriptural ethic with Kuitert's autonomous position, provides a case study of the preceding. Over against the proclivity to pragmatism, the structure of Scripture produces a theocentric alternative. The command 'not to kill' (Ex 20:13; Deut 5:17) delineates the space, points the direction, and indicates the force of revelation on the matter of life and death.

Samenvatting

THEOLOGISCHE ETHIEK EN DE HEILIGE SCHRIFT: HET SCHRIFTGEBRUIK IN DE WERKEN VAN JAMES M. GUSTAFSON, R. PAUL RAMSEY EN ALLEN D. VERHEY

Deze studie stelt de rol van de Schrift in de theologische ethiek aan de orde. Nader bepaald gaat het om een onderzoek naar de mate waarin en de wijze waarop de Schrift bepalend is voor de ethiek. Op dit onderwerp wordt ingegaan aan de hand van de werken van James M. Gustafson, R. Paul Ramsey en Allen D. Verhey, drie ethici die karakteristiek zijn voor het recente en hedendaagse Amerikaanse protestantisme. Bepalend voor de afbakening van het onderzoeksveld is derhalve de Amerikaanse en protestante context van de auteurs. De bespreking van Gustafson, Ramsey en Verhey laat de belangrijkste componenten zien van de vraag naar de rol van de Schrift in de ethiek, te weten de rol van de rede, het karakter van de interpreterende gemeenschap en de plaats die de praktijk inneemt. Deze componenten dienen vervolgens als leidende begrippen voor het hele onderzoek naar de rol van de Schrift in de theologische ethiek.

I. Inleiding: historische achtergrond en hedendaagse context

In het eerste hoofdstuk wordt de plaats van de Schrift in de Amerikaanse protestantse ethiek geschetst tegen de achtergrond van de geschiedenis en gezet in hedendaagse context. Karakteristiek voor de Amerikaanse ethiek is met name de aandacht voor de praktijk van de ethiek en de sterke neiging om, collectief en individueel, zich te richten naar een sociale norm. Daarnaast heeft de invloed van de Verlichting ertoe geleid dat men, evenals in Europa, een belangrijke plaats is gaan toekennen aan de rede als basis voor ethiek. Van elk van de drie zojuist genoemde elementen, het praktische, het collectieve en het rationele, wordt het ontstaan en de ontwikkeling historisch nagegaan. Hoofdzakelijk het Puritanisme, de "Grote Opwekking" ["Great Awakening"], en de Verlichting, hebben deze elementen ontwikkeld en hun invloed op de ethiek laten gelden. Toch werden zij pas volledig samengesmolten ten tijde van het "Sociale Evangelie" ["the Social Gospel"], waarvan Rauschenbusch de meeste markante vertegenwoordiger was. In de loop van de twintigste eeuw verschoof het theologische zwaartepunt naar de zogenoemde Neo-Orthodoxie, die in Amerika vooral verbonden is met de namen van Reinhold Niebuhr en H. Richard Niebuhr. Deze laatste, gedurende lange tijd hoogleraar aan Yale University, legde enerzijds nadruk op de transcendentie van God, en anderzijds op de relativiteit van het menselijk begrip. Hij vermengde het collectieve, het rationele en het praktische door het inzicht van de gemeenschap voor te stellen als de beslissende context voor ethische besluitvorming. Gustafson, Ramsey en – wat later – Verhey zijn allen afgestudeerd aan Yale University, en alle drie zijn, in meerdere of mindere mate, werkzaam geweest in het spoor van H. Richard Niebuhr.

Deze voorafgaande historische ontwikkelingen zijn bepalend geweest voor de wijze waarop de Schrift functioneert in de hedendaage ethische discussie binnen het Amerikaanse protestantisme. In deze discussie is "ervaring" een sleutelbegrip, wat verklaard kan worden vanuit het rationele element in het Amerikaanse ethische denken. De rol van de christelijke gemeenschap, d.w.z. het collectieve aspect, wordt beklemtoond als het kader waarin de Schrift gezag heeft en gezag ontvangt. De combinatie van het rationele en het collectieve aspect heeft er onder meer toe geleid dat de term "dialoog" een belangrijke rol is gaan spelen.

II. James M. Gustafson: het gebruik van de Schrift in de theocentrische ethiek

Hoofdstuk 2 onderzoekt de functie van de Schrift in het werk van James Gustafson. Gustafson kan geplaatst worden op het snijvlak van neo-orthodoxie en modernisme. In zijn werk komt de Schrift en het gezag daarvan als onderwerp ter sprake in drie kaders: 1) in polemische discussie met fundamentalisten over gezag; 2) als een voorbeeld van de ontwikkeling van een religieuze traditie; 3) als een bron van de christelijke theologie. In elk van deze gevallen is Gustafsons bespreking van de Schrift sterk *beperkend* van aard. Hierbij zijn vier afzonderlijke aspecten te onderscheiden, die overigens niet geheel los van elkaar staan. 1) De scheiding tussen Ervaring en Openbaring: kennis wordt opgebouwd en ontvangen via de ervaring en dit maakt de normativiteit van de Schrift onherroepelijk tot iets subjectiefs. 2) De scheiding tussen Realiteit en Moraliteit: de Schrift openbaart geen moraliteit, maar veeleer de realiteit van het evangelie, waarop de legalistische moraliteit dan een antwoord is, dat uit de gemeenschap dient op te komen. 3) De scheiding tussen Christus en de Bijbel: het gaat om geloof in Christus, en niet in de Bijbel. 4) De scheiding tussen Gezindheid en Norm: bijbelse leerstukken zijn niet eenvoudig toe te passen als normen, maar lijken op meer indirecte wijze bij te dragen aan de ontwikkeling van een christelijke gezindheid. In elk van deze punten manifesteert zich een rationele aanpak in de hantering van de normativiteit van de Schrift, waarbij het gezag wordt verplaatst naar de gemeenschap.

De manier waarop Gustafson de Schrift daadwerkelijk gebruikt komt naar voren in zijn "theocentrische ethiek". Hij omschrijft theocentrisme als de doelstelling om alles te ordenen in relatie tot God. De tegenpool ervan, antropocentrisme, richt zich puur op het welzijn van mensen, en komt duidelijk naar voren in radicaal pragmatisme, maar ook in theologieën die simpelweg draaien om de redding van de mens. Toch is de ervaring noodzakelijkerwijs het uitgangspunt, dat in het leven van een christen het beste kan worden aangeduid als vroomheid, het zich afhankelijk weten van de soevereine regering van God. Ethiek is dan een dialogisch proces, waarin sociale, culturele en individuele situaties worden doordacht vanuit een onderkennen ["discernment"] van de goddelijke regering. Gustafson staat geen casuïstiek voor, maar een dialogisme waarin de Schrift fungeert als een bron, net als b.v. de traditie. De Schrift speelt derhalve een rol op tenminste vier niveaus: 1) in de definitie van theocentrisme, doordat de Schrift in de richting wijst van een monotheïstische Godsleer; 2) in de vorming van de traditie, die meespreekt in de dialoog waarin men zoekt naar inzicht ["discernment"]; 3) in het specifiek meespreken in het proces van het verwerven van inzicht, als een neerslag van geïnterpreteerde ervaring; en 4) in de manier waarop de Schrift Christus tekent als de belichaming van afhankelijkheid van God, zoals in de synoptische evangeliën.

Theologie en ethiek behoren tot een reflectie van de tweede rang ten aanzien van de ervaring zelf. Gustafson bedrijft theologie binnen de gereformeerde traditie, in dialoog met de gegevens afkomstig uit de natuurwetenschappen. Gustafson spreekt zijn duidelijke voorkeur uit voor de gereformeerde traditie, en in het bijzonder voor drie aspecten daarvan: 1) het duidelijk uitgesproken gevoelen dat God "anders" is; 2) de diepgaande beoefening van en waardering voor de vroomheid; en 3) een duidelijke overtuiging dat alle dingen gerelateerd dienen te worden aan de machtige Ander. Gustafsons opvatting van de gereformeerde traditie is selectief en revisionistisch. Het feit dat Gustafson het belangrijk vindt om aansluiting te zoeken bij een traditie kan men beschouwen als een onderdeel van zijn methode en zijn uitgangspunt voor de ethiek. De gereformeerde traditie dient voor hem 1) als "voedingsbodem" waarop hij zijn discussie kan "kweken", en 2) als rechtvaardiging voor bepaalde theologische en ethische keuzes.

Met de ervaring als uitgangspunt, vaart Gustafson een koers die hem dicht bij Schleiermacher brengt, doordat hij God opvat als "de kracht die op ons afkomt" ["the power who bears down upon us"] en Christus als de belichaming van theocentrische vroomheid. Gustafsons antropologie benadrukt hoezeer het menselijk leven gekenmerkt wordt door afhankelijkheid; zijn soteriologie benadrukt het vergroten van inzicht en oordeelskracht. Het christelijke leven ligt in het verlengde van deze correctie van ons christen-zijn. Moraliteit wordt onderkend middels rationele denkactiviteit binnen de gemeenschap. Ethiek en theologie zijn onderling afhankelijk, want theocentrische vroomheid, die wordt beoefend in de theologie, heeft invloed op het leven van individuen en gemeenschappen. Van Troeltsch en anderen heeft Gustafson geleerd om alles te bezien binnen de grenzen van sociologische en historische kennis. De plaats waar ethische beslissingen tot stand komen is de christelijk gemeenschap, doordat zij, onder meer op basis van de Schrift, onderkent welke handelwijze het juiste theocentrische antwoord is.

III. R. Paul Ramsey: het Schriftgebruik in de christelijke ethiek

Hoofdstuk 3 onderzoekt de functie van de Schrift in het werk van R. Paul Ramsey. Ramsey staat op een tussen Barth en Reinhold Niebuhr. In zijn ethische denken vertoont Ramsey niet zozeer de neiging om afstand te creëren tussen de Schrift en moreel handelen, zoals bij Gustafson wel het geval is. Ramsey beroept zich op de Schrift zonder al te veel nadere verklaring. Hij noemt de Bijbel de traditionele bron van ethiek in de Hebreeuws-christelijke traditie. Het wezenlijke karakter van de Bijbel met het oog op de ethiek is gebaseerd op de verbinding tussen God en de christelijke ethiek.

Intussen is er wel degelijk een zekere afstand tussen Schrift en ethiek merkbaar, en wel hierin dat Ramsey poogt om, met het oog op de christelijke praktijk, één samenbindend principe te formuleren. De overeenkomsten in verschillende situaties roepen om handelings-principes. Hij zoekt een middenweg tussen puur situationisme enerzijds, en anderzijds hen die alleen maar regels voorschrijven zonder aandacht voor de concrete situatie.

Het *agape*-principe, zoals dat geleerd wordt in de Bijbel en tot uitdrukking komt in Christus, is de hoogste belichaming van de christelijke morele praktijk. Het hiaat dat ontstaat door de afwezigheid van een onmiddellijk bijbels gezag, wordt bij Ramsey gevuld door een christocentrische opvatting van de liefde. Eenmaal aangekomen bij de persoon van Christus, laat Ramsey de rest van de Bijbel niet voor wat ze is; veeleer gebruikt hij het geheel van de Bijbel om de volle betekenis van Christus in beeld te krijgen.

De term "principe" kan op twee manieren gebruikt worden. Enerzijds kan men een "principe" zien als een samenhangend idee waartoe een geheel gereduceerd kan worden, en dat in uiteenlopende situaties toegepast kan worden. Anderzijds kan een "principe" worden opgevat als iets dat wezenlijk uniek is, oneindig verschillend van alles wat meervoudig en complex is. Overigens staan deze twee betekenissen niet geheel los van elkaar. . Bij Ramsey spelen ze beide een rol: enerzijds "distilleert" hij het principe van de liefde uit de Schrift, anderzijds staat dit principe naar zijn idee in een antithetische relatie tot natuurlijke en menselijke codificatie. Anders gezegd: voor hem staat het principe van de liefde diametraal tegenover het principe dat alleen maar meer principes voortbrengt, d.w.z. de oudtestamentische wetgeving.

Ramseys maakt in zijn bespreking gebruik van sommige resultaten van het historisch-kritische bijbelonderzoek en de rationalistische nalatenschap daarvan, zoals de veronderstelling dat er mythische elementen aanwezig zijn in de Schrift. Dit vormt de aanleiding voor een nadere filosofische uitwerking van diverse bijbelse thema's. Met betrekking tot het thema van de zonde, bijvoorbeeld, ontleent Ramsey aan het existentialisme de idee van verantwoordelijkheid, die gegeven is met de mogelijkheid en de neiging tot zonde. Daarnaast plaatst hij de zonde in een sociale context , die hij ontleent aan het idealisme.

In een later stadium van zijn denken beweegt Ramsey zich meer in de richting van een normatieve ethiek waarin de liefde niet alleen als een algemeen principe fungeert, maar ook in de vorm van meer concrete principes wordt uitgewerkt. Hij stelt dat in het christelijke leven zowel regels als concrete daden een plaats hebben. Hij wijst derhalve de situationisten terecht, door te laten zien dat ook zij er niet aan ontkomen om, uitgaande van wat de liefde in een gegeven situatie vereist, generalisaties te maken die aangeven wat in soortgelijke situaties vereist is. Aan de ene kant ziet Ramsey zijn oorspronkelijke "daden-agapisme" niet geheel overboord; aan de andere kant beweegt hij zich meer in de richting van een regel-ethiek – op zijn minst één van zogeheten "samenvattende regels" (oftewel "generalisaties"). Een vergelijkbare ontwikkeling betreft Ramseys toegenomen waardering voor de plaats van de natuurwet, vooral in verband met de problematiek van de "rechtvaardige oorlog". Hij duidt zijn stellingname aan als "Christus die de natuurwet transformeert", naar analogie van H. Richard Niebuhrs adagium "Christus die de cultuur transformeert". Hoewel Ramsey prioriteit geeft aan Christus boven begrippen die doorgaans worden gehanteerd door idealisten, zoals loyaliteit, plicht, of liefde op een menselijk niveau, kan dit motief van "transformisme" toch weer niet los gezien worden van een idealistisch kader. Een opvatting van de Schrift in termen van een centraal principe heeft tenminste drie consequenties: 1) reductionisme, en het risico van eclecticisme; 2) een idealistische concentratie op het verstand en het denken; 3) een sterkere nadruk op de rol van de gemeenschap in moreel handelen.

Ramsey sluit zich aan bij het rationele element in de geschiedenis van de Amerikaanse ethiek, en wel op twee manieren. 1) Enerzijds is zijn werkwijze "rationeel" in de zin dat hij opereert op het vlak van ideeën. Ramseys methode is niet zozeer rationeel in de zin dat hij de rede boven de openbaring stelt, maar wel in die zin dat hij binnen de openbaring op rationele gronden de ene werkelijkheid boven de andere stelt. 2) Anderzijds kan Ramseys ethiek als "rationeel" aangeduid worden in verband met zijn fundamentele openheid jegens iedere vorm van filosofie (b.v. hedonisme) waarin *agape* als centraal begrip kan worden gehanteerd, en wel in het bijzonder zijn openheid jegens idealistische filosofie.

In de praktijk van Ramseys christelijke ethiek krijgt de Schrift een ruime plaats. Meer dan eens gebruikt hij directe verwijzingen naar de Schrift in een theologische en christologische kader. Belangrijke bijbelse noties zoals gerechtigheid en verbond worden gebruikt als leidraad bij het oplossen van concrete kwesties. Bij sommige kwesties, zoals die van de rechtmatige oorlog, wordt de hulp van de natuurwet ingeroepen. Daarbij geeft Ramsey duidelijk aan hoe *agape* een transformerende functie dient te vervullen, en een normatief karakter blijft houden. De praktijk van Ramseys christelijke ethiek laat zien hoe hij worstelt met de precieze en concrete verwezenlijking van het *agape*-principe in de praktijk.

IV. Allen D. Verhey: het Schriftgebruik in moreel redeneren

Hoofdstuk 4 onderzoekt de rol van de Schrift in het werk van Allen D. Verhey. Verheys werk vertoont invloeden afkomstig uit de Nederlandse gereformeerde orthodoxie, het Amerikaanse evangelicalisme, Rauschenbusch en de neo-orthodoxie. Voor Verhey is de rol die de bijbel speelt bij het christelijke spreken over moraal en bij het komen tot een christelijke morele visie een duidelijk gegeven. De traditie is verantwoordelijk voor het toepassen van de bijbel in de ethiek, als bron én als norm. Dit verschaft de kerk het basiskader voor het functioneren van de Schrift. De rol van de bijbel wordt verondersteld, middels een verwijzing naar de context waarin hij heeft gefunctioneerd en nog steeds functioneert.

In Verheys bespreking staat toekenning van gezag ["authorization"] centraal, dat wil zeggen, hoe men de stap van de Schrift naar de praktijk dient te zetten, en hoe men een bepaalde handelwijze gezag kan toekennen. In dit verband legt Verhey tenminste zeven hermeneutische beperkingen op aan de Schrift. 1) Ten eerste maakt Verhey gebruik van het werk van de theoretici Stephen Toulmin en Henry Aiken om het proces van gezagstoekenning af te bakenen, respectievelijk op het terrein van de logica en op dat van het spreken over moraal. Het centrale probleem is: welke vragen doen recht aan de Schrift? Hierachter ligt Verheys opvatting dat de Schrift niet met gezag spreekt op het niveau van de concrete moraal. Dit geheel komt voort uit een bepaalde opvatting over subject- en object-relaties, met name waar het gezaghebbende teksten betreft. Verhey meldt dat hij in dit opzicht dank verschuldigd is aan Bultmann. 2) Ten tweede stelt Verhey, naar analogie van de uitspraken van het Concilie van Chalcedon betreffende de twee naturen van Christus, dat de verbinding tussen het goddelijke en het menselijke in de Schrift zo gelegd moet worden dat beide niet met elkaar verward, maar evenmin van elkaar gescheiden worden. De stap van de bijbel naar de morele praktijk moeten gekenmerkt worden door een zorgvuldig proces van gezagstoekenning, dat zowel het menselijke als het goddelijke karakter van de Schrift erkent. 3) Ten derde hanteert Verhey een kritische benadering, waarbij hij voor de ethiek in het Nieuwe Testament een ontwikkelingsgang veronderstelt, die begint bij de oorspronkelijke ethiek van Jezus, en vervolgens verder loopt door de vroege kerk heen. Voorop staat Jezus' eschatologische antwoord-ethiek; de latere traditie vormt een illustratie van de uiteenlopende en toch samenhangende toepassing van deze ethiek. Zo brengt Verheys *kritische* hermeneutiek hem brengt tot een *paradigmatische* hermeneutiek. 4) Ten vierde dient volgens Verhey de opstanding van Jezus te functioneren als de hermeneutische sleutel die de betekenis van het Nieuwe Testament voor ons ontsluit. Deze stellingname houdt in dat het gebruik van de Schrift alleen dan gezag heeft wanneer het coherent is met de boodschap van Gods kracht in de opstanding van Jezus. 5) Ten vijfde dient men zich de christelijke morele identiteit voor te stellen in termen van beantwoording, perspectieven, disposities en principes, maar niet in termen van vaste morele regels. Volgens Verhey strookt deze benaderingswijze met de eschatologische boodschap van de gekruisigde en opgestane Christus, en met de bijbelse notie van gerechtigheid. Deze beantwoordings-hermeneutiek is zo overheersend dat iedere morele regel overeen dient te stemmen met de bijbelse notie van gerechtigheid. 6) Ten zesde volgt Verhey de aanbevelingen die Rauschenbusch doet aan de christelijke gemeenschap om bij het spreken over moraal uit te gaan van een specifiek sociaal gebruik van de Schrift. Verhey duidt deze kortweg aan als de "machtiging van het exegetische geweten" ["exegetical conscience warrant"]. Verheys toepassing van deze "machtiging" is heel duidelijk te zien in zijn bespreking van de Tien Geboden. De sociale hermeneutiek streeft ernaar, het sociale element in de bijbelse weergave van het leven en de leer van Christus naar voren te halen, alsmede de "ethiek van de permissie" op basis van de Tien Geboden en andere gegevens die vanuit de Schrift naar voren komen. 7) Ten zevende gaat Verhey in op de vraag naar de relevantie van andere bronnen. Christenen dienen deze krijgsgevangen te nemen en te brengen onder de gehoorzaamheid aan Jezus Christus (vgl. 2 Cor. 10:5).

Verhey onderstreept de rol van de christelijke Kerk als een gemeenschap waarin men spreekt over de moraal en komt tot morele visie. De diversiteit die bestaat binnen het lichaam van Christus is reden voor dialoog. Juist in de weg van deze dialoog geeft de Geest leiding aan de gemeenschap. De kerk komt bijeen rondom het Woord en weet zichzelf onderworpen aan de Here van de kerk, in wiens opstanding de bron van haar bestaan en loyaliteit ligt. Hier werkt Verhey de morele dimensie van de ecclesiologie nader uit. De christelijke gemeenschap vormt het kader waarbinnen de Schrift en de interpretatie daarvan hun plaats krijgen.

Naast het gegeven van de gemeenschap, kent Verhey ook het gegeven van de ervaring een vooraanstaande plaats toe in zijn bespreking van de functie de Schrift in het spreken over moraal. Volgens Verhey is de ervaring de hoogste beroepsinstantie als het gaat om de rechtvaardiging van het gezag. De nadruk die hij legt op de rechtvaardiging van het gezag heeft hem ertoe gebracht, gezag toe te schrijven aan het "ervaren van het gezag".

Verhey pleit voor het lezen van de Schrift in de christelijke gemeenschap, en wel op zodanige wijze dat het lezen van de Schrift een middel voor heiliging wordt. Wanneer wij de deugden beoefenen van heiligheid en heiliging, trouw en creativiteit, discipline en onderscheidingsvermogen, heeft de Schrift effect. Aangezien de "permissies" van de Tien Geboden bepalend zijn voor onze relatie tot God en andere mensen in deze wereld, staat hun sociale dimensie voorop. Ook de afzonderlijke beden van het Onze Vader vormen een basis voor een sociale gerichtheid én de verwachting van Gods koninkrijk. Ten aanzien van de kwesties abortus en genetische manipulatie legt Verhey de ethische vraagstukken aan de Schrift voor, en probeert hij een antwoord te geven dat overeenstemt met de bedoeling van de Schrift.

V. Rede, Gemeenschap, en Praktijk: een gereformeerde kritiek en voorstel

Hoofdstuk 5 is een theologisch-ethische kritiek op het werk van Gustafson, Ramsey en Verhey, alsmede een bijbehorend alternatief voorstel, nauw vervlochten met deze kritiek. Dit hoofdstuk is onderverdeeld aan de hand van de onderwerpen "rede", "gemeenschap" en "praktijk". Tegelijkertijd zijn hier de bijbehorende dogmatische *loci* in het geding, te weten die ontrent de openbaring, de kerk en de heiliging.

1. De rede

De rol van de rede komt duidelijk naar voren wanneer deze in verband wordt gebracht met het begrip openbaring. Staat de rede naast de openbaring als een bron voor christelijke ethiek? Twee problemen omtrent de Schrift hebben een uiterst belangrijke rol gespeeld voor met name Gustafson en Verhey: 1) de mogelijkheid van openbaring in de geschiedenis; en 2) de diversiteit binnen de Schrift. Bij Ramsey ging het vooral om 1) de reduceerbaarheid van de Schrift tot een principe en 2) de interactie met existentialistische en idealistische filosofie. De invloed van de filosofische hermeneutiek heeft tot gevolg gehad, dat de rede een belangrijk middel is geworden om het Schriftprobleem op te lossen. De cruciale rol van de rede bepaalt de opbouw van een christelijke en schriftuurlijke ethiek in aanzienlijke mate.

In de gereformeerde traditie, waarop alle drie de auteurs zich op uiteenlopende wijze beroepen, geldt de kennis van God als de passende dogmatische categorie als het gaat om de juiste verhouding tussen rede en openbaring. Gustafson draagt het begrip vroomheid aan als de religieuze subjectiviteit vanwaaruit de theologie, als linguïstisch-intellectuele en praktische bezigheid, bedreven kan worden. Dit houdt echter in dat theocentriciteit feitelijk neerkomt op een speciale nadruk op de transcendentie van God, zoals deze wordt verondersteld vanuit de menselijke subjectiviteit.

In de Schrift daarentegen staat vroomheid niet op zichzelf, maar zijn openbaring en vroomheid nauw verbonden. Ook bij Calvijn is openbaring onlosmakelijk verbonden met vroomheid, aangezien juist door de openbaring God de vroomheid teweegbrengt. Bijzondere openbaring is nodig vanwege de dwaasheid van ons verstand. Moraliteit dient opnieuw een plaats te krijgen in het raamwerk van de theologie, dat wil zeggen, het spreken over God dat een geloofs-antwoord vormt. Dan wordt de ethiek in haar juiste kader geplaatst, en dan kan eveneens op passende wijze gebruik worden gemaakt van de rede, aangezien het liefhebben van God – als deel van ons morele "antwoord" – mede via het verstand tot stand komt. Terecht legt Calvijn speciale nadruk op de "aangepaste" aard van alle kennis van God. Deze "aanpassing" (*accommodatio*) betekent niet dat de openbaring onduidelijk wordt, maar maakt juist dat ze begrepen kan worden. De onduidelijkheid waarvan bij openbaring sprake is dient toegeschreven te worden aan het schadelijk effect van de zonde op het verstand. Hieruit volgt dat het epistemologische soteriologisch benaderd en omschreven kan worden. In tegenstelling tot de rationele oplossing van een op rationele wijze vastgesteld Schriftprobleem, geeft Calvijn een theologische oplossing voor het probleem van het menselijk begrip.

Dit benadrukken van de hermeneutiek betekent een transpositie van het probleem van de epistemologie, dat bekend is uit de antieke filosofie. Het existentialisme heeft zich beziggehouden met de ervaring en de menselijke subjectiviteit, op zodanige wijze dat het begrijpen van de bijbelse tekst op wankele grond kwam te staan. De hermeneutiek vormt de aanleiding voor het veronachtzamen van bepaalde bijbelse motieven. Hier is de ervaring boven de openbaring gesteld, in plaats van voort te komen uit de openbaring, in de weg van het geloof.

De wet van God dient op de juiste wijze beschouwd te worden, wil men tot het juiste theologische begrip komen met het oog op de ethiek. Sinds de zondeval kan de wet niet langer begrepen worden los van de erkenning van de invloed die de zonde heeft op het verstand. Aangezien het probleem van het menselijk begrip te wijten is aan het menselijk begrip zelf, en niet aan de openbaring, kan de oplossing niet afgeleid worden uit het menselijk begrip, in de vorm van filosofie; veeleer dient de oplossing van buiten het menselijk denken te komen. De goddelijke openbaring in het Woord, inclusief de wet, verschaft kennis van God aan mensen die anders in onwetendheid zouden ronddwalen. In Christus functioneert de wet op epistemologische wijze, allereerst om de zonde aan het licht te brengen. Ze onthult het natuurlijke gebrek in onze epistemologie, en schenkt ons een nieuwe epistemologie waarmee wij dit alles gewaar kunnen worden. Ten tweede dient de wet, als weerspiegeling van Gods wezen, in de handen van Christus om God te openbaren. Dit wordt duidelijk door 1) het verband tussen mensen als "beelddragers van God" en de morele wet; 2) het verband tussen de eigenschappen van God en de eigenschappen van de wet; 3) het verband tussen Gods naam en Gods wet; en 4) het verband tussen de afzonderlijke geboden en het wezen van God, b.v. het feit dat Hij één isen geen vorm of gestalte heeft. Dit alles leert men in en door Christus. Epistemologie kan niet worden losgemaakt van soteriologie. De kracht ervan, die zichzelf bevestigt, wordt onderkend door het getuigenis van de Geest in het beoefenen van het geloof.

De neo-orthodoxie deed het positieve gebruik van het begrip geloof binnen het vakgebied der ethiek herleven door ruimte te scheppen voor confessionele en theologische ethiek. Toch was de terugkeer naar de openbaring – in ieder geval in het werk van H. Richard Niebuhr en dat van Gustafson, Ramsey en Verhey, die min of meer in zijn voetsporen zijn getreden – niet vrij van de rationele hantering van dit begrip door het theologische liberalisme. Ten gevolge hiervan is de relatie tussen de begrippen geloof en rede er één van onderlinge wedijver geworden, en heeft de beslissende normativiteit van de Schrift schade geleden.

Blaise Pascal heeft een alternatief voorgesteld voor deze onderlinge rivaliteit van geloof en rede. Geloof en rede behoren tot afzonderlijke niveaus van bestaan, respectievelijk het verstand en de wil. De filosofie van de Verlichting dacht alleen de rede nodig te hebben om te kunnen spreken over zaken van het hart. Op het niveau van de wil, waar het hart meest centraal is, beantwoordt het geloof de goedheid van God. De zinsnede *fides quaerens intellectum* geeft de wezenlijke rangorde van deze beide aan. De rede dient niet uit eigen beweging te handelen. In de theologie dient de rede het doel van "theologische screening". In de Schrift wordt de plaats van de rede aangegeven door het kader van de mens als beeld van God; daarnaast krijgt de rede een zekere functie toebedeeld op de terreinen van ethiek, liturgie en retorica. Verheys benadering in termen van "niveaus van redeneren" laat te veel ruimte voor concurrentie tussen rede en geloof, door een theologische wijze van toepassing in te ruilen voor een filosofische wijze van toepassing.

2. De gemeenschap

De concurrentie tussen rede en openbaring, en het feitelijke overwicht van de rede, heeft geleid tot het inschakelen van de grootheid "gemeenschap" in het normgevingsproces. Maar als het gezag van de Schrift bepaald wordt door de kerk, door wie of wat wordt de kerk dan bepaald? Waar het hier om gaat is de verhouding tussen Woord en kerk, een onderwerp waarover tijdens de Reformatie veel gediscussieerd is. Het is belangrijk om vast te stellen dat de kerk haar bestaan dankt aan het Woord en onderworpen is aan de norm van het Woord. Deze vaststelling stemt overeen met de aard van het geloof zoals die hierboven is uiteengezet, want kenmerkend voor het geloof is dat het bereid is en verlangt om zich te laten onderwijzen.

3. De praktijk

Wanneer het gaat om de onderlinge samenhang van van rede, gemeenschap en praktijk, zoals die gestalte krijgt in de werken van Gustafson, Ramsey en Verhey, is de verhouding tussen de praktijk en de Schrift een essentiële zaak. Hoeveel van de Schrift kan overgebracht worden naar de praktijk van de Christelijke ethiek? Een juiste opbouw van het theologische begrippenapparaat is van wezenlijk belang om pragmatisme te voorkomen, vooral met betrekking tot wet en evangelie. Wanneer men de relatie van Christus tot de Vader veronachtzaamt, wordt de relatie van Christus tot de wet verdraaid, en wordt het Oude Testament losgemaakt van het Nieuwe. Ook verspeelt men zo de structuur van de bijbelse ethiek, die vervat is in de wet, en houdt men, in het geval van Ramsey, alleen principes over. Daarom is het van groot belang om de relatie tussen Christus en de Vader op juiste waarde te schatten. Hetzelfde geldt voor de relatie tussen Christus en de Geest: erkenning van deze relatie vormt een bevestiging van de geldigheid van de wet voor de gelovige, en daarnaast wordt recht gedaan aan het gegeven dat Christus' de wet vervulld heeft.

De Tien Geboden bieden een structuur aan voor de christelijke ethiek, en liggen aan de basis van alle christelijke besluitvorming en christelijk handelen. Dit is van belang voor de kwestie van de ethische praktijk, want als de Schrift de categorieën of de basisstructuur kan verschaffen voor een christelijke ethiek, dan verandert dat het grootste deel van de ethiek aan "onze kant van de brug" (term afkomstig van J.H. Yoder). De wet mag niet losgemaakt worden uit de verbanden waarin zij in de Schrift staat.

Een vergelijking van sommige lijnen uit de structuur van een schriftuurlijke ethiek met de autonome positie van Kuitert levert een concreet voorbeeld op van wat voor effect het heeft wanneer men aan de wet als openbaringsbegrip en aan de kracht daar de juiste aandacht besteedt. Zo geldt voor het gebod "gij zult niet doden" (Ex. 20:13; Deut. 5:17) dat het de ruimte, de richting en de kracht van de openbaring aangeeft met betrekking tot de kwestie van leven en dood.

Bibliography

I. Primary Literature

1. Selected Writings of James M. Gustafson

Gustafson, James M. "Community and Time in the Christian Church: A Study of the Church from a Sociological and Social Philosophical Perspective." Ph.D. diss. Yale University, 1955.

________. "Christian Ethics and Social Policy." In *Faith and Ethics: The Theology of H. Richard Niebuhr*, ed. Paul Ramsey, 119-139. New York: Harper and Brothers, 1957.

________. *Treasure in Earthen Vessels: The Church as a Human Community*. Chicago: The University of Chicago Press, 1961.

________. "Christian Ethics." In *Religion*, ed. Paul Ramsey, 285-354. Englewood Cliffs, NJ: Prentice-Hall, 1965.

________. "Context Versus Principles: A Misplaced Debate in Christian Ethics." In *New Theology No. 3*, eds. Martin E. Marty and Dean G. Peerman, 69-102. New York: MacMillan, 1966.

________. *Christ and the Moral Life*. Chicago: The University of Chicago Press, 1968.

________. "Moral Discernment in the Christian Life." In *Norm and Context in Christian Ethics*, eds. Gene H. Outka and Paul Ramsey, 17-36. New York: Charles Scribner's Sons. 1968.

________. *The Church as Moral Decision-Maker*. Philadelphia: United Church Press (A Pilgrim Press Book), 1970.

________. "The Place of Scripture in Christian Ethics: A Methodological Study." *Interpretation* 24:4 (October 1970), 430-455.

________. "God's Transcendence and the Value of Human Life." In *Christian Ethics and the Community*, 139-49. Philadelphia: United Church Press (A Pilgrim Press Book), 1971.

________. *Christian Ethics and the Community*. Philadelphia: United Church Press (A Pilgrim Press Book), 1971.

________. "The Place of Scripture in Christian Ethics: A Methodological Study." In *Theology and Christian Ethics*, 121-145. Philadelphia: United Church Press (A Pilgrim Press Book), 1974.

________. *Theology and Christian Ethics*. Philadelphia: United Church Press (A Pilgrim Press Book), 1974.

________. *Can Ethics be Christian?* Chicago: University of Chicago Press, 1975.

________. *Protestant and Roman Catholic Ethics: Prospects for Rapprochement.* Chicago: University of Chicago Press, 1978.
________. *Ethics from a Theocentric Perspective*. Vol. 1: *Theology and Ethics*. Chicago: University of Chicago Press, 1981.
________. *Ethics from a Theocentric Perspective*. Vol. 2: *Ethics and Theology*. Chicago: University of Chicago Press, 1984.
________. "The Changing Use of the Bible in Christian Ethics." In *Readings in Moral Theology*. Vol. 4: *The Use of Scripture in Moral Theology*, eds. Charles E. Curran and Richard A. McCormick, S.J., 133-150. New York: Paulist Press, 1984.
________. "The Place of Scripture in Christian Ethics: A Methodological Study." In *Readings in Moral Theology*. Vol. 4: *The Use of Scripture in Moral Theology*, eds. Charles E. Curran and Richard A. McCormick, S.J., 151-177. New York: Paulist Press, 1984.
________. "A Response to Critics." *The Journal of Religious Ethics* 13 (Fall 1985), 185-209.
________. "Afterword." In *James M. Gustafson's Theocentric Ethics: Interpretations and Assessments*, eds. Harlan R. Beckley and Charles M. Swezey, 241-254. Macon, GA: Mercer University Press, 1988.
________. "Roman Catholic and Protestant Interaction in Ethics: An Interpretation." *Theological Studies* 50 (1989), 44-69.
________. *A Sense of the Divine: The Natural Environment from a Theocentric Perspective*. Cleveland: The Pilgrim Press, 1994.
________. *Intersections: Science, Theology, and Ethics*. Cleveland: The Pilgrim Press, 1996.

2. Selected Writings of Paul Ramsey

Ramsey, Paul. "Elements of a Biblical Political Theory." *The Journal of Religion* 29:4 (October 1949), 258-283.
________. *Basic Christian Ethics*. New York: Charles Scribner's Sons, 1950.
________. *Basic Christian Ethics*. Louisville: Westminster/John Knox Press, 1993 [orig. published 1950].
________. *War and the Christian Conscience: How Shall Modern War be Conducted Justly?* Durham, NC: Duke University Press (published for the Lilly Endowment Research Program in Christianity and Politics), 1961.
________. *Nine Modern Moralists*. Englewood Cliffs, NJ: Prentice-Hall, 1962.
________. *Deeds and Rules in Christian Ethics*. Scottish Journal of Theology Occasional Papers, No. 11. Edinburgh and London: Oliver and Boyd, 1965.
________. *Deeds and Rules in Christian Ethics*. New York: Charles Scribner's Sons, 1967.

________. "Two Concepts of General Rules in Christian Ethics." *Ethics* 76:3 (April 1966), 192-207.

________. *Who Speaks for the Church? A Critique of the 1966 Geneva Conference on Church and Society*. Nashville and New York: Abingdon Press, 1967.

________. "The Case of the Curious Exception." In *Norm and Context in Christian Ethics*, eds. Gene H. Outka and Paul Ramsey, 67-135. New York: Charles Scribner's Sons, 1968.

________. "War and the New Morality." *The Reformed Journal* 18:2 (February 1968), 25-28.

________. *The Just War: Force and Political Responsibility*. New York: Charles Scribner's Sons, 1968.

________. *Fabricated Man: The Ethics of Genetic Control*. New Haven: Yale University Press, 1970.

________. *The Patient as Person: Explorations in Medical Ethics*. New Haven and London: Yale University Press, 1970.

________. "The Biblical Norm of Righteousness." *Interpretation* 24:4 (October 1970), 419-429.

________. "Shall We Reproduce? II. Rejoinders and Future Forecast." *Journal of the American Medical Association* 220:11 (12 June 1972), 1480-1485.

________. "Abortion: A Review Article." *The Thomist* 37 (1973), 174-226.

________. *One Flesh: A Christian View of Sex Within, Outside, and Before Marriage*. Bramcote, England: Grove Books, 1975.

________. "Love and Society: The Ethics of Paul Ramsey: Some Rejoinders." *The Journal of Religious Ethics* 4 (Fall 1976), 185-237.

________. *Ethics at the Edges of Life: Medical and Legal Intersections*. New Haven and London: Yale University Press, 1978.

________. "Incommensurability and Indeterminancy in Moral Choice." In *Doing Evil to Achieve Good: Moral Choice in Conflict Situations*, eds. Richard A. McCormick and Paul Ramsey, 69-144. Chicago: Loyola University Press, 1978.

________. "Liturgy and Ethics." *The Journal of Religious Ethics* 7 (Fall 1979), 139-171.

________. "The Morality of Abortion." In *Abortion: The Moral Issues*, ed. Edward Batchelor, Jr., 73-91. New York: Pilgrim Press, 1982. [Reprinted from *Life or Death: Ethics and Options*, ed. Daniel H. Labby, 60-93. Seattle: University of Washington Press, 1968.]

________. *Speak Up For Just War Or Pacifism: A Critique of the United Bishop's Pastoral Letter "In Defense of Creation"*. University Park and London: The Pennsylvania State University Press, 1988.

________. *The Essential Paul Ramsey: A Collection*, eds. William Werpehowski and Stephen D. Crocco. New Haven: Yale University Press, 1994.

3. Selected Writings of Allen D. Verhey

Verhey, Allen D. "Natural Law in Aquinas and Calvin." In *God and the Good: Essays in Honor of Henry Stob*, eds. Clifton Orlebeke and Lewis B. Smedes, 80-92. Grand Rapids: Eerdmans, 1975.

________. "The Use of Scripture in Moral Discourse: A Case Study of Walter Rauschenbusch." Ph.D. diss. Yale University. Ann Arbor, MI: University Microfilms, 1975.

________. "Divorce and the New Testament." *The Reformed Journal* 26 (May-June 1976), 17-19; (July-August 1976), 28-31.

________. "Notes on a Controversy about the Bible." *The Reformed Journal* 27 (May 1977), 9-12.

________. "The Use of Scripture in Ethics: A Bibliographic Essay." *Religious Studies Review*, 4:28-29 (January 1978), 28-39.

________. "Test-Tube Babies." *The Reformed Journal* 28 (September 1978), 13-16.

________. "Test-Tube Babies: Somewhat Later." *The Reformed Journal* 29 (February 1979), 6-7.

________. "Again--*in vitro* fertilization." *The Reformed Journal* 29 (June 1979), 4-5.

________. "The Test-Tube Baby Boom: Technology and Parenting." *The Banner*, 14 November 1983, 9.

________. *The Great Reversal: Ethics and the New Testament.* Grand Rapids: Eerdmans, 1984.

________. "The Use of Scripture in Ethics." In *Readings in Moral Theology.* Vol. 4: *The Use of Scripture in Moral Theology*, eds. Charles Curran and Richard McCormick, S.J., 213-241. New York: Paulist Press, 1984.

________. *Living the Heidelberg: The Heidelberg Catechism and the Christian Life*. Grand Rapids: Christian Reformed Board of Publications, December 1985.

________. "Christian Community and Identity: What Difference Should They Make to Patients and Physicians Finally?" *Linacre Quarterly* 52:2 (1985), 149-169.

________. "Sanctity and Scarcity: The Makings of Tragedy (Reflections on a Crisis in Medicine)." *The Reformed Journal* 35, February 1985, 10-14.

________. "The Morality of Genetic Engineering." *Christian Scholar's Review* 14:2 (1985), 124-139.

________. "Bible in Christian Ethics." In *Dictionary of Christian Ethics*, Revised Edition, eds. James Childress and John Macquarrie, 57-61. Philadelphia: Westminster, 1986.

________ and Hessel Bouma III. "Genetic Control: On Celebration and Caution." *The Banner*, 24 March 1986, 12-14.

_______. "Patience and Humility." *The Reformed Journal* 36 (September 1986), 2-3.

_______ and Stanley Hauerwas. "From Conduct to Character: A Guide to Sexual Adventure." *The Reformed Journal* 36 (November 1986), 2-16.

_______. "The Truth and the Life." *The Reformed Journal* 37 (April 1987), 11-15.

_______. "The Doctor's Oath--and a Christian Swearing It." In *On Moral Medicine: Theological Perspectives in Medical Ethics*, eds. Stephen E. Lammers and Allen D. Verhey, 72-82. Grand Rapids: Eerdmans, 1987.

_______. "On James M. Gustafson: Can Medical Ethics Be Christian?" *Second Opinion* 7 (March 1988), 104-127.

_______. "Paul Ramsey (1913-1988)." *The Reformed Journal* 38 (April 1988), 2-3.

_______. "Medical Technology and Care: The Weakness of Power and the Power of Weakness." *Reformed Review* 41:3 (1988), 189-199.

_______. "A Response to Douglas Schuurman." *Calvin Theological Journal* 23:2 (November 1988), 231-237.

_______, with the Fellows of the Calvin Center for Christian Scholarship [Hessel Bouma III, Douglas Diekema, Edward langerak, Theodore Rottman]. *Christian Faith, Health, and Medical Practice.* Grand Rapids: Eerdmans, 1989.

_______. *The Practices of Piety and the Practice of Medicine: Prayer, Scripture, and Medical Ethics.* [The Stob Lectures of Calvin College and Calvin Seminary]. Grand Rapids: Calvin College and Seminary, 1991.

_______ and Stephen E. Lammers, eds. *Theological Voices in Medical Ethics* [A book from the Park Ridge Center for the Study of Health, Faith, and Ethics]. Grand Rapids: Eerdmans, 1993.

_______. "Biblical Ethics." In *From Christ to the World: Introductory Readings in Christian Ethics*, eds. Wayne G. Boulton, Thomas D. Kennedy, and Allen D. Verhey, 17-20. Grand Rapids: Eerdmans, 1994.

_______. "The Good Samaritan and Scarce Medical Resources." *Christian Scholar's Review* 23:3 (1994), 360-373.

_______. "Luther's 'Freedom of a Christian' and a Patient's Autonomy." In *Bioethics and the Future of Medicine: A Christian Appraisal*, eds. John F. Kilner, Nigel M. de S. Cameron, and David L. Schiedemayer, 81-92. Grand Rapids: Eerdmans, 1995.

_______. "New Testament Ethics." In *New Dictionary of Christian Ethics & Pastoral Theology*, eds. David J. Atkinson and David H. Field, 56-64. Downers Grove, IL: InterVarsity Press, 1995.

_______. "Introduction." In *Religion and Medical Ethics: looking back, looking forward*, ed. Allen Verhey, (The Institute of Religion Series on Religion and Health Care # 1.), 1-7. Grand Rapids: William B. Eerdmans Publishing Company, 1996.

________. "Scripture and Ethics: Practices, Performances, and Prescriptions." In *Christian Ethics: Problems and Prospects* [Essays in honor of James Gustafson], eds. Lisa Sowle Cahill and James F. Childress, 18-44. Cleveland: The Pilgrim Press, 1996.

II. Secondary Literature

"The Belgic Confession of Faith." In *The Psalter*, 25-37. Grand Rapids: Eerdmans, 1975.

"The Canons of Dordt." In *The Psalter*, 38-54. Grand Rapids: Eerdmans, 1975.

"The Dogmatic Constitution on Divine Revelation." In A. Robert and A. Feuillet, *Interpreting the Scriptures*, trans. by Patrick W. Skehan *et al.*, 212-224. New York: Desclee, 1969.

"The Heidelberg Catechism." In *The Psalter*, 1-18. Grand Rapids: Eerdmans, 1975.

Aalders, W. *Pascal als Apologetisch Prediker*. Ph.D. diss. Assen: van Gorcum, 1941.

Aiken, Henry David. "Levels of Moral Discourse." In *Reason and Conduct*. New York: Alfred A. Knopf, 1962.

Allen, Diogenes. *The Reasonableness of Faith: A Philosophical Essay on the Grounds for Religious Beliefs*. Washingon: Corpus Books, 1968.

Allen, Diogenes. *Three Outsiders: Søren Kierkegaard, Blaise Pascal, and Simone Weil*. Cambridge, MA: Cowley, 1983.

Allen, Diogenes. *Christian Belief in a Postmodern World: The Full Wealth of Conviction*. Louisville: Westminster/John Knox, 1989.

Anderson, Victor. "The Legacy of Pragmatism in the Theologies of D. C. MacIntosh, H. Richard Niebuhr, and James M. Gustafson." Ph.D. diss. Princeton University. Ann Arbor, MI: University Microfilms International, 1992.

Balke, W. "Apologetiek bij Calvijn?" In *Omgang met de Reformatoren*, 139-144. Kampen: De Groot Goudriaan, 1992.

Balke, W. "Het Woord van God en de ervaring volgens Calvijn." In *Omgang met de Reformatoren*, 191-202. Kampen: De Groot Goudriaan, 1992.

Bandstra, Andrew John. *The Law and the Elements of the World: An Exegetical Study in Aspects of Paul's Teaching*. Th.D. diss. Free University, Amsterdam. Kampen: Kok, 1964.

Barclay, Oliver. "The Nature of Christian Morality." In *Readings in Christian Ethics*. Vol. 1: *Theory and Method*, eds. David K. Clark and Robert V. Rakestraw, 41-49. Grand Rapids: Baker, 1994.

Barr, James. "Story and History in Biblical Theology." *Journal of Religion* 56:1 (January 1976), 1-17.

Barth, Karl. "The Strange New World Within the Bible." In *The Word of God and the Word of Man*, trans. by Douglas Horton, 28-50. New York: Harper and Row, 1928.

Barth, Karl. *Church Dogmatics: The Doctrine of Creation.* Vol. 3. Trans. by A. T. Mackay *et al.* Eds. G. W. Bromily and T. F. Torrance. Edinburgh: T. & T. Clark, 1961.

Bates, Stanley. "The Motivation to be Just." *Ethics* 85 (1974-1975), 1-17.

Battles, Ford Lewis. "True Piety According to Calvin." In *Readings in Calvin's Theology*, ed. Donald K. McKim, 192-211. Grand Rapids: Baker, 1984.

Beach, Waldo and H. Richard Niebuhr. *Christian Ethics: Sources of Living Tradition.* New York: Ronald Press, 1955.

Beckley, Harlan R. and Charles M. Swezey. *James M. Gustafson's Theocentric Ethics: Interpretations and Assessments.* Macon, GA: Mercer University Press, 1988.

Beker, E. J. "The Sovereignty of God in the Thought of H. Richard Niebuhr." *Nederlands Theologisch Tijdschrift* 15 (1960-1961), 108-130.

Berkhof, Hendrikus. "North America: From Social Gospel to Neo-Orthodoxy." In *Two Hundred Years of Theology: Report of a Personal Journey*, trans. by John Vriend, 256-286. Grand Rapids: Eerdmans, 1989.

Birch, Bruce C. and Larry L. Rasmussen. *Bible and Ethics in the Christian Life.* Minneapolis: Augsburg, 1976.

Bloesch, Donald G. *Freedom for Obedience: Evangelical Ethics for Contemporary Times.* San Francisco: Harper and Row, 1987.

Bockmuchl, Klaus. "Thc Tcn Commandmcnts: Arc Thcy Still Valid?" *Crux* 15 (December 1979): 20-25. [Reprinted in *With Heart, Mind and Strength: The Best of Crux 1979-1989*, Vol. 1, ed. Donald Munro Lewis. Langley, BC: Credo, 1990.]

Bonhoeffer, Dietrich. *Ethics.* Ed. Eberhard Bethge. Trans. by Neville Horton Smith. New York: MacMillan Company, 1965 [orig. published 1949].

Brinkerink, J. "Richard Niebuhr, een te weining bekend theoloog", *Wending* 16 (1961), 470-482.

Butler, Joseph. *Sermons.* New York: Robert Carter and Bros., 1858.

Bultmann, Rudolf. "Is Exegesis Without Presuppositions Possible?" In *Existence and Faith: Shorter Writings of Rudolf Bultmann*, ed. Schubert Ogden, 289-296. New York: Meridian Books, 1960.

Cahill, Lisa Sowle. "James M. Gustafson." In *A New Handbook of Christian Theologians*, eds. Donald W. Musser and Joseph L. Price, 178-188. Nashville: Abingdon Press, 1996.

Calvin, John. *Institutes of the Christian Religion* (Vols. 20-21 of the Library of Christian Classics.) Ed. John T. McNeill. Trans. by Ford Lewis Battles. Philadelphia: The Westminster Press, 1960.

Calvin, John. *Commentary on the Epistles of Paul the Apostle to the Corinthians.* Vol. I. Trans. by Rev. John Pringle. Grand Rapids: Eerdmans, 1948.

Cameron, Nigel M. de S. *The New Medicine: The Revolution in Technology and Ethics*. London: Hodder & Stoughton, 1991.

Cameron, Nigel M. de S. "Living Wills and the Will to Live." *Christianity Today*, 6 April 1992, 22-24.

Cartwright, Michael G. "The Uses of Scripture in Christian Ethics--After Bakhtin." *The Annual of the Society of Christian Ethics* 12 (1992), 263-276.

Childress, James F. "Scripture and Christian Ethics: Some Reflections on the Role of Scripture in Moral Deliberation and Justification." *Interpretation* 34 (1980), 371-380.

Childress, James F. and Stanley Hauerwas. "Focus on the Ethics of James M. Gustafson." *The Journal of Religious Ethics* 13:1 (Spring 1985), 1-111.

Childs, B. S. *Biblical Theology in Crisis*. Philadelphia: Westminster, 1970.

Clowney, David. "The Use of the Bible in Ethics." In *Inerrancy and Hermeneutic: A Tradition, a Challenge, a Debate*, ed. Harvie M. Conn, 211-236. Grand Rapids: Baker, 1988.

Crocco, Stephen D. "American Theocentric Ethics: A Study in the Legacy of Jonathan Edwards." Ph.D. diss. Princeton University, 1986. Ann Arbor, MI: University Microfilms International, 1985.

Curran, Charles E. *Politics, Medicine, and Christian Ethics: A Dialogue with Paul Ramsey*. Philadelphia: Fortress, 1973.

Curran, Charles. "Paul Ramsey and Traditional Roman Catholic Natural Law Theory." In *Love and Society: Essays in the Ethics of Paul Ramsey*, eds. James T. Johnson and David H. Smith, 47-66. Missoula, MT: Scholars Press, 1974.

de Jong, Jacobus. *Accomodatio Dei: A Theme in K. Schilder's Theology of Revelation.* Th.D. diss. Theologische Universiteit Kampen. Kampen: Mondiss, 1990.

Diefenthaler, Jon. *H. Richard Niebuhr: A Lifetime of Reflections on the Church and the World.* Macon, GA: Mercer University Press, 1986.

Dorn, J. H. *Washington Gladden: Prophet of the Social Gospel*. Columbus: Ohio State University Press, 1966.

Dowey, Edward A., Jr. *The Knowledge of God in Calvin's Theology*. New York: Columbia U. Press, 1952.

Drescher, Hans-Georg. "Troeltsch's Intellectual Development." In *Ernst Troeltsch and the Future of Theology*, ed. John Powell Clayton, 3-32. Cambridge: Cambridge University Press, 1976.

Drescher, Hans-Georg. *Ernst Troeltsch: His Life and Work.* London: SCM Press, 1992.

Edwards, Jonathan. *The Nature of True Virtue*. Ann Arbor, MI: University of Michigan, 1960.

Eichrodt, Walther. *Theology of the Old Testament* I. Trans. by J. A. Bakker. (The Old Testament Library.) Philadelphia: The Westminster Press, 1961.

Eshete, Andreas. "Contractarianism and the Scope of Justice." *Ethics* 85 (1974-1975), 38-49.

Evans, Donald. *Faith, Authenticity, and Morality*. Toronto: University of Toronto Press, 1980.

Exalto, K. *De enige troost: Inleiding tot de Heidelbergse Catechismus*. (reformatie reeks.) Kampen: Kok, n.d.

Ferguson, Sinclair B. *John Owen on the Christian Life*. Edinburgh: The Banner of Truth Trust, 1987.

Fiering, Norman. *Jonathan Edwards's Moral Thought and Its British Context*. Chapel Hill: University of North Carolina Press, 1981.

Flanagan, Mary Ann. "The Theological Ethics of James M. Gustafson: His Methodology and Fundamental Concerns." Ph.D. diss. Katholieke Universiteit Leuven, 1974.

Floor, L. "Die indikatief en die imperatief in die prediking." *Theologia Reformata* 17 (March 1974), 19-33.

Frei, Hans W. "Niebuhr's Theological Background." In *Faith and Ethics: The Theology of H. Richard Niebuhr*, ed. Paul Ramsey, 3-64. New York: Harper & Brothers, 1957.

Frei, Hans. *The Eclipse of Biblical Narrative*. New Haven: Yale University Press, 1974.

Frankena, William K. *Ethics*. Englewood Cliffs, NJ: Prentice-Hall, 1963.

Frankena, William K. "Love and Principle in Christian Ethics." In *Faith and Philosophy*, ed. Alvin Plantinga, 203-225. Grand Rapids: Eerdmans, 1964.

Gardner, E. Clinton. *Christocentrism in Christian Social Ethics*. Washington, D.C.: University Press of America, 1983.

Geertsema, H. G. *Van boven naar voren: wijsgerige achtergronden en problemen van het theologische denken over geschiedenis bij Jürgen Moltmann*. Ph.D. diss. Kampen: Kok, 1980.

Goldingay, John. *Theological Diversity and the Authority of the Old Testament*. Grand Rapids: Eerdmans, 1987.

Grenz, Stanley J. and Roger E. Olson. *20th Century Theology: God & the World in a Transitional Age*. Downers Grove, IL: InterVarsity Press, 1992.

Guelzo, Allen C. *Edwards on the Will: A Century of American Theological Debate*. Middletown: Wesleyean, 1989.

Guthrie, Donald. *New Testament Theology*. Downers Grove, IL: InterVarsity Press, 1981.

Hauerwas, Stanley. *Vision and Virtue*. Notre Dame, IN: University of Notre Dame Press, 1974.

Hauerwas, Stanley. *A Community of Character: Toward a Constructive Christian Social Ethic*. Notre Dame, IN: University of Notre Dame Press, 1981.

Hauerwas, Stanley. "The Moral Authority of Scripture: The Politics and Ethics of Remembering." *Interpretation* 34 (1980), 356-370. [Reprinted in *Moral Theology No. 4: The Use of Scripture in Moral Theology*, eds. Charles E.

Curran and Richard A. McCormick, S.J., 242-275. New York: Paulist Press, 1984.]

Hauerwas, Stanley. *The Peaceable Kingdom: A Primer in Christian Ethics*. Notre Dame, IN: University of Notre Dame Press, 1986.

Hauerwas, Stanley. *Unleashing the Scripture: Freeing the Bible from Captivity to America*. Nashville: Abingdon, 1993.

Hesselink, I. John. *Calvin's Concept of the Law*. (Princeton Theological Monograph Series, gen. ed. Dikran Y. Hadidian.) Allison Park: Pickwick Publications, 1992.

Hicks, Joe H. "Philosophers' Contracts and the Law." *Ethics* 85 (1974-1975), 18-37.

Hoitenga, Dewey J., Jr. "War and the New Morality." *The Reformed Journal* 18 (February 1968), 10-15.

Hoitenga, Dewey J., Jr. "Death's Door." *The Banner*, 25 January 1993, 10-11.

Hudson, Winthrop S. *Religion in America: A Historical Account of the Development of American Religious Life*. New York: MacMillan, 1987 [4th ed.].

Jaw, Paul Jin-Yuan. "The Roles of Jesus Christ in the Ethics of James M. Gustafson." Ph.D. diss. Drew University. Ann Arbor, MI: University Microfilms International,1990.

Johann, Robert O. "An Ethics of Emergent Order." In *James M. Gustafson's Theocentric Ethics: Interpretations and Assessments*, eds. Harlan R. Beckley and Charles M. Swezey, 95-118. Macon, GA: Mercer University Press, 1988.

Jonker, W. D. "Reformed theology and the identity of the Christian congregation." In *The Vitality of Reformed Theology: Proceedings of the International Theological Congress, June 20-24th 1994, Noordwijkerhout, The Netherlands*, eds. J. M. Batteau, J. W. Maris, K. Veling, 99-126. Kampen: Kok, 1994.

Johnson, James Turner. *The Quest for Peace*. Princeton: Princeton University Press, 1987.

Johnson, James T. "Just War in the Thought of Paul Ramsey." *The Journal of Religious Ethics* 19 (1991), 183-208.

Johnson, Oliver A. "The Kantian Interpretation." *Ethics* 85 (1974-1975), 58-66.

Kelsey, David H. *The Uses of Scripture in Recent Theology*. Philadelphia: Fortress, 1975.

Klapwijk, J. *Tussen Historisme en Relativisme: een studie over de dynamiek van het historisme en de wijsgerige ontwikkelingsgang van Ernst Troeltsch*. Ph.D. diss. Assen: Van Gorcum, 1970.

Kolfhaus, W. *Christusgemeinschaft bei Johannes Calvin*. Neukirchen: Krs. Moer, 1939.

Kuitert, H.M. *Suïcide: wat is er tegen? zelfdoding in moreel perspektief*. Baarn: Ten Have, 1994 [3rd ed.].

Kuitert, H. M. "Theologie en Ethiek." *Gereformeerd Theologisch Tijdschrift* 85 (1985), 1-10.

Lane, William L. *Commentary on the Gospel of Mark.* (The New International Commentary of the New Testament.) Grand Rapids: Eerdmans, 1974.

Long, Edward LeRoy, Jr. "The Use of the Bible in Christian Ethics: A Look at Basic Options." *Interpretation* 65 (1965), 149-162.

Long, Edward LeRoy, Jr. *A Survey of Recent Christian Ethics*. New York: Oxford University Press, 1982.

Long, D. Stephen. *Tragedy, Tradition, Transformation: The Ethics of Paul Ramsey*. Boulder, CO: Westview Press, 1993.

Luther, M. *Der 51. Psalm: Ein Grundkurs des christlichen Glaubens*. München: Claudius, 1983.

MacIntyre, Alasdair. *After Virtue: A Study in Moral Theory*. Notre Dame, IN: University of Notre Dame Press, 1984 [2nd ed.].

Maris, J. W. "The Vitality of Reformed Dogmatics Challenged." In *The Vitality of Reformed Theology: Proceedings of the International Theological Congress, June 20-24th 1994, Noordwijkerhout, The Netherlands*, eds. J. M. Batteau, J. W. Maris, K. Veling, 51-62. Kampen: Kok, 1994.

Marsden, George M. *Fundamentalism and American Culture: The Shaping of Twentieth-Century Evangelicalism 1870-1925*. Oxford: Oxford University Press, 1980.

Marshall, I. Howard. "Using the Bible in Ethics." In *Essays in Evangelical Social Ethics*, ed. David F. Wright, 39-58. Cape Town: Oxford University Prcss, 1981.

McCormick, Richard A., S.J. "Gustafson's God: Who? What? Where? (Etc.)." *The Journal of Religious Ethics* 13:1 (Spring 1985), 53-70.

McDermott, Gerald. *One Holy and Happy Society: The Public Theology of Jonathan Edwards*. University Park: Penn State University Press, 1992.

Meijers, S. *Objectiviteit en Existentialiteit: Een onderzoek naar hun verhouding in de theologie van Herman Bavinck en in door hem beïnvloede concepties*. Th.D. diss. Rijksuniversiteit Leiden. Kampen: Kok, 1979.

Mitchell, Basil. Morality: *Religious and Secular: The Dilemma of the Traditional Conscience*. Oxford: Clarendon Press, 1980.

Morris, Leon. *The First Epistle of Paul to the Corinthians*. (Tyndale New Testament Commentaries.) Grand Rapids: Eerdmans, 1958.

Morissey, Michael P. *Consciousness and Transcendence: The Theology of Eric Voegelin*. Notre Dame, IN: University of Notre Dame Press, 1994.

Murray, John. *Principles of Conduct: Aspects of Biblical Ethics*. Grand Rapids: Eerdmans, 1957.

Murray, John. *The Epistle to the Romans*. 2 vols. (The New International Commentary of the New Testament.) Grand Rapids: Eerdmans, 1965.

Murray, John. *Collected Writings*. 4 vols. Edinburgh: Banner of Truth, 1967-1982.

Nicholson, E. W. "The Decalogue as the Direct Address of God." *Vetus Testamentum* 28 (1977), 422-433.

Niebuhr, Reinhold. *Moral Man and Immoral Society: A Study in Ethics and Politics*. New York: Charles Scribner's Sons, 1932.

Niebuhr, H. Richard. *The Kingdom of God in America*. New York: Harper and Row, 1937.

Niebuhr, H. Richard. *The Purpose of the Church and its Ministry*. New York: Harper and Row, 1937.

Niebuhr, H. Richard. *The Meaning of Revelation*. New York: MacMillan, 1941.

Niebuhr, H. Richard. *Radical Monotheism and Western Culture*. Louisville: Westminster/John Knox, 1993 [orig. published 1943].

Niebuhr, H. Richard. *Radical Monotheism and Western Culture*. Louisville: Westminster/John Knox, 1960 [orig. published 1946].

Niebuhr, H. Richard. "The Norm of the Church." *The Journal of Religious Thought* 4 (1946-1947), 5-15.

Niebuhr, H. Richard. *Christ and Culture*. New York: Harper and Row, 1951.

Niebuhr, H. Richard. *The Responsible Self: An Essay in Christian Moral Philosophy*. New York: Harper and Row, 1963.

Niebuhr, Reinhold. *The Nature and Destiny of Man*. Vol. 2. New York: Charles Scribner's Sons, 1943.

Norton, David L. "Rawls's Theory of Justice: A 'Perfectionist' Rejoinder." *Ethics* 85 (1974-1975), 50-57.

O'Donavan, Oliver. "Obituary: Paul Ramsey (1913-88)." *Studies in Christian Ethics* 1 (1988), 82-90.

Ogletree, Thomas W. *The Use of the Bible in Christian Ethics*. Philadelphia: Fortress, 1983.

Oosterhoff, Berend Jakob. *De vreze des Heren in het Oude Testament*. Th.D. diss. Rijksuniversiteit Utrecht. Utrecht: Kemink en Zoon, 1949.

Oosterhoff, B. J. and W. Steenbergen, *Vroomheid in het Oude en Nieuwe Testament*. Apeldoornse Studies 7. Kampen: Kok, 1974.

Packer, James I. *Our Lord's Understanding of the Law of God*. Dr. G. Campbell Morgan Memorial Lecture. Glasgow: Pickering and Inglis, n.d.

Packer, J. I. *Truth & Power: The Place of Scripture in the Christian Life*. Wheaton: Harold Shaw Publishers, 1996.

Parker, T. H. L. "Book Review: E. A. Dowey, *The Knowledge of God in Calvin's Theology*." *Evangelical Quarterly* 26 (1954), 225-229.

Pascal, Blaise. *Pensées*. Ed. Louis Lafuma. Trans. by John Warrington. London: J. M. Dent and Sons, 1973.

Poythress, Vern Sheridan, *The Shadow of Christ in the Law of Moses*. Brentwood: Wolgemuth & Hyatt, 1991.

Rauschenbusch, Walter. *Christianity and the Social Crisis*. New York: MacMillan, 1908.

Rauschenbusch, Walter. *A Theology for the Social Gospel*. New York: MacMillan, 1918.

Rawls, John. *A Theory of Justice*. Cambridge: Harvard University Press, 1971.
Ridderbos, Herman. *Paulus: ontwerp van zijn theologie*. Kampen: Kok, 1966.
Royce, Josiah. *The Philosophy of Loyalty*. New York: MacMillan, 1908.
Schleiermacher, Friedrich. *The Christian Faith*. Trans. by H. R. Mackintosh and J. S. Stewart. Edinburgh: T. and T. Clark, 1928 [orig. published 1821-1822].
Schrenk, Gottlob. "εντολη." In *Theological Dictionary of the New Testament* II, eds. Gerhard Kittel and Gerhard Friedrich, trans. by Geoffrey W. Bromiley, 545-556. Grand Rapids: Eerdmans, 1968.
Schweiker, William. "Iconoclasts, Builders, and Dramatists: The Use of Scripture in Theological Ethics." *The Annual* 1986, 129-162.
Schweitzer, Albert. *The Quest of the Historical Jesus: A Critical Study of Its Progress from Reimarus to Wrede*. New York: MacMillan, 1964.
Scroggs, Robin. "The New Testament and Ethics: How Do we Get From There to Here?" In *Perspectives on the New Testament: Essays in Honor of Frank Stagg*, ed. Charles H. Talbert, 77-85. Macon, GA: Mercer University Press, 1985.
Smith, D.A. *Symbolism and Growth: The Religious Thought of Horace Bushnell*. Chico, CA: Scholars, 1981.
Smith, David H. "Religion and the Roots of the Bioethics Revival." In *Religion and Medical Ethics: looking back, looking forward*, ed. Allen Verhey, (The Institute of Religion Series on Religion and Health Care # 1.), 9-18. Grand Rapids: William B. Eerdmans Publishing Company, 1996.
Smith, Timothy L. *Revivalism and Social Reform: American Protestantism on the Eve of the Civil War*. Gloucester: Peter Smith, 1976.
Spohn, William C., S.J. *What Are They Saying About Scripture and Ethics*? New York: Paulist Press, 1984.
Stead, G. C. "How Theologians Reason." In *Faith and Logic: Oxford Essays in Philosophical Theology*, ed. Basil Mitchell, 108-131. London: George Allen & Unwin, 1957.
Steiner, George. *Real Presences*. Chicago: University of Chicago Press, 1989.
Stob, Henry. *Ethical Reflections: Essays on Moral Themes*. Grand Rapids: Eerdmans, 1978.
Stob, Henry. *Theological Reflections: Essays on Related Themes*. Grand Rapids: Eerdmans, 1981.
Stob, Henry. "Observations on Sin." *The Banner*, 11 March 1985, 16-17.
Stob, Henry. "The Concept of the Antithesis." In *Perspectives on the Christian Reformed Church*, eds. Peter De Klerk and Richard R. De Ridder, 241-258. Grand Rapids: Baker, 1983.
Stroh, Guy W. *American Ethical Thought*. Chicago: Nelson-Hall, 1979.
Swezey, Charles Mason. "What is Theological Ethics? A Study of the Thought of James M. Gustafson." Ph.D. diss. Vanderbilt University, 1978.
Thiemann, Ronald F., ed. *The Legacy of H. Richard Niebuhr*. (Harvard Theological Studies 36.) Mineapolis: Fortress, 1991.

Thiselton, Anthony C. *The Two Horizons: New Testament Hermeneutical Philosophical Description.* Grand Rapids: Eerdmans, 1980.

Thiselton, Anthony C. *New Horizons in Hermeneutics: The Theory and Practice of Transforming Biblical Preaching.* Grand Rapids: Zondervan, 1992.

Toulmin, Stephen. *The Uses of Argument.* Cambridge: Cambridge University Press, 1958.

Trimp, C. "Heilige Geest en Heilige Schrift." In *Hoe staan wij er voor? Actualiteit van het gereformeerde belijden,* eds. J. Kamphuis, W. van 't Spijker, C. Trimp, W. H. Velema, 103-137. Barneveld: De Vuurbaak, 1992.

Troeltsch, Ernst. *Religion in History: Essays.* Trans. by James Luther Adams and Walter F. Bense. Edinburgh: T. and T. Clark, 1991.

Troeltsch, Ernst. "Historical and Dogmatic Method in Theology." In *Religion in History: Essays,* trans. by James Luther Adams and Walter F. Bense, 11-32. Edinburgh: T. and T. Clark, 1991.

Tubbs, James Balfour, Jr. "Recent Theological Approaches in Medical Ethics: McCormick, Ramsey, Hauerwas, and Gustafson." Ph.D. diss. University of Virginia. Ann Arbor, MI: University Microfilms International, 1990.

van Bruggen, J. "The authority of Scripture as a presupposition in Reformed theology." In *The Vitality of Reformed Theology: Proceedings of the International Theological Congress, June 20-24th 1994, Noordwijkerhout, The Netherlands*, eds. J. M. Batteau, J. W. Maris, K. Veling, 63-83. Kampen: Kok, 1994.

van den Berg, J. "Tussen Troeltsch en Barth: Enkele Inleidende Opmerkingen Over het Leven en het Werk van de Amerikaanse Theoloog H. Richard Niebuhr." In *Gereformeerd Theologische Tijdschrift* 63 (1963), 161-175.

van Genderen, J. "De kenmerken van de kerk." In *De Kerk: Wezen, weg en werk van de kerk naar reformatische opvatting.* eds. W. van 't Spijker *et al.*, 283-397. Kampen: De Groot Goudriaan, 1990.

van Genderen, J. and W. H. Velema. *Beknopte gereformeerde dogmatiek.* Kampen: Kok, 1992.

van Genderen, J. "Openbaring en ervaring." In *Naar de norm van het Woord,* 137-151. Kampen: Kok, 1993.

van 't Spijker, W. *Gereformeerden en Dopers: gesprek onderweg.* (reformatie reeks.) Kampen: Kok, 1986.

van 't Spijker, W. "'Extra nos' en 'In nobis' bij Calvijn in pneumatologisch licht." *Theologia Reformata* 31 (1988), 271-291.

van 't Spijker, W. "Calvijn tussen Reformatie en Orthodoxie." In *Geest, Woord en Kerk: Opstellen over de geschiedenis van het gereformeerd protestantisme*, eds. C. Augustijn, W. H. Neuser, H. J. Selderhuis, 133-149. Kampen: Kok, 1991.

Velema, W. H. *Politieke prediking.* (Apeldoornse Studies 5.) Kampen: Kok, 1972.

Velema, W. H. "'De liefde is de vervulling van de wet.'" In *Uw knecht hoort: Theologische opstellen aangeboden aan W. Kremer, J. van Genderen, B. J. Oosterhoff*, eds. J. Kruis, J. Plantinga, W. van 't Spijker, J. P. Versteeg, 103-118. Amsterdam: Ton Bolland, 1979.

Velema, W. H. *Geroepen tot heilig leven*. Kampen: Kok, 1985.

Velema, W. H. *Het spreken en het preken van de Kerk*. (Apeldoornse Studies 23.) Kampen: Kok, 1987.

Velema, W. H. *Wet en Evangelie*. Kampen: Kok, 1987.

Velema, W. H. "Ethiek bij Calvijn." In *Reformatorische Stemmen verleden en heden: Bundel uitgegeven ter gelegenheid van het vijftigjarig bestaan van de Willem de Zwijgerstichting*, eds. D. H. Borgers, R. H. Bremmer, A. Noordegraaf, K. Exalto, D. Rietdijk, W.H. Velema, 193-222. Apeldoorn: Willem de Zwijgerstichting, 1989.

Velema, W. H. *Oriëntatie in de christelijke ethiek*. (Theologie in reformatorisch perspectief.) 's-Gravenhage: Boekencentrum, 1990.

Versteeg, Jan Pieter. *Christus en de Geest: Een exegetisch onderzoek naar de verhouding van de opgestane Christus en de Geest van God volgens de brieven van Paulus*. Th.D. diss. Free University, Amsterdam. Kampen: Kok, 1971.

Voegelin, Eric. *Israel and Revelation* [the first volume in a five volume work, entitled *Order and History*]. Baton Rouge: Louisiana State University Press, 1956-1987.

Vreekamp, H. "De Vreze des Heren: Een oorsprongswoord in de systematische theologie." Th.D. diss. Rijksuniversiteit Utrecht. Epe, 1982.

Warfield, Benjamin B. *Calvin and Augustine*. Ed. Samuel G. Craig. Philadelphia: The Presbyterian and Reformed Publishing Company, 1956.

Warfield, Benjamin. "Calvin's Doctrine of the Knowledge of God." In *Calvin and Augustine*, ed. Samuel G. Craig, 29-130. Philadelphia: Presbyterian and Reformed, 1956.

Wilson, Jonathan R. "From Theology of Culture to Theological Ethics: The Hartt-Hauerwas Connection." *Journal of Religion and Ethics* 23:1 (Spring 1995), 149-164.

Wright, G. E. *God Who Acts: Biblical Theology as Recital*. London: SCM Press, 1952.

Wright, Nicholas Thomas. *The Climax of the Covenant: Christ and the Law in Pauline Theology*. Minneapolis: Fortress, 1991.

Yoder, John Howard. *The Politics of Jesus*. Grand Rapids: Eerdmans, 1972.

Yoder, John Howard. *The Priestly Kingdom: Social Ethics as Gospel*. Notre Dame, IN: University of Notre Dame Press, 1984.

Yoder, John Howard. *When War is Unjust: Being Honest in Just-War Thinking*. Minneapolis: Fortress, 1984.

Yoder, John Howard. "The Hermeneutics of the Anabaptists." In *Essays on Biblical Interpretation: Anabaptist-Mennonite Perspectives*, ed. William

M. Swartley (Text-Reader Series 1), 11-28. Elkhart, IN: Institute of Mennonite Studies, 1984.

Yoder, John Howard. "Theological Revision and the Burden of Particular Identity." In *James M. Gustafson's Theocentric Ethics: Interpretations and Assessments*, eds. Harlan R. Beckley and Charles M. Swezey, 63-94. Macon, GA: Mercer University Press, 1988.

INDEX OF AUTHORS

INDEX OF SCRIPTURAL REFERENCES

INDEX OF SCRIPTURAL REFERENCES

INDEX OF SUBJECTS